Empire Builders Series: Masterclasses in Business and Law

Beyond the Pen

ALSO BY AUTHORSDOOR GROUP

Empire Builders Series: Masterclasses in Business and Law
Expert Insights Into Business Strategy and Legal Acumen

Brick by Brick: The Entrepreneur's Guide to Constructing a Company

Mark Your Territory: Navigating Trademarks in the Modern Marketplace

From Idea to Empire: Mastering the Art of Business Planning

From Idea to Empire: Abridged Edition

Beyond the Pen: Copyright Strategies for Modern Creators

Legal Ink: Navigating the Legalese of Publishing

The Empire Blueprint Series: Case Studies for Business Success
Strategies to Grow, Innovate, and Leave a Lasting Legacy

70 Case Studies in Vision, Strategy, and Personal Branding

70 Case Studies in Leadership, Innovation, and Resilience

74 Case Studies in Growth, Digital presence, and Legacy Building

AuthorsDoor Series: *Publisher & Her World*
The Surprisingly Simple Truth Behind Extraordinary Results

AuthorsDoor Advanced Series: *Publisher & Her World*
Adventures in Publishing and the Creation of Super Brands

AuthorsDoor Masterclass Series: *Publisher & Her World*
The Essential Keys to Unlocking Unstoppable Growth

Beyond the Pen

Copyright Strategies for Modern Creators

L. A. MOESZINGER

AuthorsDoor Group
an imprint of The Ridge Publishing Group

Disclaimer: Any internet addresses, phone numbers, or company or product information printed in this book are offered as a resource and are not intended in any way to be or to imply an endorsement by AuthorsDoor Leadership, nor does AuthorsDoor Leadership vouch for the existence, content, or services of these sites, phone numbers, companies, or products beyond the life of this book.

Credit: This book was reviewed for grammatical accuracy with the assistance of ChatGPT, an Artificial Intelligence tool developed by OpenAI. We utilized ChatGPT to ensure clarity and correctness throughout the text, enhancing the reading experience while preserving the author's original voice. The integration of this advanced technology played a crucial role in maintaining the linguistic precision of each chapter.

Library of Congress Control Number: 2024920984

Beyond the Pen: Copyright Strategies for Modern Creators / by L. A. Moeszinger

ISBN 978-1-956905-34-2 (e-book)

ISBN 978-1-956905-33-5 (softcover)

1. Law / Intellectual Property / Copyright. 2. Law / Intellectual Property / General. 3. Business & Economics / Industries / Media & Communications. 4. Business & Economics / Small Business. 5. Performing Arts / Business Aspects. I. Title. II. Series

Printed in the United States of America

For all the creators who turn ideas into masterpieces—may this guide empower you to protect and amplify your brilliance.

AuthorsDoor Group
Coeur d'Alene, Idaho

INTRODUCTION TO THE
AUTHORSDOOR LEADERSHIP PROGRAM

The AuthorsDoor Leadership Program, separate from the Builders Empire Series, is a new initiative designed to empower authors and publishers with the skills to effectively sell books. It features three tailored series: (1) AuthorsDoor Series: *Publisher & Her World*, (2) AuthorsDoor Advanced Series: *Publisher & Her World*, and (3) AuthorsDoor Masterclass Series: *Publisher & Her World*; each series is meticulously structured to guide participants from foundational concepts to advanced strategies in selling books, book by book, in a chronological format. The courses, offered for free on our YouTube channels—Publisher & Her World at Ridge Publishing Group, AuthorsDoor Group: Publisher & Her World, and Authors Red Door #Shorts—complement the books and workbooks, each providing unique and valuable teachings.

Explore additional resources to enhance your journey:

- Follow our blog at AuthorsRedDoor.com.
- Subscribe to our Newsletters at AuthorsDoor.com.
- Join our AuthorsDoor Strategy Forum Facebook Group.
- Connect with our Facebook Page at AuthorsDoor Group.
- Become a fan on our social media channels @AuthorsDoor1.

For feedback or questions, contact us at info@authorsdoor.com. We are here to support your journey from writing to successfully selling your books.

Warm regards,

L. A. Moeszinger #PubHerWorld

Contents

PART 4: LEADERSHIP PERSONA DEVELOPMENT

Introduction

Unlocking the Power of Copyright: Your Essential Guide to Protecting and Profiting from Creativity

So, you've created something amazing. Maybe it's a chart-topping song, a viral TikTok, a best-selling novel, or a piece of digital art that's racking up the likes on Instagram. Whatever it is, it's yours, and no one can take that from you...right? Well, that's where things get tricky. Enter the magical, maddening world of copyright law, where the line between creative freedom and legal headaches is thinner than you'd think.

Welcome to "Beyond the Pen: Copyright Strategies for Modern Creators," your witty guide through the sometimes murky, always essential terrain of intellectual property. This book isn't just for the buttoned-up legal types—it's for the dreamers, the doers, the creators out there bringing ideas to life. Whether you're an author, musician, designer, filmmaker, or digital content creator, you need to understand how copyright can work for you. Think of it as your secret weapon—

a legal force field to protect your creative kingdom from copyright trolls and opportunistic pirates.

But hold on—before you start imagining copyright as some stodgy, legal mumbo-jumbo, let's clear something up. In this book, we break down copyright law with humor, real-world examples, and clever analogies so that even the driest doctrines feel like they belong on a Netflix binge. We're not here to give you a lecture in legalese. Instead, we're here to arm you with the knowledge to turn your creativity into something that not only shines but gets paid and protected. Let's face it—what's the point of creating something brilliant if someone else swoops in and profits from your hard work?

The Copyright Safari Begins

Copyright can seem like a wild jungle—filled with statutes, case laws, and infringement beasts lurking around every corner. But don't worry—we're not sending you in unarmed. "Beyond the Pen" will be your trusty map through this tangled underbrush. We'll start with the roots of copyright law, giving you the historical backdrop so you understand why these protections exist in the first place. From there, we'll swing through the basics of copyright protection—what qualifies, what doesn't, and why the idea of "protecting the pie but not the recipe" makes perfect sense (or at least, will by the time you're done here).

Then we'll dive into the juicy details of how to actually register your copyright, transforming your brilliant ideas into fully protected intellectual property. Don't worry, we'll walk you through the legal labyrinth step-by-step, so even the most daunting processes feel like a piece of cake (or pie, but don't steal that recipe).

The Gray Areas: Fair Use and Beyond

Next, it's time to wade into the gray zone of **fair use**, that tricky place where admiration can sometimes cross into infringement territory. We'll break down the four factors that determine fair use, using everything from memes to YouTube reaction videos to illustrate the difference between harmless borrowing and crossing the legal line. Spoiler alert: quoting a line from a movie in your blog post may seem like fun, but it's a legal minefield unless you know the rules. And who doesn't want to avoid stepping on a legal landmine?

The Digital Age: AI, Blockchain, and the Future of Copyright

Now that you're warmed up, we'll throw you into the future with the cutting-edge copyright issues that are reshaping our world. Ever wondered who owns AI-generated content or how blockchain can protect your digital assets? We'll tackle these head-scratchers with a mix of futuristic wonder and practical advice, helping you prepare for the challenges of tomorrow's creative landscape.

We're living in an era where AI is generating music, writing articles, and even creating visual art—so who exactly owns these works? You? The AI? The developer who programmed it? Well, there's no clear answer yet, but you'll finish this section with enough knowledge to wade into the debate with confidence. Plus, we'll walk you through how blockchain technology and smart contracts are changing the way copyright is managed, allowing creators to track their work in real time and automate royalty payments. If this sounds like sci-fi, you're not alone—but it's very real, and it's coming fast.

Dealing with Pirates, Takedowns, and Social Media Landmines

Next, we jump into the choppy waters of digital piracy. Because let's face it, the internet is full of shady characters who'd love to snatch your content without so much as a "thanks." From spotting digital pirates to sending out cease-and-desist letters like a true legal sniper, we've got your back. You'll learn the ins and outs of DMCA takedowns and how to navigate the often convoluted process of protecting your work on platforms like YouTube, Instagram, and TikTok.

And speaking of social media—did we mention that UGC (user-generated content) is a minefield for copyright issues? Whether you're remixing, reacting, or reposting, there are a ton of copyright tripwires waiting for unsuspecting creators. This book will help you not only avoid them but also thrive in the UGC landscape by understanding your rights and fair use limits.

Global Copyright and the Next Decade of Creativity

Just when you think we've covered it all, we'll go global. Copyright laws vary significantly around the world, and if you're distributing your work internationally (or it's going viral), understanding the nuances of global copyright is crucial. We'll touch on how countries handle copyright differently, why the

Berne Convention matters, and what's on the horizon for international copyright harmonization.

We're also going to get a little Nostradamus on you and peer into the crystal ball, predicting where copyright law is heading in the next decade. Expect big things from AI, blockchain, and augmented reality, all of which are going to test the boundaries of current copyright frameworks. But with this book, you'll be ahead of the curve, ready to navigate the future with a copyright strategy that's as sharp as your creative ideas.

Where Do We Go from Here?

"Beyond the Pen" is just the beginning. Up next in the Empire Builders Series: Masterclasses in Business and Law is "Legal Ink: Navigating the Legalese of Publishing." While "Beyond the Pen" focuses on copyright strategies for protecting your creative works, "Legal Ink" will dive into the nitty-gritty of publishing contracts, royalties, and distribution rights—whether you're self-publishing or working with a traditional publisher. You'll learn how to decode legal jargon and ensure that every deal you sign serves your long-term creative and financial goals.

Ready to Dive In?

So grab your intellectual property armor—it's time to dive into the wild, wonderful, and sometimes wacky world of copyright. With "Beyond the Pen," you won't just learn how to protect your work; you'll learn how to leverage the power of copyright to build your creative empire. Because let's be honest: in a world where content is king, copyright is the crown.

Let's turn your creativity into a protected, profitable empire—one chapter at a time.

Why This Book Matters Now
More Than Ever

In the digital age, content is king, but knowing how to protect your kingdom is what separates the amateurs from the pros. With the rise of social media, self-publishing, and endless online platforms, creators today have more opportunities than ever before. But with those opportunities come significant challenges—especially when it comes to safeguarding your creative work.

The internet is a place where ideas spread like wildfire. One moment, your song is streaming on Spotify, your art is blowing up on Instagram, or your video is trending on YouTube. The next moment, someone halfway across the globe is using your content without giving you credit or compensation. That's why understanding copyright law isn't just an option—it's an absolute necessity.

Think about it: a single viral post, song, or video could open doors to major opportunities—sponsorships, licensing deals, adaptations for TV or film—but only if you own the legal rights to that work. Without proper copyright protection, you could find yourself watching from the sidelines while others profit from your creativity. And with AI-generated content, blockchain, and global distribution networks on the rise, it's more important than ever to stay one step ahead of the game.

We live in a time when content moves across borders with a single click, and the lines between what's fair use and what's infringement are increasingly blurred. Many creators unknowingly leave their work exposed, missing out on royalties, licensing fees, and legal protections. With millions of people creating and sharing every day, the risks of losing control of your intellectual property have never been higher.

But here's the good news: this book is designed to empower you with the tools, strategies, and know-how to navigate the complexities of copyright in today's fast-paced world. Whether you're a self-published author, a digital artist, a musician dropping singles on streaming platforms, or a YouTuber producing viral videos, the insights from this book will help you **take control of your creative** empire.

In a world where content theft, digital piracy, and unauthorized use are rampant, "Beyond the Pen" gives you the knowledge to protect your work, monetize it, and ensure that you—not someone else—reap the rewards of your creativity. In short, this book matters now more than ever because the stakes have never been higher for creators who want to thrive in a digital-first world.

So whether you're just starting out or are a seasoned creator looking to level up your legal knowledge, this book will be your guide to securing your rightful place in the creative landscape, making sure your ideas not only survive but prosper in the digital age.

Who This Book is For

Let's clear something up right away—copyright law isn't just for lawyers in suits or big-time corporations. It's for anyone who creates. Whether you're a seasoned professional or just getting started, this book is for you if you've ever created something you want to protect, profit from, or simply call your own.

So, who exactly are we talking about? Let's break it down:

1. Digital Content Creators

Are you a YouTuber, podcaster, or Twitch streamer? Maybe you're making videos that get thousands of views, producing killer podcasts, or live-streaming your gaming marathons to loyal followers. If so, your content is constantly at risk of being copied, reshared, or repurposed without your permission. This book is your go-to guide for protecting your video, audio, and streaming content from being ripped off, making sure that your hard-earned work isn't turning into someone else's free ride.

2. Authors and Writers

Whether you're self-publishing your first novel or cranking out content for blogs, if you're putting words into the world, copyright protection is your best friend. Maybe you've worked tirelessly on a manuscript or written a blog post that's been shared widely—do you know how to keep others from stealing your work? Or how to handle publishing contracts to make sure you retain control over your creation? This book helps you navigate these issues so you can focus on writing while knowing your work is legally protected.

3. Musicians and Songwriters

As a musician, songwriter, or producer, you've probably seen your music pop up in places you didn't expect. Maybe someone used your track without permission in a YouTube video or a remix. If you've ever wondered how to get paid every time your music is played, streamed, or licensed, this book is for you. We'll cover everything from copyright registration to licensing agreements and even how to handle digital rights management (DRM) to ensure you get your well-deserved royalties.

4. Visual Artists, Photographers, and Designers

If you're sharing your art, designs, or photos online—whether on Instagram, Behance, or Pinterest—you've likely seen your work get shared, reposted, or even sold without your consent. How do you prevent that? This book shows you how to protect your visual creations, from watermarking to licensing, and how to enforce your rights if someone misuses your work. For graphic designers, photographers, or even digital illustrators, knowing how to secure your intellectual property rights can make the difference between someone ripping off your design and you getting paid for it.

5. Filmmakers and Video Producers

In a world where video content rules, if you're a filmmaker, content producer, or even an indie documentarian, your creative works are vulnerable to unauthorized use and piracy. From dealing with rights clearances to managing the complex legal landscapes of licensing footage and music, this book will help you navigate copyright law like a pro. You'll learn how to protect your films, ensure proper licensing, and maximize your video content's revenue potential.

6. Social Media Influencers and Bloggers

If you're making waves on Instagram, TikTok, or through your own blog, your content is your brand. From viral videos to sponsored posts, your creative output has real value—and it needs real protection. Whether you're remixing content, using third-party assets, or collaborating with brands, this book will help you understand your rights and obligations under copyright law, helping you avoid the dreaded takedown notices and ensuring you can monetize your content without headaches.

7. Software Developers, Game Designers, and App Creators

In the tech world, intellectual property is everything. Whether you're coding the next big app, designing a hit indie game, or building software, copyright law is your safety net. How do you secure ownership of your code? What happens if someone copies your game's design or mechanics? This book will guide you through protecting your digital creations, from source code copyright to enforcing your rights against infringers.

8. Entrepreneurs and Small Business Owners

Are you an entrepreneur launching a creative business? If so, your brand assets—logos, slogans, marketing materials, and even website content—are prime candidates for copyright protection. This book will show you how to protect your business's intellectual property, from filing for copyright to licensing your content. You'll learn how to secure your rights, monetize your creative assets, and grow your business with confidence.

In short, if you're someone who creates—whether it's music, videos, writing, art, apps, or digital content—"Beyond the Pen" is written for you. It doesn't matter if you're an independent artist hustling to get noticed or an established creator managing a portfolio of projects. If you want to ensure that your work is protected, properly credited, and profitable, this book is your ultimate guide.

This is not just for the legal experts or corporate suits. It's for the everyday creators who want to turn their passion into a thriving career or business while making sure their rights and profits stay firmly in their own hands. Whatever you create, whoever you are—"Beyond the Pen" will help you claim, protect, and monetize your work in a world that's constantly evolving.

Debunking Copyright Myths

Before we dive deep into the strategies, tips, and legal know-how that will empower you as a creator, let's take a moment to clear up some of the biggest misconceptions about copyright. Because, let's be honest, copyright can feel like a maze of conflicting information, urban legends, and half-truths. Don't worry, though—we're here to set the record straight.

Here are some of the most common copyright myths that could be holding you back—and the facts you need to know:

Myth 1: "As soon as I create something, it's automatically protected forever."

The Reality: Yes, your work is automatically protected by copyright the moment it's created and fixed in a tangible form (whether that's a blog post, a song, or a painting), but this protection doesn't last forever. The duration of copyright protection depends on several factors, including whether you're the individual creator or part of a company, and what country you're in. Additionally, while automatic protection exists, formally registering your work gives you stronger legal rights, including the ability to sue for damages if someone infringes on your copyright. So don't just assume "I created it, therefore it's protected"—go the extra step and register it.

Myth 2: "If I change someone else's work by 10%, it's no longer copyright infringement."

The Reality: Sorry, but there's no magic 10% rule when it comes to copyright law. Whether you tweak a song, redesign a logo, or remix a video, simply changing someone else's work by a small percentage doesn't automatically make it original or exempt from copyright infringement. The law doesn't care about the percentage of change—it cares about whether the new work is transformative or still closely resembles the original. In short, a small modification doesn't free you from the need to get permission from the original creator.

Myth 3: "If it's on the internet, it's free to use."

The Reality: Just because you can see it, share it, or download it, doesn't mean you have the right to use it. The internet may feel like a treasure trove of free content, but in reality, everything you see online is protected by copyright unless it's explicitly stated otherwise (like content under a Creative Commons license or public domain works). Whether it's an image on Google, a song in a YouTube video, or a snippet from a blog post, using someone else's work without permission can land you in hot water. If you want to use content from the internet, make sure you either have permission or that it qualifies under fair use.

Myth 4: "If I don't make any money from it, it's not copyright infringement."

The Reality: Even if you're not profiting from someone else's work, copyright infringement is still copyright infringement. Whether you're using a song in a school project or posting a fan art drawing online, it doesn't matter whether you're getting paid for it. Copyright law protects the original creator's rights, regardless of whether the infringer is making a profit. The real question is whether you have permission to use that work—and if not, you could face legal consequences even if you're not cashing in.

Myth 5: "As long as I give credit to the original creator, I'm in the clear."

The Reality: Giving credit to the original creator does not automatically give you the right to use their work. While it's always good etiquette to credit the source, it doesn't bypass copyright law. If you want to legally use someone else's content, you need to get permission (through a license or other agreement), or your use must fall under fair use guidelines. Think of it this way: You wouldn't assume you could borrow someone's car just because you said, "Hey, thanks for letting me use your car!"—you still need their permission. The same goes for creative work.

Myth 6: "Fair use lets me use anything I want for educational or commentary purposes."

The Reality: Fair use is a tricky, gray area of copyright law. While it does allow for limited use of copyrighted material for purposes like education, commentary, criticism, or parody, it's not a blanket excuse to use anything and everything. Courts consider four factors when determining whether something is fair use: the purpose of the use, the nature of the original work, how much of the original work is used, and whether it affects the market for the original work. Just because you're making a video essay or writing a blog post doesn't mean you can use copyrighted material without limits. Fair use is a case-by-case judgment, not an automatic green light.

Myth 7: "Copyright only protects big artists, authors, and corporations."

The Reality: Copyright protects everyone, whether you're a big-name musician, an indie filmmaker, or someone uploading their first drawing to Instagram. If you create something original, you have rights—whether you're a multimillion-dollar company or a one-person creative operation. In fact, this book is here to make sure you, as an everyday creator, know exactly how to protect and enforce those rights just like the big players do.

Myth 8: "If I pay for it, I own the copyright."

The Reality: Buying a copy of something—whether it's a book, a painting, or a software license—doesn't mean you own the copyright. You own the physical or digital copy of the item, but the copyright—the legal ownership of the content itself—still belongs to the creator. For example, purchasing a painting doesn't give you the right to reproduce that painting on T-shirts or posters. Similarly, buying a music track or a digital image doesn't mean you can freely redistribute or modify it. To do that, you need explicit permission from the copyright holder.

Myth 9: "If I register my copyright, I'm fully protected worldwide."

The Reality: While registering your copyright in your home country is a great first step, copyright protection doesn't automatically extend worldwide. International copyright protection is governed by treaties like the Berne Convention, but the specific laws and enforcement mechanisms can vary from country to country. While the Berne Convention ensures basic protections in participating nations, enforcing your rights in foreign markets can be more challenging, especially in countries with less robust intellectual property laws. This book will help you understand how to protect your work globally and what steps you need to take for international enforcement.

By debunking these common myths, you're already ahead of the curve when it comes to understanding how copyright law actually works. Copyright isn't a mystery—it's a powerful tool for every creator, and the more you know, the better you can use it to your advantage. As we dive deeper into this book, you'll learn not only how to avoid these misconceptions but also how to **proactively protect** and **monetize** your creations with confidence.

A Promise of Real-World Application

Before we dive headfirst into the modern labyrinth of copyright law, it's worth pausing to appreciate where it all began. Like many things in history, copyright wasn't always the well-oiled legal machine we know today. In fact, the idea that someone could "own" a creative work was once as foreign as flying cars or the internet. Yet, here we are, in a world where ideas and expressions are fiercely protected, monetized, and litigated over. So, how did we get here?

Let's be honest: nobody wants to read about copyright law just for the sake of knowing it. What you need is practical, actionable advice that you can actually use in your creative journey—whether you're building your brand, selling your art, or navigating the wild world of digital content creation. That's where "Beyond the Pen" stands apart from the mountain of legal jargon out there. This isn't just a dry textbook on intellectual property—it's your real-world playbook for making copyright work for you.

Here's the promise: by the time you finish this book, you won't just understand copyright law—you'll know exactly how to use it to your advantage. We've designed "Beyond the Pen" to be packed with tips, tools, and strategies that can be applied to your day-to-day creative work. Whether you're uploading a new video, negotiating a licensing deal, or wondering if that viral meme you made is legal, this book has you covered.

Here's what you can expect in terms of real-world application:

1. How to Register Your Copyright—and Why You Need To

It's one thing to know that copyright exists, but it's another to actually use that knowledge to protect your work. In this book, you'll learn not only how to register your copyright step-by-step but also why it's crucial for defending your creations. We'll walk you through the registration process, showing you how it's more than just paperwork—it's your key to enforcing your rights if someone tries to steal or profit from your work. By the end, you'll feel confident in your ability to take action, whether it's protecting a design, song, or manuscript.

2. Fair Use: When You Can and Can't Use Others' Work

Ever wondered if you can use a clip from a movie in your YouTube review or remix a song without legal consequences? We'll dig deep into fair use, breaking down when you can legally use someone else's work without permission—and when you can't. You'll see real-life examples from industries like music, film, and social media, so you'll understand exactly how to navigate this gray area with confidence and creativity.

3. How to Protect Your Work in the Digital Age

The internet is both a blessing and a curse for creators. It gives you access to millions of eyes and ears, but it also opens the door for pirates, thieves, and unauthorized users to take your work without permission. In *Beyond the Pen*, we'll show you how to safeguard your digital assets using tools like digital rights management (DRM), watermarking, and encryption. Whether you're an artist sharing your designs online or a musician uploading tracks to streaming platforms, you'll get real-world advice on how to lock down your work and protect it from digital freeloaders.

4. Licensing Your Work for Profit

Copyright isn't just about stopping others from using your work—it's about creating opportunities for monetization. In this book, we'll guide you through the process of licensing your work to others while maintaining control over how it's used. You'll learn how to craft licensing agreements that work for you, allowing you to profit from your creations while ensuring that your intellectual property stays safe. From licensing your artwork for merchandise to licensing music for commercials, you'll see how to turn copyright into a revenue-generating machine.

5. Avoiding Copyright Pitfalls in Social Media

Navigating social media's legal landscape can be tricky, especially when it comes to using other people's content. From reposting images on Instagram to using background music in your TikToks, you'll learn the do's and don'ts of content creation on social platforms. You'll walk away with practical tips for staying on the right side of copyright law—ensuring your posts stay up and that you avoid dreaded takedown notices, demonetization, or worse, legal disputes.

6. Responding to Infringement: What to Do When Your Work is Stolen

One of the most practical sections of this book will teach you exactly what to do when someone infringes on your copyright. You'll get templates and strategies for sending cease-and-desist letters, filing DMCA takedown notices, and even pursuing legal action if necessary. By the time you're finished with this book, you'll know how to enforce your rights in both friendly and firm ways, without having to rush to a lawyer every time someone tries to rip off your work.

7. Harnessing the Power of AI, Blockchain, and Future Tech

As technology races forward, copyright law is struggling to keep up. This book doesn't just stop at the basics—we'll dive into AI-generated content, blockchain for copyright protection, and the future of smart contracts. We'll explore how to stay ahead of the curve and future-proof your creative work, so you can navigate the next decade of tech innovation with your rights intact.

8. International Copyright: Protecting Your Work Globally

The internet makes your work instantly available across the globe—but does that mean it's protected everywhere? In "Beyond the Pen," you'll learn how international copyright treaties work, and how to ensure your rights are protected whether your book is being read in Tokyo or your song is streaming in Paris. You'll discover real-world strategies for securing your creations across borders, giving you peace of mind that your work is safe, no matter where it travels.

This isn't a theoretical exploration of copyright law—it's a hands-on, practical guide to making sure you control your work, monetize it smartly, and protect it fiercely. By the time you finish reading "Beyond the Pen," you'll be equipped with the tools and confidence to turn your creative ideas into secure, profitable ventures. No more guessing, no more hesitation—you'll be empowered to make informed decisions that protect both your art and your livelihood.

So buckle up. This book is going to arm you with the knowledge to navigate the legal landscape of copyright with clarity and precision—no matter what you create or where you create it.

Success Stories and Cautionary Tales

To truly understand the importance of copyright protection and its practical applications, let's step into the shoes of creators who've been there—those who've successfully wielded copyright as a tool for protection and profit, and those who've learned the hard way what happens when copyright is left unattended.

These success stories and cautionary tales will give you a real-world perspective on how critical copyright law is for protecting your creative work and how it can make or break your career. Whether you're a new creator or an industry veteran, these examples show that copyright matters—and what happens when you either harness it or neglect it.

Success Story 1: The Indie Musician Who Fought Back—and Won

Imagine you're an indie musician. You've poured your heart and soul into recording an album. A few months after release, you're excited to see one of your songs featured in a viral YouTube video—but hold on. Did anyone ask you for permission? Did you get paid for that?

For one indie musician, the answer was "no." His song was used without permission in an ad that blew up on social media, gaining millions of views—and major profits for the brand. Instead of letting it slide, he leveraged copyright law to reclaim control of his work. After registering his copyright and sending a cease-and-desist letter, the company agreed to settle and pay hefty licensing fees. His copyright knowledge didn't just protect him—it led to financial compensation and wider exposure for his music.

The Lesson: By understanding your copyright and registering your work, you have the power to protect and monetize it—even after others have tried to misuse it. Being proactive in copyright protection can turn a potential infringement disaster into a financial victory.

Success Story 2: The Designer Who Turned Copyright Into Cash

Let's say you're a graphic designer who creates stunning visuals for clients and personal projects. One day, you notice a huge e-commerce site selling t-shirts with one of your designs. No credit, no royalties, no permission. What do you do?

This designer didn't let it slide. She had already registered her design with the U.S. Copyright Office, so she was able to send the company a legally enforceable notice. Instead of going through the courts, she negotiated a licensing deal that allowed the company to sell her design, while she collected royalties on every sale. This turned what could have been theft into a profitable licensing agreement—one she controlled.

The Lesson: Copyright isn't just about preventing theft—it's about creating opportunities. By protecting your designs, you can license your work to others on your terms, giving you new income streams and wider exposure.

Cautionary Tale 1: The Filmmaker Who Lost Control

On the flip side, imagine you're an independent filmmaker who has worked tirelessly on a passion project, pouring in countless hours and your life savings. Your film finally makes it to an international film festival and gains traction—only for you to discover someone is streaming your film online without your permission. You didn't register your copyright because you assumed your work was automatically protected.

Unfortunately, without proper registration, your legal options are limited. You can't pursue damages, and stopping the illegal streaming is a logistical nightmare. In this case, the filmmaker lost revenue and the chance to control where and how their film was shown.

The Lesson: Registering your copyright is essential for enforcing your rights. Without that key step, you're left vulnerable to piracy and unauthorized use, losing both control and potential earnings from your work.

Cautionary Tale 2: The Social Media Star Who Got Burned

Picture this: You're a rising social media influencer with a massive following on TikTok. You use a popular song in the background of your viral videos, assuming it's no big deal—everyone's doing it, right? But one day, you receive a DMCA takedown notice. The song's owner has flagged your content for copyright infringement, and now your entire account is at risk of being demonetized or even banned.

You didn't think to check whether you had the rights to use the music or whether there were licensing options. Now, you're scrambling to keep your account and income intact, realizing too late that a few extra steps could have saved you the headache.

The Lesson: Just because everyone is doing it doesn't mean it's legal. As a content creator, knowing your copyright boundaries—especially when using others' work—is critical. Copyright issues on social media can lead to takedowns, demonetization, or worse, so it pays to be informed about fair use and licensing rules.

These success stories and cautionary tales show how understanding and applying copyright law can lead to either triumph or turmoil. Whether you're protecting your work from thieves or looking to monetize it through licensing, copyright isn't just a legal concept—it's a tool that can shape the course of your creative career.

By learning from these examples, you can avoid the pitfalls that trip up so many creators and follow the paths of those who've successfully turned copyright into a protective shield and a profit-making machine. Through "Beyond the Pen," you'll gain the skills to take control of your creations and ensure that your hard work works for you—not someone else.

How Copyright Powers Monetization

Here's the part every creator wants to know about: how to make money from your creative work. Whether you're an artist, writer, musician, or digital content creator, your work has value—and copyright is the key to unlocking its full monetization potential. When you understand how to leverage copyright, you're not just protecting your intellectual property—you're creating opportunities to generate income from it in multiple ways.

In this section, we'll break down how copyright powers monetization and why it's one of the most important tools in your creative arsenal. Let's explore how copyright turns your work into a financial asset.

1. Licensing Your Work: Getting Paid for Others to Use It

One of the most effective ways to monetize your copyrighted work is through licensing. A copyright license allows others to use your work in exchange for payment, but you retain ownership of the intellectual property. The beauty of licensing is that it lets you control how, where, and for how long your work is used, while also ensuring that you get paid every time someone benefits from your creativity.

There are various types of licensing deals, such as:

- **Exclusive Licenses**: Where you give one entity the exclusive right to use your work within a specific market or context.

- **Non-Exclusive Licenses**: Where you allow multiple parties to use your work simultaneously, often in different regions or formats.

- **Royalty-Based Licensing**: Where you receive ongoing payments (royalties) based on the use or sales of your work.

For example, if you're a musician, you can license your songs to filmmakers, advertisers, or streaming services, earning money each time your track is used. Visual artists can license their work to appear on merchandise, album covers, or in marketing materials. Licensing allows your work to reach broader audiences while ensuring that your efforts are compensated.

The Power of Licensing: Licensing transforms your copyrighted work into a recurring revenue stream. Instead of being paid once for your work, you can generate ongoing income as long as others continue to use it. It's one of the most scalable ways to monetize your intellectual property without giving up ownership.

2. Selling Reproduction Rights: Expanding Your Revenue

Selling reproduction rights is another way to leverage your copyright for income. Reproduction rights give others the ability to reproduce your work—whether that's a print of your painting, a reprint of your article, or a copy of your song on a compilation album. You can sell reproduction rights for a one-time fee or royalty payments, depending on the deal.

Let's say you're a photographer and a magazine wants to use one of your images for a feature. By selling them the right to reproduce your photo in their publication, you're earning money from something you've already created—without giving up ownership of the original image. The same goes for authors who allow their works to be reprinted in anthologies or translated into other languages. You control how your work is used and can charge accordingly.

The Power of Reproduction Rights: Selling reproduction rights allows you to monetize your work across different platforms and formats. It's an easy way to expand your audience and increase your revenue, all while keeping control over your original creation.

3. Royalty Streams: Passive Income from Copyrighted Work

One of the biggest advantages of owning your copyright is the ability to collect royalties—payments you receive whenever your work is sold, streamed, or used by others. Think of royalties as passive income—once your work is out in the world, you can continue to earn from it long after the initial creation is done.

For example:

- Musicians earn royalties every time their song is streamed on platforms like Spotify or played on the radio.
- Authors receive royalties on every book sold, whether it's in print, ebook, or audiobook form.
- Visual artists may earn royalties when their work is licensed for products like posters, T-shirts, or home decor.

Royalty streams provide a continuous flow of income, even as you move on to new projects. If you negotiate your royalty rates wisely, a single piece of work can become a long-term source of revenue.

The Power of Royalties: Royalties allow you to make money from the ongoing use of your work. With smart licensing and distribution deals, your copyright can become a sustainable income source that pays you for years to come.

4. Merchandising and Product Sales: Turning Creations into Goods

Copyright also allows you to monetize your work by turning it into physical products. Think about famous franchises like Harry Potter or Star Wars—these brands aren't just known for their movies or books. They've expanded into everything from T-shirts and toys to theme parks. That's the power of merchandising.

Even on a smaller scale, as a creator, you can turn your original artwork, designs, or brand into merchandise. Whether it's selling prints, branded apparel, or even digital downloads, copyright enables you to control the commercialization of your creations. You decide how your work is used, and by capitalizing on your brand's popularity, you can build a whole new revenue stream through merchandising.

The Power of Merchandising: Once your work has a following, merchandising can significantly expand your income. From selling physical products to offering limited-edition items, this is an opportunity to capitalize on your creative output beyond the original work itself.

5. Exclusive Content and Paywalls: Monetizing Access

In the digital age, another powerful way to monetize your copyrighted work is by monetizing access. Whether through subscription services, patron platforms, or paywalls, you can charge audiences for access to your work. This model has been successfully used by content creators across industries, from writers who offer exclusive blog posts behind paywalls to podcasters who provide premium episodes to paying subscribers.

For instance, artists on Patreon or writers on Substack can offer exclusive content, early access to new works, or behind-the-scenes material for their paying supporters. With the protection of copyright, you can ensure that this exclusive content isn't copied or distributed without your permission—giving you control over your income and audience reach.

The Power of Paywalls: Charging for access allows you to directly monetize your relationship with your audience, providing additional income without relying solely on licensing or sales. Copyright ensures that your exclusive content remains just that—exclusive to those who value it enough to pay.

6. Selling or Transferring Rights: When It Makes Sense to Sell Your Copyright

Sometimes, creators decide it's in their best interest to sell or transfer their copyright to someone else. This might happen when a company offers to purchase the rights to a song, a script, or a design outright. While this means giving up future control of the work, it can also result in a large one-time payment or long-term collaboration that benefits the creator financially.

For example, an indie filmmaker might sell the rights to a script to a production studio, earning a significant upfront payment that allows them to finance their next project. In this case, copyright allows the creator to negotiate a sale that reflects the full value of their work.

The Power of Selling Rights: While selling your copyright means giving up control, it can also be a strategic move if you need an influx of capital or want to partner with a larger entity that can take your work to the next level.

Copyright is more than just protection—it's a monetization machine that allows you to turn your creativity into a diverse range of income streams. Whether you're selling reproduction rights, licensing your work, collecting royalties, or turning your designs into products, copyright powers the entire process. By mastering copyright law, you can unlock countless opportunities to profit from your work while maintaining control over how it's used.

In "Beyond the Pen," we'll guide you through each of these monetization strategies, showing you how to make your work not only protected but profitable. Because at the end of the day, it's not just about creating—it's about ensuring that your creativity translates into long-term financial success.

Copyright in a Connected World

Welcome to the digital age, where your creative work can be shared with just a click, liked by thousands in seconds, and—unfortunately—stolen just as quickly. As a creator in a connected world, you're no longer operating within a bubble. The moment you upload your artwork, song, book, or video, it's potentially exposed to a global audience—and with that exposure comes both opportunities and risks.

Today's interconnected digital platforms have completely changed the way we create, distribute, and consume content. While this offers unprecedented reach, it also poses new challenges when it comes to protecting your intellectual property across borders, time zones, and platforms. To thrive in this hyper-connected world, you need to understand how copyright law operates on a global scale and how to adapt to the ever-evolving legal landscape.

In this section, we'll explore how copyright works in an international, digital-first environment and what you need to know to protect your creative empire.

1. The Global Reach of Your Creative Work

The internet doesn't recognize borders, and neither does your audience. Whether you're an artist in New York, a musician in Tokyo, or a writer in Johannesburg, your work has the potential to go global in an instant. But while your content is accessible worldwide, the rules that govern how it's protected can vary significantly depending on where it's being used or consumed.

Most countries have copyright laws that offer protection to creators, and many of these laws are harmonized through international agreements like the Berne Convention. This means that if you publish a book in the U.S., you'll have some level of copyright protection in countries that are part of these treaties. However, each country has its own unique approach to copyright enforcement, and the process of defending your rights in a foreign country can be complex and daunting.

What You Need to Know:

- Global distribution is a double-edged sword. It allows you to reach new markets and audiences, but it also exposes your work to potential infringement in countries where copyright laws may be weaker or harder to enforce.

- International treaties, such as the Berne Convention, provide a baseline of protection in many countries, but you need to be aware of country-specific differences in copyright enforcement and legal procedures.

2. International Copyright Treaties: How They Work

You might be wondering, "Do I need to file for copyright in every country where my work is used?" Fortunately, no. International copyright protection is governed by several key treaties that simplify the process and ensure your work is protected globally without needing to register in each country individually.

The most important of these is the Berne Convention for the Protection of Literary and Artistic Works, which has over 175 member countries. Under this treaty, when you create and copyright a work in one member country, it's automatically protected in all the other member countries. This provides broad coverage for most creators, but it's not foolproof—enforcement mechanisms still vary by country.

Other important treaties include:

- The Universal Copyright Convention (UCC): Another global treaty that provides protection in countries not part of the Berne Convention.

- TRIPS Agreement: Part of the World Trade Organization (WTO) framework, which sets minimum standards for copyright protection in international trade.

What You Need to Know:

- International treaties provide a foundational level of protection for your work in multiple countries, but they don't eliminate the need for local legal action in the case of infringement.

- Being aware of the limitations of these treaties and the specific copyright laws in key markets can help you be proactive in protecting your rights.

3. Digital Piracy: A Global Threat

In this connected world, digital piracy is one of the biggest threats to creators. From illegal streaming sites to file-sharing platforms, your work can be copied, distributed, and monetized without your consent by anyone with an internet connection. And while anti-piracy measures have improved over time, pirates are constantly finding new ways to exploit digital content across borders.

The challenge for creators is that piracy is a global issue, but copyright enforcement tends to be local. A website hosting pirated versions of your work might be based in a country with weak copyright enforcement, making it difficult to shut them down. Additionally, digital platforms often have different takedown policies depending on their location, and the process of fighting piracy can feel like a never-ending game of whack-a-mole.

What You Need to Know:

- Digital piracy can occur from anywhere in the world, and stopping it often requires a combination of legal action, takedown requests, and technological tools like digital rights management (DRM).

- Familiarize yourself with the takedown procedures for global platforms like YouTube, Instagram, and others to ensure you can quickly address any infringement.

4. Social Media and Copyright in the Global Arena

Social media platforms have revolutionized the way we share content. Whether you're uploading your latest design to Instagram, releasing a music video on YouTube, or sharing a short story on your blog, your work is immediately visible to a worldwide audience. But these platforms come with their own copyright challenges, especially when it comes to user-generated content, reposting, and fair use.

Each platform has its own set of rules for how they handle copyrighted material, and the processes for issuing DMCA takedown notices or reporting infringement can vary. Moreover, what's considered "fair use" in one country might not be the same in another. As a creator, you need to be aware of how these platforms function globally and how to protect your work on them, especially as your audience grows internationally.

What You Need to Know:

- Different social media platforms have different copyright policies, and you need to understand how they handle takedown notices, content ID systems, and copyright claims across borders.

- International audiences might interact with your work in ways that trigger copyright issues, so be proactive in monitoring your content on a global scale.

5. Enforcing Your Rights Across Borders

So what happens if someone in another country copies your work? How do you go about enforcing your copyright in a global context? This is where things get complicated.

Enforcing your rights internationally often requires working with local legal experts in the country where the infringement occurred. This can be time-consuming and costly, but it's sometimes the only way to protect your work. In some cases, filing a DMCA takedown or issuing a cease-and-desist letter might be enough to stop the infringement. But in others, you may need to pursue legal action in a foreign court.

While international treaties provide a framework for protection, the reality of enforcement is that you'll need to navigate the local legal system. That's why it's important to be prepared and to consider proactive strategies for safeguarding your work globally.

What You Need to Know:

- Legal enforcement across borders can be challenging but necessary. You may need to hire local legal help or work with international law firms specializing in intellectual property.

- Proactive measures—such as registering your work with relevant copyright offices, using technological tools like DRM, and working with platforms' copyright systems—can help reduce the risk of infringement and streamline enforcement if issues arise.

Copyright in a connected world isn't just about knowing the laws in your home country—it's about understanding the global landscape of intellectual property. As a modern creator, your audience, your opportunities, and your risks are all global. To truly protect your creative empire, you need to be aware of the international rules, potential pitfalls, and tools at your disposal.

In "Beyond the Pen," we'll help you navigate these complexities, showing you how to protect your work from digital pirates, leverage global platforms to your advantage, and make sure your copyright is enforced around the world. With the right strategies, you can build an **international presence** while keeping your intellectual property safe from the growing challenges of a connected world.

The Fun Factor

Let's face it—copyright law doesn't exactly scream "fun," does it? You might be expecting dry legal jargon, endless case studies, and more footnotes than your brain can handle. But here's where "Beyond the Pen" stands out from the crowd: we believe learning about copyright shouldn't feel like reading a tax manual. In fact, we're here to show you that understanding copyright can be just as creative, engaging, and exciting as the work you're trying to protect.

That's why this book is infused with a healthy dose of wit, humor, and real-world examples that bring legal concepts to life. We'll be dropping pop culture references, making analogies you won't forget, and breaking down complex laws into digestible, relatable pieces. Our goal isn't just to help you grasp copyright law—it's to make sure you enjoy the process along the way.

Think of copyright law like a game of strategy—one where you get to play both creator and protector. As you move through the chapters, you'll start to see how mastering copyright is less about memorizing rules and more about unlocking new opportunities for your creative work. It's about feeling empowered—knowing that you've got the tools to protect your art, negotiate deals, and profit from your ideas without losing your sanity.

Why Learning Copyright Can Be Fun

1. **Pop Culture Meets Legal Genius**: Throughout this book, we're going to use examples from music, movies, memes, and social media to illustrate how copyright works in the real world. You'll learn about famous copyright battles (from YouTubers to blockbuster films) and see how the same rules apply to your creative projects.

2. **Relatable Analogies**: Ever wondered how a meme can go from a funny internet joke to a copyright lawsuit? Or how remixing a song is like trying to tweak someone else's recipe without getting sued? We've got you covered. We'll break down tough concepts with memorable analogies that help you understand how copyright operates in everyday scenarios.

3. **A Practical Approach**: This isn't just about reading the law—this is about putting it into practice. We'll walk you through scenarios where you'll apply copyright principles to your own creative work. Whether you're trying to figure out if you can use a song in your podcast or how to stop someone from ripping off your design, we'll give you hands-on tips that you can use immediately.

4. **Cheeky Humor**: Legal books don't have to be boring, and "Beyond the Pen" proves it. We're going to keep things light, fresh, and full of humor, because let's face it—learning is better when it's entertaining. You might even laugh out loud a few times while learning the ins and outs of copyright.

5. **Real Stories, Real People**: From indie creators to big brands, you'll get stories of real-world copyright successes and failures. These cautionary tales and victory laps will keep you engaged, and show you how the strategies in this book have played out in high-stakes copyright dramas. And trust us, these stories are anything but boring.

Empowerment Through Knowledge

By the end of this book, we want you to walk away not only smarter about copyright but also more confident in your creative journey. Copyright isn't something to dread or ignore—it's something to embrace. Once you've got the fundamentals down, you'll see how copyright can work for you, turning potential legal headaches into opportunities for profit and growth.

With the fun factor cranked up, you'll find yourself breezing through concepts that might have seemed intimidating before. You'll understand how to avoid copyright pitfalls, leverage your rights for maximum gain, and feel ready to navigate the modern creative landscape with a smile on your face.

It's Not Just Fun—It's Your Creative Superpower

At the end of the day, copyright law is your creative superpower—and getting a handle on it doesn't have to feel like pulling teeth. By blending humor, practical advice, and real-world relevance, "Beyond the Pen" makes copyright not just accessible, but enjoyable. You'll be laughing, learning, and leveling up your creative game all at once.

So let's get started! With witty examples, relatable stories, and a little bit of fun, we'll turn copyright into one of your greatest assets—no law degree required.

PART ONE

Copyright:
The Essentials

In the dizzying digital age where every tweet, snap, and post could be the next big thing, safeguarding your creative output is more than a necessity—it's an art. "Copyright: The Essentials," the first grand chapter of "Beyond the Pen: Copyright Strategies for Modern Creators," serves as your indispensable guide through the intricate dance of copyright law. With wit sharp enough to slice through the thickest legal tomes, this section disentangles the complexities of rights, registrations, and royalties, making them as palatable as your morning coffee. Here, we equip modern creators not just with the shield to guard their creative domains but with the savvy to navigate the ever-evolving battleground of intellectual property. Ready your pens and pixels—this journey transforms from daunting to empowering, one clever clause at a time.

The Copyright Landscape: An Introduction to Copyright Law

"Understanding copyright is not just about protecting your work; it's about empowering it. Knowledge of the law turns your creativity into a sustainable business." — SHONDA RHIMES, TELEVISION PRODUCER AND WRITER

Welcome to the wilds of the Copyright Landscape, a realm where creative minds roam free and the stakes are as high as your last viral post. Here in Chapter One, we embark on a spirited safari through the tangled underbrush of Copyright Law, a field so riddled with legal labyrinths that even the bravest of souls may feel a twinge of trepidation. Fear not, intrepid creator, for you are not alone on this journey.

As we venture forth, we'll decipher the ancient runes known as statutes and confront the legendary beasts known as case laws. We'll uncover the mystical incantations required to register your work and invoke the powerful protections that guard it. From the hallowed halls of the Library of Congress to the shadowy corners of online platforms, copyright law spans a complex network of rules that determine who gets to share, shape, and monetize creative works.

Think of this chapter as your trusty map through this bewildering terrain. We'll demystify the principles that underpin copyright ownership, infringement, and fair use with cheeky analogies and real-world examples that bring the driest doctrines to vibrant life. By the end of this tour, you'll not only understand your rights but also how to enforce them, ensuring that your creative works serve you— and not the other way around.

So grab your gear and let's set off—the Copyright Landscape awaits, and its secrets are yours to claim. After all, in the world of creation, knowledge isn't just power; it's profit.

The Roots of Copyright Law: A Historical Perspective

Before we dive headfirst into the modern labyrinth of copyright law, it's worth pausing to appreciate where it all began. Like many things in history, copyright wasn't always the well-oiled legal machine we know today. In fact, the idea that someone could "own" a creative work was once as foreign as flying cars or the internet. Yet, here we are, in a world where ideas and expressions are fiercely protected, monetized, and litigated over. So, how did we get here?

The story of copyright traces back to the printing press—a revolutionary invention that made mass distribution of written works possible. Suddenly, authors were no longer bound by the limitations of hand-copying their manuscripts; they could share their creations with the world. But this freedom also opened the door to rampant copying by others. Books were reprinted without the author's permission or any compensation. The need for regulation became painfully clear.

Enter the Statute of Anne in 1710. Widely regarded as the world's first formal copyright law, this British statute was designed to give authors control over their work—at least for a limited time. It granted creators the exclusive right to print and sell their works for 14 years, with the possibility of renewal for another 14 years if the author was still alive. For the first time, authors were recognized as having rights over their intellectual creations, separate from the publishers who often held all the power.

This early version of copyright was born from the struggle to balance the interests of creators, publishers, and the public. As societies progressed, so too did the laws protecting creative works. The United States followed suit with its first copyright law in 1790, inspired by the Statute of Anne, giving American authors exclusive rights to their works for 14 years with a renewal option. Over time, copyright law expanded to cover more forms of creative expression—art, music, and even the digital works that dominate today.

From these early laws, the concept of intellectual property began to take root, transforming the creative landscape. Copyright law evolved as technology advanced, adapting to new mediums and challenges. Today, copyright not only protects written works but also movies, software, visual art, and virtually any form of expression that can be fixed in a tangible form.

By understanding the roots of copyright, we gain insight into its original purpose: to encourage creativity by protecting creators. And while the landscape has grown more complex, this core mission remains the same. Without copyright, the motivation to innovate, express, and share might well have been smothered under a mountain of unchecked replication. So, as we set off on this journey, remember: copyright law isn't just a set of rules; it's the backbone of the creative economy.

What Is Copyright: Defining the Core Concepts

Now that we've uncovered the roots of copyright law, it's time to get down to the nitty-gritty: what exactly is copyright, and what does it mean for you, the creator? At its core, copyright is a form of legal protection that grants the creator of an original work exclusive rights over how that work is used. In simple terms, it's a way to ensure that you control who can share, copy, and benefit financially from your creation. Whether you're writing a novel, composing a song, designing a logo, or producing a video, copyright gives you the legal power to determine how others can use your work.

The Elements of Copyright

To truly understand copyright, we need to break it down into its basic elements:

1. **Originality**: For something to be eligible for copyright protection, it must be an original creation. This doesn't mean it has to be completely groundbreaking—after all, many works are inspired by existing ideas. However, the expression of those ideas must be unique to you. Simply copying someone else's work won't cut it.

2. **Fixed in a Tangible Medium**: Copyright protection doesn't apply to ideas floating around in your head. Your work must be "fixed" in some kind of tangible medium, meaning it needs to exist in a physical or digital form. This could be a book, a painting, a song recording, a website, or even software code. The moment your work takes on a fixed form, copyright protection kicks in.

3. **Exclusive Rights**: As the creator, copyright grants you a bundle of exclusive rights, including:

     o   The right to reproduce the work (i.e., make copies).

     o   The right to distribute copies of the work (sell, lease, or lend).

     o   The right to create derivative works (adaptations, translations, etc.).

     o   The right to publicly perform or display the work (important for music, plays, and visual art).

These rights mean that you have the final say on who can copy, share, or alter your work. However, you can also choose to license these rights to others—either for free or for a fee.

4. **Term of Protection**: Copyright doesn't last forever, though it does last quite a long time. In most cases, copyright protection lasts for the

creator's lifetime plus an additional 70 years after their death. For works created by corporations or anonymous authors, the term generally lasts 95 years from the date of publication or 120 years from the date of creation, whichever comes first.

What Copyright Protects (and What It Doesn't)

Copyright applies to a broad range of creative works, including:

- Literary works (books, articles, poems)

- Visual art (paintings, sculptures, photographs)

- Musical works (compositions, sound recordings)

- Motion pictures and videos

- Software and code

- Websites and digital content

However, not everything qualifies for copyright protection. Ideas, procedures, systems, and methods of operation aren't protected—only the way they're expressed is. For example, you can't copyright the concept of a cooking technique, but you can copyright a cookbook that explains it. Likewise, facts and data are not eligible for copyright, although a unique presentation or compilation of those facts might be.

The Importance of Copyright for Creators

Copyright gives creators control over their work—control that is essential for protecting your creative investment. Without copyright, anyone could take your work and use it without credit or compensation. It serves as both a defensive shield and a potential source of income. You can sell, license, or transfer your copyright rights to others, opening up revenue streams through royalties, merchandising, and more.

In summary, copyright is your key to safeguarding your creative assets. It's the legal framework that allows you to maintain control, dictate how your work is used, and ensure that your creations benefit you and not just someone else looking for a free ride. Understanding these core concepts will empower you to navigate the copyright landscape with confidence, knowing that your work is protected from the moment you bring it to life.

The Legal Labyrinth: How to Register Your Copyright

So, you've poured your heart and soul into creating something amazing, and now you're ready to make sure it's protected. While copyright protection technically begins the moment your work is "fixed" in a tangible form, there's an additional step that can give you even stronger legal ground: registering your copyright. This section will guide you through the process of registering your work, from filing forms to understanding why it's worth the effort.

Why Register Your Copyright?

You may be wondering, "If my work is automatically protected by copyright, why bother registering it?" The answer lies in the legal advantages that come with formal registration. While registration isn't required to claim copyright, it's a crucial tool if you ever want to enforce your rights in court. Here's why:

- **Evidence of Ownership**: Registration provides a public record of your copyright claim. It's official proof that you are the owner of the work, and this can be invaluable if there's ever a dispute over authorship.

- **Legal Leverage**: If someone infringes on your copyright, you can't file a lawsuit until the work is registered. And if you register your work before the infringement occurs (or within three months of publication), you may be eligible for statutory damages and attorney's fees, rather than just actual damages, which can be hard to prove.

- **Global Reach**: Though copyright protection is largely national, many countries have treaties in place that respect the copyrights of foreign works. Registering your copyright in your home country can strengthen your claims abroad.

The Step-by-Step Process for Registration

Navigating the copyright registration process can seem daunting, but fear not— it's actually quite straightforward once you know the steps. Here's a breakdown of how to register your work with the U.S. Copyright Office (or similar agencies if you're outside the U.S.):

1. **Prepare Your Work for Submission**. Before you start the registration process, make sure you have a complete, finalized version of your work ready. You'll need to submit a copy as part of your application, and it should be in a form that accurately reflects the finished product. For written works, this might be a manuscript or book. For visual art, it could be a digital file or photograph of the artwork.

2. **Create an Online Account with the U.S. Copyright Office**. Head to the U.S. Copyright Office's website and create an account through their eCO (Electronic Copyright Office) portal. This is where you'll file your application, upload your work, and pay the registration fee. If your work is a group effort or falls into a special category, you may have to fill out additional forms or provide more information.

3. **Fill Out the Application**. The application will ask for key details about your work, including:

   o **Title of the work**: If it's part of a series, include the series title as well.

   o **Type of work**: Indicate whether it's a literary work, a visual work, a sound recording, etc.

   o **Author(s)**: List yourself (or others) as the creator(s) of the work.

   o **Date of creation**: When was the work completed? If it's been published, you'll also need the publication date.

   o **Claimant**: This is usually the same as the author, but it can also be a company or someone else if the rights have been transferred.

Make sure all the information you provide is accurate and matches what you're submitting. Errors or omissions can lead to delays in processing—or worse, your application might be rejected.

4. **Pay the Registration Fee**. The registration fee varies depending on the type of work and how you submit it. For most online submissions, the fee is around $35 to $55. While it might feel like just another expense, think of it as an investment in your creative future. For physical submissions, the fee is usually higher and processing times longer.

5. **Submit a Copy of Your Work**. You'll need to upload a digital copy of your work if you're registering online. For physical works, you may have to mail a hard copy to the Copyright Office. This is called a deposit, and it becomes part of the official record. Don't worry—this doesn't give the government or anyone else the right to use your work; it's simply to have a record of what was registered.

6. **Receive Your Certificate of Registration**. Once your application is processed, you'll receive a formal certificate of registration from the Copyright Office. This can take several months, so be patient! Your registration will be effective as of the date the Copyright Office receives your complete application, not the date the certificate is issued.

Special Considerations: Group Registrations, Derivative Works, and Joint Authors

If you're working on something outside the typical solo project—such as a collaboration or a work that builds on an existing creation—there are a few extra details to keep in mind:

- **Group Works**: If you're registering multiple works (like a series of blog posts or photographs), the Copyright Office may allow group registration. This can save you time and money, but specific rules apply depending on the type of work.

- **Derivative Works**: If your work is based on or incorporates another creator's copyrighted work, you'll need to make sure you have permission or that your use qualifies as fair use. You'll also need to be clear in your registration about what parts of the work are original to you.

- **Joint Authors**: If you're registering a work created by multiple people, all authors should be listed on the application. Copyright is then shared equally among all authors unless there's a written agreement stating otherwise.

What Happens After Registration?

Once your copyright is registered, you've got a solid legal foundation to protect your work. From here, you can confidently share, license, or sell your creation, knowing that you have formal protection if anyone tries to infringe on your rights. And if infringement does occur, your registration is your first line of defense in a legal battle, giving you the leverage to seek damages and protect your creative legacy.

In short, while navigating the copyright registration process may seem like a trek through legal territory, it's one worth taking. Registration offers a level of protection and peace of mind that is invaluable in the competitive world of creative industries. So, don't skip this crucial step—register your work and make sure your creative investment is secured for the long haul.

Fair Use and Infringement: Navigating the Gray Areas

As we venture deeper into the Copyright Landscape, we now find ourselves in one of the murkiest and most contested areas: Fair Use and Infringement. These two concepts often seem like opposing forces in a tug-of-war between creators, consumers, and the law. Understanding the difference between protecting your work and respecting the rights of others is essential to navigating this gray zone without stepping into legal quicksand.

What Is Fair Use?

Fair use is a legal doctrine that allows limited use of copyrighted material without needing permission from the copyright owner. The idea behind it is to promote freedom of expression, particularly in contexts like commentary, criticism, news reporting, research, and education. Fair use acts as a safeguard, ensuring that copyright law doesn't become a tool for stifling creativity, academic discourse, or social critique.

However, fair use is not a blanket license to use someone else's work freely. Instead, it's determined on a case-by-case basis, meaning that there are no hard-and-fast rules about what qualifies. Courts look at several factors when deciding whether a particular use falls under fair use:

1. **The Purpose and Character of the Use**: Is the use transformative? Does it add new meaning, expression, or value to the original work, or is it simply copying? Courts are more likely to rule in favor of fair use if the work is used for commentary, criticism, parody, education, or research. Commercial uses, especially those that directly profit from the original work, are less likely to qualify as fair use.

2. **The Nature of the Copyrighted Work**: Creative works like fiction, music, and art are given stronger copyright protections than factual works. The more creative and unique the original work, the less likely courts will rule in favor of fair use.

3. **The Amount and Substantiality of the Portion Used**: How much of the original work did you use? The smaller the portion, the better your chances of claiming fair use. However, even if you use a small portion, courts may rule against fair use if you take the "heart" of the work, or the most recognizable and important part.

4. **The Effect on the Market**: Does your use of the work harm the market value or potential earnings of the original? If your use could replace the original or serve as a substitute, it's less likely to be considered fair use. This factor often holds significant weight in court decisions, as copyright law is designed to protect the financial interests of creators.

Common Examples of Fair Use

To give you a better sense of how fair use works in practice, here are a few common scenarios where it may apply:

- **Commentary and Criticism**: If you're reviewing a book, movie, or piece of music, quoting or using small excerpts from the original work to back up your opinions is typically considered fair use. For instance, a YouTube reviewer may include clips from a movie to provide context for their critique.

- **Parody**: Parody involves mimicking or imitating an original work for comedic effect or social commentary. Since parody adds new meaning to the original work and isn't simply copying it, courts often view it as fair use.

- **Educational Use**: Teachers, researchers, and students can use portions of copyrighted works for educational purposes under fair use. This is especially common in classroom settings or academic papers where materials are used for analysis and learning rather than profit.

- **News Reporting**: Journalists often use small portions of copyrighted works to report on current events. Whether it's a still image from a newsworthy movie premiere or a short video clip during a news broadcast, fair use helps ensure the free flow of information.

What Is Copyright Infringement?

In contrast to fair use, copyright infringement occurs when someone uses a copyrighted work without permission in a way that violates the owner's exclusive rights. Infringement can take many forms, from copying and distributing a book to posting someone else's music or artwork online without their consent.

Copyright infringement doesn't require the infringer to profit from the use—simply reproducing or displaying someone else's work without permission is enough to constitute infringement. However, not all unauthorized uses are treated equally. There are both innocent infringement (where the person didn't know the work was copyrighted) and willful infringement (where the person knew the work was copyrighted and used it anyway). Courts tend to be more lenient on innocent infringers but can impose harsh penalties on willful infringers, including hefty fines or damages.

Avoiding Copyright Infringement

So, how can you avoid becoming an infringer? Here are a few key tips:

- **Always Get Permission**: If you want to use someone else's work, the safest route is to ask for permission or obtain a license. Many creators or copyright holders are happy to allow use of their work if you credit them properly or agree on terms of compensation.

- **Know the Limits of Fair Use**: Don't assume that all uses for criticism, parody, or education automatically qualify as fair use. Always assess your use against the four factors to make an informed decision. When in doubt, consult a legal expert.

- **Use Public Domain or Creative Commons Works**: Works in the public domain are free from copyright and can be used without permission. Similarly, some creators release their works under Creative Commons licenses, which allow for certain uses with minimal restrictions.

- **Create Your Own Content**: The best way to avoid infringement is to create your own original content. If you're inspired by someone else's work, put your unique spin on it—transform it into something new and different, rather than simply copying.

Consequences of Copyright Infringement

Infringing on someone's copyright can have serious legal consequences. If you're sued for infringement, you could be ordered to pay actual damages (the losses suffered by the copyright owner), statutory damages (set amounts determined by law), and attorney's fees. If the infringement is willful, the fines could range from $750 to $150,000 per work. In extreme cases, infringement can even result in criminal charges, particularly when the violation involves piracy or large-scale distribution.

Even if you believe your use qualifies as fair use, copyright disputes can be expensive and time-consuming. The burden of proof falls on the defendant to prove fair use, so it's always better to err on the side of caution and avoid potential infringement in the first place.

Finding the Balance Between Fair Use and Infringement

Fair use and copyright infringement represent two sides of the same coin—both vital to a healthy creative ecosystem. On one hand, copyright encourages creators to invest in their work by offering legal protection. On the other hand, fair use allows for commentary, innovation, and learning, ensuring that creativity isn't stifled by overly restrictive laws.

As a creator, learning how to strike this balance is key to both protecting your own work and respecting the rights of others. Armed with the knowledge from this chapter, you're ready to navigate these gray areas and make informed decisions that keep you on solid legal ground.

After all, creativity thrives when we build on the work of others in a way that's transformative, respectful, and legally sound.

Quick Tips and Recap

- **Copyright Protection is Automatic**: Your work is protected by copyright the moment it's fixed in a tangible form—no need to register, though registration provides extra legal benefits.

- **Understand the Core Elements of Copyright**: To qualify, your work must be original, fixed in a tangible medium, and eligible for protection (ideas and facts aren't covered).

- **Exclusive Rights Matter**: Copyright grants you the right to reproduce, distribute, create derivative works, and publicly perform or display your work.

- **Registration is Key for Enforcement**: While not required, registering your work provides official proof of ownership and enables you to take legal action against infringers.

- **Fair Use is Flexible**: The four factors of fair use—purpose, nature, amount, and effect on the market—determine whether your use is protected, but it's assessed on a case-by-case basis.

- **Avoid Infringement**: Get permission, respect fair use limits, and consider using public domain or Creative Commons works to avoid legal issues.

- **Infringement Has Consequences**: Fines, damages, and legal fees can pile up if you infringe someone's copyright, so always tread carefully when using others' works.

- **Balance Fair Use and Protection**: Protect your own rights while also ensuring you respect the rights of others—this balance is crucial for the creative ecosystem.

Claim Your Creation: Establishing Copyright Ownership

"Claiming ownership of your creative work is the first step towards turning your art into an asset. Secure your rights, and you secure your future."— JEFF BEZOS, FOUNDER OF AMAZON

Chapter Two: "Claim Your Creation: Establishing Copyright Ownership" invites you on a quest to secure the golden fleece of the creative world— ownership. In this chapter, we'll scale the dizzying heights of legal documentation and delve into the arcane rituals of registration that mark you as the undisputed lord of your creative domain.

Think of this as planting your flag on the moon, but instead of a barren rock floating in space, it's your artwork, your manuscript, or that catchy jingle that everyone hums in the shower. Establishing copyright ownership isn't just about staking claim; it's about setting the stage for future royalties, rights, and perhaps, if you play your cards right, a legacy that outlives the fleeting fame of internet virality.

We'll navigate through the oft-overlooked nuances of joint authorship and derivative works, ensuring you know who owns what, when, and how much. This chapter is packed with tips, tricks, and tales of caution—a veritable treasure map that leads to the 'X' marking not buried treasure, but something far more valuable: your peace of mind in a world where creative assets are the true currency.

So cinch up your intellectual property belts, creators. We're about to make it official, in ink, on paper, and within the hallowed databases of copyright offices worldwide. After all, in the kingdom of content, the one who holds the copyright crown rules supreme.

The Power of Ownership: Why Copyright Matters

In the vast realm of creativity, your work is more than just an expression of your ideas—it's a valuable asset. Establishing copyright ownership is like setting a lock on that treasure chest, ensuring that only you hold the key. But why exactly does copyright ownership matter so much? Because in a world where intellectual property is one of the most powerful currencies, ownership isn't just a formality—it's your foundation for control, profit, and protection.

Ownership Equals Control

The most immediate benefit of establishing copyright ownership is that it gives you complete control over your work. This means you decide who can use it, how it can be used, and when. Whether it's a book, a painting, a song, or a piece of software, copyright law empowers you to:

- Reproduce the work and make copies.
- Distribute the work, either by selling it, licensing it, or sharing it freely.
- Create Derivative Works, such as adaptations, translations, or remixes.
- Display or Perform the work publicly.

Without clear ownership, others may exploit your work without permission, profiting off your efforts or diminishing the value of what you've created. When you claim your creation through copyright, you become the gatekeeper, deciding how it moves through the world.

Profits and Royalties: Monetizing Your Creativity

Copyright ownership isn't just about keeping others from using your work—it's about ensuring that you profit from it. When you own the copyright, you have the power to license your work to others for use in exchange for payment, whether it's a one-time fee or ongoing royalties. This is how authors, musicians, filmmakers, and creators across industries turn their art into income.

For instance, if you write a book, owning the copyright allows you to sell publishing rights, license film adaptations, or create audiobook versions—all generating revenue streams. When your creation becomes popular, copyright ensures that you receive the financial rewards for your talent and hard work.

In today's digital age, your work could go viral in an instant, reaching millions. Copyright ownership makes sure that when the world wants a piece of what you've created, the value flows back to you—not to someone who simply copied and reposted it.

Protecting Against Infringement

Unfortunately, the world of creativity is rife with opportunities for others to copy, steal, or misuse your work. Establishing copyright ownership arms you with the legal tools to protect yourself from infringement. If someone uses your work without permission, you have the right to:

- Send cease-and-desist notices demanding they stop using your work.
- Sue for damages, especially if they profited from your creation.
- Recover attorney's fees and potentially statutory damages if you registered your copyright before the infringement occurred.

Without legal ownership, you're left vulnerable, unable to enforce your rights. Registering your copyright makes it clear to the world—and to the courts—that this work is yours, giving you the power to defend it and demand justice when necessary.

Building a Legacy

Establishing copyright ownership also plays a critical role in securing your creative legacy. Copyright lasts for your lifetime plus 70 years in most countries, meaning that your heirs can continue to benefit from your creations long after you're gone. If your work becomes iconic or timeless, this ownership can generate long-term wealth for your family or estate.

Think of authors like J.R.R. Tolkien, musicians like Prince, or even filmmakers like Stanley Kubrick. Their estates continue to earn significant income from their creations because they secured copyright ownership. The same principle applies to anyone creating work today—whether you're writing the next great novel or designing a viral app, copyright ownership ensures your legacy endures beyond the spotlight of today's attention.

Copyright: The Backbone of Creative Industries

At its core, copyright ownership is what makes the creative economy thrive. It provides the legal framework for creators to exchange ideas, build upon existing works, and monetize their innovations. Without ownership, creators would lack the incentive to invest time, effort, and resources into their projects. Why spend years writing a book or composing a symphony if anyone can take it and profit without your permission?

Copyright allows creators to confidently pursue their passions, knowing that their efforts are protected and rewarded. This protection fuels the growth of industries like publishing, music, film, and digital media, where intellectual property is the most valuable asset.

In conclusion, copyright ownership matters because it gives you control, helps you profit from your creativity, protects you from infringement, and secures your legacy. Whether you're just starting out or already established, planting your flag in the ground by establishing ownership is the first step in turning your creative work into a lasting, protected, and valuable asset.

The Registration Process: From Creation to Ownership

Now that you understand why copyright ownership is vital, it's time to walk through how to officially establish that ownership. While your work is automatically protected by copyright the moment it's created, registering your copyright provides an additional layer of security that solidifies your claim and opens up avenues for legal protection and enforcement.

Let's break down the process from creation to formal ownership, so you can ensure that your creative work is safeguarded to the fullest extent of the law.

Step 1: Preparing Your Work for Registration

Before diving into the paperwork, ensure your work is in its final, complete form. Copyright protects your expression of an idea, not the idea itself, so the work must be tangible—whether it's a written manuscript, a digital file, a painting, or a song recording.

Make sure the version of your work that you're registering reflects the completed product. If you're registering a work in progress, understand that any future revisions or updates may require separate registrations.

Step 2: Determine the Correct Copyright Office or Agency

Depending on where you live or where your work will be distributed, you'll need to register with the appropriate copyright office. In the United States, this is done through the U.S. Copyright Office. Other countries have their own agencies, such as:

- **UK**: Intellectual Property Office (IPO)
- **Canada**: Canadian Intellectual Property Office (CIPO)
- **European Union**: European Union Intellectual Property Office (EUIPO)

If your work will be distributed internationally, most countries recognize foreign copyrights thanks to treaties like the Berne Convention. However, registering in your home country first is usually the best step.

Step 3: Complete the Registration Application

Once your work is ready and you know where to register, it's time to complete the registration application. In most countries, this can be done online, which speeds up the process considerably. Here's what you'll typically need to provide:

1. **Title of the Work**: Be specific about the title. If your work is part of a larger series, include both the series title and the title of the individual work.

2. **Type of Work**: Indicate whether it's a literary work, sound recording, visual artwork, software code, etc. The copyright office needs this information to categorize your work appropriately.

3. **Author Information**: Provide the names of all authors or creators involved in the work. If the work was created as part of employment or under contract, this should be noted.

4. **Creation and Publication Date**: You'll need to specify when the work was created and whether it has been published. If it's unpublished, you can still register it, but you should note that in your application.

5. **Claimant Information**: This is usually the same as the author, but if ownership has been transferred (for example, to a company), you'll need to indicate the new owner.

6. **Rights or Licenses**: If you're licensing parts of the work to others or sharing authorship with collaborators, include these details in the application. This ensures that rights are clear and unambiguous.

Step 4: Submit a Copy of Your Work

Along with the registration form, you'll need to provide a deposit—a copy of the work you're registering. For online submissions, this is typically a digital file. For physical works like sculptures, paintings, or analog media, you may need to send in a physical copy.

The deposit becomes part of the public record, and while it won't be used commercially or distributed, it serves as evidence of what exactly you're registering. This protects you in the event of future disputes over the work's originality or authorship.

Step 5: Pay the Registration Fee

There is a fee associated with copyright registration, and it varies depending on the type of work and how you submit it. Online registration is generally the cheapest and fastest route, with fees in the U.S. typically ranging from $35 to $85. Physical submissions or registrations for multiple works, like a collection of photographs or a series of written works, may incur higher fees.

While the fee may seem like an additional burden, it's a small price to pay for the peace of mind and legal protections that registration provides.

Step 6: Receive Your Certificate of Registration

After you submit your application, deposit, and payment, your work will be reviewed by the copyright office. This process can take a few months, depending on the volume of submissions. Once everything is approved, you'll receive a Certificate of Registration—a formal document that confirms your copyright claim.

It's important to note that your copyright protection is retroactive to the date the office receives your complete application, not the date the certificate is issued. This means your work is protected during the waiting period.

Why Registration is Worth It

While registration isn't mandatory to claim copyright ownership, it offers significant advantages. Here's why it's worth the effort:

- **Legal Protection**: If someone infringes on your work, you can't file a lawsuit without first registering your copyright. Registration gives you the standing to pursue legal action and recover damages.

- **Evidence of Ownership**: Your registration creates a public record, which acts as proof that you own the work. This can be crucial if someone else tries to claim ownership or if a dispute arises.

- **Statutory Damages and Attorney's Fees**: If your work is registered before infringement occurs, or within three months of publication, you may be eligible for statutory damages (predetermined compensation) and attorney's fees in the event of a lawsuit. Without registration, you're limited to recovering actual damages, which can be difficult to prove and often results in lower compensation.

- **International Recognition**: Many countries honor foreign copyrights, but having your work registered in your home country strengthens your claim abroad. This is especially important in the digital age, where works can quickly reach a global audience.

Special Cases: Group Registrations, Unpublished Works, and Derivatives

Depending on your situation, there may be additional considerations:

- **Group Registrations**: If you're registering multiple works, like a series of blog posts or a collection of photographs, you may qualify for group registration. This can save time and money, but it's important to follow the specific rules for these cases.

- **Unpublished Works**: You can register works before they're published. This is especially useful for manuscripts or projects in development, as it establishes ownership early on. However, you may need to update your registration once the work is published.

- **Derivative Works**: If your new work builds upon an existing copyrighted work (either your own or someone else's), make sure to clearly define which parts of the work are original to you. This is important for protecting your new creation without infringing on prior copyrights.

Conclusion: Your Work, Your Rights

Registering your copyright is more than just ticking a box—it's the official declaration that your creative work is yours. The registration process solidifies your ownership, grants you the legal tools to protect your creation, and ensures that you can fully benefit from it. By taking this step, you're not just safeguarding your current work—you're building a foundation for future creations and securing your place in the creative world.

In the end, the time and effort you invest in registering your copyright is an investment in your creative future. The next time your masterpiece reaches the public, you'll have the peace of mind knowing that your ownership is not just implied but documented and protected.

Joint Authorship and Ownership: Sharing the Crown

Collaboration can lead to some of the most exciting and innovative creations in the world of art, literature, music, and beyond. But when two or more creative minds come together, the question of ownership becomes a little more complex. Who holds the rights? How are profits divided? Who gets to make decisions about how the work is used? This is where joint authorship comes into play, and understanding the rules of shared ownership is essential for any successful creative partnership.

In this section, we'll explore the ins and outs of joint authorship and ownership, helping you navigate the delicate balance of collaboration so that everyone involved in a project gets the credit—and the rights—they deserve.

What Is Joint Authorship?

Joint authorship occurs when two or more people collaborate to create a single work, and they intend to merge their contributions into an inseparable whole. Think of a songwriting duo, co-authors of a book, or artists creating a joint mural. The key is that each contributor must contribute something original and creative, and all parties must agree that the work will be a joint creation.

For a work to be considered jointly authored, two important criteria must be met:

1. **Intent to Collaborate**: The creators must have intended to work together to produce a unified whole. For instance, if two writers each contribute chapters to the same book, intending it to be published as a single, cohesive piece, this qualifies as joint authorship.

2. **Creative Contribution**: Each contributor must provide more than just an idea—they must make a tangible, creative contribution to the work.

25

For example, someone providing research or edits may not qualify as a joint author unless their contribution involves original creativity.

Joint Ownership: What You Need to Know

When a work is considered to have joint authorship, the copyright ownership is shared among the authors, and this has several important implications. Each co-owner has certain rights and responsibilities that must be understood to avoid future conflicts.

1. **Equal Ownership by Default**: In the absence of any written agreement stating otherwise, copyright law generally assumes that each author owns an equal share of the work—regardless of how much they contributed. This means that even if one author wrote 90% of the work and the other wrote 10%, they both own 50% of the copyright unless they agree otherwise in writing.

2. **Independent Use**: Each joint author has the right to use or license the work independently without needing the permission of the other authors—as long as they share any profits from the use with the other co-owners. For example, if one songwriter licenses a jointly written song to a film, they must split the profits with their co-writer, but they don't need the co-writer's approval to make the deal.

3. **Decisions on Derivative Works**: Joint owners also have the right to create derivative works, such as adaptations, without the other owners' consent, as long as any resulting profits are shared. This can lead to tension if one author creates a spin-off or adaptation that the other owners don't agree with, making it essential to have agreements in place.

4. **Transfer of Ownership**: Any joint author can transfer or sell their share of the copyright, but the buyer will then only own that specific portion of the work. The remaining co-owners will continue to own their shares. This can create complex situations where new owners are introduced into the mix, often leading to legal disputes if not handled carefully.

The Importance of a Written Agreement

While the law provides default rules for joint ownership, it's always best to have a written agreement in place before you start a collaboration. This agreement can clearly define:

- **Ownership Shares**: If you don't want an automatic 50-50 split, specify the percentages of ownership based on the contribution.

- **Decision-Making Power**: Clarify who has the authority to license, sell, or adapt the work and under what conditions. This can prevent future conflicts over how the work is used or monetized.

- **Profit Splits**: Spell out exactly how profits will be divided. This can include royalties, licensing fees, and any future income from derivative works.

- **Credit and Attribution**: Ensure that each author's contribution is acknowledged in the way they prefer, whether that's on the cover of a book, in film credits, or in liner notes for an album.

A well-crafted joint authorship agreement not only avoids disputes but also sets clear expectations and keeps the collaboration running smoothly. It gives all parties the confidence that their contributions are valued and their rights protected.

Special Cases in Joint Authorship

Joint authorship can get especially tricky in certain situations. Here are a few cases where it's important to be extra vigilant about defining ownership:

- **Work-for-Hire**: If one person is hired to contribute to a project, their contributions might not qualify for joint authorship. Instead, the work is considered a "work-for-hire," and the employer retains full ownership unless otherwise specified. For example, if a graphic designer is hired to create an illustration for a book, they typically don't own the copyright to that work—the author or publisher does.

- **Collaborations Across Mediums**: In cases where a work involves multiple mediums, such as a play with an original score, the rights and ownership can become even more complex. Each contributor—whether a playwright or composer—needs to have their respective rights clearly outlined in the agreement.

- **Posthumous Contributions**: If a joint author passes away, their ownership of the work transfers to their heirs or estate, but the other living co-authors retain their rights. The new heirs may then enter into any decisions or agreements concerning the work's future use.

Avoiding Future Disputes: Best Practices for Joint Creators

To ensure that joint authorship remains a harmonious collaboration rather than a legal battle waiting to happen, consider the following best practices:

- **Communicate Openly**: From the outset, be transparent with your co-authors about expectations, contributions, and goals for the project. Regular communication can prevent misunderstandings.

- **Agree on Attribution**: Discuss and agree on how each author will be credited, both in the final product and in any future marketing or derivative works.

- **Establish Ownership and Licensing Terms Early**: Don't wait until the project is finished to figure out ownership shares and how the work can be used. The earlier you hammer out the details, the fewer surprises there will be later.

- **Consult Legal Advice**: Especially for larger or high-stakes projects, having a legal professional review your joint authorship agreement can save you from potential disputes down the line.

Conclusion: Collaboration Done Right

Joint authorship and shared ownership don't have to be a thorny issue if approached with clarity, communication, and proper planning. While creative partnerships can be some of the most rewarding, they require a solid foundation to ensure that everyone gets fair credit, rights, and profits from their contributions.

By understanding the legal framework of joint authorship and putting agreements in place, you and your co-creators can focus on what matters most—bringing your collaborative vision to life. When done right, sharing the crown of ownership can lead to a creative kingdom that thrives for years to come.

Derivative Works and Licensing: Extending Your Creative Kingdom

Once you've established ownership over your creative work, the next step is often to explore how to expand its reach. Whether through licensing your work to others or creating derivative works, the possibilities for building upon your creation are vast. These strategies not only extend the life and influence of your work but can also open up new revenue streams and opportunities for growth.

In this final section, we'll break down the key concepts of derivative works and licensing, helping you understand how to retain control while allowing your creative kingdom to expand in ways that benefit you.

What Are Derivative Works?

A derivative work is a new creation that is based on, or derived from, an existing copyrighted work. It could take many forms, such as:

- A movie adaptation of a book.

- A sequel to a novel.

- A remix or sampling of a song.

- A translation of a book into another language.

- A video game based on a comic book.

The critical factor is that the derivative work incorporates elements of the original work but transforms or adds new content, making it a unique creation in its own right. However, the original creator retains significant control over how derivative works are created and used.

Your Rights as a Copyright Owner Over Derivative Works

As the copyright owner, you have the exclusive right to create or authorize derivative works. No one else can adapt, modify, or build upon your original creation without your permission. This control is one of the key powers of copyright ownership and allows you to protect the integrity of your work while also benefiting financially from new versions.

Here's why understanding your rights over derivative works is essential:

- **Control Over Adaptations**: If someone wants to adapt your novel into a screenplay or turn your painting into a piece of merchandise, they must first get your permission. You can negotiate the terms of this use, including how much creative freedom they have and how you will be compensated.

- **Retaining Credit and Profits**: As the owner of the original work, you are entitled to both credit and royalties from any derivative work. Even if someone else creates the adaptation, you still have a claim to the profits because the new work is based on your creation.

- **Protecting Your Legacy**: Derivative works can either enhance or diminish the reputation of the original. By retaining control, you ensure that any adaptations align with your vision and maintain the quality or message you intended. For instance, an author may want final approval over how their characters are portrayed in a film adaptation to avoid misrepresentation.

Licensing: Sharing Your Creation Without Losing Ownership

If you want to let others use your work but don't want to give up ownership, licensing is the perfect solution. A copyright license allows you to grant permission for someone else to use, distribute, or create derivative works based on your creation—without transferring your rights entirely.

Licensing is a powerful way to extend your creative reach, allowing others to help spread your work while you maintain control and receive financial benefits. There are several types of licenses you can grant, depending on your goals and how much control you want to retain:

1. **Exclusive License**: You grant one individual or entity the exclusive right to use or create derivative works based on your original. For example, a publisher may receive an exclusive license to distribute your book,

meaning no other publishers can do so. Exclusive licenses often come with higher compensation but may limit your ability to work with others.

2. **Non-Exclusive License**: You grant permission to multiple individuals or entities to use your work. For instance, you might license a song for use in multiple commercials or allow several artists to create merchandise based on your artwork. Non-exclusive licenses give you more flexibility to work with various partners while still earning royalties from each one.

3. **Limited License**: A license that restricts how, where, or for how long the licensee can use your work. For example, you may grant a film studio a license to adapt your novel into a movie, but only for a period of five years, after which the rights revert to you.

4. **Creative Commons License**: This is a more flexible type of license where you can allow others to use your work freely under specific conditions. You can choose whether to allow modifications, whether to require attribution, or whether commercial use is permitted. Creative Commons is popular among creators who want to share their work more openly while still retaining some control.

Key Considerations When Licensing Your Work

Licensing can be a lucrative and effective way to expand your creative empire, but it's essential to manage it carefully. Here are some important considerations:

- **Retain Legal Counsel**: Licensing agreements can be complex, and it's crucial to have a legal professional draft or review the terms to ensure your interests are protected. Clear terms prevent disputes down the line and ensure that both parties understand their rights and obligations.

- **Set Royalty Rates**: One of the main benefits of licensing is the potential for ongoing income. Make sure your agreement includes clearly defined royalty rates that outline how much you will earn from the use or sale of your work. These royalties could be based on a percentage of sales, a flat fee, or a combination of both.

- **Define Usage Rights**: Be specific about how the licensee can use your work. For example, are they allowed to make changes or adaptations? Can they sublicense the work to others? Defining these terms helps you maintain control over how your creation is used.

- **Territory and Duration**: Your license can specify geographic limits (e.g., the license only applies in North America) or time limits (e.g., the license is valid for five years). These limits allow you to maximize the value of your work in different markets over time.

The Benefits of Licensing and Derivative Works

Expanding your creative kingdom through licensing and derivative works has numerous benefits:

- **Increased Exposure**: By licensing your work to others, you tap into new markets and audiences that you might not have reached on your own. For instance, licensing your artwork for merchandise could introduce your brand to a broader audience beyond art collectors.

- **Ongoing Income**: Licensing allows you to continue earning from your work without constantly creating something new. For example, licensing a song to be used in multiple commercials or films can generate consistent royalty payments over time.

- **Creative Expansion**: Derivative works provide opportunities to see your creation reimagined in new forms. A novel can become a film or TV show, a painting can be turned into digital art, or a song can be remixed into different genres—all while crediting you as the original creator.

Conclusion: Expanding Your Creative Kingdom

Derivative works and licensing offer a pathway to grow your creative legacy, allowing others to build upon your original work while still giving you control and financial benefits. Whether you're licensing your work for commercial use or creating spin-offs that reach new audiences, these strategies provide endless possibilities for expanding the reach and impact of your creation.

By understanding your rights and carefully managing how your work is used, you can extend your creative kingdom without losing ownership. In the end, the power of copyright is not just in protecting what you've already made—but in giving you the freedom to shape where your creative journey will take you next.

Quick Tips and Recap

- **Register Your Work for Maximum Protection**: While copyright is automatic, registering your work provides stronger legal protection and allows you to take action in case of infringement.

- **Define Joint Ownership Clearly**: If you're collaborating, ensure that you have a written agreement specifying ownership shares, decision-making authority, and how profits will be divided.

- **Control Derivative Works**: As the copyright owner, you have the exclusive right to create or authorize derivative works—protect this right to ensure your vision remains intact.

- **Use Licensing to Expand Your Reach**: Licensing allows others to use your work while you retain ownership. Make sure licensing agreements are clear about terms, royalties, and usage rights.

- **Keep Written Agreements**: Always have formal agreements in place for collaborations, joint ownership, or licensing deals to prevent disputes and ensure that everyone's rights are protected.

- **Consult Legal Counsel**: When dealing with complex ownership or licensing issues, getting legal advice can save you from potential conflicts and ensure you're making the best decisions for your work.

- **Extend Your Creative Legacy**: Through licensing and derivative works, you can extend the life and reach of your creation, potentially generating ongoing income while maintaining control.

What's Covered? The Scope of Copyright Protection

"Copyright doesn't cover everything, but understanding its boundaries can transform how effectively you protect and leverage your creative works." — J. K. ROWLING, AUTHOR

Chapter Three, "What's Covered? The Scope of Copyright Protection," pulls back the curtain on the magic show that is copyright law. Here, we demystify what's protected under the shimmering dome of copyright and what remains in the public domain, free for all like snacks at a party.

Think of copyright as a VIP pass at a festival. It doesn't get you everywhere—you can't swing backstage just because you penned a catchy tune or snapped a poignant photo—but it does give you a whole lot of exclusive access. This chapter explores the boundaries of this pass, detailing what types of works can strut down the copyright runway (hint: originality is your best outfit) and which ones are left dancing in the rain.

From novels to software, and from architecture to ad jingles, we'll chart out the territories where your copyright reigns supreme. We'll also tip-toe around the edges where ideas meet expression, helping you understand why you can copyright a novel recipe for apple pie, but not the idea of pie itself. Yes, it's a bit like explaining why your dog can't be vegan—it makes sense, but it's complicated.

So, buckle up and keep your hands inside the vehicle at all times. This ride through the scope of copyright protection promises to be as enlightening as it is entertaining. After all, who said legal boundaries couldn't have a bit of flair?

Original Works: What Qualifies for Copyright Protection

Copyright protection doesn't cover everything under the sun. Instead, it applies to original works of authorship—those creations that spring from your mind and are fixed in some kind of tangible form. Understanding what qualifies for protection is key to safeguarding your creative efforts, so let's dive into what makes a work copyrightable.

The Two Key Elements of Copyright Protection

For a work to qualify for copyright protection, it must meet two essential criteria: it must be original, and it must be fixed in a tangible medium. Let's break down each of these components.

1. **Originality**

   o   Originality is the foundation of copyright law. To be eligible for protection, your work must be independently created by you and not copied from someone else. It doesn't need to be a groundbreaking or completely unique idea, but the way you express that idea must be your own. In other words, originality doesn't mean the idea itself is new—it's how you've expressed it that matters.

For example, you can't copyright the concept of a love story, but you can copyright the way you've written a particular love story with your own characters, dialogue, and setting. Similarly, a photographer can't copyright the idea of a sunset, but they can copyright their unique photograph of one.

Originality also requires a minimum level of creativity, though the threshold is fairly low. Even simple works like a photograph or a logo design can qualify as long as there's some degree of creative decision-making involved.

2. **Fixed in a Tangible Medium**

   o Copyright protection only applies to works that are "fixed" in a tangible form that others can see, hear, or touch. This means the work must exist in a concrete way, such as a written manuscript, a recorded song, a painting, a digital file, or even a sculpture.

Ideas floating around in your head aren't protected by copyright. If you come up with a brilliant concept for a novel but haven't written it down or typed it out, it isn't eligible for protection. The moment your ideas are fixed in a tangible form, whether on paper, on a canvas, or in a digital format, copyright protection kicks in automatically.

What Types of Works Are Protected?

Copyright law casts a wide net over many different types of works. As long as the work is original and fixed, it can be protected. Here's a look at some of the most common categories of copyrightable works:

1. **Literary Works**

   o This category includes not just books and novels but also poems, essays, articles, blog posts, and even software code. If it's written and fixed, it qualifies. Keep in mind that short phrases, titles, or slogans generally don't meet the threshold for copyright protection (though they may be eligible for trademark protection).

2. **Musical Works**

    o   Both the composition of a song (the notes, melody, and harmony) and the recording of that song are eligible for copyright protection. Lyrics, when written down, are also considered a form of literary work and are protected under copyright law. It's important to note that the composition and the sound recording can be two separate copyrighted works.

3. **Dramatic Works**

    o   Plays, screenplays, and scripted performances are protected, along with any accompanying music or choreography. The protection covers the specific expression of the performance, not the overall theme or concept.

4. **Choreographic Works**

    o   Original dance choreography is protected when it's recorded or notated in some way. However, social dances or simple routines might not qualify for protection.

5. **Pictorial, Graphic, and Sculptural Works**

    o   Visual art, including paintings, drawings, photographs, sculptures, and even architectural designs, are protected by copyright. The design of useful objects, like furniture, may also qualify if the design incorporates original, creative elements.

6. **Audiovisual Works**

    o   Movies, TV shows, documentaries, and online videos fall under this category. The protection covers both the visual elements (the film itself) and the accompanying sounds (the soundtrack).

7. **Architectural Works**

    o   The design of buildings and structures is protected, as long as the design incorporates creative expression. Copyright law, however, doesn't cover the functional aspects of a building, like safety features or utility.

8. **Software and Computer Programs**

    o   Source code and object code for software programs are considered literary works and are protected under copyright law. The functionality of the software itself, however, may be eligible for patent protection, not copyright.

What About Compilations and Collective Works?

In addition to original works, copyright law also protects compilations and collective works. These are works that consist of material selected and arranged in a way that demonstrates creativity, even if the individual parts of the compilation aren't original.

*   **Compilations**: If you've collected data, images, or text from various sources and arranged them in a unique way (like a database or an anthology), the selection and organization of those elements can be protected by copyright. However, the individual components remain protected by their own copyrights.

*   **Collective Works**: Collective works, like magazines, anthologies, or albums, consist of multiple distinct works assembled together. The overall compilation is protected, but each individual work within the collection retains its own copyright.

Why Originality Matters

The concept of originality is crucial because copyright law seeks to protect creativity and expression—not common ideas or information. For instance, if copyright applied to ideas or facts, it would stifle innovation and prevent others from building on existing knowledge. That's why originality is the bedrock of copyright protection. Your specific expression of an idea is safeguarded, but the idea itself remains open for others to explore.

Conclusion: Protect What You Create

Understanding what qualifies for copyright protection is essential for any creator. Your original works—whether they're novels, songs, paintings, or software—are valuable assets that deserve legal protection. By ensuring your creations are both original and fixed in a tangible form, you unlock the full scope of copyright law's protective power, allowing you to safeguard your intellectual property and control how it's used. In the next section, we'll explore what's not covered by copyright, and why some things, like ideas and facts, remain outside its reach.

Excluded from Coverage: Ideas, Facts, and Public Domain

While copyright law grants broad protection over creative works, not everything under the creative sun qualifies. There are important exclusions—things that, no matter how innovative or clever, fall outside the boundaries of copyright protection. In this section, we'll explore what isn't covered by copyright law, focusing on ideas, facts, and works in the public domain, and why these exclusions matter.

Ideas vs. Expression: The Crucial Distinction

One of the most fundamental tenets of copyright law is the separation between ideas and the expression of those ideas. Copyright protects the way ideas are expressed in tangible form, not the ideas themselves. Here's how that breaks down:

- **Ideas**: The raw concepts, themes, or principles behind a creative work are not eligible for copyright protection. This means that anyone can take the same idea and express it differently. For example, the concept of a superhero who saves the world is not protected—only the specific way a particular superhero is created, described, and portrayed in a story or comic book.

- **Expression**: The way you choose to bring that idea to life—the dialogue, characters, visual art, or music that represents it—is protected by copyright. This is why you can have dozens of romantic comedies based on the same idea of two unlikely people falling in love, but each individual movie is protected as its own unique work.

This distinction is essential because it promotes innovation while ensuring creators can't monopolize basic concepts. If copyright applied to ideas, it would block others from creating anything remotely similar, which would be a major roadblock to creative progress.

Facts and Data: Not Eligible for Copyright

Similar to ideas, facts are not protected by copyright. Facts are seen as part of the public knowledge and therefore available for anyone to use and share. You can't claim ownership over historical events, scientific data, or objective truths, no matter how much research you put into discovering or compiling them.

For example:

- You can't copyright the fact that the sun rises in the east or that George Washington was the first president of the United States.

- If you write a book about Washington's presidency, you can copyright the specific expression of that information—how you present and interpret the facts. But the facts themselves remain unprotected and can be used freely by others.

This exclusion is crucial for fostering the free flow of information, especially in academic, scientific, and journalistic contexts. If facts were copyrightable, it would hinder the ability of researchers, historians, and others to access and share important knowledge.

Procedures, Methods, and Systems

In addition to ideas and facts, procedures, methods, systems, and concepts are not protected by copyright law. This includes things like:

- Recipes (the list of ingredients and steps)

- Mathematical formulas

- Instructions for assembling something

- Business methods or technical processes

While you can't copyright the actual method or process, you can copyright the specific text or expression that describes it. For instance, a cookbook's introduction, explanations, or photography may be protected by copyright, but the recipe itself is not. Similarly, you can't copyright a scientific method, but you can protect the way you've written about it in a research paper.

If you invent something like a process, system, or method, you may need to look into patent protection instead of copyright. Patents protect inventions and technical innovations, not creative expression.

Works in the Public Domain

Not all works are protected by copyright indefinitely. After a certain period, they enter the public domain, where anyone is free to use, adapt, or build upon them without permission. Once a work is in the public domain, it can be reproduced, modified, and shared without fear of infringement.

Works can enter the public domain in several ways:

1. **Expiration of Copyright**: In most countries, copyright protection lasts for the life of the author plus 70 years. After that period, the work enters the public domain. For works created by corporations or under pseudonyms, copyright typically lasts 95 years from publication or 120 years from creation, whichever is shorter. For example, many of Shakespeare's plays and Beethoven's symphonies are in the public domain.

2. **Failure to Comply with Formalities**: In the past, works could fall into the public domain if their copyright owners failed to renew protection or follow formal registration procedures. However, modern copyright law automatically protects works upon creation, making this much less common today.

3. **Voluntary Dedication**: An author can choose to dedicate their work to the public domain, relinquishing their exclusive rights and allowing others to freely use the work. For example, some creators release works under licenses like Creative Commons Zero (CC0), which allows anyone to use the work without restriction.

4. **Government Publications**: In many countries, works created by government agencies or employees as part of their official duties are automatically placed in the public domain. This is to encourage

transparency and public access to information. For instance, reports from the U.S. government, like a weather forecast or a legal statute, are free for public use.

Why These Exclusions Matter

The exclusions from copyright protection serve a vital purpose in maintaining a balance between encouraging creativity and promoting access to ideas and information. If everything were protected by copyright—ideas, facts, methods—the creative landscape would be stifled, and innovation would be restricted.

- **Encouraging Innovation**: By allowing ideas, facts, and methods to remain free for use, copyright law ensures that others can build on existing knowledge. This promotes progress in fields like science, art, and technology, where new discoveries and innovations often rely on the work of others.

- **Access to Knowledge**: Keeping facts and data in the public domain ensures that researchers, journalists, and educators can freely share information. Copyright law's focus on protecting creative expression—rather than knowledge itself—encourages the spread of education and understanding without unnecessary legal barriers.

- **Creative Freedom**: When a work enters the public domain, it opens the door for future creators to reinterpret, remix, and reimagine the original. For example, many modern adaptations of classic literature or public domain stories have resulted in new, innovative works that bring older content to new audiences.

Conclusion: Knowing What's Free and What's Protected

As a creator, it's essential to understand not just what's protected by copyright, but also what isn't. Ideas, facts, methods, and public domain works remain open for everyone to use, ensuring a healthy exchange of knowledge and inspiration. While your expression of an idea is safeguarded, the idea itself is not—and that's a good thing. It means the creative world is constantly evolving, with space for new voices and perspectives to build on the ideas that came before.

In the next section, we'll explore the specific categories of works that are protected by copyright, breaking down the types of creative expressions that fall under its protective shield.

Types of Protected Works: A Breakdown by Category

Copyright protection covers a wide range of creative works, provided they meet the key requirements of originality and being fixed in a tangible form. These works span numerous categories, from written literature to software code. In this section, we'll break down the various types of works that enjoy copyright protection, along with examples for each category, to give you a clear understanding of what falls under the copyright umbrella.

1. Literary Works

When most people think of literary works, novels and short stories come to mind. But the category is much broader than that. It includes anything written that can be fixed in a readable format. Whether it's a physical book, an article, or a digital document, the written word is protected by copyright.

Examples:

- Books, novels, and essays

- Poems, blog posts, and articles

- Academic papers and research reports

- Software code (often overlooked but falls under literary works)

What's Not Covered: Titles, slogans, short phrases, and common expressions are not protected by copyright. They're often too minimal or widely used to meet the originality requirement.

2. Musical Works and Sound Recordings

Music enjoys strong copyright protection, both in terms of the musical composition (the melody, harmony, and arrangement) and the sound recording itself (the recorded performance of the song). These two are treated separately, meaning a composer may hold the copyright for the composition, while a recording artist or producer might hold the copyright for the sound recording.

Examples:

- Sheet music, scores, and song compositions

- Recorded music, whether on a CD, streaming service, or digital file

- Lyrics to songs (protected as literary works)

What's Not Covered: Simple rhythmic patterns or short sequences of notes may not meet the threshold for originality.

3. Dramatic Works

Dramatic works include plays, screenplays, and scripts for performances. These works are protected in their written form and in any recorded or performed versions. A dramatic work can involve spoken dialogue, movement, and even music, but it's the way all these elements are combined into a cohesive narrative that's protected by copyright.

Examples:

- The script for a stage play or musical

- Screenplays for movies and TV shows

- Radio dramas or spoken-word performances

What's Not Covered: Simple ideas or themes for a drama aren't protected—only the script's specific expression.

4. Choreographic Works

Choreography involves the creative arrangement of movements, often set to music, and is protected under copyright when it's written down, recorded, or otherwise fixed in a tangible form. While a dance performed live may not be automatically protected, once it's recorded or notated, the choreographer's creative work is safeguarded.

Examples:

- Ballet routines or modern dance choreography

- Choreographed stage performances or music video dances

What's Not Covered: Simple, commonly known movements (e.g., walking, jumping, or social dances) are not protected by copyright.

5. Pictorial, Graphic, and Sculptural Works

Visual art forms are strongly protected by copyright, whether they exist in traditional media or digital formats. This category includes everything from paintings and drawings to photographs and sculptures. The key is that the visual work must be original and fixed in some tangible way, like on canvas, film, or digital media.

Examples:

- Paintings, drawings, and illustrations

- Photographs and posters

- Sculptures and 3D artwork

- Architectural drawings or blueprints (though the physical building itself falls under a different category)

What's Not Covered: Functional objects that incorporate artistic design (e.g., furniture) may not always be fully protected, as the design may serve a utilitarian purpose.

6. Audiovisual Works

Audiovisual works combine sound and visuals into a unified piece, such as movies, TV shows, and online videos. Copyright protection covers both the visual and audio components. The protection ensures that filmmakers, animators, and video creators retain control over their work and can license it for distribution or adaptations.

Examples:

- Feature films, documentaries, and short films

- TV shows, web series, and online video content (e.g., YouTube videos)

- Animated movies or cartoons

What's Not Covered: Simple concepts, themes, or unrecorded visual ideas are not protected. You can't copyright the idea of a superhero team, but you can protect the specific portrayal of one in a film.

7. Architectural Works

The design of buildings and structures is also protected by copyright, as long as the design is creative and original. This protection applies to the architectural plans as well as the building itself, although the functional elements of the structure—like staircases, walls, and windows—are not protected. It's the creative design and artistic aspects that copyright law shields.

Examples:

- Blueprints or technical drawings for buildings

- Completed architectural works like museums or iconic homes

- Design plans for bridges, parks, or public spaces

What's Not Covered: Functional or structural elements that are necessary for the building's operation (e.g., doors, load-bearing walls) are not protected.

8. Software and Computer Programs

In today's digital age, software is another significant category of protected works. The source code and object code that make up computer programs are treated as literary works under copyright law. Copyright protection allows developers to retain control over their software, preventing unauthorized use or copying.

Examples:

- Source code for software applications

- Web-based programs and mobile apps

- Video game code

What's Not Covered: The actual functionality or design of the software (like how the software operates or performs tasks) may be eligible for patent protection, but not copyright.

9. Compilations and Collective Works

This category covers works that compile existing content in a creative way. While the individual pieces in a compilation or collective work may be protected by their own copyrights, the way the content is selected, arranged, and presented can itself be a copyrightable expression.

Examples:

- Anthologies or collections of short stories, poems, or essays

- A curated photo book or art exhibition catalog

- Databases or collections of data, as long as the selection and arrangement involve original creativity

What's Not Covered: The individual works in the compilation retain their own copyrights, so you'd need permission to use them if they're not already in the public domain.

Conclusion: The Creative Spectrum of Copyright Protection

Copyright law provides robust protection for a wide variety of creative works, from the written word to visual art, and from music to computer programs. By recognizing what's covered and how these categories apply to different types of works, you gain a better understanding of how your creations can be protected under copyright law. Whether you're a writer, artist, musician, or software developer, your original expressions of creativity are shielded by copyright, giving you the power to control how they're used and shared.

In the next section, we'll explore how long this protection lasts and what happens when a work enters the public domain.

Duration and Limitations: How Long Copyright Protection Lasts

Copyright protection doesn't last forever. While it grants creators exclusive rights over their works for a significant period, there comes a point when the protection expires, and the work enters the public domain, becoming free for anyone to use. Understanding the duration of copyright and its limitations is essential for managing your intellectual property effectively.

In this section, we'll explore how long copyright protection lasts, the factors that influence this duration, and the limitations that shape how your work can be used even while it's protected.

How Long Does Copyright Last?

The length of copyright protection depends on several factors, including when the work was created, whether it has been published, and who owns the copyright. The duration has evolved over time, but modern copyright law generally offers a lengthy period of protection.

Here's a breakdown of the most common rules for how long copyright lasts today:

1. **Works Created by an Individual (After January 1, 1978)**

   o For works created by an individual, the copyright lasts for the life of the author plus 70 years. This means that after the author's death, their heirs or estate can continue to benefit from the work for another 70 years. After that period, the work enters the public domain, where it can be freely used by anyone.

   o **Example**: If an author writes a novel in 2000 and passes away in 2040, the copyright would last until 2110 (2040 + 70 years).

2. **Works Made for Hire, Corporate Authorship, or Anonymous/Pseudonymous Works**

   o For works created under a corporate entity, works made for hire, or works published anonymously or under a pseudonym, the copyright lasts for the shorter of:

- 95 years from the date of publication, or

- 120 years from the date of creation.

  o **Example**: If a company publishes a film in 1990, the copyright would expire in 2085 (1990 + 95 years).

3. **Works Published Before 1978**

   o For works published before January 1, 1978, copyright durations can be more complex due to the changes in copyright law over the years. These works were typically granted an initial term of 28 years with the possibility of a renewal term. However, the 1976 Copyright Act extended protection for works that were still under copyright, adding 67 years to the renewal term. As a result, these works enjoy protection for a total of 95 years from the date of publication.

   o **Example**: A book published in 1940 would remain under copyright until 2035 (1940 + 95 years).

What Happens When Copyright Expires?

Once the copyright term expires, the work enters the public domain, which means it is no longer protected by copyright law. Anyone can use, reproduce, or modify the work without asking for permission or paying royalties. This is why many classic works of literature, art, and music are freely available and widely adapted into new forms.

For example:

- Shakespeare's plays, which are in the public domain, can be freely performed, adapted, and modified without legal restrictions.

- Classical music compositions by composers like Beethoven and Mozart are also in the public domain, allowing modern musicians to record or reinterpret them without infringing copyright.

Public domain works are a rich resource for creators, as they offer the freedom to build on timeless ideas and cultural treasures without needing to navigate legal permissions.

Limitations on Copyright: Fair Use, Public Access, and More

While copyright gives creators control over their works, it comes with certain limitations that ensure a balance between protecting intellectual property and promoting public access to information and culture. These limitations include:

1. **Fair Use**

   o   Fair use allows others to use copyrighted material without permission in certain circumstances. It's a legal doctrine designed to encourage freedom of expression, scholarship, commentary, and criticism. Fair use is typically determined by considering factors like the purpose of the use (e.g., educational or transformative), the amount of the work used, and the effect on the market for the original work.

   o   **Examples of Fair Use**:

   ▪   Quoting a book in a literary review or academic paper.

   ▪   Using brief clips from a movie for commentary or parody.

   ▪   Repurposing a work in a transformative way that adds new meaning, such as creating a mashup or remix.

2. **Educational Use**

   o   In some cases, copyright law provides special exceptions for educational purposes. For example, teachers and students may use copyrighted materials in a classroom setting for teaching, research, and study without needing permission from the copyright holder.

   o   However, these exceptions are limited, and they don't apply to commercial use or for-profit education.

3. **Compulsory Licensing**

   o   In certain cases, the law allows for compulsory licensing, where the copyright holder must allow others to use their work under specific conditions and in exchange for a set fee. This is common in the music industry, where songwriters and music publishers are required to grant licenses to others who want to record their music after it has been published.

o   Compulsory licensing ensures that creative works can continue to be distributed and enjoyed by the public while still compensating the original creators.

4.   **Public Access to Government Works**

o   In many countries, including the United States, works created by the government are automatically placed in the public domain. This means that government publications, reports, and data are freely available to the public and can be used, shared, or repurposed without restriction.

When Copyright Can Be Challenged or Waived

In some instances, creators may voluntarily waive their copyright or dedicate their works to the public domain. This can be done through licenses like Creative Commons, which allow creators to specify how their works can be used by others while retaining certain rights.

- **Creative Commons Licenses**: These licenses let creators share their work more freely while giving others permission to use, adapt, or build upon it, often with certain conditions like requiring attribution or prohibiting commercial use.

- **Public Domain Dedication**: Some creators opt to release their works into the public domain, giving up all copyright protections and allowing anyone to use the work without limitations.

Conclusion: The Lifespan of Creativity

Copyright protection gives creators a powerful tool to control how their works are used, but that protection isn't endless. By understanding how long copyright lasts and the limitations placed on it, you can better manage your creative assets and ensure your works remain protected for as long as possible. Whether your work eventually enters the public domain or is licensed for public use, knowing the lifespan of your rights helps you make informed decisions about how your creations will live on.

In the next chapter, we'll explore how to defend those rights when someone crosses the line into copyright infringement and what steps you can take to protect your work from unauthorized use.

Quick Tips and Recap

- **Copyright Lasts for Life + 70 Years**: For individual creators, copyright protection generally lasts for the life of the author plus 70 years, giving you and your heirs long-term control over your work.

- **Corporate Works Last 95 or 120 Years**: Works made for hire or owned by corporations are protected for either 95 years from publication or 120 years from creation, whichever is shorter.

- **Works Enter the Public Domain When Protection Expires**: Once copyright protection ends, the work enters the public domain, allowing anyone to use, reproduce, or modify it freely.

- **Fair Use Allows Limited Use Without Permission**: Certain uses like criticism, commentary, education, and parody may be allowed under fair use without requiring permission from the copyright owner.

- **Government Works Are in the Public Domain**: In many countries, government-created works are automatically public domain, ensuring public access to important information and data.

- **Creative Commons Licenses Let You Share on Your Terms**: You can use a Creative Commons license to specify how others can use your work while retaining some control over certain rights.

- **Copyright Can Be Challenged or Waived**: Creators can voluntarily waive their copyright or dedicate works to the public domain, allowing others to use their creations freely.

CHAPTER FOUR

The Clock is Ticking: Copyright Duration and Rights

"Copyright ensures that your creative labor isn't just for today—it's a legacy that extends well beyond your lifetime. It's about making sure your voice, your vision, remains alive and well for generations."
— WALT DISNEY, FOUNDER OF THE WALT DISNEY COMPANY

Welcome to Chapter Four, "The Clock is Ticking: Copyright Duration and Rights," where we delve into the sands of time governing your precious creations. Just like your favorite dairy product, copyright has an expiration date—though thankfully, it lasts a bit longer than the milk in your fridge.

In this chapter, we'll explore the lifespan of copyright, from the moment of creation to that bittersweet day it joins the public domain. Think of it as a countdown timer that starts the second your brainchild hits the canvas, the page, or the airwaves. We'll answer burning questions like, "How long does this party last?" and "Can my grandkids ride the royalty train?"

With a timeline stretching over the life of the author plus seventy years post-mortem (or even longer in some club-level countries), copyright ensures that your work can provide for your descendants, possibly inspiring family squabbles for generations to come. And for our corporate creators, we'll decipher the magic number of 95 years from publication or 120 years from creation—whichever is shorter—ensuring your company's mascot can retire in style.

By the end of this chapter, you'll not only understand how to keep the clock ticking in your favor but also how to plan a legacy that could outlive you. Ready to wind up your copyright clock? Let's get ticking!

Copyright Timeline: From Creation to Expiration

Every copyrighted work embarks on a journey that begins the moment it's created and continues for decades, often beyond the creator's lifetime. This journey is governed by the laws of copyright duration, which determine how long the creator (or their heirs) can control the use and distribution of the work before it enters the public domain. In this section, we'll break down the key phases of the copyright timeline, from the moment your work is born to the day its protection expires.

When Does Copyright Protection Begin?

Copyright protection kicks in the moment your original work is fixed in a tangible medium. This means that as soon as you write down your story, record a song, or snap a photograph, it's automatically protected under copyright law—no formal registration is required (though registering your work does provide legal advantages).

Fixation simply means that the work is recorded in a way that others can perceive, whether on paper, canvas, film, or in digital form. Ideas floating in your head aren't protected by copyright—only once they take a concrete form do they qualify for protection.

Copyright Duration for Individual Works

For works created by individuals, copyright protection lasts for the life of the author plus 70 years. This means that you, the creator, retain exclusive rights to your work throughout your lifetime, and after your death, these rights pass to your heirs or estate for an additional 70 years. During this period, your family or estate can continue to manage the work, licensing it for commercial use, reprinting it, or collecting royalties.

Example:

- An author writes a novel in 2024. The author passes away in 2070. Copyright protection for that novel lasts until 2140 (2070 + 70 years). During those 70 years after the author's death, the estate or heirs can continue to profit from the work.

Corporate, Anonymous, and Work-for-Hire Durations

The rules are different when it comes to works created by corporations, works made for hire, or anonymous and pseudonymous works. These works don't follow the "life of the author" rule since they're not directly tied to an individual creator's lifespan. Instead, they are protected for either:

- 95 years from the date of publication, or
- 120 years from the date of creation (whichever is shorter).

This applies to works like corporate logos, advertisements, and other works produced by employees as part of their job duties. For example, if a company creates a mascot in 2024, the copyright protection could last until 2119, ensuring that the company controls the character for nearly a century.

Example:

- A corporation releases a movie in 2020. The movie's copyright will last until 2115 (2020 + 95 years).

The Countdown Begins: Key Moments in the Copyright Timeline

Once your work is fixed in a tangible medium, the countdown to copyright expiration begins. Here are the key phases in the copyright lifecycle:

1. **Creation and Fixation**: The work is created and fixed in a tangible medium. From this point, copyright protection is automatic.

2. **Life of the Author**: During the author's lifetime, they retain full control over their work, including the right to reproduce, distribute, perform, and license it.

3. **Post-Mortem Protection (Life + 70 Years)**: After the author's death, the copyright protection extends for 70 additional years, allowing the author's estate or heirs to manage and profit from the work.

4. **Expiration and Public Domain**: After the copyright term expires (life + 70 years for individual works or 95 years/120 years for corporate/anonymous works), the work enters the public domain, where it is no longer protected by copyright law and is free for anyone to use without permission.

What Happens When Copyright Expires?

When a copyright expires, the work enters the public domain. Once in the public domain, the work can be freely used, copied, modified, and distributed by anyone without the need to seek permission or pay royalties. This is why classic works like Shakespeare's plays or Beethoven's symphonies can be freely adapted into films, performances, and modern music.

Entering the public domain doesn't diminish the value of a work—it can actually lead to a creative resurgence. For example, public domain works are often used as the basis for new interpretations, mashups, and reimagined versions in modern art, film, and music.

How Copyright Duration Has Evolved

Copyright duration has changed over time. Earlier copyright laws, like those in the U.S. before the 1976 Copyright Act, provided shorter terms of protection (often 28 years, with the option to renew for another 28). But as copyright laws evolved globally, protection periods have been extended to better safeguard creators' rights and allow their works to provide income for future generations.

The current life + 70 years standard in many countries, like the U.S. and those in the European Union, reflects a balance between protecting creators' rights and eventually making works available to the public without restriction.

Conclusion: Navigating the Copyright Timeline

Understanding the copyright timeline is crucial for managing your creative assets effectively. Whether you're an individual creator or part of a corporate team, knowing how long your work will be protected helps you plan for its future. For individual creators, this means securing a legacy that lasts well beyond your lifetime. For corporations, it means retaining control over valuable intellectual property for nearly a century.

In the next section, we'll explore how these timelines apply specifically to individual works, corporate creations, and anonymous works, helping you maximize the benefits of copyright protection for years to come.

Life + 70 Years: Individual Copyright Duration

For individual creators, copyright protection is designed to last far beyond the creator's lifetime, ensuring their intellectual property remains under their control and can continue to benefit their heirs. This rule, commonly referred to as life plus 70 years, is the standard in many countries around the world, including the United States, the European Union, and others. Let's break down how this works and why it's such an important part of copyright law.

What Does "Life + 70 Years" Mean?

For works created by individuals, copyright protection lasts for the entire life of the author plus an additional 70 years after their death. This means that the creator enjoys exclusive rights over their work throughout their lifetime, and after they pass away, their heirs or estate will retain control for another 70 years. During this extended period, the work can still generate income through royalties, licensing, or sales.

The "life + 70 years" rule applies to works where the authorship is clear and tied to a specific individual or group of individuals (like co-authors). The countdown starts the moment the work is fixed in a tangible medium—whether that's writing, recording, or capturing the work in some other form.

Why the Extra 70 Years?

The extra 70 years after the author's death serve a few purposes:

1. **Benefit to Heirs or Estate**: Copyright law is designed to provide for the author's descendants, allowing the work to continue generating revenue for their family or estate. This is especially important for creators who depend on their work as a source of income or want to leave a financial legacy for their heirs.

2. **Cultural and Economic Stability**: The extended period allows works to be continuously managed and licensed, ensuring they remain accessible in the marketplace. This helps preserve the creator's artistic or literary legacy while continuing to generate value.

3. **International Harmonization**: Many countries follow the "life + 70 years" rule as a standard, creating consistency across borders. This makes it easier for creators to navigate copyright law globally, ensuring that their work is protected internationally under similar terms.

Example of Life + 70 Years in Action

Let's say an author writes and publishes a novel in 2025. If the author lives for another 40 years, passing away in 2065, the copyright on that novel will continue for an additional 70 years beyond the author's death. This means that the work will be protected until 2135 (2065 + 70 years). During this time, the author's heirs or estate will retain exclusive rights to control how the work is used, whether through sales, adaptations, or licensing agreements.

Multiple Authors: Co-Creation and Joint Works

In cases where a work has multiple authors, the duration of copyright protection is based on the life of the last surviving author plus 70 years. This ensures that all co-creators have equal protection and that their joint work remains protected until 70 years after the last contributor passes away.

Example:

- Two co-authors write a book together in 2020. One author dies in 2050, and the other dies in 2060. The copyright for the book will last until 2130 (2060 + 70 years), based on the lifespan of the last surviving author.

What Happens After 70 Years?

Once the life + 70 years term expires, the work enters the public domain, meaning it is no longer protected by copyright and can be freely used by anyone without the need for permission or payment. This transition is essential for ensuring that cultural works eventually become available for public use and can inspire new generations of creators.

When a work enters the public domain, it can be:

- **Reproduced**: Anyone can copy or distribute the work without asking for permission.

- **Adapted**: The work can be transformed, remixed, or reinterpreted in new ways, such as creating modern film adaptations of classic novels.

- **Commercialized**: The public domain status allows businesses to commercialize the work, such as producing new editions of a book or incorporating it into other media.

How Heirs Can Manage Copyright

During the 70 years after an author's death, their heirs or estate have the same rights that the author held during their lifetime. This includes the ability to:

- **License the Work**: Heirs can grant permission for others to use or adapt the work in exchange for royalties or fees.

- **Enforce Copyright**: The estate can take legal action if someone uses the work without permission, just as the original author could have done.

- **Control the Legacy**: The heirs may have control over how the work is presented, ensuring that the author's legacy is preserved according to their wishes.

Many well-known authors, musicians, and artists have estates that continue to manage their works long after their deaths, ensuring their intellectual property is properly monetized and their creative legacy is respected.

Exceptions to the Rule

While the life + 70 years standard applies to most individual works, there are a few exceptions:

1. **Anonymous or Pseudonymous Works**: For works where the author's identity is unknown or hidden behind a pseudonym, the copyright duration is not based on the author's lifespan. Instead, the work is protected for 95 years from the date of publication or 120 years from the date of creation, whichever is shorter.

2. **Works Made for Hire**: If a work was created as part of employment or under contract (for example, a designer creating a logo for a company), the employer or client typically holds the copyright, and the duration follows the rules for corporate works (95 years from publication or 120 years from creation).

Conclusion: Protecting Your Legacy

The "life + 70 years" rule ensures that creators retain control over their work for their entire lifetime, with the added benefit of passing those rights on to their heirs for an additional seven decades. This long duration allows for sustained income from creative works and ensures that the creator's legacy can be managed and preserved by their family or estate.

By understanding how copyright duration works, you can plan for the future of your creative assets, ensuring that your work continues to provide value even after you're gone. In the next section, we'll explore how corporate and anonymous works differ from individual works in terms of copyright duration and rights.

Corporate and Anonymous Works: Special Duration Rules

Not all works are created by individual authors, and copyright law treats corporate, anonymous, and pseudonymous works differently than those tied to a named individual. These types of works have their own unique duration rules, designed to account for the fact that the creator might be a company, organization, or an unnamed individual. In this section, we'll explore how copyright duration is calculated for corporate works, works made for hire, and anonymous/pseudonymous works, breaking down the special rules that apply to each.

Works Made for Hire and Corporate Authorship

A work made for hire is a creation made as part of someone's job or under a contract, where the copyright is owned by the employer or the person who commissioned the work, rather than the individual creator. Corporate authorship also falls under this category, which includes any work created by employees within the scope of their employment or commissioned works where the parties have agreed in writing that the work is made for hire.

Instead of the life + 70 years rule that applies to individual authors, the copyright duration for works made for hire and corporate works follows this formula:

- 95 years from the date of publication, or
- 120 years from the date of creation, whichever is shorter.

This extended protection ensures that businesses and corporations can retain control over their intellectual property for nearly a century.

Example:

A company releases an advertising campaign in 2025. The copyright on that campaign will last until 2120 (2025 + 95 years). If the company never publishes the campaign but creates it in 2025, the copyright would last until 2145 (2025 + 120 years), though it would expire at 2120 if it were published.

What Qualifies as a Work Made for Hire?

To be considered a work made for hire, the work must fit into one of two categories:

1. **Created by an Employee**: If the work is created by an employee within the scope of their job, the employer automatically owns the copyright, and it's considered a work made for hire. This includes things like:

   o Logos and branding materials created by an in-house designer.

   o Software or code written by a company's developers.

   o Reports, articles, or presentations created by employees.

2. **Commissioned Works**: If a work is commissioned, it can also qualify as a work made for hire if both parties agree in writing. However, commissioned works must fit into one of these categories:

   o A contribution to a collective work (e.g., an anthology or magazine).

   o A part of a motion picture or audiovisual work.

   o A translation.

   o A supplementary work (e.g., a foreword or appendix).

   o A compilation.

   o An instructional text.

   o A test or test answer key.

   o An atlas.

Without a written agreement or if the work doesn't fall into one of these categories, the individual creator retains the copyright, even if it was commissioned.

Anonymous and Pseudonymous Works

Anonymous and pseudonymous works are those where the author's identity is either unknown or concealed. These works follow the same duration rules as corporate and work-for-hire creations, with copyright lasting:

- 95 years from the date of publication, or

- 120 years from the date of creation, whichever comes first.

This rule ensures that even when the author's identity is hidden or unknown, the work is still protected for an extended period. However, if the author's identity becomes known during the copyright term, the duration may switch to the life + 70 years rule, depending on the circumstances.

Example:
A writer publishes a novel under a pseudonym in 2020. If their identity remains concealed, the copyright will last until 2115 (2020 + 95 years). If the author later reveals their identity, the copyright could shift to the life + 70 years duration, depending on when they disclose it.

Why These Special Rules?

The rules for corporate and anonymous works exist to address the unique nature of these creations. Since companies, organizations, or anonymous individuals don't have a natural lifespan like individual authors, copyright protection needs to be defined differently to ensure these works remain valuable assets for their owners while also eventually entering the public domain.

For companies, intellectual property like logos, advertising, and software can hold value for many years. The longer protection period (95 or 120 years) ensures that businesses retain control over their creative assets for as long as possible, allowing them to benefit from their investments in marketing, product design, and content creation.

For anonymous or pseudonymous works, these rules offer protection even when the creator's identity is concealed, ensuring that the work is still protected from misuse and that the author (or their estate) can benefit if their identity is later revealed.

The Importance of Contractual Agreements

When it comes to corporate or commissioned works, clear contractual agreements are essential. If you're hiring someone to create a work for your business, having a written agreement that explicitly states the work is made for hire ensures that your company holds the copyright, not the creator. Without this agreement, the individual may retain copyright, complicating future use, licensing, or distribution of the work.

On the other hand, if you're an individual creator working on a commissioned project, make sure you understand whether your work will be classified as a work made for hire. Knowing who holds the copyright can affect your ability to use, modify, or license the work in the future.

What Happens When the Copyright Expires?

Just like with individual works, when the copyright on a corporate, anonymous, or work-for-hire creation expires, the work enters the public domain. At this point, anyone can use, reproduce, or adapt the work without seeking permission or paying royalties.

Many iconic characters, logos, and works created by corporations eventually enter the public domain. For example, some of the earliest comic book characters and logos are now part of the public domain, allowing modern creators to reinterpret or repurpose them.

Conclusion: Planning for Corporate and Anonymous Works

Whether you're managing a company's intellectual property or creating works under a pseudonym, understanding the special duration rules for corporate, work-for-hire, and anonymous creations is essential. These extended timelines ensure that businesses can retain control over their assets for decades, while anonymous creators enjoy protection even without revealing their identities.

By ensuring proper agreements are in place and understanding how these rules apply, you can make informed decisions about how your work is protected and how to manage your creative assets for the long haul. In the next section, we'll discuss what happens when copyright protection ends and how works transition into the public domain.

Renewals, Extensions, and Public Domain: What Happens After Expiration

Like all things, copyright protection has a lifespan. While copyright durations are lengthy, eventually, every work's protection ends, and the work enters the public domain. But before that final transition, some works may be eligible for renewals or extensions, depending on when they were created. In this section, we'll explore what happens when a copyright expires, the possibilities for renewing or extending protection, and what it means for a work to enter the public domain.

The Public Domain: Free for All

When a copyrighted work's protection expires, it enters the public domain. This means the work is no longer under any copyright restrictions and can be freely used by anyone. No one needs to ask permission or pay royalties to reproduce, modify, adapt, or distribute the work.

The public domain is vital for fostering creativity and cultural development. It allows new creators to build upon the ideas, themes, and expressions of the past without fear of infringing copyright. Many iconic works that have entered the public domain continue to inspire modern adaptations and reinterpretations, contributing to ongoing creative innovation.

Examples of Public Domain Works:

- **Classic literature**: Works by authors like William Shakespeare, Charles Dickens, and Jane Austen are in the public domain, leading to countless adaptations, spin-offs, and reinterpretations.

- **Music**: Classical compositions by Beethoven, Mozart, and other long-gone composers are part of the public domain, allowing musicians to freely perform and record these pieces without restrictions.

- **Art and Film**: Early films and artwork from the 19th and early 20th centuries are now public domain, allowing creators to remix and share these works.

Copyright Renewals and Extensions

While today's copyright laws provide lengthy protections—life + 70 years for individual works and up to 95 years for corporate works—older works were subject to shorter protection periods. In the past, copyright terms were typically much shorter, often lasting just 28 years with the option to renew for an additional term. These renewal periods were important for keeping older works protected.

Example of the Old System:

- A book published in 1950 may have been granted an initial copyright term of 28 years, meaning it would expire in 1978. The copyright holder would need to file for a renewal to extend protection for another 28 years (until 2006). If they failed to renew it, the work would enter the public domain.

The renewal system changed with the 1976 Copyright Act in the U.S., which extended copyright terms and eliminated the need for renewals for works created after January 1, 1978. Today, works automatically receive their full term of protection without needing renewal, but works created before 1978 may still have been subject to renewal rules.

The 1998 Copyright Term Extension Act (Mickey Mouse Protection Act)

In 1998, the U.S. Congress passed the Copyright Term Extension Act, also known informally as the Mickey Mouse Protection Act, because it was heavily influenced by corporate interests in preserving the copyrights of valuable intellectual properties, including Disney's iconic Mickey Mouse character.

This act extended copyright terms by an additional 20 years:

- For individual authors, the term became life + 70 years (previously life + 50 years).

- For corporate or work-for-hire creations, the term became 95 years from publication or 120 years from creation, whichever is shorter.

This extension was designed to delay the entry of valuable works into the public domain, allowing copyright holders more time to benefit financially from their creations.

What Happens When Copyright Expires?

Once a copyright expires, the work enters the public domain, where it can be freely used without restriction. This transition is crucial because it allows culture, art, and knowledge to become more accessible over time.

When a work enters the public domain:

1. **Reproduction is Free**: Anyone can copy, publish, or share the work without asking permission.

2. **Adaptation is Allowed**: The work can be modified, adapted, or reimagined in new forms. For example, public domain books can be turned into movies, plays, or sequels without needing to seek rights.

3. **Commercial Use**: Businesses can commercialize the work, selling products or services based on it. For example, publishers can print and sell classic literature or make audio versions of public domain books.

Examples of Famous Public Domain Works

Many works that have entered the public domain continue to shape culture today:

- "Dracula" by Bram Stoker: With copyright long expired, countless films, novels, and TV series have reinterpreted this classic horror story.

- "Pride and Prejudice" by Jane Austen: As a public domain work, this novel has inspired everything from faithful film adaptations to modern retellings like "Pride and Prejudice and Zombies."

- "The Nutcracker" by Tchaikovsky: Every year, new performances, recordings, and adaptations of this ballet are produced, thanks to its public domain status.

Planning for Copyright Expiration: When Should You Care?

As a creator or a business managing intellectual property, understanding when your works will enter the public domain is essential for planning their future. If your work is nearing the end of its copyright term, consider how you can make the most of it before it enters the public domain. You may want to explore licensing, new adaptations, or reissues that can capitalize on the final years of protection.

For creators working with public domain materials, the expiration of copyrights offers a wealth of opportunity. By building on classic works, you can create new, transformative projects that resonate with modern audiences.

Conclusion: The End of Copyright and the Beginning of Public Access

Copyright protection serves an essential purpose by giving creators exclusive rights to their work for a set period. However, all copyrights eventually expire, allowing the work to enter the public domain, where it can be freely used by anyone. This transition is crucial for the continued growth of culture and creativity, giving future generations access to the art, music, literature, and knowledge of the past.

Whether you're managing your own works or looking to draw inspiration from public domain creations, understanding the rules around copyright expiration and the public domain can help you make informed decisions about how to protect, use, and share creative assets. In the next chapter, we'll explore the legal mechanisms available to enforce your copyright and protect your creations from infringement.

Quick Tips and Recap

- **Works Enter the Public Domain After Copyright Expires**: Once a copyright expires, the work enters the public domain, allowing anyone to use, reproduce, or adapt it without permission.

- **Modern Copyright Requires No Renewal**: For works created after January 1, 1978, copyright lasts for the full term (life + 70 years or 95 years for corporate works) without requiring renewal.

- **Older Works May Have Required Renewal**: Works published before 1978 were subject to shorter terms and needed to be renewed. If the renewal wasn't filed, these works may already be in the public domain.

- **Copyright Term Extensions**: The 1998 Copyright Term Extension Act added 20 years to existing copyright durations, ensuring longer protection for both individual and corporate works.

- **Public Domain Fosters Creative Freedom**: Once a work enters the public domain, it can be freely used, adapted, or commercialized, opening the door for new interpretations and creative projects.

- **Monitor Expiration Dates for Your Work**: As a copyright holder, keep an eye on when your work is set to expire so you can make the most of it before it enters the public domain.

- **Public Domain is a Resource for New Creations**: Creators can draw inspiration from public domain works to create new, transformative art, literature, or media without worrying about copyright infringement.

A Global Perspective: Navigating International Copyright

"In the digital age, your work can travel faster and further than ever before. It's essential to understand international copyright laws to ensure your creations are respected worldwide." — REED HASTINGS, CO-FOUNDER AND CEO OF NETFLIX

Chapter Five, "A Global Perspective: Navigating International Copyright," takes us on a world tour of copyright laws, where the rules aren't just different—they're a whole new game. Think of this as your passport to understanding how your creations fare when they jet-set across borders.

As we globetrot from country to country, you'll see how your copyrighted work can rack up more stamps in its passport than a luxury travel blogger. From the cobblestone streets of Paris to the neon lights of Tokyo, each stop brings its own flavor of protection and pitfalls. We'll explore how treaties like the Berne Convention act like a Eurail pass, offering a baseline of protection across multiple countries, while others might require a bit more legwork to ensure your work isn't served up like a local delicacy.

Whether you're a filmmaker in Finland or a songwriter in South Africa, understanding the nuances of international copyright law is crucial. It's not just about knowing where your rights start and end—it's about strategizing how to expand your creative empire without stepping on international toes.

So, pack your bags and bring your lawyer, because we're about to navigate the complex, sometimes confusing, but always fascinating world of international copyright. Let's make sure your creations feel at home, no matter where in the world they might find themselves.

The Berne Convention: A Global Standard for Copyright Protection

Like all things, copyright protection has a lifespan. While copyright durations are lengthy, eventually, every work's protection ends, and the work enters the public domain. But before that final transition, some works may be eligible for renewals or extensions, depending on when they were created. In this section, we'll explore what happens when a copyright expires, the possibilities for renewing or extending protection, and what it means for a work to enter the public domain.

When your work crosses borders, so do the rules that govern its protection. But thanks to the Berne Convention, a global agreement signed by over 180 countries, creators have a reliable foundation of copyright protection that applies across many different legal systems. The Berne Convention is the cornerstone of international copyright law, and it simplifies the complex web of global regulations, ensuring that creators' rights are recognized worldwide.

Let's break down what the Berne Convention is, how it works, and why it's critical for anyone looking to protect their creative works internationally.

What Is the Berne Convention?

The Berne Convention for the Protection of Literary and Artistic Works, commonly known as the Berne Convention, was first established in 1886 in Berne, Switzerland. Its main goal is to provide international copyright protection for creative works across borders. Signatory countries, known as Berne Union members, agree to honor the copyright laws of other member countries, meaning that when you create a work in one country, it automatically receives protection in all the other member nations.

The convention has undergone several updates to adapt to the evolving nature of intellectual property, but the core principles remain the same. For creators, this means you can focus on your craft, knowing that your work is shielded by a standard set of rules in most of the world's major markets.

Key Principles of the Berne Convention

The Berne Convention lays out several key principles that ensure creators have strong and consistent protection internationally:

1. **Automatic Protection**: One of the most significant advantages of the Berne Convention is that copyright protection is automatic. The moment your work is created and fixed in a tangible form; it is protected not just in your home country but also in all the other member countries. This means there's no need to register your work separately in each nation, which saves time and legal costs.

2. **National Treatment**: Under the principle of national treatment, creators from one Berne Union country are entitled to the same level of protection in any other member country as that country's own citizens. For example, if you're an author from the U.S., your book will receive the same copyright protection in France as a French author's work would.

3. **Minimum Standards**: The Berne Convention sets minimum standards for copyright protection that all member countries must follow. These standards include:

- o **Duration**: Copyright must last at least the life of the author plus 50 years, although many countries, including the U.S. and those in the European Union, have extended this to life plus 70 years.

- o **Exclusive Rights**: The convention guarantees that creators have exclusive rights over their work, including the rights to reproduce, distribute, perform, and adapt it.

- o **Moral Rights**: In addition to economic rights, the Berne Convention recognizes moral rights for creators, which allow them to maintain the integrity of their work and receive attribution, even if they no longer hold economic rights.

4. **No Formalities Required**: Unlike some countries' domestic copyright laws, which may require registration to enforce copyright (as is the case in the U.S.), the Berne Convention stipulates that no formalities are required to receive protection. This means you don't need to file paperwork, display a copyright notice, or register your work to be protected internationally. The act of creation itself is enough to ensure protection.

How the Berne Convention Works in Practice

So how does the Berne Convention function in real life when your work travels across borders?

Let's say you're a filmmaker based in Italy, and you've just completed a short film. The film is protected by Italian copyright law the moment it's fixed in a tangible form. Thanks to the Berne Convention, your film is now automatically protected in the other 180+ member countries, from Argentina to Japan, without you needing to file any additional paperwork or pay any registration fees.

If someone in Canada, for instance, decides to screen your film without permission, you can rely on Canadian copyright law, backed by the Berne Convention, to protect your rights and seek remedies for infringement. Canada will treat your work as if it were created by a Canadian filmmaker, providing the same legal protections available to its own citizens.

Limitations of the Berne Convention

While the Berne Convention offers significant protection, it's not without limitations. Here are a few things to keep in mind:

1. **Enforcement Varies by Country**: The Berne Convention provides a common framework, but the enforcement of copyright laws can vary greatly between countries. While most nations offer strong protections on paper, the reality of pursuing copyright infringement cases can differ depending on local legal systems, resources, and the level of intellectual property awareness in that country.

2. **Minimum Standards, Not Maximum**: The Berne Convention sets minimum standards, but individual countries can offer more generous terms of protection. For instance, while the convention requires a minimum copyright term of life + 50 years, some countries extend protection to life + 70 years or beyond. However, countries cannot provide less protection than the convention requires.

3. **Moral Rights Not Universally Enforced**: While the Berne Convention requires member countries to recognize moral rights (such as the right to attribution and the right to protect the integrity of the work), not all countries enforce these rights equally. In some nations, moral rights are less emphasized than economic rights, meaning creators may find it challenging to assert these rights in certain jurisdictions.

4. **Non-Berne Countries**: While most of the world's major markets are Berne Convention members, a few countries are not. In non-Berne countries, you may need to take additional steps to ensure your work is protected.

How to Maximize Your Protection Under the Berne Convention

Here are a few strategies to make the most of the Berne Convention's protections:

- **Understand Local Laws**: Even with Berne Convention protection, familiarize yourself with local copyright laws in the countries where your work is distributed. This will help you better navigate any nuances or additional requirements specific to each market.

- **Consider Registration in Key Markets**: While the Berne Convention doesn't require registration, some countries offer additional benefits (like access to certain legal remedies) if your work is registered domestically. For example, registering your copyright in the U.S. allows you to seek statutory damages in case of infringement.

- **Monitor for Infringement**: International copyright protection is powerful, but it requires vigilance. Use digital tools and professional services to monitor global use of your work and identify any instances of unauthorized reproduction, distribution, or adaptation.

- **Work with Local Experts**: If you're operating in a foreign market, working with local legal experts or copyright lawyers can help ensure your rights are respected and that you can take swift action if they're infringed upon.

Conclusion: The Berne Convention's Role in Protecting Your Creative Empire

The Berne Convention simplifies the complex web of international copyright laws by providing a baseline of protection in over 180 countries. It ensures that your work is automatically protected across borders, offering you peace of mind as you expand your creative reach globally. By understanding the principles and limitations of the Berne Convention, you can strategically protect your work and assert your rights no matter where in the world your creations land.

In the next section, we'll explore how copyright laws vary by region, and what you need to know about the differences in protection between key global markets.

Regional Differences: Understanding Variations in Copyright Laws

While the Berne Convention provides a strong foundation for international copyright protection, copyright laws still vary significantly from country to country. Each region has its own legal framework, enforcement practices, and unique interpretations of copyright. Understanding these regional differences is crucial when protecting your work globally, as even small variations can have a major impact on how your rights are recognized and enforced.

In this section, we'll explore the key differences in copyright laws across major regions, including the United States, the European Union, Asia, and developing markets. Knowing these distinctions can help you navigate the international copyright landscape and make informed decisions about where and how to protect your creative works.

The United States: Registration and Enforcement

The United States is a Berne Convention member, which means that works are automatically protected by copyright from the moment they are created and fixed in a tangible form. However, the U.S. adds a layer of complexity with its optional registration system. While you don't need to register your work to gain copyright protection, doing so provides important legal advantages, especially if you want to enforce your rights in court.

Key Features of U.S. Copyright Law:

- **Registration Benefits**: While not mandatory, registering your work with the U.S. Copyright Office provides additional legal benefits, including the ability to claim statutory damages and attorney's fees in case of infringement. Without registration, you're limited to seeking actual damages, which can be harder to prove.

- **Fair Use Doctrine**: The U.S. has a broad interpretation of fair use, allowing for certain unlicensed uses of copyrighted material for purposes such as criticism, commentary, education, and parody. The four factors that determine fair use include the purpose of the use, the nature of the copyrighted work, the amount used, and the effect on the market for the original work.

- **Term of Protection**: U.S. copyright lasts for life + 70 years for individual works and 95 years from publication for corporate or work-for-hire creations. These durations are aligned with Berne Convention standards.

Enforcement: U.S. copyright law allows creators to file lawsuits against infringers, but registration is required to take full advantage of the legal system. The U.S. courts take copyright infringement seriously, and the availability of statutory damages makes the U.S. an attractive venue for protecting and enforcing rights.

European Union: Harmonization with Room for Flexibility

The European Union has taken significant steps to harmonize copyright laws across its member states, ensuring that creators enjoy a relatively consistent level of protection regardless of which EU country they're in. The EU follows the life + 70 years rule, and the InfoSoc Directive (Directive 2001/29/EC) is a key piece of legislation that ensures strong protection for creators across the region.

Key Features of EU Copyright Law:

- **Harmonization Across Member States**: While copyright laws are generally aligned across the EU, each member state has the flexibility to implement specific exceptions and limitations. For example, some countries may have stricter rules on private copying or more lenient fair use policies. It's important to understand these local nuances when operating within the EU.

- **Moral Rights Protection**: Moral rights are strongly protected in many EU countries. These include the right to be credited for your work and the right to prevent alterations that could damage your reputation. Unlike economic rights, moral rights often remain with the creator even if the work's copyright has been transferred.

- **Database Rights**: The EU has special protections for databases under the Database Directive (Directive 96/9/EC), offering additional protection for creators of structured collections of data. This is an important distinction for those working in tech, research, or industries reliant on large-scale data compilation.

Enforcement: Enforcement can vary by country, but the EU provides tools like cross-border injunctions and has made efforts to streamline enforcement across member states. The European Union Intellectual Property Office (EUIPO) is also a valuable resource for creators seeking to protect their work across multiple EU countries.

Asia: A Mix of Traditional and Emerging Markets

Asia is a diverse region when it comes to copyright laws, with countries like Japan and South Korea boasting robust intellectual property protection, while emerging markets such as India and China continue to evolve their enforcement practices.

Key Features of Copyright Law in Asia:

- **Japan and South Korea**: Both countries are members of the Berne Convention and provide strong copyright protection. Japan's copyright law includes moral rights, similar to many EU countries, while South Korea offers broad protections for both creators and performers, with a robust enforcement system for copyright infringement.

- **China**: As a member of the Berne Convention, China offers copyright protection for works created domestically and abroad. However, enforcement in China can be challenging due to widespread piracy and inconsistent legal practices. In recent years, the Chinese government has made efforts to strengthen intellectual property laws and improve enforcement, but navigating the system still requires patience and local expertise.

- **India**: India's copyright law is aligned with the Berne Convention, and the country has seen significant improvements in enforcement in recent years. However, enforcement can still be slow, and piracy remains a major issue, particularly in the film and music industries.

Enforcement: Enforcement practices in Asia vary widely. In Japan and South Korea, copyright infringement is taken seriously, with strong legal remedies available for creators. In countries like China and India, enforcement may require more resources and local support, as navigating the courts can be more challenging.

Latin America: Evolving Laws with Room for Growth

Latin American countries like Brazil, Argentina, and Mexico are Berne Convention members, but copyright protection and enforcement vary significantly across the region. While most Latin American countries adhere to the life + 70 years rule, enforcement can be inconsistent, and piracy is a major issue in the region.

Key Features of Latin American Copyright Law:

- **Moral Rights**: Many Latin American countries place a strong emphasis on moral rights, similar to EU countries. This allows creators to retain control over how their work is attributed and used, even after transferring economic rights.

- **Collective Management Organizations**: In countries like Brazil and Argentina, collective management organizations (CMOs) play a critical role in enforcing copyright and collecting royalties for creators. These organizations can be valuable allies for creators seeking to monetize their work in the region.

Enforcement: Enforcement can be inconsistent, particularly in countries with high levels of piracy. However, governments across the region are taking steps to strengthen copyright laws and improve enforcement mechanisms.

Conclusion: Navigating Regional Variations in Copyright Law

While the Berne Convention provides a baseline of protection, navigating copyright laws across different regions requires an understanding of the unique legal frameworks and enforcement practices in each country. From the strong registration benefits in the U.S. to the moral rights protections in the EU and the challenges of enforcement in Asia and Latin America, each region offers its own mix of opportunities and obstacles for creators.

By familiarizing yourself with these regional differences, you can make more informed decisions about where to register your work, how to enforce your rights, and how to navigate the complexities of international copyright law. In the next section, we'll explore practical strategies for protecting your work abroad and enforcing your rights when operating in foreign markets.

How to Protect Your Work Abroad: Registration and Enforcement

Expanding the reach of your creative work beyond your home country is a thrilling step, but it also comes with the challenge of protecting your intellectual property across different legal systems. While the Berne Convention provides automatic copyright protection in most countries, ensuring your rights are fully enforceable abroad often requires extra steps. In this section, we'll dive into how you can effectively register your work in foreign markets and the strategies for enforcing your rights when infringement occurs.

Do You Need to Register Your Work Abroad?

Under the Berne Convention, your work is automatically protected in all member countries from the moment it is created and fixed in a tangible form. However, some countries offer additional legal benefits if you register your work locally. Registration isn't always required, but it can provide advantages, such as:

1. **Enhanced Legal Remedies**: In some countries, registration allows you to access certain legal remedies that wouldn't be available otherwise. For example, in the United States, registering your work with the U.S. Copyright Office before an infringement occurs or within three months of publication allows you to claim statutory damages and attorney's fees in court. Without registration, you may only be able to seek actual damages, which can be harder to prove.

2. **Easier Proof of Ownership**: Registration creates a public record of your copyright ownership, which can simplify the process of proving that the work is yours in the event of a dispute. This can be particularly useful in countries where enforcement mechanisms are less robust or where proving ownership in court can be difficult without formal documentation.

3. **Deterrent Effect**: Having your work registered in key markets can act as a deterrent to potential infringers, signaling that you take copyright enforcement seriously and are prepared to defend your rights.

Where Should You Register Your Work?

While the Berne Convention eliminates the need for separate registration in each country, you may want to consider registering your work in countries where you expect to have significant commercial activity or where infringement is more likely. Here are a few key markets where local registration can be beneficial:

- **United States**: As mentioned earlier, registration with the U.S. Copyright Office provides important legal advantages, particularly when it comes to accessing statutory damages in infringement cases. The U.S. is a large market for books, music, films, and digital content, making it a common choice for registration.

- **European Union**: While individual EU countries don't require registration, the European Union Intellectual Property Office (EUIPO) provides registration for trademarks and designs, and it offers resources for copyright enforcement. For creators operating in multiple EU countries, this can be a useful resource for coordinating protection across borders.

- **China**: Despite being a member of the Berne Convention, China's enforcement of copyright can be challenging, particularly due to widespread piracy. Registering your work with the China National Copyright Administration (CNCA) provides a stronger foundation for enforcing your rights and taking legal action against infringers.

- **Japan and South Korea**: Both countries have strong copyright laws and enforcement mechanisms. Registration isn't required for protection, but it can simplify the legal process if you need to take action against infringers. Local registration helps establish clear proof of ownership and can make it easier to resolve disputes in these markets.

- **Brazil and India**: In emerging markets like Brazil and India, local registration can strengthen your ability to enforce copyright. These countries have robust creative industries but can be challenging when it comes to navigating legal systems for enforcement. Registering your work in these markets can help cut through red tape and provide formal documentation of your rights.

How to Register Your Work Internationally

If you decide that registering your work in a foreign market is beneficial, here are some steps you can take:

1. **Identify Key Markets**: Consider where your work is most likely to be distributed, sold, or infringed. These might be countries where you have significant sales, where your audience is located, or where piracy is a known issue.

2. **Use Local Copyright Offices**: Most countries have a national copyright office where you can register your work. Each country's process will vary, but in general, you will need to submit:

   o A copy of your work (either in physical or digital form).

   o Proof of your identity or ownership of the work.

   o A registration fee, which varies depending on the country and type of work.

3. **Consult Local Experts**: If you're entering a foreign market with complex copyright laws, consider hiring a local lawyer or legal expert who specializes in intellectual property. They can guide you through the registration process and ensure that your rights are fully protected.

4. **Monitor for Infringement**: Once your work is registered, it's important to monitor its use in foreign markets. This can be done through digital tools that track unauthorized distribution or through local legal services that specialize in IP protection.

Enforcing Your Copyright Abroad

Registering your work is just the first step—ensuring your rights are enforced is the real challenge, especially in countries with different legal systems and levels of enforcement. Here are some strategies for enforcing your copyright abroad:

1. **Hire Local Legal Representation**: When dealing with copyright infringement in a foreign country, local legal expertise is invaluable. A local lawyer familiar with that country's legal system and enforcement

practices will help you navigate the process and increase your chances of success in court or through settlement.

2. **Leverage Treaties and Agreements**: Many countries have signed on to international treaties, like the TRIPS Agreement (Trade-Related Aspects of Intellectual Property Rights) under the World Trade Organization (WTO), which sets minimum standards for intellectual property enforcement. These treaties provide a common framework for enforcing rights internationally, but enforcement mechanisms can still vary by country.

3. **Use Digital Monitoring Tools**: In today's digital age, copyright infringement often happens online. Using digital tools like Content ID for YouTube, DMCA takedown notices, and web-based IP monitoring services can help you track and remove unauthorized uses of your work online. Some services even specialize in tracking global piracy and offering rapid takedown solutions.

4. **Partner with Collective Management Organizations (CMOs)**: In some countries, CMOs play a key role in enforcing copyright and collecting royalties on behalf of creators. These organizations can help you manage your rights, license your work, and ensure you receive payment when your work is used in foreign markets. For example, music creators often rely on CMOs like ASCAP (U.S.), SACEM (France), or JASRAC (Japan) to manage performance and broadcasting rights internationally.

5. **Pursue Legal Action**: If infringement occurs and you can't reach a settlement through negotiations, you may need to pursue legal action. This can involve filing lawsuits in foreign courts, which requires familiarity with local laws and processes. While this can be time-consuming and expensive, successful lawsuits can lead to damages, cease-and-desist orders, and greater protection for your work.

Conclusion: Protecting Your Creative Empire Abroad

Protecting your work internationally requires a proactive approach. While the Berne Convention offers automatic protection, registering your work in key markets can provide added legal advantages and make enforcement easier. By working with local legal experts, monitoring for infringement, and using digital tools, you can safeguard your creations no matter where they travel.

In the next section, we'll explore the complexities of international licensing and royalties, providing practical tips on how to manage global contracts, collect royalties from foreign markets, and maximize your creative income across borders.

Navigating International Licensing and Royalties

As your creative work reaches a global audience, licensing your intellectual property abroad and collecting royalties can become an essential part of your income strategy. Navigating international licensing involves negotiating contracts that comply with different legal systems, while ensuring that you are compensated properly through royalty collection across various countries. This section explores how to manage international licensing agreements and maximize royalties from foreign markets.

What is International Licensing?

International licensing allows you to authorize others to use, distribute, or adapt your work in foreign markets while you retain ownership of the copyright. Licensing agreements can vary based on the type of work—whether it's a book, a song, a film, or software—and typically involve granting certain rights to a licensee in exchange for royalty payments.

Licensing is a powerful way to expand the reach of your work and tap into new revenue streams without the need to personally handle distribution in every market. However, crafting a successful international licensing agreement requires careful consideration of local laws, market dynamics, and terms of payment.

Key Elements of International Licensing Agreements

When negotiating international licensing agreements, several key elements must be clearly defined to protect your rights and ensure you receive fair compensation. Here are some of the critical components to include:

1. **Territory**: Specify which countries or regions the license covers. You may choose to license your work globally or limit it to certain markets. Being selective about the territory can allow you to strike different deals in different regions, maximizing revenue.

Example: You might grant exclusive rights to distribute your book in Europe to one publisher, while keeping the rights to distribute in Asia for yourself or another partner.

2. **Exclusivity**: Determine whether the license is exclusive or non-exclusive. An exclusive license gives the licensee the sole right to use the work in the specified territory, whereas a non-exclusive license allows you to license the work to multiple parties.

   o **Exclusive license**: The licensee is the only entity allowed to use or distribute your work in a specific region.

   o **Non-exclusive license**: Multiple parties can use or distribute the work in the same territory.

3. **Rights Granted**: Clearly define what specific rights you are granting. These can include:

   o Reproduction rights (e.g., printing books, making copies).

   o Distribution rights (e.g., selling physical or digital products).

   o Performance rights (e.g., playing music or performing a play).

   o Adaptation rights (e.g., turning a book into a film or TV series).

4. **Term**: Specify how long the license will last. Some agreements are for a fixed period (e.g., 5 years), while others might be ongoing until terminated. Clearly define renewal and termination clauses to give both parties flexibility.

5. **Royalty Structure**: One of the most important aspects of a licensing agreement is how royalties will be calculated and paid. Common royalty structures include:

   o **Flat-rate royalties**: A set amount paid per use, sale, or performance.

- o **Percentage-based royalties**: A percentage of the revenue generated from the sale or use of your work.

- o **Advance payments**: Some licensing agreements involve an advance payment, which is recoupable against future royalties.

6. **Payment Terms**: Establish how and when royalties will be paid. International transactions may involve currency conversions and international banking transfers, so it's important to clarify how payments will be processed and ensure compliance with local tax laws.

7. **Dispute Resolution**: Given the complexities of international business, it's essential to include a dispute resolution clause that specifies how conflicts will be resolved. This may involve arbitration, mediation, or a specific country's court system.

Managing Royalties Across Borders

Once your work is licensed internationally, the next step is collecting royalties from multiple regions. However, the process of tracking and collecting royalties can be challenging, especially when dealing with different currencies, laws, and collection systems. Here's how to ensure you receive what you're owed:

1. **Use Collective Management Organizations (CMOs)**: In many countries, CMOs help manage and collect royalties on behalf of creators. For example, musicians may work with performing rights organizations (PROs) like ASCAP (U.S.), PRS (UK), or JASRAC (Japan), which track the use of their music and collect royalties from broadcasters, venues, and digital platforms.

For creators of other types of works, such as authors or visual artists, there are equivalent organizations that collect royalties for uses such as public lending, reproduction, or exhibitions. Joining a CMO can help streamline the royalty collection process and ensure you're compensated when your work is used in foreign markets.

2. **Monitor Licensing Agreements**: Regularly review your licensing agreements to ensure that you are being paid correctly. Royalty reports from your licensees should provide detailed information about how your

work is being used, how many copies have been sold or distributed, and how much revenue has been generated. Make sure these reports are accurate and aligned with your contract terms.

3. **Negotiate Currency Terms**: When working internationally, exchange rates can significantly impact your earnings. Negotiate terms that account for currency fluctuations, or specify the currency in which you prefer to be paid. Having clear payment methods (e.g., wire transfers, PayPal) can also reduce delays or discrepancies in payment.

4. **Consider Tax Implications**: Each country has different tax laws regarding royalty payments, and international agreements may be subject to withholding taxes. For example, if you're a U.S. author receiving royalties from the UK, the UK might withhold a portion of your earnings for tax purposes unless there is a tax treaty in place. Consult with tax experts or financial advisors to ensure you're complying with local laws and maximizing your net income.

5. **Use Digital Tools for Global Tracking**: Today's digital platforms can help creators track the use of their work across the globe. Tools like YouTube's Content ID, streaming platform dashboards, and digital rights management (DRM) systems provide insights into how your work is being used, helping you monitor licensing compliance and potential infringement.

International Licensing Pitfalls to Avoid

While licensing your work internationally can be highly lucrative, it also comes with risks. Here are a few common pitfalls to watch out for:

-   **Poorly Defined Contracts**: Incomplete or vague contracts can lead to confusion or disputes down the line. Always ensure that your licensing agreements are comprehensive and clearly outline all terms, including rights, royalties, and dispute resolution.

-   **Lack of Local Expertise**: If you're not familiar with the legal systems and business practices of a foreign market, it's easy to make costly mistakes. Partnering with local experts or legal advisors can help you navigate unfamiliar territory and protect your interests.

- **Inconsistent Royalty Payments**: Some licensees may underreport usage or delay payments. Keep an eye on your royalty reports and don't hesitate to follow up if something seems amiss. If necessary, consider including audit rights in your contract, allowing you to review the licensee's financial records if discrepancies arise.

- **Infringement in Foreign Markets**: While licensing agreements provide legitimate ways to distribute your work, piracy and unauthorized use are still significant risks. Be vigilant about monitoring for infringement and take action when necessary, whether through legal means or by issuing takedown notices on digital platforms.

Conclusion: Maximizing Revenue Through International Licensing

Licensing your work internationally opens the door to new markets and revenue streams, but it requires careful planning and management. By negotiating clear licensing agreements, working with collective management organizations, and diligently monitoring royalties, you can ensure that your creative empire thrives on the global stage.

In the next chapter, we'll explore the challenges of defending your copyright and intellectual property in the digital age, where technology has created both unprecedented opportunities and significant risks for creators worldwide.

Quick Tips and Recap

- **Automatic Protection Under the Berne Convention**: Your work is automatically protected in over 180 countries without registration, but registering locally in key markets can offer added benefits.

- **Consider Registration in Key Markets**: In countries like the U.S., China, and Brazil, registering your work locally can strengthen your legal position and offer access to additional remedies, such as statutory damages.

- **Define Licensing Agreements Clearly**: When negotiating international licensing deals, be clear about the territory, exclusivity, rights granted, and royalty structure. These terms ensure you control how your work is used abroad.

- **Monitor Royalty Payments**: Use digital tools and partner with CMOs (Collective Management Organizations) to track royalties from foreign markets and ensure you are paid accurately.

- **Negotiate Currency and Payment Terms**: Avoid currency fluctuations eating into your earnings by specifying payment terms and currency in your licensing agreements.

- **Leverage Digital Monitoring Tools**: Tools like YouTube's Content ID and other DRM systems can help you track where your work is being used and detect infringement across borders.

- **Consult Local Experts for Foreign Markets**: Legal systems and business practices vary by country. Partnering with local advisors ensures you understand the nuances of foreign markets and protect your work effectively.

- **Watch Out for Infringement**: Stay vigilant about unauthorized use and take swift action against infringement, whether through legal action or digital takedown notices.

PART TWO

Mastering Fair Use

and Infringement

Welcome to Part Two: "Mastering Fair Use and Infringement," where we tread the fine line between inspiration and imitation. This section is like a masterclass in navigating a minefield blindfolded—you'll learn how to dance through the legal loopholes without blowing your foot off. We'll dissect the perplexing world of fair use, peeling back the layers to reveal when it's perfectly legal to borrow a bit of brilliance and when you're just stealing someone else's thunder. From cheeky memes to scholarly citations, we decode the dos and don'ts, ensuring you can riff on others' ideas without risking a courtroom showdown. Strap in, creators—it's time to play it smart in the wild west of copyright law.

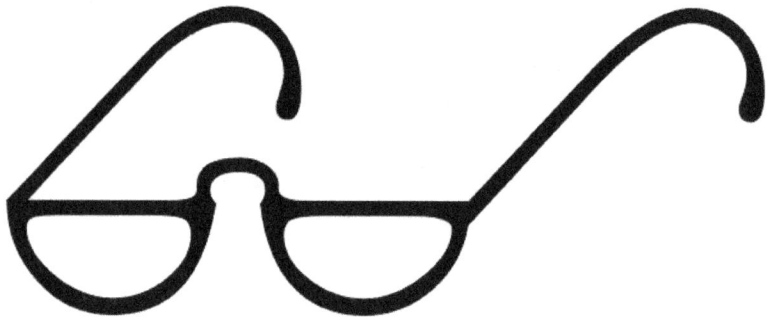

Fair Play or Fair Use?: Understanding the Concept of Fair Use

"Fair use is not just a legal defense—it's a vital part of how we innovate and create. Understanding it is essential for anyone who wants to engage with and build upon the cultural dialogue." — LAWRENCE LESSIG, PROFESSOR AND CO-FOUNDER OF CREATIVE COMMONS

Chapter Six, "Fair Play or Fair Use?: Understanding the Concept of Fair Use," dives into the heart of copyright's most nebulous territory. Think of fair use as the playground of the intellectual property world—a place where rules are absolutely crucial, yet somehow, everyone interprets them differently.

Here, we unpack the four factors of fair use—like ingredients in a secret recipe— that determine whether you're playing nicely or just playing with fire. We'll explore how something as simple as quoting a movie in a blog post can be akin to tiptoeing through a legal minefield. With vivid examples and cautionary tales, we'll show you how to wield the power of fair use like a seasoned pro, not a reckless renegade.

This chapter isn't just about staying out of trouble; it's about mastering the art of borrowing brilliance. Whether you're a filmmaker using a snippet of someone else's song or a teacher copying pages of a textbook, understanding fair use is like having a backstage pass to the world of creative expression. So, let's roll out the red carpet and demystify these complex guidelines, ensuring you know exactly when and how you can legally stand on the shoulders of giants.

The Four Factors of Fair Use: Breaking Down the Basics

Fair use is a powerful concept in copyright law, providing a legal defense that allows people to use copyrighted material under certain circumstances without seeking permission from the rights holder. However, it's not a straightforward, black-and-white rule. Whether a particular use qualifies as "fair" depends on a careful balancing of four key factors. These factors help courts determine if your use of copyrighted content is lawful or if you've crossed the line into infringement.

In this section, we'll break down the four factors of fair use, explaining how they are applied in real-world cases and what they mean for creators.

1. Purpose and Character of the Use

The first factor looks at the purpose and character of your use. Courts will ask: *Why are you using the copyrighted material, and in what way?* This factor tends to favor uses that are transformative—meaning they add something new or give the work a different meaning, message, or purpose. The more your use differs from the original, the more likely it is to be considered fair use.

Questions to Consider:

- Is the use for a non-commercial, educational, or nonprofit purpose (which tends to favor fair use)?

- Is the use transformative—does it alter the original work with new expression, meaning, or message?

- Are you using the material for criticism, commentary, parody, news reporting, or research?

Example:

A documentary filmmaker using short clips of a news broadcast to comment on media bias may qualify as fair use, because the clips are used to criticize the news media—a different purpose than the original intent of the broadcast.

On the other hand, simply reproducing someone's work with little or no change to its original purpose (for example, reposting a full image from an art collection on a commercial website) is unlikely to be seen as fair use.

2. Nature of the Copyrighted Work

This factor considers the nature of the copyrighted work being used. Courts are more likely to favor fair use if the material is factual or non-fiction rather than a highly creative or artistic work. The reasoning here is that creative works deserve stronger protection, whereas factual information is considered more necessary for public discourse and knowledge sharing.

Questions to Consider:

- Is the work factual (like a textbook or news article) or creative (like a novel or a painting)?

- Is the work published or unpublished? (Unpublished works generally get more protection, as the creator has not yet had the opportunity to decide how to present their work.)

Example:

Using short excerpts from a research article in an educational context is more likely to be considered fair use than using large parts of a novel or song, which would typically have a more creative nature.

3. Amount and Substantiality of the Portion Used

The third factor looks at how much of the original work you've used, both in terms of quantity and quality. Using smaller portions of a work is generally more likely to qualify as fair use, especially if you're using only what's necessary to make your point. However, even using a small amount can tip the scales against fair use if the portion used represents the heart of the work—the most important or recognizable part.

Questions to Consider:

- How much of the original work are you using? (Is it a few sentences or a significant portion of a book or movie?)

- Is the portion you're using the most critical or memorable part of the work?

Example:

A music reviewer using a 10-second clip of a song to illustrate a point about the artist's style might be seen as fair use, as they are using only a small part. However, using the song's iconic chorus or its most recognizable part could weigh against fair use, even if the clip is brief.

4. Effect on the Market for the Original Work

The final and often most crucial factor is the effect of the use on the potential market for the original work. Courts want to know whether your use of the copyrighted material is likely to harm the original creator's ability to profit from their work. If your use could replace the original in the marketplace—such as by offering a free alternative that undercuts sales—then it's less likely to be considered fair use.

Questions to Consider:

- Does your use of the work compete with the original, reducing its market value?

- Could your use cause the original creator to lose licensing opportunities or sales?

Example:

If you upload a full movie to YouTube without permission, even if it's for educational purposes, you could negatively impact the market for the original film. Viewers may choose to watch your uploaded version instead of purchasing or streaming the movie legally, which would harm the creator's ability to profit from their work.

Conversely, if you're using a small excerpt of a movie in a classroom setting or to create a critical analysis video, it's unlikely to affect the market for the film, and your use is more likely to be considered fair.

Weighing the Four Factors

It's important to remember that these factors are balanced together. No single factor is decisive on its own. Courts look at how all four factors interact in a given situation, and the outcome of a fair use claim depends on the specifics of the case.

- Transformative uses—those that add new meaning or value to the original—are often given more weight, even if a large portion of the work is used.

- Non-commercial, educational, and commentary uses are generally favored.

- Commercial uses or those that affect the market for the original work negatively are more likely to be challenged.

Conclusion: Understanding the Balance of Fair Use

Fair use is a flexible, case-by-case doctrine, and it often comes down to balancing these four factors. By understanding the purpose of your use, the nature of the work, the amount you're using, and how your use affects the original's market value, you can better navigate the complexities of fair use. This balancing act ensures that while creators can protect their work, others still have room for commentary, critique, education, and creative innovation.

In the next section, we'll dive deeper into transformative use, one of the most critical aspects of fair use, and explore how adding new meaning or value to a work can significantly shift the balance in favor of fair use.

Transformative Use: The Heart of Fair Use

At the core of fair use lies the concept of transformative use—a principle that can make or break a fair use defense. Transformative use refers to taking a copyrighted work and adding new meaning, message, or purpose that distinguishes it from the original. The more a use transforms the original work, the more likely it is to be considered fair use, even if large portions of the work are used. In this section, we'll dive deep into transformative use, why it's so important in fair use cases, and how creators can leverage it to stay on the right side of the law.

What Is Transformative Use?

A transformative use takes the original work and modifies it in a way that gives it new expression, context, or insight. The focus is not on whether the use benefits the user but whether it adds something new—whether it creates an original work that is distinct from the copyrighted material it draws upon.

Example of Transformative Use:
A book reviewer uses several quotes from a novel in a review. The quotes are used to critique the author's writing style, plot structure, and character development. In this case, the review transforms the original work by adding commentary and analysis, making it distinct from the novel itself. This use would likely be considered fair use.

In contrast, simply reproducing large excerpts of the novel without adding any original commentary or analysis would not be transformative and therefore might not qualify for fair use.

How Transformative Use Tips the Balance in Fair Use Cases

Transformative use is often the most important factor in determining whether a particular use qualifies as fair use. Courts tend to favor cases where the copyrighted material is used in a way that transforms its purpose or meaning. If a work is deemed transformative, even other factors, such as the amount of the work used, may carry less weight.

Transformative use is not just about changing the original but about repurposing it in a new way that benefits society—whether through criticism, commentary, parody, or educational insights.

Types of Transformative Use

Here are some common ways that copyrighted works can be transformed and therefore considered fair use:

1. **Parody**: A parody takes an original work and humorously imitates or exaggerates it to make a social or political commentary. Parody is one of the clearest examples of transformative use because it adds new meaning through satire or critique.

Example:

A comedian creates a parody of a popular song, changing the lyrics to poke fun at the music industry. Because the new lyrics serve as a commentary on the original work and its context, this is likely to be seen as fair use.

2. **Commentary and Criticism**: Using portions of a copyrighted work to analyze, critique, or comment on it is transformative, as the purpose is to evaluate or assess the original, adding new insights or viewpoints.

Example:

A film critic uses short clips from a movie in a YouTube video to analyze the director's unique visual style. By adding commentary and insights, the critic transforms the movie clips from simple entertainment into educational content.

3. **Educational Use**: In some cases, educational uses that add new context or insight to a copyrighted work can be transformative, especially when the work is used for purposes like teaching or research.

Example:

A professor copies a few pages of a novel to distribute in class for a literary analysis lesson. Because the purpose is educational, and the discussion adds new meaning to the text, this may qualify as fair use.

4. **Research and Scholarship**: When copyrighted material is used for research or scholarship purposes, such as quoting from a work in a

research paper or using excerpts in academic studies, it may be seen as transformative, provided the use adds value through analysis or context.

5. **Remixes and Mashups**: Digital and visual artists often use transformative elements when creating mashups, remixes, or collages that combine various copyrighted works. By rearranging, remixing, or altering the original material to create something new, these works can often be considered transformative.

Example:

A visual artist creates a collage from several magazine covers, altering the images to critique the way media portrays beauty standards. Because the artwork adds new commentary and shifts the purpose of the original images, it could be considered fair use.

When Use Is Not Transformative

On the flip side, using a work in a way that does not significantly alter its meaning or purpose may not be considered transformative. Here are some examples where a use might fail to meet the transformative threshold:

- **Direct Reproduction**: If a work is copied or reproduced in its entirety, without any significant changes to its meaning, message, or context, it's unlikely to be considered fair use. For example, simply reposting a photo from a photographer's portfolio on social media without adding any commentary or new context is not transformative.

- **Minimal Changes**: Making small or superficial alterations to a work, such as cropping a photo or changing a few words in a song, does not constitute a meaningful transformation. For instance, changing the background color of a painting without adding new meaning would not be transformative.

- **Commercial Uses Without Added Value**: If a copyrighted work is used purely for commercial gain without adding any new value or message, it's less likely to qualify as transformative use. Selling T-shirts with someone else's artwork printed on them without permission, for instance, would not be considered transformative.

Why Transformative Use Is Essential for Creators

For creators, understanding transformative use is key to leveraging the fair use defense while respecting the boundaries of copyright law. Whether you're producing videos, art, music, or written content, transforming the original work by adding new insights or perspectives is crucial to staying within legal limits.

Transformative use also empowers creators to build upon existing works in meaningful ways. By remixing, analyzing, or commenting on copyrighted content, you can engage in creative expression without infringing on someone else's intellectual property. The result is a balance between protecting original creators and allowing for innovation, critique, and educational use.

Conclusion: Mastering the Art of Transformation

Transformative use lies at the heart of the fair use doctrine. By adding new meaning, purpose, or commentary to an existing work, you can shift the balance in favor of fair use—even when using a significant portion of the original material. Whether you're a content creator, educator, artist, or researcher, understanding how to transform the material you're using is essential to building a strong fair use defense. In the next section, we'll explore real-world examples of fair use across different industries and look at how courts have applied the four factors and transformative use in practice.

Fair Use in Action: Examples Across Industries

Understanding fair use in theory is important, but seeing it applied in real-world situations makes the concept clearer. The fair use doctrine impacts various industries, from entertainment to education, journalism, and digital media. By examining how courts have ruled on different cases, we can see how the four factors of fair use, especially transformative use, come into play. In this section, we'll explore examples of fair use in action across multiple industries to show how creators can navigate the boundaries of fair use while minimizing risk.

1. Fair Use in Film and Television

The entertainment industry frequently deals with fair use, particularly in documentaries, parodies, and reviews. The use of short clips, commentary, or transformative remixes is common, but creators must be careful not to cross into infringement.

Example 1: Documentaries
Documentaries often use clips from films, TV shows, or news broadcasts to provide context or commentary. In these cases, the clips are typically brief and accompanied by transformative content—such as analysis, critique, or commentary.

Case Example:
In the documentary *Super Size Me*, filmmaker Morgan Spurlock used McDonald's logos, advertisements, and promotional materials throughout the film. Because these visuals were used to critique the fast-food industry and convey the film's overall message about fast food's health impact, the court found that Spurlock's use of McDonald's intellectual property was transformative and qualified as fair use.

Takeaway: Using brief clips in a documentary, especially when the purpose is to critique or analyze, is more likely to qualify as fair use, provided that the use is transformative and doesn't replace the market for the original work.

2. Fair Use in Education and Research

Fair use plays a crucial role in the academic world, where educators, researchers, and students frequently rely on copyrighted materials for teaching, learning, and analysis. The use of copyrighted materials in an educational setting is often favored under the fair use doctrine, but it's not a blanket exemption—how much material is used and its purpose are critical factors.

Example 2: Textbook Excerpts in the Classroom
A teacher photocopies several chapters from a copyrighted textbook and distributes them to students for classroom discussion. The teacher argues that this is for educational purposes, but the court must consider the amount of the material used and whether the use impacts the market for the textbook.

Case Example:
In *Cambridge University Press v. Becker*, a group of publishers sued Georgia State University for allowing professors to distribute large amounts of copyrighted academic content to students through course reserves. The court found that while some uses were fair, others were not, particularly when large portions of the works were used without transformative value and when the use directly impacted the market for academic books.

Takeaway: Educational use is often favored, but it must still respect fair use limits. Using only the amount necessary for educational purposes, and ensuring that the material is not available for free or on a large scale, helps to meet fair use standards.

3. Fair Use in Journalism and Commentary

News outlets and commentators frequently rely on fair use when reporting on current events or offering criticism or commentary. The use of copyrighted content for news reporting or to critique public figures and events often falls under fair use, provided it's not overly extensive and serves a new, transformative purpose.

Example 3: News Reporting Using Video Clips
News outlets often include short clips from copyrighted video footage to report on events or provide analysis. These clips are typically brief and are used in a context that adds new meaning or value to the original material.

Case Example:
In *Nunez v. Caribbean International News Corp.*, a Puerto Rican newspaper published photos of a local model that had been previously copyrighted by the photographer. The court found that the photos were used for news reporting purposes, specifically in articles discussing the controversy surrounding the model's images. The use of the photos was deemed transformative and fell under fair use.

Takeaway: In journalism, using copyrighted material in a transformative way to report on or comment about the content is more likely to be considered fair use, especially when the use is limited in scope.

4. Fair Use in Parody and Satire

One of the clearest examples of transformative use is in parody. Parody takes elements of the original work but exaggerates or distorts them to create humor or social commentary. Courts often view parody as a strong example of fair use because the purpose is to create something new that directly comments on the original.

Example 4: Parody Songs
Musicians or comedians who create parody songs often use the melodies or lyrics of the original work but alter them for comedic or critical effect.

Case Example:
In *Campbell v. Acuff-Rose Music*, the rap group 2 Live Crew parodied Roy Orbison's song *Oh, Pretty Woman*. The court found that the parody was transformative because it added a new, comedic twist to the original and was not likely to replace the market for Orbison's version. Despite using significant portions of the original, the parody was deemed fair use.

Takeaway: Parody is one of the strongest forms of fair use because it adds significant new meaning or commentary to the original work, provided that it does not harm the market for the original.

5. Fair Use in Digital Media and Social Platforms

In the age of social media and user-generated content, creators are constantly remixing, commenting on, and sharing copyrighted content online. While platforms like YouTube, Instagram, and TikTok have made it easier for creators to remix and reuse content, the rules of fair use still apply.

Example 5: Reaction Videos on YouTube
YouTubers who create reaction videos—where they watch and respond to copyrighted movies, music, or TV shows—often rely on fair use to avoid infringement. The key factor is whether the reaction adds significant commentary or criticism, transforming the original work into something new.

Case Example:
In *Equals Three, LLC v. Jukin Media, Inc.*, YouTube creator Equals Three used viral videos from Jukin Media to create comedic commentary. The court ruled

that while some of the videos were used in a transformative way, others were not sufficiently transformative, and Equals Three was found liable for infringement.

Takeaway: Reaction videos or remixes must clearly add new meaning or commentary to the original material to qualify as fair use. Simply re-posting or reacting without substantial transformation is less likely to be protected.

Conclusion: Fair Use as a Creative Tool

Fair use allows creators in various industries to incorporate copyrighted material into new works, whether for criticism, education, journalism, or entertainment. However, the boundaries of fair use are not always clear-cut. Understanding how courts apply the four factors in different contexts helps creators navigate the complexities of fair use and avoid legal pitfalls.

In the next section, we'll discuss the risks and limitations of fair use, outlining when fair use doesn't apply and how to avoid common mistakes that could lead to infringement claims.

Risks and Limitations: When Fair Use Doesn't Apply

While fair use can be a valuable tool for creators, educators, and journalists, it is not a free pass to use copyrighted material without consequence. The line between fair use and copyright infringement can be thin, and even well-intentioned uses may fall outside the protection of fair use if the four key factors aren't properly considered. In this final section, we'll explore the risks and limitations of fair use, highlighting scenarios where it doesn't apply and providing strategies to help you avoid potential legal trouble.

When Fair Use Doesn't Apply

Fair use is flexible but not without boundaries. Here are common situations where creators, businesses, and educators may run into trouble if they assume fair use without fully understanding its limits.

1. Commercial Use Without Transformation

One of the biggest red flags for courts when evaluating fair use is whether the copyrighted material was used for commercial purposes without sufficient transformation. If you are using copyrighted work purely for commercial gain, and the use is not transformative (i.e., it doesn't add new meaning, message, or purpose), courts are more likely to view it as infringement.

Example:
Selling T-shirts or other merchandise with copyrighted images or song lyrics, without altering the original meaning or context, is a commercial use that's unlikely to qualify as fair use. Since the purpose is purely commercial, and the original work is being used without adding anything new, this is not considered transformative.

2. Using the "Heart" of the Work

Even if you use a small portion of a work, using the most recognizable or essential part of it (often referred to as the "heart" of the work) can weigh heavily against a fair use defense. Courts have ruled that even brief excerpts can be infringing if they are the most memorable or important part of the original work.

Example:
A YouTube creator uploads a reaction video that includes the entire climax of a blockbuster movie. Even though the clip may be short, the fact that it contains the most critical and recognizable part of the film would likely disqualify it from fair use because it uses the "heart" of the original.

3. Non-Transformative Copying

If your use of a copyrighted work doesn't transform the original in a meaningful way, it is unlikely to be considered fair use. Simply copying or reproducing content without adding new meaning, value, or commentary falls outside the boundaries of fair use.

Example:
Re-posting someone's article on your blog without adding your own commentary or analysis is not considered transformative. You're simply copying the original work without offering anything new, and this could lead to an infringement claim.

4. Harming the Market for the Original Work

One of the most significant factors in determining fair use is whether your use of the copyrighted material negatively impacts the market for the original work. If your use competes with or replaces the original—such as offering a free alternative—courts are more likely to view it as infringement.

Example:
A website offers free downloads of copyrighted music, even if the purpose is to promote lesser-known artists. This harms the market for legitimate music sales and streaming services and would not be considered fair use, as it diminishes the creator's ability to profit from their work.

5. Using Unpublished Works

Courts are generally more protective of unpublished works, as the creator has not yet had the opportunity to control how and when their work is introduced to the public. Using unpublished materials without permission is less likely to be considered fair use, even if your purpose is educational or non-commercial.

Example:
A researcher discovers unpublished letters from a famous author and publishes them in full without permission. Because these letters were unpublished and the author's estate still controls their release, this would likely be considered copyright infringement, not fair use.

Risks of Misusing Fair Use

Misapplying fair use can result in serious legal and financial consequences. Here are the risks of assuming that your use qualifies as fair use without properly assessing the four factors:

1. **Copyright Infringement Lawsuits**: If a copyright holder believes you've misused their work, they may file a copyright infringement lawsuit against you. This can lead to significant legal costs, statutory damages, and injunctions that prevent you from continuing to use the work. Even if your use was unintentional or non-commercial, courts may still find you liable for infringement.

2. **Cease-and-Desist Orders**: Before filing a lawsuit, a copyright holder may send you a cease-and-desist letter. This is a formal request to stop using the copyrighted material and to remove it from any public platforms. Ignoring a cease-and-desist order can lead to further legal action.

3. **Monetary Damages**: If a court rules against your fair use defense, you may be required to pay statutory damages or actual damages to the copyright holder. Statutory damages can range from hundreds to thousands of dollars per instance of infringement, depending on whether the court deems your infringement willful.

4. **Reputation Damage**: Misusing fair use, especially in highly visible projects, can damage your reputation and credibility. Copyright holders may take public legal action against you, impacting your professional relationships and standing in your industry.

How to Minimize Risk When Claiming Fair Use

Although fair use is a flexible doctrine, there are ways to minimize risk and protect yourself from infringement claims:

1. **Transform the Material**: The more you can transform the original work by adding new meaning, purpose, or context, the stronger your fair use defense will be. Commentary, criticism, parody, and educational uses are more likely to be considered fair use, especially if they alter the original in a meaningful way.

2. **Use Only What's Necessary**: When possible, use only the amount of material necessary to achieve your purpose. If a few seconds of a song or a short excerpt from a book are enough to make your point, avoid using more than is required. This reduces the risk of being seen as overreaching.

3. **Consider the Market Impact**: Always ask yourself if your use will impact the market for the original work. If you're offering an alternative that could replace the original or harm its sales potential, fair use is less likely to apply. Ensure that your use doesn't undermine the original creator's ability to profit from their work.

4. **Get Legal Advice**: If you're unsure whether your use qualifies as fair use, consider seeking legal advice from an intellectual property lawyer. They can assess your specific situation, guide you through the fair use factors, and help you make informed decisions about using copyrighted material.

Conclusion: Navigating the Risks of Fair Use

Fair use is an essential tool for creators, educators, and commentators, allowing them to engage with copyrighted material in meaningful and transformative ways. However, it's crucial to recognize the limits of fair use and avoid assuming that it applies in every situation. By understanding the risks, carefully considering the four factors, and using copyrighted material responsibly, you can navigate the complexities of fair use while protecting your work from legal challenges.

In the next chapter, we'll explore how digital platforms and the internet have reshaped the boundaries of copyright and fair use, offering both new opportunities and significant challenges for creators in the digital age.

Quick Tips and Recap

- **Fair Use Isn't Automatic**: Always evaluate the four factors of fair use—purpose, nature, amount used, and market impact—before using copyrighted material.

- **Transformative Use is Key**: The more you change the meaning, message, or purpose of the original work, the more likely your use will qualify as fair use.

- **Commercial Use Requires Care**: If you're using copyrighted material for profit, ensure your use is transformative, as purely commercial uses are less likely to qualify for fair use.

- **Don't Use the "Heart" of the Work**: Avoid using the most recognizable or central part of a work, as this can weigh heavily against a fair use claim.

- **Educational Uses Aren't Automatic**: Just because the use is educational doesn't guarantee fair use; the amount used and market impact still matter.

- **Unpublished Works Get Extra Protection**: Using unpublished works is less likely to qualify as fair use, as courts tend to give more weight to the creator's control over initial publication.

- **Check for Market Impact**: If your use could replace or compete with the original work in the marketplace, fair use is unlikely to apply.

- **Consider Legal Advice**: When in doubt, consult a copyright lawyer to evaluate your fair use claim and avoid potential infringement risks.

- **Use Only What You Need**: Use the smallest portion necessary to achieve your purpose, and avoid overusing copyrighted material.

By keeping these tips in mind, you can better navigate the complexities of fair use and protect yourself from legal risks.

Real-World Scenarios: Practical Applications of Fair Use

"Understanding fair use is like learning the rules of chess—you need to know how each piece moves to play the game effectively. It's about making informed choices in the creative process."
— KEN BURNS, DOCUMENTARY FILMMAKER

Chapter Seven, "Real-World Scenarios: Practical Applications of Fair Use," is where theory meets the road—or, more accurately, where it hits the YouTube comments section. We're not just talking about fair use; we're applying it in the trenches of everyday creativity. This chapter is like a boot camp for your brain, preparing you to navigate the complex scenarios where fair use can either be your shield or your Achilles' heel.

Here, we dissect real-life cases from classrooms to newsrooms, and from your garage-based podcast to blockbuster film productions. We'll explore how a documentary filmmaker can use clips without permission, why your favorite YouTuber can (sometimes) get away with using trademarked music, and when an educator can copy a book chapter for class without facing a lawsuit. It's a whirlwind tour of copyright battles fought and won (or lost) on the grounds of fair use.

Equipped with this practical knowledge, you'll be able to spot fair use opportunities and pitfalls as if you had copyright-law goggles on. By the end of this chapter, you'll feel more confident in your ability to use others' creations in ways that are not only legal but also ethically sound. So let's dive into the deep end of fair use—it's time to learn by example, one fascinating case study at a time.

Educational Use and Classroom Copies: Fair Use in Academic Settings

The use of copyrighted materials in educational settings is one of the most common scenarios where **fair use** is invoked. Teachers, professors, and students often rely on copyrighted content—whether it's copying chapters from textbooks, showing clips from movies, or using articles in class discussions. While education is generally viewed as a "favored" purpose under the fair use doctrine, it doesn't give blanket permission to use copyrighted material freely. In this section, we'll explore how fair use applies in academic settings, the factors that determine whether a specific use is legal, and real-world cases that highlight both the opportunities and limitations of fair use in education.

Fair Use Factors in Education

While educational use is generally favored in fair use cases, it still requires balancing the four key factors:

1. **Purpose and Character of the Use**: Educational purposes, particularly non-commercial ones, tend to favor fair use. However, this factor alone is not enough—how the material is used matters, and courts will look for transformative uses that add new meaning or context to the work.

112

2. **Nature of the Copyrighted Work**: Courts are more likely to favor fair use when the original work is factual rather than creative, such as using a chapter from a textbook versus reproducing a short story.

3. **Amount and Substantiality of the Portion Used**: Even in educational settings, using too much of the original work or copying the "heart" of it can weigh against fair use. Teachers should be mindful to use only the portion necessary for their educational purpose.

4. **Effect on the Market for the Original Work**: One of the most important factors in educational use is whether the copying or distribution of material could harm the market for the original work. For example, if a professor distributes full textbook chapters to students, it could replace the need for students to purchase the textbook, potentially harming sales.

Common Educational Uses and Their Fair Use Implications

Let's break down some common scenarios in education and whether they're likely to qualify as fair use.

1. Copying Chapters from Textbooks

Professors and teachers often want to distribute copies of textbook chapters for classroom use. While the purpose is clearly educational, this type of use often faces scrutiny based on the amount used and the potential harm to the textbook market.

Case Example: Cambridge University Press v. Becker
In this landmark case, Georgia State University was sued by several academic publishers for allowing professors to upload copyrighted textbook chapters to the university's digital course reserves. The professors did this to provide students with free access to essential reading materials.

The court applied the four fair use factors and found a mixed result: while copying small excerpts for educational use was deemed fair use, copying entire chapters was not. The court ruled that reproducing large portions of textbooks could harm the market, as students might opt not to purchase the textbooks.

Takeaway: Copying small portions (a few pages or sections) of a textbook for academic purposes is more likely to qualify as fair use, but copying entire chapters or full works generally won't, especially if it impacts sales.

2. Showing Films or Clips in Class

Using film clips in an educational setting, such as showing a movie scene to illustrate a historical event or analyze filmmaking techniques, is another common scenario in education. This kind of use is often considered fair use, provided it is done in a classroom setting and the clips are short and relevant to the lesson.

Example:

A history professor shows a two-minute scene from the movie *Schindler's List* during a lecture on the Holocaust. The use is educational, non-commercial, and the clip is only a small part of the larger film. This scenario is likely to qualify as fair use, especially if the professor uses the clip to offer commentary or analysis.

Takeaway: Showing brief, relevant clips from films or TV shows in a classroom setting is generally favored under fair use, as long as it serves an educational purpose and doesn't involve showing the entire work.

3. Copying Articles for Classroom Discussions

Teachers and professors often distribute copies of news articles, research papers, or scholarly journals to facilitate classroom discussions. Since these works are typically factual and educational, they are more likely to be considered fair use, especially when only portions of the articles are used.

Example:

A sociology professor copies two pages from a 20-page academic article and distributes them to students for a class discussion. The excerpt is used to highlight specific points, and the full article is not reproduced. This use is likely to be considered fair use because it is educational, limited in scope, and doesn't replace the need for students to access the full article.

Takeaway: Copying small portions of factual articles for educational use is more likely to fall under fair use, but distributing full articles or extensive excerpts could weigh against fair use, especially if the material is otherwise available for purchase.

Fair Use in Digital Education

The rise of online learning has created new challenges and opportunities for fair use in education. With the increase in virtual classrooms, digital course materials, and remote learning platforms, the boundaries of fair use in education have evolved.

1. Uploading Copyrighted Material to Online Course Platforms

In digital classrooms, educators often want to upload copyrighted materials (such as articles, book chapters, or videos) to platforms like Blackboard, Google Classroom, or Canvas. While the educational purpose is clear, educators must still respect fair use limits and avoid overuse of copyrighted materials.

Example:
A professor uploads a short academic article to an online platform for students to read as part of a class assignment. Since the work is factual, limited in scope, and serves an educational purpose, this is likely to qualify as fair use. However, uploading entire textbooks or copyrighted books without permission, even for educational purposes, would likely violate fair use.

Takeaway: Digital education can still rely on fair use, but the same principles apply—use only what's necessary, and avoid uploading full works that could impact the market for the original material.

2. Using Copyrighted Images in Presentations

In both physical and virtual classrooms, teachers often use copyrighted images in PowerPoint slides or other presentations to illustrate points or facilitate learning. While this is usually fine for educational purposes, using a large number of copyrighted images, or using them outside of the classroom setting (such as sharing presentations publicly online), may cross the line into infringement.

Example:
A professor uses several copyrighted photographs in a presentation to analyze media portrayals of climate change. The presentation is used solely for educational purposes, shown only to students, and the images are integral to the analysis. This is likely to qualify as fair use.

Takeaway: Use of copyrighted images in classroom presentations is generally safe under fair use, provided they are used for educational purposes and not shared publicly without permission.

Risks and Best Practices for Educators

While fair use is a powerful defense for educators, it's important to recognize its limits and follow best practices:

1. **Use Only What's Necessary**: Copy or distribute only the portion of the work that is necessary for the educational objective. This reduces the risk of exceeding fair use limits.

2. **Avoid Using Full Works**: In most cases, copying or distributing entire books, films, or articles is unlikely to qualify as fair use. Stick to short excerpts, clips, or summaries.

3. **Ensure Educational Purpose**: Always ensure that the use of copyrighted material serves a legitimate educational purpose and doesn't replace the need for students to purchase the original material.

4. **Consider Licensing Options**: For materials that don't clearly fall under fair use (such as full textbook chapters), consider licensing options or direct students to purchase the material.

5. **Be Cautious with Digital Distribution**: When distributing copyrighted material online, make sure it is accessible only to students enrolled in the course and is not available for public access.

Conclusion: Navigating Fair Use in Academic Settings

Fair use in education is an essential tool that allows teachers and students to use copyrighted materials for learning, research, and academic discourse. However, even in academic settings, there are limits. By understanding how fair use applies and carefully considering the four factors, educators can ensure that they respect copyright law while still making the most of educational opportunities.

In the next section, we'll shift focus to digital media, where platforms like YouTube and podcasts have sparked countless fair use debates. We'll explore how content creators navigate the tricky waters of using copyrighted materials online.

YouTube, Podcasts, and Social Media: Fair Use in Digital Media

In the age of digital media, platforms like YouTube, podcasts, Instagram, and TikTok have revolutionized how we create and share content. With this explosion of user-generated content comes a significant challenge: how to legally incorporate copyrighted materials under the fair use doctrine. Whether it's using music, video clips, or memes, creators often walk a fine line between innovation and copyright infringement. In this section, we'll explore how fair use applies to digital media, highlighting real-world examples and the key considerations that creators need to keep in mind to avoid legal pitfalls.

Fair Use in the Context of Digital Platforms

Digital media platforms allow creators to produce and share content that often includes snippets of existing work. Fair use can provide a legal defense for some of these uses, but it's important to evaluate the four fair use factors in the context of digital media:

1. **Purpose and Character of the Use**: Is the content transformative? This is the critical factor for most social media and video content. If you're adding commentary, criticism, parody, or education to the original work, it's more likely to qualify as fair use.

2. **Nature of the Copyrighted Work**: While creative works like songs and movies are more heavily protected, their use in a transformative way, especially in critique or commentary, can still fall under fair use.

3. **Amount and Substantiality of the Portion Used**: Using a smaller portion of the copyrighted work, and avoiding its most significant or iconic parts, increases the chances of a successful fair use defense.

4. **Effect on the Market**: If your use impacts the market for the original work—such as offering a free alternative to the original content—it's less likely to qualify fair use.

1. Fair Use in YouTube Videos

YouTube is a hotbed for fair use disputes, with creators frequently incorporating copyrighted music, video clips, and images into their videos. From reaction videos to reviews and parodies, creators often rely on fair use to defend their inclusion of copyrighted material. However, just because a use is on YouTube doesn't mean it automatically qualifies as fair use.

Example 1: Reaction Videos
Reaction videos are one of the most popular types of content on YouTube, where creators watch and react to a video or movie in real time, often using portions of the original work in their reaction.

Case Example: Equals Three, LLC v. Jukin Media, Inc.
In this case, *Equals Three*, a YouTube channel known for creating comedic commentary videos about viral clips, was sued by *Jukin Media* for using its viral videos without permission. The court ruled that some uses were transformative—such as when Equals Three provided substantial commentary and analysis—but others were not, especially when the original clips were merely played without much added content.

Takeaway: Reaction videos are more likely to be protected under fair use when they add significant commentary or analysis to the original content. Simply watching and reacting without transforming the original video is less likely to be considered fair use.

Example 2: Movie Reviews and Criticism
Creators who review movies or TV shows often include short clips from the original works to illustrate their points. These clips can fall under fair use if they are used for the purpose of criticism, commentary, or analysis and are not too extensive.

Example:
A YouTube movie reviewer includes short, non-essential clips from a film to critique the director's style and discuss its narrative. This is likely to qualify as fair use because it's transformative and serves the purpose of criticism, rather than simply reproducing the original film.

Takeaway: When using clips from films or TV shows, brevity and context matter. Using small, relevant clips in a review is more likely to be fair use, especially when the purpose is transformative, such as providing critique or analysis.

2. Fair Use in Podcasts

Podcasts often incorporate copyrighted content, such as music, audio clips, or interviews. While podcasting can fall under fair use, the same rules apply— creators must use copyrighted content in a transformative way, and the amount used should be limited to what is necessary to make a point.

Example 3: Music Snippets in Podcasts

Many podcasters want to use popular songs to set the tone for an episode or illustrate a discussion. However, using full songs or large portions of music can be risky unless it's clear that the use is transformative and doesn't impact the market for the original song.

Example:

A podcast that analyzes the cultural impact of a famous band plays a short 10-second clip of a song to highlight a point in the discussion. Since the podcast is using the clip for commentary and analysis and only uses a small portion of the song, it's more likely to be considered fair use. In contrast, playing a full song as background music during the podcast without adding any commentary would likely be infringement.

Takeaway: Use only short excerpts of music and ensure that the use adds value, such as commentary or education, rather than simply enhancing the atmosphere of the podcast.

3. Fair Use in Social Media (Instagram, TikTok, and Memes)

On social media platforms like Instagram and TikTok, creators often incorporate popular songs, images, or video clips into their content. While these platforms encourage creative expression, it's essential to remember that using copyrighted content without permission can still lead to copyright claims.

Example 4: Using Music in TikTok Videos

TikTok users frequently incorporate popular music into their videos. While TikTok has licensing agreements with many music labels that allow users to use certain tracks, not all content is covered by these agreements.

Example:

A TikTok creator uses a popular song in a dance video and uploads it to the platform. If TikTok has a licensing agreement for the song, the creator is in the clear. However, if the song is not licensed and the use is purely for entertainment without adding commentary or analysis, it could be considered infringement if uploaded elsewhere without proper rights.

Takeaway: Platforms like TikTok may provide licensing agreements for music, but creators should check platform rules and avoid using unlicensed music when sharing content on other platforms where protections may not apply.

Example 5: Memes and Social Media Commentary

Memes often rely on images, videos, or phrases from copyrighted works, adding humor or commentary that transforms the original content.

Example:

A meme that uses a still image from a popular movie but alters the context with new, humorous text can be considered transformative, especially if it adds commentary or satire. This type of use is often protected under fair use because it repurposes the original content in a creative and transformative way.

Takeaway: Memes that add new meaning, commentary, or humor to copyrighted works are more likely to be considered fair use, as they transform the original content into something new.

4. Monetization and the Market Effect

One of the most significant issues for creators on platforms like YouTube and Instagram is monetization. If a creator is generating revenue from content that includes copyrighted material, it can impact the original work's market, making a fair use defense more challenging.

Example 6: Monetized YouTube Videos

A YouTuber creates a video essay using clips from several blockbuster films. While the video provides commentary and analysis, the YouTuber is monetizing the video through ads. If the clips used are extensive or replace the need to watch the original films, this could negatively affect the market for the films and hurt the creator's fair use defense.

Takeaway: Monetizing content that includes copyrighted material is riskier because it could harm the market for the original work. To strengthen a fair use defense, creators should use only what is necessary and ensure the content is transformative.

Strategies for Using Copyrighted Content in Digital Media

To avoid copyright claims while creating digital content, here are some key strategies:

1. **Be Transformative**: Always add commentary, criticism, or analysis to the copyrighted material you're using. The more you transform the original, the stronger your fair use defense.

2. **Keep It Brief**: Use only the portion of the work necessary to make your point. Avoid using large or essential parts of the original content.

3. **Check Licensing**: Platforms like YouTube and TikTok may have licensing agreements for certain content. Make sure to check the platform's guidelines before using copyrighted material.

4. **Use Public Domain and Royalty-Free Content**: Whenever possible, use public domain works or royalty-free music and images to avoid copyright issues altogether.

5. **Disclose Fair Use**: Include a fair use disclaimer in your video or podcast descriptions, explaining that the content is used for transformative purposes like commentary, education, or parody. While this doesn't guarantee protection, it shows good faith in applying fair use.

Conclusion: Fair Use in the Digital Age

Fair use provides creators on platforms like YouTube, TikTok, and podcasts with a powerful tool to incorporate copyrighted content legally, but it's essential to understand its limits. By focusing on transformative uses, keeping portions small, and avoiding negative impacts on the original work's market, digital creators can make the most of fair use while avoiding legal risks.

In the next section, we'll explore how **journalists and news outlets** use copyrighted material for reporting, criticism, and commentary, showing how fair use operates in the world of journalism.

News Reporting and Criticism: Navigating Fair Use in Journalism

Fair use plays a crucial role in journalism, enabling reporters, critics, and commentators to incorporate copyrighted material into their work without seeking permission. Whether it's quoting text, using video clips, or incorporating images, journalists rely on fair use to provide commentary, analysis, and factual reporting on current events. However, fair use in journalism comes with its own set of challenges, particularly when it comes to balancing the use of copyrighted material with the four fair use factors. In this section, we'll explore how journalists and news outlets navigate fair use, provide real-world examples, and discuss best practices for ensuring compliance.

1. Purpose and Character of Use in Journalism

Journalistic uses of copyrighted material generally fall under commentary, criticism, or news reporting, which are strongly favored purposes for fair use. However, even in journalism, the use must be transformative and not simply reproduce the original work without adding new value or context.

Example:
A news website uses short clips from a controversial political speech to provide analysis and fact-check the speaker's claims. This use would likely be considered fair use because the clips are used to comment on and critique the speech, rather than simply broadcasting it in full.

Takeaway: In journalism, using copyrighted material for criticism, commentary, or fact-checking is generally more likely to qualify as fair use, especially when the original content is transformed by the journalist's analysis or reporting.

2. Nature of the Copyrighted Work: Factual vs. Creative

The nature of the copyrighted work is also a significant factor in fair use. Courts are more likely to favor fair use when the copyrighted material is factual, such as news reports or educational content, rather than creative works like films or novels. Since journalism often involves reporting on factual events, this tends to weigh in favor of fair use.

Example:

A news outlet quotes from a government report to explain how certain policies may affect the economy. Since the original report is factual in nature and the journalist's use involves reporting on public policy, this use would likely fall under fair use.

Takeaway: When using factual works (such as government reports, studies, or news footage), journalists are more likely to benefit from fair use than if they were using highly creative works, such as movies or songs.

3. Amount and Substantiality: How Much Is Too Much?

Even in the context of news reporting, the amount of the copyrighted work used must be limited to what is necessary to achieve the journalistic purpose. Using too much of the original work, or using its most essential parts, could tip the balance against fair use.

Example:

A journalist writes a critical review of a new book and includes two paragraphs from the original text to support their argument. Since the journalist is only quoting a small portion of the book and using it for the purpose of commentary, this would likely qualify as fair use.

However, if the journalist were to include an entire chapter of the book in the review, that could weigh against fair use, as it may affect the market for the book and use more than is necessary for critique.

Takeaway: In journalism, it's important to use only the portion of the work necessary to make your point. Avoid using large sections of text or extensive video clips unless they are absolutely critical to the story.

4. Effect on the Market for the Original Work

One of the most critical factors in determining fair use is whether the journalist's use of the copyrighted material affects the market for the original work. If the use could replace or compete with the original—such as making the original unnecessary for consumers—fair use is less likely to apply.

Example:
A news outlet reports on a popular film and includes a 10-second clip in the video segment to illustrate a key point in the movie's plot. Because the clip is brief, and the report provides analysis that encourages viewers to watch the film, it is unlikely to harm the market for the film and would likely be considered fair use.

In contrast, if the news outlet were to stream the entire film or show extensive clips without providing commentary or analysis, it could harm the market by offering a substitute for watching the movie, thus weighing against fair use.

Takeaway: Journalists should ensure that their use of copyrighted material doesn't replace the need for the original work. Use short clips, quotes, or excerpts that complement the reporting, rather than offering a complete or competitive substitute.

5. Real-World Examples of Fair Use in Journalism

Example 1: Quoting Text in News Articles
Journalists frequently quote copyrighted text, such as from books, speeches, or articles, in their reporting. As long as the quote is used for commentary, analysis, or reporting, and the amount used is limited, this is generally protected by fair use.

Case Example:
In *Leibovitz v. Paramount Pictures Corp.*, photographer Annie Leibovitz sued Paramount for using a photograph in an advertisement that parodied her iconic image of a pregnant Demi Moore. The court ruled that the advertisement was a parody and thus a transformative use, meaning it was protected under fair use.

While this case involved an advertisement, the same principle applies to journalism: the use of copyrighted images or text in a transformative way—such as for commentary or criticism—can be considered fair use.

Takeaway: Quoting text in news articles for the purpose of reporting or critique is often protected under fair use, provided the amount used is reasonable and serves a specific journalistic purpose.

Example 2: Using Video Clips in News Broadcasts

Television news programs frequently use short video clips to report on events, such as political speeches, movie trailers, or press conferences. When used for the purpose of news reporting or commentary, these clips are generally protected by fair use, but the length and context of the clips matter.

Case Example:

A news station airs a brief 15-second clip from a controversial political ad during a segment that analyzes the ad's impact on public opinion. Since the clip is used to provide commentary and is only a small portion of the full ad, this is likely to qualify as fair use.

However, if the station were to air the entire ad without providing any analysis or context, it could be seen as substituting for the original and may not qualify as fair use.

Takeaway: When using video clips in news reporting, keep the clips short and contextualized. Provide analysis or commentary that transforms the original content, rather than simply broadcasting it.

6. Fair Use Pitfalls in Journalism

While fair use offers journalists significant leeway in using copyrighted materials, there are potential pitfalls to watch out for:

- **Using Too Much of the Work**: Even in reporting, using large portions of a copyrighted work—such as streaming full interviews or films—without adding transformative content can cross the line into infringement.

- **Commercial Use Without Transformation**: If a news outlet uses copyrighted material solely for commercial gain without adding commentary or analysis, it may be considered infringement. For example, if a website republishes an entire news article or image gallery without permission, this could harm the market for the original content.

- **Misinterpreting the Fair Use Defense**: Journalists should avoid assuming that any use of copyrighted material in a news report automatically qualifies as fair use. The use must still meet the criteria of the four factors, particularly transformation and market impact.

Best Practices for Journalists Using Copyrighted Material

To avoid legal challenges while using copyrighted content in news reporting, journalists should follow these best practices:

1. **Transform the Material**: Add commentary, analysis, or criticism to the original content. The more transformative the use, the stronger your fair use defense.

2. **Keep It Brief**: Use short quotes, excerpts, or clips that serve the purpose of your reporting. Avoid using large portions of the original work.

3. **Use Factual Works**: When possible, use factual works (such as news reports or government documents) rather than creative works, as factual works are more likely to qualify as fair use.

4. **Check the Market Impact**: Make sure your use doesn't harm the market for the original work. If your report could replace the need for consumers to access the original content, it may not qualify as fair use.

5. **Provide Credit**: While attribution is not a requirement for fair use, giving credit to the original creator can show good faith and may reduce the risk of legal challenges.

Conclusion: Fair Use as a Journalistic Tool

Fair use is an essential tool for journalists, enabling them to use copyrighted material for commentary, criticism, and reporting without infringing on the rights of the original creator. However, journalists must be mindful of how they use copyrighted content, ensuring that the use is transformative, limited in scope, and doesn't harm the market for the original work.

In the next section, we'll explore how filmmakers, documentarians, and visual artists navigate fair use in the creative world, highlighting key examples and best practices for using copyrighted material in artistic projects.

Film, Documentaries, and Art: Creative Uses of Copyrighted Material

In the worlds of film, documentaries, and visual art, creators often incorporate copyrighted material to comment on, critique, or reinterpret the original works. Whether using footage in a documentary, sampling music in a film, or referencing iconic images in visual art, the concept of fair use is essential to many creative projects. However, just like in journalism, artists must be mindful of the four factors of fair use and consider how transformative their work is to avoid copyright infringement. In this section, we'll explore how filmmakers, documentarians, and artists can legally incorporate copyrighted materials, using real-world examples and practical strategies.

1. The Importance of Transformative Use in Creative Works

In the context of artistic and creative projects, the transformative nature of the use is often the most critical factor in determining fair use. If the copyrighted material is altered in a way that adds new meaning, message, or purpose, it's more likely to qualify as fair use. For filmmakers, documentarians, and artists, this means that their use of copyrighted content should go beyond simple reproduction and instead serve a new, original purpose—such as commentary, critique, or artistic expression.

Example:
A documentary filmmaker uses a 15-second clip from a news broadcast to critique media coverage of a political event. The clip is used not to simply replay the event but to highlight biases in the reporting. Since the clip is being used in a transformative way, this would likely be considered fair use.

Takeaway: In creative works, transforming the original content to serve a new purpose—whether through critique, commentary, or artistic reinterpretation—strengthens the fair use defense.

2. Fair Use in Documentary Films

Documentary filmmakers often rely on fair use to include copyrighted material, such as historical footage, news clips, music, or images. Because documentaries frequently offer commentary or critique on real-world events or social issues, they often meet the criteria for transformative use. However, filmmakers must still carefully consider how much of the original work is used and ensure that their use does not harm the market for the original.

Example 1: Historical Footage in Documentaries

A documentary about the Vietnam War includes short clips of televised news broadcasts from the 1960s to illustrate how the media portrayed the conflict at the time. The filmmaker uses only the portions necessary to support the documentary's argument and adds analysis to each clip.

Takeaway: Using short, relevant excerpts of historical footage in a documentary, especially when providing commentary or analysis, is likely to be considered fair use. The key is using only what's necessary and transforming the original through critique or storytelling.

Example 2: Music in Documentaries

Music is often used in documentaries to set the tone or underscore emotional moments. However, using entire songs or large portions of them without permission can be risky, especially if the music is central to the scene and not transformative.

Case Example: *Bill Graham Archives v. Dorling Kindersley Ltd.*
In this case, the publisher of a historical book about rock music used small images of concert posters created by Bill Graham, a famous promoter. These images were used to provide historical context, and the court ruled that the use was transformative and fair. The posters were reproduced in a reduced size and served a different purpose than originally intended.

Takeaway: When using copyrighted images or music in documentaries, make sure that they are necessary for context and commentary and not simply for aesthetic purposes.

3. Fair Use in Narrative Films

Fair use in narrative films is more complex, as filmmakers often want to use copyrighted content in ways that enhance storytelling or mood. Whether it's including a copyrighted song in a key scene or referencing another filmmaker's iconic shots, narrative filmmakers must ensure that their use is transformative and limited in scope.

Example 3: Referencing Films in a Satirical Comedy

A satirical comedy references several famous movies, using short clips and recreating iconic scenes with a humorous twist. Since the clips are used to create new meaning through satire and parody, this would likely be considered transformative.

**Case Example: *Campbell v. Acuff-Rose Music, Inc.*

This landmark case involved 2 Live Crew's parody of Roy Orbison's song *Oh, Pretty Woman*. The Supreme Court ruled that the parody was transformative because it added new meaning and commentary to the original song, even though it used substantial portions of the original. This ruling reinforced the idea that parody and satire can qualify as fair use if they provide social or artistic commentary.

Takeaway: In narrative films, parody, satire, and critique are often considered fair use, especially when they transform the original work and add new layers of meaning.

4. Fair Use in Visual Art

Visual artists frequently reference or incorporate copyrighted images, works of art, and pop culture in their creations. While artistic expression is strongly protected by fair use, artists must still ensure that their use of copyrighted material is transformative and does not simply reproduce the original work without adding new meaning or purpose.

Example 4: Appropriation Art

Appropriation artists, such as Andy Warhol, often use existing images in their work to comment on culture, consumerism, and art itself. For instance, Warhol's famous *Campbell's Soup Cans* series used a recognizable commercial logo but transformed it into a statement about mass production and art.

Case Example: *Cariou v. Prince*

In this case, the artist Richard Prince used photos from Patrick Cariou's book in a series of transformative works that altered the original images by adding new elements and changing the context. The court ruled that Prince's use of Cariou's photos was transformative and therefore protected by fair use, as the new works added significant artistic value beyond simple reproduction.

Takeaway: In visual art, appropriation and transformation are key to fair use. Artists should ensure that their work adds new meaning or commentary, rather than merely copying or reproducing existing works.

5. Potential Pitfalls and Best Practices for Filmmakers and Artists

While fair use provides essential protection for creative expression, there are some common pitfalls that filmmakers and artists should avoid:

- **Using Full Works Without Transformation**: Incorporating a full song, movie clip, or image without adding commentary, critique, or new meaning is less likely to qualify as fair use. For example, using a full song in a film's soundtrack purely for mood or atmosphere, without permission, could lead to copyright infringement.

- **Commercial Uses Without Transformation**: Commercial use of copyrighted material is more likely to be scrutinized, especially if the use is not transformative. For instance, selling merchandise that reproduces copyrighted images without adding artistic value can be seen as infringement.

- **Failing to Consider Licensing**: In cases where fair use is uncertain, such as when using music or extensive clips, filmmakers and artists should consider licensing the material. Licensing provides legal certainty and avoids potential legal disputes.

Best Practices for Filmmakers and Artists

1. **Transform the Original Work**: Add new meaning, context, or commentary to the copyrighted material. The more you transform it, the more likely it is to qualify as fair use.

2. **Use Only What's Necessary**: Limit the amount of copyrighted material you use to what is absolutely necessary for your creative purpose. Avoid using large portions or the heart of the work.

3. **Consider Licensing**: When in doubt, especially with music or large portions of film footage, seek permission or obtain a license to use the copyrighted material.

4. **Provide Context and Commentary**: Whether in a documentary or visual art, ensure that copyrighted material is used to support commentary, critique, or artistic expression. Adding context can strengthen your fair use defense.

Conclusion: Creative Uses of Copyrighted Material

For filmmakers, documentarians, and artists, fair use allows for creative freedom while balancing the rights of original creators. By transforming the original work, limiting the amount used, and ensuring that the use does not harm the market for the original, creators can navigate the complexities of fair use while maintaining their artistic vision.

In the next chapter, we'll explore the rise of the digital age and how it has reshaped the landscape of fair use and copyright protection in the era of streaming, social media, and global connectivity.

Quick Tips and Recap

- **Transformative Use is Key**: Always aim to add new meaning, context, or artistic value to copyrighted material in your creative work.

- **Use Only What's Necessary**: Limit your use of copyrighted material to the portions that are essential for your purpose, whether it's commentary, critique, or artistic expression.

- **Documentaries Can Use Brief Clips**: When using video or audio clips in documentaries, keep them brief and ensure they serve a clear commentary or analytical purpose.

- **Consider Licensing for Full Works**: If your project relies heavily on copyrighted music, film, or art, consider obtaining licenses to avoid legal risks, especially if the use isn't transformative.

- **Parody and Satire Are Strong Defenses**: Works of parody and satire, which comment on or mock the original, are more likely to be considered fair use as they often transform the original meaning.

- **Artistic Appropriation Requires Transformation**: Visual artists should ensure their work appropriates and transforms the original content, offering new insights or commentary rather than simply reproducing it.

- **Beware of Commercial Uses**: Commercial projects using copyrighted material are scrutinized more heavily. If your project is for profit, ensure it significantly transforms the original work.

By keeping these tips in mind, creators in film, documentaries, and visual art can use copyrighted materials effectively while staying within the boundaries of fair use.

Caught in the Act: Handling Copyright Infringements

"When dealing with copyright infringements, remember it's not just about defending your work; it's about upholding the respect for creativity itself."— DAVID BOWIE, MUSICIAN AND SONGWRITER

Chapter Eight, "Caught in the Act: Handling Copyright Infringements," is where we roll up our sleeves and delve into the nitty-gritty of what happens when the copyright cookie crumbles. Think of this chapter as your guide to the Wild West of intellectual property disputes, where the good, the bad, and the ugly come out to play.

So, someone used your work without a nod or a wink in your direction? Or maybe you're the one who got a little too inspired by someone else's genius? Fear not, for here we outline the duels and deals of copyright law enforcement. We'll show you how to send a cease and desist with the charm of a Jane Austen protagonist and the precision of a sniper. We'll explore the legal battlegrounds from courtroom dramas to settlement whispers, giving you the playbook on how to handle accusations with the poise of a diplomat and the strategies of a general. Whether you're defending your creative fortress or waving a white flag, this chapter provides the armor and the tools to engage in copyright conflicts with confidence and savvy. Ready your legal lances, creators, because it's time to learn how to joust in the courts of law and public opinion.

Recognizing Infringement: How to Spot When Your Copyright is Violated

Copyright infringement occurs when someone uses your creative work without permission in a way that violates your exclusive rights as the copyright holder. While some uses may fall under fair use, others can clearly cross the line, infringing on your intellectual property rights. In this section, we'll break down how to recognize copyright infringement, providing you with the tools to protect your work from unauthorized use and knowing when to take action.

1. What is Copyright Infringement?

Copyright infringement happens when someone uses a copyrighted work in a way that violates one or more of the exclusive rights granted to the copyright holder. These exclusive rights include the right to:

- Reproduce the work (e.g., making copies of a book, photograph, or song).

- Distribute the work (e.g., selling or sharing the work without permission).

- Display or perform the work publicly (e.g., showing a film or performing a play).

- Create derivative works (e.g., making adaptations or remixes of the original work).

If someone uses your work in any of these ways without permission and outside of fair use exceptions, they are infringing on your copyright.

2. Common Signs of Copyright Infringement

Spotting infringement can sometimes be straightforward, like seeing an unauthorized copy of your book for sale online. Other times, it requires a more careful analysis. Here are some common signs that your work may have been infringed:

- **Uncredited Use**: If you see your work (text, images, videos, etc.) used by someone else without giving you proper credit, this could be an infringement, especially if they haven't sought permission.

- **Unauthorized Distribution**: If someone is distributing copies of your work—whether physical or digital—without your consent, this violates your right to control the distribution of your content.

- **Derivative Works Without Permission**: If your work has been remixed, altered, or used to create a derivative piece without your approval, this is also a form of infringement. This could include someone creating new artwork from your original design or remixing your song.

- **Unauthorized Sales or Monetization**: If you discover someone profiting from your work by selling or licensing it without permission, this is a serious form of infringement that directly impacts your ability to earn revenue from your creation.

- **Plagiarism or Direct Copying**: If a person or organization copies large portions of your work and presents it as their own, this is not only plagiarism but also copyright infringement. This can occur in written content, visual art, music, and even software code.

3. How to Verify an Infringement Claim

Before taking action, it's important to verify whether what you've observed constitutes actual copyright infringement. Not all uses of copyrighted material are illegal. Here are some key questions to help you determine if an infringement has occurred:

- **Is the work copyrighted?** Your work must be original and fixed in a tangible form to be protected by copyright. If it meets these criteria, it is protected from the moment of creation, even without formal registration (though registration is necessary for litigation).

- **Do you own the rights?** Ensure that you are the rightful copyright holder. For example, if you created the work as part of a work-for-hire agreement, the company or individual that hired you may own the copyright.

- **Is the use covered by fair use or other exceptions?** Consider whether the unauthorized use might qualify as fair use. Fair use allows limited use of copyrighted material for purposes such as criticism, commentary, news reporting, teaching, or research. The four factors of fair use (purpose, nature, amount used, and market effect) need to be analyzed to determine if the use is legal.

Example:

If a blogger quotes a short passage from your book in a review, this could be considered fair use. However, if they publish entire chapters without your consent, it's more likely to be infringement.

- **Has the material been used commercially?** Commercial uses of your work (such as someone selling prints of your artwork) are less likely to qualify for fair use and more likely to be an infringement.

- **How much of your work was used?** Even small excerpts can be infringing if they represent the "heart" of your work. Using a key element of your work in a way that removes its creative essence may cross the line into infringement.

4. Digital Infringement: The Online Wild West

In today's digital age, copyright infringement is rampant online, with content being copied and shared across websites, social media, and file-sharing platforms. Here are some specific types of digital infringement to watch for:

- **Website or Social Media Use**: If someone has posted your photos, videos, or other content on their website or social media without permission, this is likely infringement. Even "reposting" without credit, unless the work is shared under a Creative Commons license, could be an infringement.

- **Piracy on File-Sharing Sites**: If your work is being distributed on piracy websites or peer-to-peer networks (e.g., illegal downloads of your ebook or film), this is a serious form of copyright violation.

- **Content Scraping**: This happens when someone copies large amounts of text or images from your website and reposts it on their own without permission. It's a common issue for bloggers and online businesses.

5. Tools and Resources for Detecting Infringement

Thankfully, there are many tools available that can help you detect when your work is being used without permission:

- **Google Reverse Image Search**: If your photos or artwork are being used without permission, you can upload your images to Google's reverse image search tool to find websites where they appear.

- **Content ID on YouTube**: If you create videos or music, YouTube's Content ID system can help identify when your content is used in other videos. You can choose to block the video, track its performance, or monetize it.

- **Plagiarism Checkers**: Tools like Copyscape, Grammarly, and Turnitin can help you identify when written content has been copied and reposted online without your permission.

- **Digital Rights Management (DRM)**: DRM systems can be used to protect digital products like ebooks, software, and videos from unauthorized distribution or copying.

6. What to Do if You Suspect Copyright Infringement

Once you've recognized that someone has used your work without permission, here are the steps to take:

1. **Document the Infringement**: Take screenshots, save URLs, and collect any evidence that shows how your work is being used. This

documentation will be critical if you need to send a cease and desist letter or file a lawsuit.

2. **Check Fair Use or Licensing**: Ensure that the use doesn't fall under fair use or an existing license (such as Creative Commons or another type of open license).

3. **Reach Out to the Infringer**: In some cases, a friendly email or direct message can resolve the issue. Some infringers may not realize they've violated your copyright and may comply by taking down the content.

4. **Send a Cease and Desist Letter**: If reaching out informally doesn't work, a cease and desist letter is the next step. This formal notice requests that the infringer stop using your work and provides legal consequences if they don't comply (more on this in the next section).

5. **Consider Legal Action**: If the infringer refuses to comply or the infringement has caused significant harm (e.g., lost revenue), you may want to consult a lawyer and consider filing a lawsuit for damages.

Conclusion: Spotting and Responding to Copyright Infringement

Recognizing copyright infringement is the first step in protecting your intellectual property. Whether it's through direct copying, unauthorized distribution, or commercial exploitation of your work, infringement can take many forms. By understanding the signs of infringement, using the right tools to track unauthorized use, and knowing when to take action, you can safeguard your creative rights and maintain control over your work.

In the next section, we'll explore how to send a **cease and desist** letter—your first line of defense in addressing copyright infringement and getting the infringer to stop without heading straight to court.

Cease and Desist: The First Line of Defense

When you discover that someone is using your copyrighted material without permission, the cease and desist letter is often the first step in defending your intellectual property. It's a formal way to assert your rights and demand that the infringer stop their unauthorized use of your work. The beauty of a cease and desist letter is that it can often resolve the situation without the need for a lengthy (and costly) legal battle. In this section, we'll break down how to draft an effective cease and desist letter, what to include, and how to handle responses.

1. What is a Cease and Desist Letter?

A cease and desist letter is a formal notice sent to an individual or organization that you believe is infringing on your copyright. The letter outlines the unauthorized use, explains your rights as the copyright holder, and demands that the infringing party stop using your work immediately. If ignored, the letter also serves as a precursor to legal action, giving the infringer a chance to comply before things escalate.

2. When to Send a Cease and Desist Letter

Before jumping into litigation, a cease and desist letter is a strategic way to address copyright infringement. You should send one if:

- **You've confirmed infringement**: You have gathered evidence that your copyrighted material is being used without permission, and the use doesn't fall under fair use or any licensing agreement.

- **The use is harmful**: The infringer is profiting from your work or causing harm to your ability to monetize it (e.g., selling pirated versions of your book or distributing your content without authorization).

- **Informal requests haven't worked**: If you've tried reaching out directly to the infringer and they've ignored your request to stop or remove the material, it's time to escalate with a formal letter.

3. Key Components of a Cease and Desist Letter

A well-drafted cease and desist letter is professional, clear, and firm in tone. It should assert your rights but remain diplomatic—there's no need to be overly aggressive. Here's what to include:

1. Your Identity and Ownership of the Copyright. Begin by identifying yourself as the copyright holder and stating your legal rights to the material. This could include mentioning when the work was created and registered, if applicable. Make it clear that you are the rightful owner of the work in question.

Example:
"I, [Your Name], am the creator and copyright owner of the original work titled [Work Title], which was created on [Creation Date] and is registered with the U.S. Copyright Office under registration number [Registration Number] (if applicable)."

2. Description of the Infringement. Clearly state how the infringing party is using your work without permission. Be specific—cite where and how the work is being used, such as on a website, social media, or in a publication. Include URLs, screenshots, or other evidence of the infringement to support your claim.

Example:
"It has come to my attention that you have used my copyrighted photograph on your website, [Website URL], without obtaining my permission. This use constitutes copyright infringement as it violates my exclusive right to reproduce and distribute my work."

3. Request to Stop the Infringement. Firmly request that the infringer stop using your work immediately. This is the core demand of the cease and desist letter. You can also request that they take specific actions, such as removing the content from their website or social media.

Example:
"I hereby demand that you immediately cease and desist from using my copyrighted material and remove it from your website [or any other platform]. Failure to comply within [X] days will result in further legal action."

4. Deadline for Compliance. Set a reasonable deadline for the infringer to respond and comply with your demands. Typically, a period of 7 to 10 days is common, giving them enough time to take down the content or respond with their position.

Example:

"I expect to receive confirmation of compliance with this demand no later than [Date], after which I will consider further legal actions if the infringement continues."

5. Legal Consequences. Politely but firmly explain the legal consequences of non-compliance. Mention that failure to stop the infringement may result in legal action, such as a lawsuit seeking damages, injunctive relief, and recovery of legal fees.

Example:

"Should you fail to comply with this request, I will have no choice but to pursue legal remedies, including but not limited to filing a lawsuit for copyright infringement, seeking damages and injunctive relief, as well as recovery of attorneys' fees."

6. Signature and Contact Information. Sign the letter and provide your contact information so the infringer can easily reach you to discuss the matter or confirm compliance.

4. Tone and Approach: Polite but Firm

When drafting a cease and desist letter, it's important to strike the right tone. While you need to assert your rights, there's no need to be overly aggressive or hostile. In many cases, the infringer may not have realized they were violating your copyright, and a professional, respectful tone can lead to a quicker resolution.

- **Polite but firm**: Be clear in your demands without sounding overly threatening. This encourages cooperation rather than confrontation.

- **Stay professional**: Avoid emotional language or insults. The goal is to resolve the issue, not escalate it unnecessarily.

- **Give them a chance to correct the issue**: The cease and desist letter is often enough to resolve the problem without legal action. Give the infringer a chance to comply before pursuing more aggressive measures.

5. What Happens After Sending a Cease and Desist

After you've sent the cease and desist letter, there are a few possible outcomes:

1. The Infringer Complies. In many cases, the infringer will comply by removing the infringing material and confirming that they will no longer use your work without permission. This is the ideal outcome—your rights are restored without having to go to court.

2. The Infringer Ignores the Letter. If the infringer ignores your cease and desist letter or continues to use your work, you may need to escalate the situation. This could involve consulting with a lawyer and considering legal action.

3. The Infringer Disputes the Claim. In some cases, the infringer may respond with a defense, such as claiming fair use or that they have a license to use your work. At this point, it's important to evaluate the validity of their claim and decide whether to pursue further legal action.

6. When to Seek Legal Help

If the infringer refuses to comply with the cease and desist letter or disputes your claim, it may be time to seek legal assistance. An intellectual property attorney can help you assess the situation, negotiate with the infringer, and file a lawsuit if necessary.

- **Legal advice**: If you're unsure whether to send a cease and desist letter or how to handle a response, an attorney can guide you through the process.

- **Filing a lawsuit**: If the infringement is significant or causing you financial harm, legal action may be necessary to seek damages and protect your work.

7. Cease and Desist Letters in the Digital Age

In the digital era, cease and desist letters can also be used to address online copyright infringement. For instance, if your content is being distributed on a website or social media platform, you can send a cease and desist letter to the platform's administrators, requesting that they remove the infringing material.

- **DMCA Takedown Notices**: For online content, sending a Digital Millennium Copyright Act (DMCA) takedown notice to the infringer's hosting provider or platform can be an effective way to have infringing content removed.

Conclusion: The Power of the Cease and Desist Letter

A cease and desist letter is a powerful tool for addressing copyright infringement without escalating the issue to court. By clearly asserting your rights and requesting the infringer to stop using your work, you can often resolve the matter quickly and professionally. However, if the infringer ignores or disputes your claim, you may need to consider further legal action to protect your intellectual property.

In the next section, we'll explore legal remedies, such as lawsuits and settlements, and guide you through what happens when cease and desist letters aren't enough to stop the infringement.

Legal Remedies: Navigating Lawsuits and Sentiments

When a cease and desist letter fails to resolve copyright infringement, or the infringing party disputes your claim, the next step is to consider legal action. This can involve filing a lawsuit to protect your rights or negotiating a settlement to avoid drawn-out court battles. In this section, we'll guide you through the process of pursuing legal remedies, from initiating a lawsuit to reaching settlements, and help you understand the pros and cons of each path.

1. When to Consider Filing a Lawsuit

Filing a lawsuit should generally be a last resort, but there are situations where it becomes necessary. You may need to pursue legal action if:

- **Significant financial harm has occurred**: The infringer's actions have caused you to lose revenue, such as when someone is selling unauthorized copies of your work or using it commercially without permission.

- **The infringement is ongoing**: Despite attempts to stop the infringer, such as sending a cease and desist letter, they continue to use your work without authorization.

- **The case involves a large-scale violation**: In cases where your work has been widely distributed (e.g., piracy or mass production of unauthorized goods), legal action may be the only way to stop the infringement and seek damages.

- **Negotiation has failed**: If informal efforts to resolve the issue have been ignored or dismissed, a lawsuit can force the infringer to take the matter seriously.

2. The Process of Filing a Copyright Infringement Lawsuit

Filing a lawsuit involves several steps, from gathering evidence to the formal court process. Here's an overview of what to expect when you decide to take legal action for copyright infringement:

Step 1: Gather Evidence. Before filing a lawsuit, you'll need to collect evidence of the infringement. This includes:

- Screenshots or printouts of where the infringing material is being used (websites, social media, stores, etc.).

- Proof of your copyright ownership (e.g., copyright registration, creation dates, and original files).

- Evidence of any cease and desist letters you've sent and the infringer's response (if any).

- Any financial losses you've incurred as a result of the infringement (e.g., loss of sales, licensing opportunities, or damage to your brand).

Step 2: Consult an Attorney. It's important to have a copyright attorney guide you through the process of filing a lawsuit. An attorney can help you assess the strength of your case, determine the appropriate legal strategies, and represent you in court.

Step 3: File a Complaint. Your attorney will file a complaint with the court, which formally outlines your allegations of copyright infringement and the relief you are seeking. Relief may include:

- **Injunctive relief**: A court order to stop the infringer from using your work.

- **Monetary damages**: Compensation for the financial losses you've suffered as a result of the infringement.

- **Statutory damages**: Fixed damages that may be awarded even if you can't prove actual financial losses, provided your work was registered with the U.S. Copyright Office prior to the infringement or within three months of publication.

Step 4: Discovery Process. After the lawsuit is filed, both parties enter the discovery phase, where they gather and exchange evidence related to the case. This can include depositions, requests for documents, and interrogatories.

Step 5: Trial or Settlement. The case may proceed to trial, where both parties present their evidence and arguments before a judge or jury. Alternatively, the case may be resolved before reaching trial through a settlement agreement (more on settlements below).

3. Remedies Available in a Copyright Infringement Lawsuit

There are several remedies available to copyright holders who win a lawsuit or reach a settlement:

- **Injunctive Relief**: The court can issue an injunction, ordering the infringer to stop using your work. This prevents further harm and unauthorized use of your intellectual property.

- **Monetary Damages**: There are two types of damages you may be awarded:

  - **Actual Damages**: These are based on the financial losses you suffered as a result of the infringement. You will need to show evidence of how the infringement impacted your revenue or licensing opportunities.

○ **Statutory Damages**: If your work was registered with the U.S. Copyright Office before the infringement, you can seek statutory damages ranging from $750 to $30,000 per work infringed. In cases of willful infringement, statutory damages can increase to $150,000 per work.

- **Attorney's Fees**: In some cases, the court may order the infringer to pay your legal costs and attorney's fees, especially if the infringement was willful.

- **Destruction of Infringing Goods**: The court may order the destruction of unauthorized copies of your work, such as pirated goods or counterfeit merchandise.

4. Settlements: An Alternative to Going to Trial

In many cases, lawsuits are resolved before trial through a settlement. Settling can be a quicker and less expensive option for both parties, avoiding the unpredictability of a trial verdict. A settlement is a negotiated agreement where the infringer agrees to certain terms—such as stopping the use of your work and paying damages—in exchange for you dropping the lawsuit.

Advantages of Settling:

- **Cost-Effective**: Settlements are generally less expensive than a full trial, as they avoid lengthy court proceedings and additional legal fees.

- **Faster Resolution**: Litigation can take months or even years, whereas settlements can be reached in a matter of weeks or months, providing a quicker end to the dispute.

- **More Control Over the Outcome**: In a settlement, both parties can negotiate the terms, whereas a trial outcome is left to the judge or jury's discretion.

What to Include in a Settlement Agreement:

- **Cease Use**: The infringer agrees to immediately stop using your work and remove any infringing materials.

- **Monetary Compensation**: The infringer agrees to pay damages, which can include both actual damages (your financial losses) and a settlement amount to compensate for the unauthorized use.

- **Licensing Agreement** (Optional): In some cases, rather than prohibiting use entirely, you might agree to license your work to the infringer for a fee, allowing them to continue using it under legal terms.

- **Confidentiality Clause**: Some settlements include a clause that prevents either party from publicly discussing the terms of the agreement, protecting your reputation and theirs.

Example of a Settlement: In 2011, Coldplay and guitarist Joe Satriani reached a confidential settlement after Satriani accused the band of copying a melody from one of his songs for their hit single *Viva La Vida*. Rather than pursuing the matter in court, the two parties agreed to settle, avoiding a potentially damaging public trial.

5. The Pros and Cons of Litigation vs. Settlement

Litigation Pros:

- **Higher Damages**: A successful lawsuit may result in higher damages than what could be negotiated in a settlement, especially if the infringement was willful.

- **Court Order**: An injunction from the court can provide a powerful and enforceable legal order to stop the infringer from continuing their activities.

Litigation Cons:

- **Expensive**: Lawsuits can be costly, especially if they go to trial. Legal fees, court costs, and expert witness expenses can add up quickly.

- **Time-Consuming**: Litigation can take months or even years to resolve, creating uncertainty and prolonged stress for both parties.

- **Unpredictable Outcome**: There's no guarantee of success in court, and the outcome is ultimately in the hands of the judge or jury.

Settlement Pros:

- **Faster and Cheaper**: Settling is often quicker and less expensive than going to trial, saving both time and money.

- **Control Over Terms**: Settlements allow you to negotiate the terms and reach a mutually agreeable resolution.

Settlement Cons:

- **Lower Compensation**: You may not receive as much compensation in a settlement as you could win in court, especially if the infringer is unwilling to pay a large sum.

Conclusion: Choosing the Right Path for Legal Remedies

When faced with copyright infringement, you have several legal remedies available. Whether you choose to pursue litigation or negotiate a settlement depends on the severity of the infringement, the potential for damages, and your willingness to invest time and money in a legal battle. By understanding the pros and cons of each approach and seeking the right legal guidance, you can protect your intellectual property and recover any losses caused by unauthorized use.

In the next section, we'll discuss defending against infringement claims, outlining what to do if you're accused of copyright infringement and how to build a defense or reach a resolution.

Defending Against Infringement Claims: What to Do When Accused

Receiving a copyright infringement claim can be unsettling, especially if you didn't intend to violate anyone's intellectual property rights. However, it's important to remain calm, assess the situation carefully, and respond appropriately. In this section, we'll explore how to handle accusations of copyright infringement, whether the claims are valid or not, and the steps you can take to resolve the situation, including building a defense or negotiating a settlement.

1. Understand the Nature of the Claim

The first step when accused of copyright infringement is to fully understand the nature of the claim. Review the details provided in the **cease and desist letter** or **complaint** to determine what specific work is involved and how the claimant believes you've infringed on their rights.

Key questions to ask:

- **What is the work in question?** Identify the copyrighted material you're being accused of infringing on.

- **How have you used the work?** Determine whether you have used the material in a way that might be considered infringement (e.g., reproducing, distributing, or creating a derivative work).

- **Did you have permission or a license?** If you have a license or permission from the copyright holder, it may be a misunderstanding or a contractual issue rather than an infringement.

- **Is it a fair use scenario?** Consider whether your use falls under the **fair use** doctrine, particularly if your use is for purposes like criticism, commentary, education, or parody.

Example:
You run a blog and use an image found on the internet without realizing it's copyrighted. The photographer sends you a cease and desist letter demanding that you stop using the image and pay damages. In this case, you must determine if you have a legitimate defense (such as fair use) or if you'll need to comply with their demands.

2. Review Your Options: Comply, Defend, or Settle

Once you've understood the claim, you have three main options for how to proceed:

1. Comply with the Demands. If the claim appears to be legitimate, and you realize you've used copyrighted material without permission, the simplest solution is to comply with the demands. This typically involves removing the infringing content, halting its use, and possibly compensating the copyright holder for any losses.

Steps to Take:

- **Remove the infringing material**: Take down any content that infringes on the copyright holder's rights (e.g., removing an image from your website).

- **Negotiate a license or settlement**: In some cases, the copyright holder may be willing to grant you a license to continue using the material for a fee, avoiding legal action.

- **Pay compensation** (if necessary): If the copyright holder has suffered financial losses due to your use, they may demand damages, which you can negotiate.

2. Defend Yourself. If you believe the claim is unfounded or that your use qualifies as fair use, you may choose to defend yourself. This could involve responding to the cease and desist letter, explaining why your use is lawful, or preparing a defense in court if the matter escalates.

Defenses to Consider:

- **Fair Use**: If your use is transformative (e.g., for commentary, parody, or education), you may have a strong fair use defense.

- **Permission or License**: If you had permission from the copyright holder or a valid license, you can provide proof to counter the infringement claim.

- **Public Domain**: If the work is in the public domain, meaning it's no longer under copyright protection, your use is likely lawful.

- **Innocent Infringement**: While not a complete defense, claiming that the infringement was unintentional can sometimes reduce the amount of damages, especially if you take immediate corrective action.

Example:
A YouTuber uses a brief clip from a movie in a video review. The movie studio sends a cease and desist letter claiming infringement. The YouTuber believes the

use qualifies as fair use because the clip is short and used for commentary. They prepare a defense explaining why the use is transformative and non-commercial.

3. Negotiate a Settlement. If the claim is valid but you want to avoid a lengthy legal battle, negotiating a settlement may be the best course of action. In a settlement, you and the copyright holder agree on terms to resolve the dispute without going to court. This could involve removing the content, paying damages, or agreeing to a licensing arrangement.

Benefits of Settling:

- **Avoids costly litigation**: Settling is usually quicker and less expensive than going to court.

- **Limits reputational damage**: Settling the matter privately can prevent public exposure and preserve your reputation.

- **Control over the outcome**: In a settlement, both parties have more control over the terms, rather than leaving the decision to a judge.

Example:
An artist accidentally incorporates a copyrighted photograph into their artwork. The photographer demands compensation. The artist negotiates a settlement where they agree to pay a fee and credit the photographer in future uses of the work, avoiding further legal action.

3. Responding to a Cease and Desist Letter

If the copyright holder sends you a cease and desist letter, it's important to respond thoughtfully. You should avoid ignoring the letter, as doing so can escalate the situation to a lawsuit. Here's how to respond effectively:

Step 1: Acknowledge the Letter. Promptly acknowledge receipt of the cease and desist letter. You can respond professionally without admitting guilt, simply stating that you are reviewing the matter.

Example:
"Dear [Copyright Holder], I acknowledge receipt of your cease and desist letter dated [Date]. I am currently reviewing the claims and will respond in more detail shortly."

Step 2: Investigate the Claim. Take time to investigate the claim and gather any evidence that supports your position (e.g., fair use arguments, licensing agreements, or proof that the work is in the public domain).

Step 3: Decide Your Course of Action. Once you've investigated, decide whether to comply, negotiate, or defend yourself, and craft a formal response to the copyright holder based on your decision.

- If complying, clearly state that you will cease using the material and take any corrective actions.

- If defending, outline why you believe your use is lawful (e.g., under fair use) and provide supporting evidence.

- If negotiating, propose terms for a settlement, such as licensing fees or removing the content in exchange for avoiding litigation.

4. Building a Defense: What You Need

If you decide to defend yourself against a copyright infringement claim, you'll need to build a strong defense based on evidence and legal arguments. Here's what you'll need to gather:

- **Proof of Permission or Licensing**: If you have written permission or a license to use the copyrighted material, provide these documents as evidence.

- **Fair Use Analysis**: If you believe your use falls under fair use, conduct a thorough analysis of the four factors of fair use and how they apply to your case.

- **Proof of Public Domain**: If the work is in the public domain, provide evidence showing that the copyright has expired or that the work was never copyrighted.

- **Innocent Infringement Argument**: If the infringement was accidental, such as using an image mistakenly thought to be free, you can argue for a reduction in damages based on your innocent intent, particularly if you took immediate action to correct the issue.

5. When to Seek Legal Help

If you're unsure about how to respond or if the case is complex, it's advisable to seek legal counsel from a copyright attorney. An attorney can help you evaluate the strength of the claim, advise you on the best course of action, and represent you in negotiations or court if necessary.

Consider seeking legal help if:

- You're unsure whether your use qualifies as fair use.

- The copyright holder is demanding substantial damages.

- The case involves significant financial or reputational risk.

- The infringement involves large-scale distribution, such as through a website or business.

Conclusion: Defending Yourself with Confidence

Facing a copyright infringement claim can be daunting, but by taking the time to understand the nature of the claim and your options, you can handle the situation with confidence. Whether you choose to comply, negotiate, or defend yourself, the key is to act thoughtfully and strategically. By gathering evidence, building a solid defense, and seeking legal help when necessary, you can resolve the matter and protect your rights.

In the next chapter, we'll explore the digital landscape of copyright law, including the challenges and opportunities that come with protecting and managing intellectual property in an increasingly online world.

Quick Tips and Recap

- **Understand the claim**: When accused of copyright infringement, review the claim carefully to determine the specific work involved and how it was allegedly misused.

- **Evaluate your options**: You can choose to comply, defend, or negotiate a settlement depending on the validity of the claim and your use of the material.

- **Comply if necessary**: If the claim is valid, remove the infringing content, negotiate a settlement, or seek a licensing agreement to resolve the issue.

- **Consider fair use**: If your use of the material qualifies as fair use (e.g., for commentary, criticism, or education), you may have a strong defense.

- **Defend your rights**: If you believe the claim is unfounded or if you have permission, build a defense based on fair use, licenses, or public domain arguments.

- **Respond to cease and desist letters professionally**: Always acknowledge and respond to cease and desist letters promptly, outlining your position or agreeing to comply.

- **Consider settling**: Settlements can save time and legal costs, especially if both parties can agree on compensation or licensing terms without litigation.

- **Seek legal help if needed**: When facing a complicated claim or potential litigation, consult with a copyright attorney to ensure your rights are protected.

By following these steps, you can effectively handle a copyright infringement claim, whether you're complying, negotiating, or defending yourself.

When Disputes Arise: Resolution and Litigation

"Effective resolution of disputes doesn't always mean winning in the courtroom; sometimes it means knowing when to compromise and when to stand firm. That's the art of litigation."
— RUTH BADER GINSBURG, U.S. SUPREME COURT JUSTICE

Chapter Nine, "When Disputes Arise: Resolution and Litigation," is your all-access pass to the drama-filled arena of copyright battles, where tensions are high and the stakes even higher. It's the legal equivalent of a reality TV showdown—only the players are lawyers, and the game is played in courtrooms instead of on sound stages.

Here, we'll guide you through the labyrinth of legal proceedings, from the first murmurings of a dispute to the gavel's final bang in court. Think of this chapter as a backstage tour, where we reveal how to negotiate settlements that could put a Hollywood dealmaker to shame, and where we unveil the strategies that turn courtroom ordeals into masterclasses in rhetoric and reasoning.

This isn't just about surviving the legal storm; it's about navigating it with the finesse of a seasoned captain. We'll decode the legal jargon, simplify the procedural play-by-plays, and even provide a few pro tips on when to fight, when to settle, and when to walk away. Buckle up, because whether you're aiming for a swift settlement or bracing for a court battle, this chapter will ensure you're armed and ready for whatever comes your way.

Early Stages of Disputes: Negotiation and Mediation

When a copyright dispute first arises, the initial reaction might be to prepare for a courtroom showdown, but litigation should often be the last resort. The early stages of a dispute provide a valuable opportunity for negotiation and mediation, two powerful tools that can help resolve issues quickly, cost-effectively, and without the stress of a court battle. In this section, we'll explore how to navigate the initial stages of a copyright dispute, using negotiation and mediation to find a resolution before things escalate into litigation.

1. The Importance of Early Resolution

Resolving a copyright dispute early can save time, money, and resources for both parties. Court cases can drag on for months, even years, and the costs associated with legal representation, court fees, and lost productivity can be significant. By addressing the dispute early on, you increase your chances of reaching a favorable resolution while maintaining control over the outcome.

Benefits of Early Resolution:

- **Cost savings**: Avoiding litigation can significantly reduce legal fees and court costs.

- **Time efficiency**: Resolving the issue quickly allows you to focus on your business or creative work, rather than getting bogged down in a lengthy legal process.

- **Relationship preservation**: Early negotiations can preserve professional relationships, which might be damaged by a more adversarial court battle.

- **Control over the outcome**: In negotiation and mediation, you have more control over the terms of the settlement, rather than leaving the decision to a judge.

2. Negotiation: Finding Common Ground

Negotiation is often the first step in resolving a copyright dispute. This informal process involves direct communication between the parties (or their lawyers) to work out a solution that satisfies both sides. The goal of negotiation is to come to a mutually agreeable resolution that avoids the need for formal litigation.

Key Strategies for Effective Negotiation:

- **Understand your position**: Before entering into negotiations, assess the strength of your case. Is there clear evidence of copyright infringement, or could the accused party claim fair use? Understanding your legal standing will help you negotiate more effectively.

- **Be clear about your goals**: Decide in advance what you hope to achieve through negotiation. Do you want the other party to stop using your work? Are you seeking financial compensation, or would a licensing agreement resolve the issue? Knowing your objectives will guide the negotiation process.

- **Remain professional and focused**: Negotiation should be conducted professionally, without letting emotions get in the way. Keep discussions focused on the facts of the case and potential solutions.

- **Be open to compromise**: In many cases, both parties will need to make concessions to reach an agreement. Be willing to compromise on certain points in exchange for a faster and less expensive resolution.

Example:

A photographer discovers that a magazine has used one of her photos without permission in a print issue. Instead of filing a lawsuit immediately, she sends a letter to the magazine, requesting compensation for the unauthorized use of her image. The magazine agrees to pay a licensing fee and credits her in future issues. This negotiation avoids a lengthy legal battle and results in a favorable outcome for both sides.

3. Mediation: A Neutral Party to Facilitate Resolution

If direct negotiations stall or the parties cannot reach an agreement, mediation offers a structured, yet non-adversarial, alternative. In mediation, a neutral third party (the mediator) helps both sides communicate, identify areas of agreement, and explore potential solutions. While the mediator does not have the authority to impose a decision, they can guide the discussion and help facilitate a compromise.

Benefits of Mediation:

- **Confidentiality**: Mediation is a private process, meaning the details of the dispute and the resolution remain confidential, unlike a court case, which becomes part of the public record.

- **Cost-effectiveness**: Mediation is generally less expensive than litigation, as it avoids the high costs of court proceedings and legal fees.

- **Faster resolution**: Mediation can often resolve disputes more quickly than litigation, allowing both parties to move on without prolonged disruption.

- **Voluntary and flexible**: Mediation allows both parties to retain control over the outcome, as any agreement is reached voluntarily and can be tailored to meet their specific needs.

The Mediation Process:

1. **Selection of a mediator**: Both parties agree on a neutral mediator, often a legal professional with experience in copyright law or dispute resolution.

2. **Opening statements**: Each party presents their position, outlining the facts of the case, their concerns, and what they hope to achieve.

3. **Facilitated discussion**: The mediator helps guide the conversation, encouraging open communication and exploring potential solutions. The

mediator may meet with both parties together or separately (called caucusing) to discuss options privately.

4. **Proposing solutions**: The mediator helps the parties brainstorm and propose solutions, often suggesting creative compromises that address both sides' concerns.

5. **Reaching an agreement**: If both parties agree on a resolution, the mediator will help them draft a formal settlement agreement. This agreement is legally binding and can be enforced by the courts if necessary.

Example:

A freelance writer discovers that one of his articles has been reprinted without permission on a popular website. The website owner claims that the use falls under fair use, while the writer disagrees. After negotiations fail, both parties agree to enter mediation. With the mediator's help, they reach an agreement where the website pays a fee for past use and licenses the article for future use, allowing the writer to be compensated without the need for litigation.

4. When Negotiation and Mediation Fail

While negotiation and mediation can resolve many disputes, there are situations where these methods do not lead to a satisfactory outcome. If the other party refuses to cooperate, denies liability, or is unwilling to offer fair compensation, it may be necessary to escalate the matter to litigation.

However, entering into formal litigation should be considered only after all attempts at negotiation and mediation have been exhausted. Litigation is costly, time-consuming, and unpredictable. The decision to proceed to court should be based on a thorough evaluation of the risks, costs, and potential outcomes.

5. Best Practices for Successful Dispute Resolution

To increase your chances of resolving a copyright dispute early, here are some best practices to keep in mind:

*   **Document everything**: Keep records of all communications with the infringing party, including emails, phone calls, and any offers made

during negotiation or mediation. This documentation can be critical if the dispute escalates to litigation.

- **Stay flexible**: Be open to creative solutions that might not involve money. For example, a licensing agreement or partnership could turn a negative situation into a business opportunity.

- **Maintain professionalism**: Even if the other party is uncooperative, remain calm and professional throughout the process. Emotional reactions can harm your credibility and make it harder to reach an agreement.

- **Know when to walk away**: If the dispute is relatively minor and not worth the time, energy, or financial investment, it may be best to walk away and focus on more important matters.

Conclusion: Early Resolution as a Strategic Advantage

The early stages of a copyright dispute are a critical opportunity to resolve issues without resorting to litigation. By approaching the dispute with a clear strategy, engaging in good-faith negotiations, or enlisting the help of a mediator, you can often achieve a faster, less expensive, and more satisfactory outcome. When negotiation and mediation are successful, you avoid the risks and costs of a courtroom battle while still protecting your intellectual property.

In the next section, we'll explore what happens when disputes do escalate to litigation, providing a detailed overview of the litigation process and how to navigate a copyright lawsuit.

Litigation Basics: What to Expect in a Copyright Lawsuit

When negotiation and mediation fail to resolve a copyright dispute, the next step is often litigation. Taking a case to court can feel daunting, but understanding the basic steps of a copyright lawsuit can help you navigate the process more confidently. This section will break down the phases of a copyright lawsuit, from filing the initial complaint to the trial itself, and provide insights into what to expect at each stage.

1. The Decision to File a Lawsuit

Filing a lawsuit should be a last resort, only pursued after other resolution methods (like negotiation or mediation) have been exhausted. Before proceeding, consider the costs, time commitment, and potential risks. Litigation can be expensive and time-consuming, but if your copyright has been seriously violated, and you stand to suffer significant financial or reputational damage, legal action may be the best course.

2. Filing the Complaint: Starting the Lawsuit

A copyright lawsuit begins with the filing of a complaint in federal court. The complaint is a legal document that outlines your allegations, including:

- **Who you are**: Your identity as the plaintiff and your ownership of the copyrighted work in question.

- **The infringer**: The identity of the defendant(s) who allegedly infringed your copyright.

- **The facts**: A detailed account of how your copyright was infringed, including specifics such as where, when, and how the infringement occurred.

- **Legal basis**: A statement of the laws being violated (in this case, the U.S. Copyright Act).

- **Relief sought**: A request for remedies, which could include monetary damages, an injunction to stop the infringer from using your work, or statutory damages.

After filing the complaint, the defendant is served with a copy and must respond, typically within 20 to 30 days. The defendant's response, called an answer, will either deny or admit the allegations and may include defenses like fair use or lack of copyright ownership.

3. The Discovery Phase: Gathering Evidence

Once the lawsuit has been filed and the defendant has answered, both parties enter the discovery phase. This is the pre-trial process where each side gathers evidence to support their case. Discovery involves:

- **Interrogatories**: Written questions that each party sends to the other, which must be answered under oath. These questions help clarify the facts of the case and the positions of each party.

- **Document Requests**: Requests for documents or records relevant to the case. For example, you might request emails, sales records, or contracts that show how the defendant used your work.

- **Depositions**: Oral testimony given under oath. Both parties may be deposed (interviewed) by the opposing counsel to gather more information and assess the strength of the other side's arguments.

- **Expert Testimony**: In complex cases, both parties may bring in experts (such as economists or media experts) to offer opinions on issues like damages or the originality of the work in question.

The discovery process can be lengthy and labor-intensive, but it's critical for building a strong case. This is where the bulk of the evidence will be collected and where key facts will be established.

4. Pre-Trial Motions: Setting the Stage for Court

Before the case goes to trial, either party may file pre-trial motions to resolve certain issues or narrow the scope of the dispute. Common pre-trial motions include:

- **Motion to Dismiss**: The defendant may ask the court to dismiss the case if they believe the complaint is legally insufficient. For example, they might argue that the plaintiff doesn't actually own the copyright or that the use in question is protected by fair use.

- **Summary Judgment**: Either party may file a motion for summary judgment, arguing that the facts of the case are so clear that the judge can decide without a trial. For instance, if both parties agree on the facts, but disagree on the legal interpretation, the court may resolve the matter without a jury.

Pre-trial motions can sometimes result in an early resolution, either by dismissing the case or narrowing down the issues to be decided at trial.

5. Going to Trial: Presenting Your Case in Court

If the case is not resolved through pre-trial motions or a settlement, it proceeds to trial. At trial, both parties present their evidence and arguments, and the case is decided by a judge or jury. Here's what to expect at trial:

- **Opening Statements**: Both sides give opening statements, outlining their case and what they intend to prove.

- **Presentation of Evidence**: The plaintiff (the person bringing the lawsuit) presents their case first, introducing evidence such as documents, expert testimony, and witness statements. The defendant then has the opportunity to present their defense.

- **Cross-Examination**: Both sides have the opportunity to cross-examine witnesses and challenge the evidence presented by the other party.

- **Closing Arguments**: After all the evidence has been presented, both sides give closing arguments, summarizing their case and urging the judge or jury to rule in their favor.

- **Verdict**: The judge or jury delivers a verdict based on the evidence. If the plaintiff wins, the court may award damages and issue an injunction to stop the infringement.

6. Remedies in a Copyright Lawsuit

If you win the lawsuit, the court will award remedies to compensate for the infringement. Remedies can include:

- **Injunctive Relief**: The court may issue an injunction ordering the infringer to stop using your copyrighted work.

- **Actual Damages**: You may be awarded actual damages, which compensate you for the financial harm caused by the infringement. This could include lost sales, licensing fees, or profits the infringer made from using your work.

- **Statutory Damages**: If your work was registered with the U.S. Copyright Office before the infringement, you may choose to receive statutory damages, which are set amounts that can range from $750 to

$30,000 per infringement. In cases of willful infringement, statutory damages can increase to as much as $150,000.

- **Attorney's Fees**: In some cases, the court may order the defendant to pay your attorney's fees, especially if the infringement was deliberate.

7. The Appeals Process

If either party is unhappy with the outcome of the trial, they can appeal the decision to a higher court. An appeal doesn't involve re-trying the case but focuses on whether the trial court made any legal errors. The appellate court will review the trial record and issue a decision, which could affirm, reverse, or modify the original judgment.

Appeals can prolong the legal process, so it's important to weigh the costs and benefits before deciding whether to pursue one.

8. Weighing the Costs of Litigation

Litigation is expensive and time-consuming, so it's important to evaluate whether it's worth pursuing. Costs to consider include:

- **Attorney's Fees**: Lawyers charge by the hour, and complex cases can require hundreds of hours of work.

- **Court Costs**: Filing fees, deposition costs, and other court expenses can add up quickly.

- **Time**: Litigation can take months or even years, and the time spent in court may distract from your creative or business activities.

- **Emotional Toll**: Lawsuits can be stressful and emotionally draining, especially when they involve high stakes.

9. Alternative Paths: Settling During Litigation

Even after a lawsuit has been filed, it's still possible to **settle** the dispute before the case goes to trial. In fact, many copyright cases are settled during the discovery phase or after pre-trial motions. Settlement can offer a quicker, less costly resolution and allow both parties to control the outcome.

- **Settlement Negotiations**: You can negotiate a settlement at any point during the litigation process. Settlements typically involve the defendant agreeing to stop the infringement and paying compensation, either in the form of damages or licensing fees.

- **Mediation**: Some courts require parties to attempt mediation before going to trial. Mediation is a chance for both sides to work with a neutral third party to negotiate a resolution.

Conclusion: Navigating the Litigation Process with Confidence

Litigation is a complex and often lengthy process, but it's sometimes the only way to fully protect your copyright and recover damages for infringement. Understanding the steps involved—from filing a complaint to presenting your case at trial—can help you navigate the legal system with greater confidence. By weighing the costs, gathering strong evidence, and working with an experienced attorney, you'll be prepared to defend your intellectual property rights in court if necessary.

In the next section, we'll explore settlement strategies in more depth, providing insights into how to negotiate favorable terms and avoid the risks of a full-blown trial.

Settlements: Reaching a Resolution
Outside of Court

When faced with a copyright dispute, pursuing a settlement is often a more cost-effective, quicker, and less stressful alternative to a full-blown trial. Settlements allow both parties to resolve the issue on mutually agreed terms, avoiding the unpredictability and costs associated with litigation. In this section, we'll explore how settlements work, when they make sense, and strategies for negotiating a favorable resolution outside of court.

1. Why Consider a Settlement?

Litigation can be expensive, time-consuming, and unpredictable. Even if you have a strong case, taking a dispute all the way through trial doesn't guarantee the outcome you want. Settling can provide several advantages:

- **Cost Savings**: Settlements generally save both parties significant legal fees. Lawsuits can involve months of legal work, with lawyers charging by the hour. Settling early reduces the costs associated with discovery, depositions, expert witnesses, and court fees.

- **Faster Resolution**: A lawsuit can take months or even years to conclude, while a settlement can be reached in a matter of weeks or months. This quicker resolution allows both parties to move forward without the drawn-out stress of a court case.

- **Certainty and Control**: A settlement gives both parties more control over the outcome. In a trial, a judge or jury decides the case, and their ruling may not align with either party's expectations. In a settlement, the parties can negotiate terms that meet their specific needs and avoid the uncertainty of a court decision.

- **Confidentiality**: Settlements can be kept private, whereas trial outcomes become part of the public record. For those concerned about reputation or business relationships, keeping the details of the dispute out of the public eye can be beneficial.

Example:

An independent artist discovers that their illustration has been used in a major ad campaign without permission. Rather than take the company to court, where the outcome is uncertain and the costs are high, the artist negotiates a settlement. The company agrees to pay damages and license the work for future use. The artist avoids a lengthy legal battle and is compensated for the infringement.

2. When to Settle: Factors to Consider

Settling isn't always the right decision, but there are several factors that might lead you to consider it as a viable option:

- **Strength of Your Case**: If your case is strong but the costs of litigation outweigh the potential benefits, settling might be a practical solution. For example, if the financial gain from a court ruling is likely to be small, settling early can save you time and money.

- **The Other Party's Position**: If the other party has a valid defense—such as fair use—or if the infringement was unintentional, settling may be preferable to a long, drawn-out legal process. In such cases, the outcome in court may be less favorable, so a negotiated agreement may serve your interests better.

- **Financial Considerations**: If the infringer lacks the resources to pay significant damages, taking them to court may result in a hollow victory, where you win but receive little compensation. In these cases, negotiating a settlement that provides some compensation, even if less than you might win in court, could be a better outcome.

- **Preserving Relationships**: If you have an ongoing relationship with the other party (for example, if the infringer is a business partner, client, or collaborator), settling amicably can preserve that relationship, while a court battle might damage it beyond repair.

Example:

A writer discovers that their short story has been used in an anthology without permission. While they could pursue a lawsuit, they realize that the publisher is a small independent press with limited resources. Instead of seeking damages that the press might struggle to pay, the writer negotiates a licensing fee and ensures proper credit is given in future editions. This settlement resolves the issue quickly and preserves the writer's relationship with the publisher.

3. Key Elements of a Settlement Agreement

A settlement agreement is a legally binding contract between the parties that outlines the terms of the resolution. This agreement will typically include the following elements:

- **Cessation of Infringement**: The infringer agrees to stop using the copyrighted material immediately and to refrain from any further unauthorized use.

- **Monetary Compensation**: The infringer may agree to pay damages, which could include compensation for past use of the work and, in some cases, future licensing fees.

- **Licensing Agreement**: In some cases, the parties may agree to a licensing arrangement, allowing the infringer to continue using the work in exchange for payment. This can be a win-win solution, as it avoids further infringement while providing the copyright holder with ongoing compensation.

- **Confidentiality Clause**: Many settlement agreements include a confidentiality clause, which prevents either party from discussing the details of the settlement publicly. This can be important for protecting both parties' reputations.

- **Release of Claims**: In exchange for the settlement, the copyright holder agrees to drop the lawsuit or to refrain from filing any future claims related to the same infringement. This provides the infringer with legal certainty and protection against future litigation.

Example:

A musician finds that one of their songs was sampled without permission in a popular online video. Rather than go to court, the musician negotiates a settlement where the video creator agrees to pay a fee for the past use of the song and enters into a licensing agreement for future use in additional videos. The settlement includes a confidentiality clause and a release of claims, ensuring that the issue is resolved without further legal action.

4. Strategies for Successful Settlement Negotiations

To reach a successful settlement, it's important to approach negotiations with a clear strategy and an open mind. Here are some key strategies to keep in mind:

- **Know Your Bottom Line**: Before entering settlement negotiations, know what you're willing to accept. This could be a specific amount of compensation, the removal of infringing content, or a licensing deal. Having a clear bottom line will help guide your negotiations.

- **Be Open to Compromise**: Settlements often require both parties to make concessions. Be prepared to compromise on some aspects of your demands to reach a mutually agreeable solution. For example, you might agree to accept a lower payment in exchange for a licensing deal that allows future use of your work.

- **Keep Emotions in Check**: Copyright disputes can be personal, especially when your creative work is involved. However, it's important to approach settlement discussions with a clear, rational mindset. Focus on the facts of the case and the potential benefits of settling, rather than getting caught up in emotional responses.

- **Leverage Mediation**: If direct negotiations stall, consider bringing in a neutral third party to mediate the settlement. A mediator can help facilitate productive discussions and suggest creative solutions that might not have been considered.

- **Put Everything in Writing**: Once a settlement has been reached, make sure the agreement is put in writing and signed by both parties. A formal written settlement is legally binding and provides protection for both parties.

Example:

A graphic designer discovers that their artwork has been used in an advertising campaign without permission. During settlement negotiations, the designer is willing to accept a lower compensation fee in exchange for a licensing deal that allows the ad agency to continue using the work, with proper credit and ongoing royalty payments. The agreement is formalized in a written settlement that both parties sign.

5. Common Pitfalls to Avoid in Settlement Negotiations

While settlements offer many advantages, there are common pitfalls that can derail the process:

- **Failing to Research**: Before entering negotiations, research the other party's financial situation and the potential value of your claim. This will help you determine whether the settlement offer is fair and whether the other party can realistically pay the amount you're seeking.

- **Unrealistic Expectations**: Don't expect to receive the same amount in a settlement as you might win in court. Settlements typically involve compromise, so be prepared to accept a lower amount in exchange for a quicker, less risky resolution.

- **Overly Aggressive Tactics**: Pushing too hard for an unrealistic settlement or making aggressive demands can backfire, causing the other party to walk away from negotiations. Aim for a collaborative, problem-solving approach rather than an adversarial one.

- **Neglecting to Consult a Lawyer**: Even if you're pursuing a settlement, it's important to have a lawyer review the terms of the agreement. This ensures that your interests are protected and that the settlement is enforceable.

Conclusion: Achieving a Favorable Settlement

Settlements provide an effective way to resolve copyright disputes without the risks and expenses of a courtroom battle. By understanding the key elements of a settlement agreement, approaching negotiations strategically, and being open to compromise, you can often achieve a favorable outcome that protects your intellectual property and compensates you for any harm caused by infringement.

In the next section, we'll explore the final stage of the dispute resolution process: going to trial. We'll break down what happens in a copyright trial and offer tips for presenting a strong case in court.

Going to Trial: Courtroom Strategies and Outcomes

When settlement negotiations fail or the parties cannot reach an agreement, a copyright dispute may proceed to trial. While litigation is often a last resort due to its complexity and cost, it's sometimes the only way to fully protect your intellectual property. In this section, we'll walk through the trial process, explore courtroom strategies for presenting a strong case, and discuss potential outcomes, including damages and other remedies.

1. Preparing for Trial: Building Your Case

Going to trial is a major undertaking, and success hinges on preparation. A well-prepared case will be built on strong evidence, legal arguments, and careful attention to detail. Before stepping into the courtroom, here are some key steps you'll need to take:

- **Gather Evidence**: Collect all relevant documents, communications, and other evidence to support your claim. This might include copyright registrations, records of the infringement, emails, contracts, and financial statements that show any economic harm caused by the infringement.

- **Work with Expert Witnesses**: Expert testimony can play a critical role in copyright cases. For instance, an expert witness might testify about the value of your work, the originality of your creation, or the financial impact of the infringement.

- **Develop a Clear Legal Argument**: Work with your attorney to craft a clear and compelling legal argument. This will involve interpreting the relevant copyright laws and applying them to the specific facts of your case. You'll need to show that the defendant violated your exclusive rights as a copyright holder and explain the harm that the infringement caused.

- **Prepare for Cross-Examination**: Anticipate the defendant's arguments and prepare to defend your position under cross-examination. This includes reviewing your evidence and being ready to explain your position clearly and confidently in court.

2. The Trial Process: What to Expect

A copyright trial is a formal, structured process, with both parties presenting evidence and arguments before a judge or jury. Here's an overview of what to expect at trial:

- **Opening Statements**: Both parties begin by presenting their opening statements. These are summaries of each side's case, explaining what they intend to prove. The plaintiff (the copyright holder) goes first, followed by the defendant (the alleged infringer).

- **Plaintiff's Case**: As the copyright holder, you'll present your evidence first. This may include documents, emails, copyright registrations, and financial records that show the extent of the infringement. You'll also call witnesses to testify, such as yourself, your attorney, or expert witnesses who can provide technical or financial insights.

- **Cross-Examination**: After you present your case, the defendant's attorney will have the opportunity to cross-examine your witnesses. They may try to discredit your evidence, challenge your copyright claim, or argue that their use of your work was lawful under fair use or another legal defense.

- **Defendant's Case**: After your case is presented, the defendant will present their evidence and call their own witnesses. They may argue that their use of the copyrighted material was legally permissible or that the copyright was not valid. They may also attempt to show that the infringement caused little or no harm to your business.

- **Closing Arguments**: Once all evidence has been presented, both sides deliver their closing arguments. This is the final opportunity for each party to persuade the judge or jury by summarizing the key points of the case and explaining why they deserve a favorable ruling.

- **Verdict**: After closing arguments, the judge or jury will deliberate and issue a verdict. In a jury trial, the jury will decide whether the defendant infringed your copyright and, if so, what damages should be awarded. In a bench trial (where there is no jury), the judge makes these determinations.

3. Courtroom Strategies: Presenting a Strong Case

To increase your chances of success in a copyright trial, it's important to focus on key courtroom strategies. Here are some tips for presenting a compelling case:

- **Tell a Clear and Consistent Story**: Jurors (or judges) need to understand how the infringement occurred, why it was unlawful, and the harm it caused you. Present your evidence in a logical, easy-to-follow sequence that ties everything together.

- **Focus on the Law**: Copyright law is complex, and not all jurors or even judges are experts. Your attorney should clearly explain the relevant copyright laws, including the rights you hold as a copyright owner, how those rights were violated, and why the defendant's defenses (such as fair use) don't apply.

- **Use Expert Testimony Wisely**: Expert witnesses can make or break your case. A financial expert might calculate the damages you've suffered due to the infringement, while an industry expert could testify to the originality or market value of your work. Make sure your expert testimony is clear and well-supported by facts.

- **Anticipate the Defendant's Arguments**: Expect the defendant to challenge your case by arguing that their use of the work was lawful (such as under fair use), that they had permission, or that your copyright isn't valid. Prepare to address these arguments head-on during cross-examination and in your closing arguments.

4. Potential Outcomes: What You Could Win or Lose

The outcome of a copyright trial can vary widely depending on the strength of the evidence, the nature of the infringement, and the judge or jury's interpretation of the law. Here are some potential outcomes:

- **Monetary Damages**: If you win, the court may award you damages to compensate for your losses. These damages can include:

    o **Actual Damages**: The court may award you compensation for the financial harm you've suffered due to the infringement. This could include lost sales, licensing fees, or other economic losses.

    o **Statutory Damages**: If your copyright was registered before the infringement occurred, you may be entitled to statutory damages. These damages can range from $750 to $30,000 per work, or up to $150,000 per work in cases of willful infringement.

    o **Defendant's Profits**: In some cases, the court may require the defendant to pay you any profits they earned from using your copyrighted material.

- **Injunctions**: The court may issue an injunction to stop the defendant from using your work. This can prevent further infringement and protect your future rights as a copyright holder.

- **Attorney's Fees**: In some cases, the court may order the defendant to pay your legal fees, especially if the infringement was deliberate or willful.

Example:

A photographer wins a lawsuit against a company that used her images in a national advertising campaign without permission. The court awards her statutory damages, orders the company to stop using the photos immediately, and requires the company to pay her attorney's fees. The photographer is compensated for the unauthorized use of her work and can enforce the court's order to prevent further infringement.

5. Losing at Trial: What Happens Next?

If you lose the case, you may be ordered to pay the defendant's legal fees or face other financial penalties. However, losing at trial doesn't always mean the end of the road. You have the right to appeal the decision if you believe that legal errors were made during the trial. Appeals can result in a new trial, a reversal of the decision, or a reduction in the damages awarded.

6. Weighing the Costs and Risks of Trial

Going to trial is a major financial and emotional investment. Before pursuing litigation, carefully weigh the costs and potential outcomes. Trials are unpredictable, and even with a strong case, there's no guarantee of success. Consider whether the potential damages are worth the expense of litigation, and always consult with your attorney to evaluate the risks and rewards.

Conclusion: Mastering the Courtroom

A copyright trial can be a long, complex, and challenging process, but with proper preparation and a strong legal strategy, you can protect your creative rights and secure the compensation you deserve. By presenting clear evidence, anticipating the defendant's arguments, and working closely with legal experts, you can navigate the courtroom with confidence and achieve a successful outcome.

In the next chapter, we'll explore appeals and enforcement, providing guidance on what to do if you win or lose at trial, and how to ensure that court-ordered damages or injunctions are enforced effectively.

Quick Tips and Recap

- **Prepare thoroughly**: Gather all relevant evidence, including copyright registrations, documents, and expert testimony, to build a strong case.

- **Understand the legal arguments**: Work with your attorney to develop a clear legal strategy that outlines how the defendant infringed on your copyright and why their defenses (like fair use) don't apply.

- **Use expert witnesses wisely**: Expert testimony on damages, market value, or originality can strengthen your case significantly.

- **Anticipate the defendant's arguments**: Be ready to address defenses like fair use or claims that the work isn't protected by copyright.

- **Maintain clarity in your presentation**: Present your evidence in a logical, easy-to-follow manner that helps the judge or jury understand how the infringement occurred and the harm it caused.

- **Weigh the costs**: Litigation can be expensive and time-consuming. Evaluate whether the potential damages justify the costs and risks of going to trial.

- **Be prepared for cross-examination**: Expect the defendant to challenge your evidence and arguments. Stay calm and confident during cross-examination.

- **Focus on the outcome**: If you win, you could be awarded actual damages, statutory damages, or an injunction to stop the infringement. Consider whether appealing or settling is a better option if the verdict doesn't go in your favor.

By following these steps, you can navigate the complexities of a copyright trial and protect your creative rights effectively.

CHAPTER TEN

Shield Your Work: Preventive Measures Against Infringement

"Protecting your work is not about building barriers; it's about ensuring that your creativity can thrive safely in a world full of opportunities—and threats."— TIM COOK, CEO OF APPLE

Chapter Ten, "Shield Your Work: Preventive Measures Against Infringement," is where we transition from defense to fortress-building. Think of this as the home security system for your intellectual property—no moats or dragons required, just smart, strategic safeguards to keep the copyright bandits at bay.

In this chapter, we'll walk you through a series of clever yet practical steps to protect your creations. From watermarking your visuals like a street artist tags a masterpiece, to registering your works as if you're tucking them into the safest vault. We'll even delve into the digital realms of copyright management, where technology serves as both the lock and the key.

By the time you turn the last page, you'll be equipped with an arsenal of tools to not just deter potential infringers but to do so with the swagger of a seasoned creator who knows their work deserves the highest shield. So, sharpen those pencils and tighten those security settings—your creative empire isn't going to protect itself!

Copyright Registration: The First Line of Defense

When settlement negotiations fail or the parties cannot reach an agreement, a copyright dispute may proceed to trial. While litigation is often a last resort due to its complexity and cost, it's sometimes the only way to fully protect your intellectual property. In this section, we'll walk through the trial process, explore courtroom strategies for presenting a strong case, and discuss potential outcomes, including damages and other remedies.

When it comes to safeguarding your creative work, copyright registration is the foundation upon which all other preventive measures are built. While your work is automatically protected by copyright the moment it is created and fixed in a tangible form, registering it with the U.S. Copyright Office (or the appropriate authority in your country) provides several key benefits that strengthen your legal position in the event of infringement. In this section, we'll explore the importance of copyright registration, the steps involved, and why it's a critical first line of defense for protecting your creations.

1. Why Register Your Copyright?

Even though your work is protected by copyright as soon as it's created, registering it provides several important legal advantages. Here are the primary reasons to register your work:

- **Legal Proof of Ownership**: Registration provides a public record that you own the copyright to the work. This official record is invaluable in legal disputes, as it establishes the date of creation and ownership, which can help prove your case if someone challenges your rights.

- **Eligibility for Statutory Damages**: If your work is registered prior to the infringement (or within three months of publication), you are eligible to seek statutory damages in a lawsuit. Statutory damages can range from $750 to $30,000 per work, and up to $150,000 for willful infringement. Without registration, you may only be eligible for actual damages, which can be harder to prove and may result in a lower payout.

- **Ability to File a Lawsuit**: In the U.S., you cannot file a copyright infringement lawsuit unless your work is registered. Even if you don't plan to go to court, having the option to file a lawsuit is a powerful deterrent to potential infringers. Many cases are settled out of court once the infringer realizes the work is registered and the copyright holder is serious about enforcing their rights.

- **Protection Against Infringement**: Registered works are more likely to deter infringers, as they can easily verify your ownership through the public record. Registration serves as a warning that you have taken legal steps to protect your intellectual property.

2. When Should You Register?

To maximize the legal protection offered by copyright registration, it's best to register your work as soon as possible. Here are some key moments to consider:

- **Immediately after creation**: Registering your work shortly after it's created ensures you're protected from day one and gives you the full range of legal options, including the ability to seek statutory damages and attorney's fees in the event of infringement.

- **Before publication**: If you plan to distribute your work to the public, it's a good idea to register it before publication. This provides legal protection in case someone tries to copy or distribute your work without permission after it's released.

- **Within three months of publication**: In the U.S., you can still qualify for statutory damages if you register your work within three months of publication. This grace period allows you to take advantage of the additional legal benefits of registration, even if you didn't register immediately after creation.

3. The Copyright Registration Process

Registering your copyright is a straightforward process, but it's important to follow each step carefully to ensure your registration is valid. Here's how to do it:

Step 1: Determine Eligibility. Make sure your work is eligible for copyright protection. Copyright protects original works of authorship that are fixed in a tangible medium of expression. This includes:

- Literary works (e.g., books, articles, poems)

- Visual art (e.g., photographs, paintings, illustrations)

- Music (both the composition and sound recordings)

- Films and audiovisual works

- Dramatic works (e.g., plays, scripts)

- Software and databases

- Architectural designs

Ideas, facts, and works that haven't been fixed in a tangible form (like unwritten speeches) are not eligible for copyright protection.

Step 2: Complete the Application. To register your work, you'll need to complete an application with the U.S. Copyright Office or the relevant authority in your country. The application typically requires the following information:

- **Title of the work**: The name or title of your creative work.

- **Type of work**: Identify what category your work falls under (e.g., literary, visual, musical).

- **Date of creation**: Provide the date the work was created or first fixed in a tangible form.

- **Author information**: Your name and contact information.

- **Claimant information**: If the copyright is being claimed by someone other than the author (such as a publisher or company), their information must be provided.

Step 3: Submit a Copy of Your Work. You'll need to submit a copy of your work as part of the registration process. This is called a deposit copy and will become part of the public record. For online registrations, digital copies of the work can often be submitted. For physical works, such as books or paintings, you may need to mail in a physical copy or photograph.

Step 4: Pay the Filing Fee. A registration fee must be paid when you submit your application. The cost varies depending on the type of work and the method of filing. Online applications are usually less expensive than paper submissions. In the U.S., the fee typically ranges from $35 to $85.

Step 5: Receive Your Registration Certificate. Once your application is processed and approved, you'll receive a certificate of registration. This document serves as official proof of your copyright ownership and can be used in court if you need to file a lawsuit.

4. International Copyright Registration

If you plan to distribute or sell your work internationally, it's important to understand that copyright laws vary by country. However, many countries honor foreign copyrights under international treaties like the Berne Convention, which allows copyright holders to protect their works in over 170 member countries. You may not need to register your work in every country, as your U.S. registration (or registration in your home country) may already provide protection abroad. However, if you're concerned about infringement in a specific country, you may choose to register your work in that country's copyright office for added protection.

5. Common Misconceptions About Copyright Registration

Myth 1: I don't need to register because my work is already protected. While it's true that your work is automatically protected by copyright upon creation, registration provides additional legal benefits that you won't have otherwise, such as the ability to sue for statutory damages and attorney's fees.

Myth 2: Registration is too complicated or expensive. The registration process is relatively simple and inexpensive compared to the potential costs of an infringement lawsuit. The small investment in time and money can pay off significantly if you ever need to enforce your rights in court.

Myth 3: I can't register unpublished works. You can and should register your work even if it hasn't been published yet. Unpublished works are just as eligible for copyright registration as published ones, and registering early provides stronger protection against potential infringers.

Conclusion: Why Copyright Registration Is Essential

Copyright registration is your first line of defense against infringement, providing legal proof of ownership and giving you access to statutory damages, attorney's fees, and the ability to file a lawsuit if necessary. By registering your work as soon as possible, you're taking a proactive step in protecting your creative assets and ensuring that you have the legal tools needed to defend your intellectual property.

In the next section, we'll explore additional digital tools and strategies, such as watermarking and content management systems, to further protect your work in the online world.

Watermarking and Digital Tools: Protecting Visual and Digital Content

In the age of the internet, where images, videos, and other forms of digital content can be easily copied, shared, or altered, it's more important than ever to protect your creations. While copyright registration provides legal protection, watermarking and other digital tools offer practical, everyday defenses against unauthorized use. In this section, we'll explore how watermarking, metadata, and other digital rights management tools can help safeguard your work in the online world.

1. Watermarking: A Visual Deterrent

Watermarking is one of the simplest yet most effective ways to protect your visual content, such as photographs, illustrations, and digital artwork. By adding a visible or invisible mark to your work, you make it clear that the image is copyrighted and that unauthorized use is not permitted. Watermarking serves two key purposes:

- **Deterrence**: Watermarks discourage potential infringers from stealing or misusing your work. A visible watermark with your name or logo makes it clear who owns the image and signals that you're serious about protecting your intellectual property.

- **Ownership Proof**: If your work is copied and shared without permission, a watermark serves as clear evidence of ownership. Even if the image circulates online, the watermark remains visible, ensuring that you're credited as the creator.

Types of Watermarks:

- **Visible Watermarks**: These are easily seen and usually placed in a prominent area of the image, such as the corner or center. Common visible watermarks include your name, logo, or website URL. While visible watermarks offer strong protection, they can sometimes detract from the aesthetics of your image, so it's important to find a balance between protection and presentation.

- **Invisible Watermarks**: Invisible or digital watermarks are embedded in the image file itself but aren't visible to the naked eye. These watermarks use special software to encode information like your name or copyright details within the image's metadata. Invisible watermarks are useful because they don't interfere with the image's appearance, but they still provide a layer of protection by allowing you to trace the image back to its source.

Example:

A photographer posts high-quality images of a landscape on their portfolio website. To prevent others from downloading and using the images without permission, they add a visible watermark with their logo in the bottom-right corner. If someone shares the image on social media without credit, the watermark remains intact, ensuring the photographer is still recognized as the creator.

2. Metadata: Embedding Copyright Information

Another way to protect your visual and digital content is by embedding metadata into your files. Metadata is information about the file—such as the author's name, copyright status, and creation date—that's stored within the file itself. Unlike visible watermarks, metadata doesn't affect the appearance of the image, video, or other digital content, but it provides important legal information about the work.

How Metadata Protects Your Work:

- **Proof of Ownership**: Embedding your name and copyright information in the metadata ensures that anyone who accesses the file can see who created it and who holds the rights to it.

- **Tracking and Attribution**: Metadata helps track how and where your work is being used. Many websites and platforms automatically display metadata, allowing you to receive proper credit when your work is shared or reposted.

- **Legal Evidence**: If someone claims your work as their own, the metadata can serve as proof of ownership, strengthening your case in a copyright dispute.

How to Add Metadata: Most image-editing software, such as Adobe Photoshop or Lightroom, allows you to add metadata when you save your files. Common metadata fields include:

- **Creator's Name**: Your name or business name.

- **Copyright Information**: A copyright notice that indicates the work is protected.

- **Creation Date**: The date the work was created or published.

- **Contact Information**: Your email or website URL, so potential users can contact you for licensing inquiries.

3. Digital Rights Management (DRM): Controlling Access to Your Work

Digital Rights Management (DRM) tools go a step beyond watermarking and metadata by allowing you to control how your digital content is accessed, copied, and distributed. DRM is commonly used for digital media such as e-books, music, software, and video content. It prevents unauthorized users from accessing, downloading, or sharing your work without permission.

How DRM Works:

- **Access Control**: DRM systems can restrict who is allowed to view, download, or use your work. For example, e-books with DRM protection can only be opened on authorized devices, preventing users from sharing the file with others.

- **Copy Protection**: DRM can limit the number of times a file can be copied or prevent copying altogether. This ensures that your content isn't widely distributed without your approval.

- **License Management**: DRM allows you to manage licenses for your digital content, granting users specific rights (e.g., a limited-time license to use an image or download a song). Once the license expires, the user can no longer access the content.

Example:

A self-published author sells e-books through an online platform that uses DRM. The DRM system restricts the number of times the e-book can be shared or copied, ensuring that only paying customers can access it. The author can also set expiration dates for promotional downloads, controlling how long readers have access to free copies.

4. Content ID Systems: Automated Protection for Audio and Video

For creators who produce audio and video content, Content ID systems are a powerful tool for preventing unauthorized use. Content ID is commonly used by platforms like YouTube to detect when copyrighted material, such as music or videos, is used in user-generated content without permission.

How Content ID Works:

- **Automatic Detection**: Platforms that use Content ID scan uploaded content (such as videos) for matches with copyrighted material. If a match is found, the platform can take action, such as blocking the video, muting the audio, or allowing the copyright holder to monetize the content.

- **Control Over Usage**: As the copyright holder, you can set your preferences for how your work is treated when detected. For example, you might allow others to use your music in their videos but require that you receive a portion of the ad revenue generated.

- **Protection Against Piracy**: Content ID systems help protect against piracy by automatically flagging unauthorized uploads of your work, reducing the need for manual takedown requests.

Example:

A musician uploads their original song to YouTube's Content ID system. Later, if another user uploads a video that uses the song without permission, Content ID detects the match and either removes the video or gives the musician the option to monetize the content by running ads on the video.

5. Other Digital Tools for Monitoring and Protection

In addition to watermarking, metadata, and DRM, there are several other digital tools you can use to monitor and protect your work:

- **Reverse Image Search**: Use tools like Google Reverse Image Search or TinEye to search for unauthorized uses of your images online. These tools scan the web for visual matches, allowing you to identify websites or platforms where your images may have been used without permission.

- **Google Alerts**: Set up Google Alerts for your name, business, or specific works. You'll receive email notifications whenever your work or related keywords are mentioned online, making it easier to track where and how your content is being shared.

- **DMCA Takedown Services**: If you discover that your work has been used without permission, many websites and platforms offer a DMCA takedown service, allowing you to request the removal of infringing content. Some services, such as DMCA.com, also provide monitoring tools to help you keep track of unauthorized use.

Conclusion: Layering Digital Defenses

Protecting your visual and digital content in the online world requires a multi-layered approach. Watermarking, metadata, DRM, and Content ID systems all serve as practical tools that deter potential infringers and provide proof of ownership if your work is misused. By incorporating these digital defenses into your creative process, you'll be able to share your work confidently while keeping it shielded from unauthorized use.

In the next section, we'll explore proactive strategies for monitoring your intellectual property online and catching potential infringements early, so you can take swift action to protect your rights.

Monitoring Your Work: Keeping an Eye on Potential Infringement

In today's digital world, where content can spread rapidly across platforms and be repurposed in seconds, keeping track of your creative work is a critical part of protecting it from unauthorized use. While copyright registration, watermarking, and digital tools help protect your creations, active monitoring is key to catching potential infringements early. This section will explore strategies and tools to help you monitor your work online, so you can quickly detect and respond to any unauthorized use.

1. Why Monitoring Is Essential

Even with copyright protections in place, infringement can still occur. Monitoring your work allows you to catch unauthorized uses before they cause significant harm. This proactive approach not only helps you maintain control over your creations but also provides an opportunity to resolve issues quickly, often before they escalate into legal battles.

Benefits of Monitoring:

- **Early Detection**: Spotting infringements early allows you to take swift action, whether through a cease and desist letter or a Digital Millennium Copyright Act (DMCA) takedown notice. Early action can prevent further distribution of your work and mitigate financial losses.

- **Preserving Your Brand**: By keeping an eye on where and how your work is being used, you can ensure that your brand and reputation remain intact. Unauthorized use, especially if altered or misrepresented, can harm your image or dilute the value of your creations.

- **Maintaining Control**: Monitoring your work helps you stay in control of how it's shared, distributed, or monetized. This is especially important if you offer licensing agreements or rely on content monetization for income.

2. Reverse Image Search: Tracking Visual Content

One of the most effective ways to monitor your visual content—such as photographs, artwork, and graphics—is by using reverse image search tools. These tools scan the web for images that match or closely resemble your work, allowing you to identify where it has been used without your permission.

Popular Reverse Image Search Tools:

- **Google Reverse Image Search**: Google's reverse image search allows you to upload an image or provide an image URL, and the search engine will return websites where the image appears. This tool is widely used and highly effective for finding unauthorized uses of visual content across the internet.

- **TinEye**: TinEye is another reverse image search engine that specializes in finding where images are used online. It's particularly helpful for tracking down altered versions of your work, such as cropped or resized images.

How to Use Reverse Image Search:

1. Upload your image or paste the URL into the search tool.

2. Review the search results to see where your image is being used.

3. If you find unauthorized uses, document the evidence (such as screenshots and URLs) and take the necessary action to protect your work, whether that's contacting the infringer or filing a takedown notice.

Example:

A digital illustrator frequently uploads their work to their website and social media accounts. To monitor for unauthorized use, they regularly use Google Reverse Image Search to see if any of their illustrations have been posted on other websites without permission. When they find their artwork being sold as prints on a third-party site, they contact the platform to have the listing removed.

3. Google Alerts: Monitoring Mentions of Your Work

For creators of written content, audio, video, or even visual content, Google Alerts can be a powerful tool to monitor when and where your work is mentioned online. Google Alerts notifies you whenever a specified keyword or phrase appears in new web content, such as blog posts, news articles, or forums.

How to Set Up Google Alerts:

1. Go to the Google Alerts page (google.com/alerts).

2. Enter keywords related to your work, such as your name, business name, or the title of a specific piece of content.

3. Customize the settings, including how often you receive notifications (e.g., daily, weekly) and where to receive them (e.g., your email).

4. Google will send you email notifications whenever it detects new mentions of your keywords, allowing you to track where your work is being discussed or shared.

Best Practices for Google Alerts:

- **Be specific with keywords**: Use specific phrases or titles to avoid being overwhelmed by irrelevant results. For example, if you've written an article titled "The Creative Journey," set an alert for the full title rather than just "creative journey" to avoid unrelated content.

- **Monitor your name and brand**: Set alerts for your name, website, and any associated branding to ensure that your work is being properly attributed when shared or discussed online.

Example:

An author who publishes articles across multiple platforms sets up Google Alerts for their name and the titles of their most popular works. One day, they receive an alert that a significant portion of one of their articles has been copied and reposted on a blog without credit. The author contacts the blog owner to request proper attribution or removal of the article, ensuring their work is protected.

4. Social Media Monitoring: Protecting Your Content on Social Platforms

Social media is a double-edged sword for creators—it's a powerful platform for sharing and promoting your work, but it also increases the risk of your content being copied, reposted, or misused without permission. To stay on top of this, you'll need to actively monitor social platforms where your content might be shared.

Tools for Social Media Monitoring:

- **Mention**: Mention is a social media and web monitoring tool that tracks brand mentions, keywords, and hashtags across various platforms, including Twitter, Facebook, Instagram, and YouTube. You can set up alerts for mentions of your name, business, or specific works, helping you track how your content is being shared.

- **Hootsuite**: Hootsuite's social media management platform includes monitoring features that allow you to track mentions of your work or brand in real-time across multiple social media networks. You can also respond to mentions directly from the platform, making it easier to address unauthorized uses or misrepresentations.

- **TweetDeck**: If Twitter is a major platform for your work, TweetDeck is a free tool that allows you to set up custom columns to monitor specific keywords, hashtags, or mentions of your handle. This helps you track how your content is being shared and spot any potential infringements.

Best Practices for Social Media Monitoring:

- **Set up alerts for relevant hashtags**: Many social platforms rely heavily on hashtags. Use monitoring tools to track hashtags associated with your work, such as your name, product, or creation.

- **Engage with mentions**: When your work is shared or discussed on social media, engage with users and ensure that your content is being credited appropriately. If you find instances of unauthorized use, reach out directly to the user or platform to resolve the issue.

Example:

A musician frequently uploads short clips of their songs to Instagram and TikTok. To ensure their work is credited, they use Mention to monitor hashtags related to their music. When they find a user reposting a song clip without credit, they reach out to the user and request proper attribution or removal, preventing unauthorized sharing of their music.

5. DMCA Takedown Requests: Removing Infringing Content

If you discover that your work is being used without permission, one of the most effective ways to address the issue is by filing a DMCA takedown request. The Digital Millennium Copyright Act (DMCA) provides copyright holders with a way to request that infringing content be removed from websites, social media platforms, or online marketplaces.

How to File a DMCA Takedown Request:

1. **Identify the Infringement**: Document the infringing content, including screenshots, URLs, and any relevant details. This will help you build your case for the takedown request.

2. **Submit the Request**: Most platforms have specific procedures for submitting DMCA takedown requests. Typically, you'll need to provide information such as:

   o Your contact details

   o A description of the copyrighted work

   o The location (URL) of the infringing content

      o   A statement affirming that the use is unauthorized and that you are the copyright holder

3. **Wait for Removal**: Once your request is processed, the platform will remove or disable access to the infringing content. In some cases, the user may dispute the claim, at which point further legal action may be required.

Example:

A graphic designer finds that their original artwork is being sold as prints on an online marketplace without their permission. The designer files a DMCA takedown request with the platform, providing evidence that they hold the copyright to the work. The platform removes the listing, protecting the designer's rights and preventing further unauthorized sales.

Conclusion: Stay Proactive in Monitoring Your Work

Monitoring your work is an essential part of protecting your intellectual property in the digital age. By using tools like reverse image search, Google Alerts, social media monitoring platforms, and DMCA takedown requests, you can stay ahead of potential infringements and take action before they cause significant harm. Being proactive in keeping an eye on your content ensures that you maintain control over how your work is shared and used.

In the next section, we'll dive into licensing and contracts, exploring how you can set clear boundaries and expectations for others who want to use your work legally while still retaining ownership and control.

Licensing Contracts: Setting Boundaries and Expectations

Licensing your creative work can be a lucrative and beneficial way to expand your audience, collaborate with other creators, and generate revenue. However, without clear contracts and licensing agreements in place, you risk losing control over how your work is used or facing unauthorized exploitation. In this final section, we'll explore how to use licensing agreements and contracts to set clear boundaries and expectations, allowing others to legally use your work while you retain ownership and control.

1. What Is Licensing?

A license is a legal agreement that grants someone permission to use your copyrighted work under specific conditions. As the copyright owner, you can choose how your work is licensed, setting terms that outline what rights you're granting, for how long, and for what purpose. Licensing allows you to maintain ownership of your work while allowing others to legally use it, often in exchange for a fee or royalty.

Common Types of Licenses:

- **Exclusive License**: In an exclusive license, you grant one party the exclusive right to use your work for a specific purpose. This means that no one else, including you, can use the work for that purpose during the term of the license.

- **Non-Exclusive License**: A non-exclusive license allows you to grant permission to multiple parties to use your work. This is common for stock photography, music licensing, or software distribution, where multiple users can access and use the same work.

- **Single-Use License**: This type of license permits the licensee to use your work only once, such as in a single advertisement, blog post, or printed product.

- **Limited-Time License**: A limited-time license allows the licensee to use your work for a specific period. After the license expires, they must stop using the work or renegotiate the agreement for continued use.

Example:

A freelance illustrator licenses one of their digital artworks to a magazine under a non-exclusive license. This agreement allows the magazine to use the artwork for one issue, while the illustrator retains the right to license the same artwork to other clients.

2. The Importance of Written Contracts

When licensing your work, it's crucial to have a written contract in place. A handshake agreement or verbal understanding can lead to misunderstandings or disputes down the line. A formal written contract ensures that both you and the licensee understand the terms of use, and it provides legal protection in case of infringement or breach of agreement.

What Should Be Included in a Licensing Contract?:

- **Scope of the License**: Clearly define what rights you're granting. This includes specifying how the work can be used (e.g., print, digital, broadcast), whether the license is exclusive or non-exclusive, and whether the licensee can modify the work.

- **Duration of the License**: Specify the length of time the license is valid. Is it for a one-time use, a year-long campaign, or an indefinite period? Make sure the terms are clear to avoid any confusion once the license expires.

- **Territory**: Define where the licensee can use the work. Is it limited to certain countries or regions, or can it be used globally? For example, a license for an advertising campaign may be limited to a specific geographic area.

- **Payment Terms**: Outline how and when you will be compensated for the use of your work. This could be a one-time fee, a recurring royalty, or payment based on sales or usage. Be sure to include details on how royalties will be calculated and when they'll be paid.

- **Attribution**: Specify how you will be credited for your work. This ensures that you receive proper attribution whenever the work is displayed, published, or broadcast.

- **Restrictions**: Include any limitations or restrictions on how the work can be used. For example, you might restrict the use of your work in certain industries or prevent the licensee from sublicensing the work to third parties.

- **Termination and Renewal**: Define the conditions under which the agreement can be terminated, such as failure to pay royalties or breach of contract. Additionally, include terms for renewing the license if both parties wish to continue the agreement after it expires.

Example:

A musician licenses one of their songs to a film production company for use in a movie trailer. The contract specifies that the song can be used for the trailer only (not in the movie itself), limits the use to a six-month promotional period, and outlines a flat fee for the license. The contract also includes a clause requiring the production company to credit the musician whenever the trailer airs.

3. Common Licensing Pitfalls and How to Avoid Them

While licensing can be an excellent way to monetize your work, it's important to be aware of potential pitfalls that can arise if the terms are unclear or too broad. Here are some common licensing challenges and how to avoid them:

- **Overly Broad Licensing Terms**: Be cautious about granting too many rights in a single agreement. If a license allows for unlimited use of your work across all platforms and territories, you may lose control over where and how your work is used. To avoid this, limit the license to specific uses, time periods, and territories.

- **Lack of Clarity on Modifications**: Some licenses may allow the licensee to modify your work (e.g., cropping, color adjustments, or reformatting). If you're uncomfortable with your work being altered, be sure to include a clause that restricts modifications or requires your approval before any changes are made.

- **Inadequate Payment Terms**: Ensure that the payment terms are clearly defined, whether it's a flat fee, a royalty percentage, or another arrangement. Avoid agreements that don't specify when and how you'll be paid, as this can lead to delays or disputes.

- **Failure to Register the Contract**: In some countries, copyright licenses must be registered with the local copyright office to be enforceable. Make sure to check the requirements in your jurisdiction to ensure your licensing agreement is legally binding.

Example:

A photographer licenses one of their images to a clothing brand for use in a promotional campaign. However, the contract doesn't specify whether the brand can alter the image. Later, the photographer discovers that the brand heavily modified the photo without their consent. To avoid this issue in the future, the photographer adds a clause in all licensing agreements that requires approval for any alterations to their work.

4. Licensing for Different Mediums

The terms of your licensing agreement may vary depending on the type of creative work you're licensing. Here's how licensing typically works for different mediums:

- **Photography and Visual Art**: When licensing visual works, such as photography or illustrations, the agreement should specify where and how the image can be used (e.g., online, in print, on merchandise). Be sure to clarify whether the license allows for editing or manipulation of the image.

- **Music**: Music licensing often involves multiple types of rights, such as the rights to the composition, performance, and recording. For example, a license might grant the right to use a song in a commercial, while another license might be needed to perform the song live or distribute it on streaming platforms.

- **Writing and Literary Works**: Licensing written works, such as articles, essays, or books, typically involves granting permission for publication in specific formats (e.g., print, digital, or audiobook). You may also grant permission for translations or adaptations, but be sure to specify these rights clearly in the contract.

- **Software**: Software licenses often include terms related to distribution, installation, and updates. It's important to clarify whether the licensee has the right to modify or resell the software and how long they can access updates or technical support.

Example:

A self-published author licenses the audiobook rights for their novel to an audio production company. The contract specifies that the license applies only to the audio format and grants the company exclusive rights for a period of three years. The author retains the rights to publish the book in print and e-book formats separately.

5. Sublicensing: Allowing Third Parties to Use Your Work

In some cases, you may grant a licensee the right to sublicense your work to third parties. For example, a licensing agreement with a publisher might allow them to sublicense your work to a foreign publisher for translation and distribution in another country. If you choose to allow sublicensing, be sure to set clear limits on how it can be done and how you will be compensated for sublicensed uses.

Best Practices for Sublicensing:

- **Set Clear Terms**: Define what types of sublicenses are allowed, and whether the licensee needs your approval before sublicensing your work.

- **Specify Payment Terms**: Ensure that you receive a fair share of any sublicensing revenue. This could be a percentage of the royalties or a flat fee.

- **Limit Sublicensing Rights**: If you don't want your work sublicensed to certain industries or regions, include restrictions in the contract.

Example:

A software developer licenses their application to a tech company for distribution. The agreement allows the company to sublicense the software to other firms for installation on company devices, but it includes a clause that prevents sublicensing to competitors in the same industry.

Conclusion: Protecting Your Work with Licensing Agreements

Licensing agreements are essential for protecting your creative work while allowing others to use it legally. By setting clear boundaries and expectations through a well-crafted contract, you can maintain control over how your work is used, ensure proper compensation, and avoid potential disputes. Whether you're licensing visual art, music, writing, or software, taking the time to create detailed and enforceable agreements will safeguard your intellectual property and help you make the most of your creative efforts.

In the next chapter, we'll dive into the digital landscape of copyright management, exploring how online platforms and content creation technologies are shaping the future.

Quick Tips and Recap

- **Always use a written contract**: Verbal agreements can lead to disputes. A clear, written contract ensures both parties understand the terms of the license.

- **Define the scope of the license**: Specify what rights you're granting (exclusive or non-exclusive), how the work can be used, and where it can be distributed (e.g., print, digital, or global use).

- **Set time limits**: Include a clear start and end date for the license, and outline the process for renewal if applicable.

- **Clarify payment terms**: Whether it's a flat fee, royalties, or a combination, clearly outline how and when you'll be compensated for the use of your work.

- **Address modifications**: If you don't want your work altered, add a clause that restricts modifications or requires your approval before any changes are made.

- **Include attribution**: Specify how you should be credited for your work to ensure you receive proper recognition.

- **Consider sublicensing carefully**: If you allow sublicensing, set limits on how and where it can be done, and ensure you're fairly compensated for any sublicenses.

- **Review the contract regularly**: As your work expands into new markets or mediums, update your contracts to reflect any changes in licensing terms.

By following these steps, you can create strong licensing agreements that protect your work, define expectations, and ensure fair compensation for your creative efforts.

Mastering Strategic Leadership

Part Three, "Mastering Strategic Leadership," serves up a hearty blend of wisdom and wit, essential for anyone looking to steer their ship through the choppy waters of modern leadership. This isn't just about holding the wheel; it's about charting a course where others see only open sea. We'll dive deep into the traits that define a strategic leader: vision sharp enough to spot trends on the horizon, charisma that can turn skeptics into loyal crew members, and a knack for decision-making that feels more like chess than checkers. Get ready to captain your enterprise with a mix of boldness and brains, navigating through storms with a grin, because here, every challenge is just another adventure in your leadership odyssey.

Licensing: Basics of Licensing Agreements

"Licensing is the art of monetizing your creativity without giving away
your control. It's about building partnerships that respect your vision
and reward your innovation."— RICHARD BRANSON,
FOUNDER OF VIRGIN GROUP

Chapter Eleven, "Licensing: Basics of Licensing Agreements," is your front-row ticket to the dazzling world of licensing—where creativity meets commerce, and everyone wants a piece of the pie. Here, we strip away the legal jargon and dive into the nuts and bolts of licensing agreements with the ease of a seasoned negotiator at a flea market.

Think of licensing as the art of letting someone else throw a party with your beloved creations, while you still get to control the guest list and take home a slice of the cake. We'll explore the different flavors of licensing—from exclusive to non-exclusive—and how to pick the perfect blend that doesn't just resonate with your business goals but also sings in harmony with your brand's essence.

By the time you finish this chapter, you'll be crafting licensing agreements that protect your interests while maximizing your profits, all without selling your soul to the corporate devils. Ready to turn your creations into a thriving marketplace? Let's turn these legal complexities into your next big opportunity!

Types of Licensing Agreements: Exclusive vs. Non-Exclusive

When it comes to licensing your creative work, one of the first decisions you'll face is choosing between an exclusive or non-exclusive licensing agreement. Each type of agreement has its own advantages and limitations, depending on your goals, the type of work you're licensing, and how much control you want to retain over your intellectual property. In this section, we'll break down the key differences between exclusive and non-exclusive licenses and help you determine which one is the best fit for your specific situation.

1. What is an Exclusive License?

An exclusive license grants one licensee the sole right to use your work in a specific way, often for a particular market or territory. When you issue an exclusive license, you cannot grant the same rights to anyone else, and in some cases, you may not be able to use the work yourself for the same purpose during the term of the agreement.

Advantages of an Exclusive License:

- **Higher Value**: Because the licensee has exclusive rights to your work, they may be willing to pay a higher fee or offer more favorable terms. Exclusive licenses are often more attractive to companies or individuals who want to stand out by offering something unique or proprietary.

- **Increased Control**: You can maintain tighter control over how your work is used, as only one party is permitted to use it for the specified purpose. This can prevent oversaturation of your work in the marketplace, helping to maintain its value.

- **Stronger Relationship**: Exclusive licenses can foster a closer, more collaborative relationship with the licensee, as both parties are more invested in the success of the work. This can lead to long-term partnerships and additional opportunities for future collaborations.

Limitations of an Exclusive License:

- **Limited Flexibility**: By granting exclusive rights, you're locking yourself into a single agreement, which limits your ability to license the work to others or use it for yourself. This can be a downside if you later find more lucrative opportunities or want to diversify how your work is used.

- **Risk of Lost Revenue**: If the licensee doesn't fully capitalize on the work's potential, you could miss out on additional revenue that might have been generated through multiple non-exclusive licenses.

Example:

A photographer grants an exclusive license to a fashion magazine to use one of their images for a cover photo. This means the photographer cannot license the same image to another magazine or publication for the duration of the agreement. In return, the magazine pays a premium for the exclusive use of the image, knowing they have the sole right to use it in their industry.

2. What is a Non-Exclusive License?

A non-exclusive license allows you to grant the same rights to multiple parties, meaning that several different licensees can use your work simultaneously for similar purposes. This type of license is common in industries like stock photography, music licensing, and software distribution, where the work can be widely distributed without losing value.

Advantages of a Non-Exclusive License:

- **Greater Flexibility**: Non-exclusive licenses give you the freedom to license your work to multiple parties, allowing you to tap into different markets or industries without being restricted to a single deal. You can also continue to use the work yourself or offer it to new licensees in the future.

- **Ongoing Revenue**: With non-exclusive licenses, you can generate ongoing revenue from the same work by licensing it to multiple parties. This can be especially valuable for digital or reproducible content, such as software, music, or stock images, where the work can be reused in different contexts without diminishing its appeal.

- **Lower Commitment**: Non-exclusive licenses don't require the same level of commitment or risk as exclusive licenses, making them ideal for short-term or lower-stakes projects. If one licensee doesn't generate much revenue, you still have the opportunity to profit from other deals.

Limitations of a Non-Exclusive License:

- **Lower Value**: Because the licensee doesn't have exclusive rights to the work, they may be less willing to pay a premium for the license. Non-exclusive licenses tend to have lower fees compared to exclusive agreements, but the ability to grant multiple licenses can make up for this over time.

- **Potential for Oversaturation**: If your work is licensed to too many parties or used too widely, it may lose its uniqueness and appeal. This can be a particular concern for creative works like art, photography, or fashion, where exclusivity often adds value.

Example:

A music producer grants non-exclusive licenses to several filmmakers and content creators, allowing them to use one of their tracks in their respective projects. Each licensee pays a smaller fee, but the producer can issue the same license to many clients, generating steady revenue without giving up control of the track.

3. Deciding Between Exclusive and Non-Exclusive Licenses

The decision to offer an exclusive or non-exclusive license depends on your goals, the nature of your work, and the market you're targeting. Here are some factors to consider when choosing between the two:

- **Value of Exclusivity**: If exclusivity adds significant value to your work (such as in fashion, design, or high-end photography), an exclusive license may be more attractive to potential licensees and provide a higher return. If your work can be easily reused in multiple contexts (like music or software), a non-exclusive license may be a better fit.

- **Market Demand**: Consider how your work will be used and whether the demand for exclusivity justifies the limitations. For example, if you're licensing stock photography that can be used by a variety of clients, non-exclusive licenses make sense. However, if you're licensing artwork for a one-of-a-kind product or campaign, exclusivity might be more valuable.

- **Long-Term Strategy**: Think about how the license fits into your long-term business goals. An exclusive license might provide a quick financial boost, but a non-exclusive license could generate steady, ongoing income. If you plan to use or license the work in multiple ways over time, non-exclusive licenses may offer more flexibility.

- **Collaborative Relationships**: If you're looking to build a strong relationship with a key partner, an exclusive license can create opportunities for closer collaboration and future projects. Non-exclusive licenses, on the other hand, are more transactional and don't typically foster long-term partnerships.

Example:

An illustrator creates a set of digital designs and must decide how to license them. For a high-end fashion brand looking for a unique pattern for their new collection, the illustrator might offer an exclusive license at a premium. Meanwhile, for generic products like mugs or t-shirts sold online, they may offer non-exclusive licenses to multiple print-on-demand companies, maximizing revenue across various platforms.

Conclusion: Choosing the Right License for Your Work

The choice between an exclusive and non-exclusive license is one of the most important decisions you'll make when licensing your work. Both types of agreements offer distinct advantages, and the right choice depends on your creative vision, financial goals, and the specific needs of your market. By carefully weighing the benefits and limitations of each option, you can tailor your licensing strategy to protect your interests while maximizing the value of your intellectual property.

In the next section, we'll explore the key elements of a licensing agreement, breaking down what every contract should include to ensure that your rights are protected and both parties are clear on their obligations.

Key Elements of a Licensing Agreement

A well-crafted licensing agreement is essential for protecting your intellectual property while allowing others to use your work under agreed-upon terms. Every licensing agreement should include clear and specific elements that outline the rights and responsibilities of both parties, define the scope of use, and ensure that you are compensated fairly. In this section, we'll break down the key elements of a licensing agreement, ensuring that you cover all the bases and avoid potential legal or financial pitfalls.

1. Scope of the License

The scope of the license defines exactly how, where, and for what purpose the licensee can use your work. This is one of the most critical elements of a licensing agreement, as it establishes the boundaries for the use of your intellectual property.

Key considerations for the scope:

- **Type of Use**: Specify how the work can be used. For example, is it being licensed for commercial use (e.g., in advertisements, products), or is it for personal use (e.g., in a private collection)? If it's software, are you licensing it for distribution, modification, or integration into another product?

- **Medium**: Clearly define where and in what format your work can be used. Is it for print, digital, broadcast, or multimedia platforms? Will it be used online, in physical products, or both?

- **Exclusivity**: Clarify whether the license is exclusive (only one licensee can use the work) or non-exclusive (multiple parties can license the work). This will impact how widely the work can be distributed and by whom.

Example:

An author licenses their book for use in a podcast. The agreement specifies that the book can be narrated for the podcast but cannot be modified or adapted into other formats, such as a film or an audiobook, without further permission.

2. Duration of the License

The duration of the license sets the length of time the licensee can use the work. This can be a fixed period (e.g., one year) or indefinite, depending on the agreement. The duration should be clearly stated to avoid misunderstandings about when the license expires.

Types of duration clauses:

- **Fixed-Term License**: A license that is valid for a specific period, such as six months, one year, or five years. After the term ends, the licensee must stop using the work unless the agreement is renewed.

- **Perpetual License**: A license that grants the licensee the right to use the work indefinitely. While this can be convenient for long-term collaborations, it may limit your ability to reclaim or re-license the work later.

- **Renewal Clauses**: If you want to give the licensee the option to continue using the work after the original term expires, include a renewal clause that outlines the conditions for renewal, such as additional fees or changes to the scope of use.

Example:

A clothing designer licenses a pattern to a fashion brand for a period of two years. After the license expires, the fashion brand can no longer use the pattern unless they negotiate a new agreement.

3. Territory

The territory defines the geographic area in which the licensee can use your work. This element is especially important for works that can be distributed globally, such as films, software, or online content.

Options for territory clauses:

- **National License**: Limits the use of the work to a specific country or region. For example, a license might allow the work to be used only in the United States or the European Union.

- **Global License**: Grants the licensee the right to use the work worldwide. This is common for digital products or content that will be distributed via the internet.

- **Regional Licenses**: You can issue different licenses for different regions. For example, you might grant an exclusive license to a publisher in North America while offering a non-exclusive license to another publisher in Europe.

Example:
A filmmaker licenses their documentary to a distribution company for the North American market. The agreement specifies that the company can distribute the film only in the U.S. and Canada, while the filmmaker retains the rights to license the film in other regions.

4. Payment Terms

One of the most important parts of a licensing agreement is how you will be compensated for the use of your work. The payment terms should be clear and detailed, outlining the amount, method, and timing of payments.

Common payment structures:

- **Flat Fee**: The licensee pays a one-time fee for the rights to use the work. This is common for short-term or single-use licenses.

- **Royalties**: You receive ongoing payments based on the licensee's sales or usage of the work. Royalties are often calculated as a percentage of sales or profits and may be paid quarterly, annually, or as specified in the agreement.

- **Advance + Royalties**: The licensee pays an upfront advance (a lump sum) and then pays additional royalties once the work generates revenue. The advance is typically non-refundable and deducted from future royalties.

- **Milestone Payments**: Payments are made at specific points in time or after certain milestones are reached. This is common in software licensing or complex projects where development stages are important.

Example:

A musician licenses a song to a video game developer. The agreement includes an upfront fee of $5,000 plus a 5% royalty on any in-game purchases related to the song. Royalties are paid out quarterly based on the developer's sales reports.

5. Attribution and Credit

In many creative industries, proper attribution or credit is just as important as financial compensation. The licensing agreement should specify how you will be credited for your work and where that credit will appear.

Attribution clauses should include:

- **Location of Credit**: Where and how your name or brand will be displayed. For example, will your name appear in the credits of a film, on a product label, or within a digital interface?

- **Format of Credit**: The exact wording of how you want to be credited. You might specify that your name must appear in a specific size or position (e.g., "Photography by [Your Name]").

Example:

A photographer licenses an image to a travel magazine. The agreement specifies that the photographer's name must appear in the photo credit on the page where the image is used, with the wording "Photo by [Photographer's Name]."

6. Restrictions and Limitations

Every licensing agreement should clearly state any restrictions or limitations on how the work can be used. This helps ensure that your intellectual property is not misused or exploited beyond the intended purpose.

Common restrictions:

- **No Modifications**: Specify whether the licensee is allowed to modify or alter your work. If you don't want your work to be edited, resized, or changed in any way, include a clause that prohibits modifications without your approval.

- **Sublicensing**: Decide whether the licensee can sublicense your work to third parties. If you want to retain control over who uses your work, you may choose to prohibit sublicensing or require that any sublicenses be approved by you.

- **Field of Use**: Limit the use of the work to a specific industry or product category. For example, you might license a design for use on clothing but restrict its use on other products like mugs or posters.

Example:
A graphic designer licenses a logo to a tech startup. The agreement specifies that the logo cannot be altered or used in any other context (such as on merchandise) without the designer's prior approval.

7. Termination and Breach Clauses

The termination clause outlines how and when the agreement can be terminated, either by mutual agreement or due to breach of contract. It should also define what constitutes a breach of the agreement, such as failure to make payments, unauthorized use of the work, or violation of any restrictions.

Key elements to include:

- **Termination for Cause**: Define the specific conditions under which the agreement can be terminated, such as failure to pay royalties, misuse of the work, or breach of exclusivity.

- **Notice Period**: Specify how much notice is required before terminating the agreement. This is typically 30, 60, or 90 days, giving both parties time to address any issues or disputes.

- **Consequences of Breach**: Outline what happens if the licensee breaches the agreement. This may include immediate termination of the license, legal action, or financial penalties.

Example:

A software developer licenses a program to a business with a clause that allows for termination if the business fails to pay the agreed royalties within 30 days of the due date. The agreement also specifies that if the license is terminated, the business must immediately stop using and distributing the software.

Conclusion: Crafting a Strong Licensing Agreement

A well-structured licensing agreement is essential for protecting your intellectual property and ensuring a successful collaboration with the licensee. By clearly defining the scope, duration, territory, payment terms, attribution, restrictions, and termination clauses, you can set clear boundaries and expectations that benefit both parties. Taking the time to carefully craft your licensing agreements will help you maintain control over your work while maximizing its value.

In the next section, we'll explore the negotiation process, providing strategies and tips for securing favorable terms in your licensing agreements while maintaining strong relationships with your licensees.

Negotiating Licensing Terms: Strategies for Success

Negotiating a licensing agreement can be both an art and a science, requiring you to balance protecting your intellectual property with creating an appealing deal for the licensee. A successful negotiation results in an agreement that benefits both parties, providing you with fair compensation and the licensee with clear rights to use your work. In this section, we'll explore strategies to help you negotiate licensing terms effectively, ensuring that you walk away with a favorable deal while maintaining control over your creative assets.

1. Know the Value of Your Work

The first step in any successful negotiation is understanding the value of your work. Before entering negotiations, take time to assess the market value of your intellectual property based on factors such as its uniqueness, demand, and potential commercial appeal. Research what similar works have been licensed for and how they're being used in the market. This knowledge will empower you to negotiate from a position of strength and avoid undervaluing your work.

Factors to consider when valuing your work:

- **Market Demand**: How popular or in-demand is your work? The higher the demand, the more leverage you have to negotiate favorable terms.

- **Uniqueness**: Is your work one-of-a-kind or easily replicated? Unique works, like original art or exclusive music compositions, typically command higher licensing fees.

- **Potential for Commercial Use**: Assess the potential revenue your work can generate for the licensee. For example, if your work will be featured in a major advertising campaign or sold as a product, its value increases significantly.

Example:

A software developer who has created a groundbreaking app should understand the market demand for similar apps and how much they've been licensed for. This allows the developer to confidently ask for a higher licensing fee and favorable terms during negotiations.

2. Be Clear About Your Priorities

Before you enter into negotiations, identify your key priorities and non-negotiables. These might include the licensing fee, attribution, restrictions on modifications, or geographic limitations. Understanding what's most important to you will help guide the negotiation process and ensure you don't compromise on the elements that matter most.

Common priorities to consider:

- **Financial Compensation**: Are you seeking a flat fee, royalties, or a combination of both? Make sure you're clear about what kind of payment structure works best for you.

- **Control Over Usage**: How much control do you want over how your work is used? For example, if you're licensing artwork or music, you may want to set strict limits on alterations or sublicensing.

- **Duration**: Decide how long you're comfortable licensing your work. Shorter durations provide more flexibility for future licensing opportunities, while longer terms offer stability and potentially higher payments.

Example:

An illustrator negotiating a license for their artwork might prioritize maintaining the ability to license the work to other companies (non-exclusive rights) while ensuring the work isn't modified without their permission.

3. Be Prepared to Compromise

While it's important to know your priorities, successful negotiations often require some level of compromise. Being flexible on less critical terms can help you build a better relationship with the licensee and increase the chances of closing the deal. However, make sure that any compromises you make still protect the core value of your work and align with your long-term goals.

Strategies for effective compromise:

- **Identify Trade-Offs**: Be willing to make concessions on secondary issues (such as geographic restrictions or exclusivity) in exchange for better terms in your priority areas (like payment or usage rights).

- **Negotiate for Royalties**: If a flat fee isn't meeting your expectations, consider negotiating for royalties or performance-based payments as a way to increase your potential earnings over time.

- **Offer Trial Periods**: If the licensee is hesitant about long-term commitments, suggest a **trial period** or a short-term license with the option to renew. This gives both parties flexibility while allowing you to secure a deal.

Example:

A songwriter negotiating a license for their music may offer a longer-term license (three years instead of one) in exchange for a higher royalty percentage on any sales generated by the song's use in advertisements.

4. Understand the Licensee's Position

To negotiate effectively, it's important to understand the licensee's perspective and business needs. Are they looking for exclusive rights to set themselves apart from competitors? Do they need the work for a specific project, campaign, or product launch? By understanding their objectives, you can better tailor your negotiation strategy and offer solutions that align with their goals while protecting your interests.

Questions to ask during negotiations:

- **How does the licensee intend to use your work?** Understanding their plans helps you set appropriate restrictions and tailor the license to fit their needs.

- **What is their budget?** Knowing their budget range allows you to adjust your offer or suggest payment structures that work for both parties (e.g., upfront fees with smaller royalties).

- **What timeline are they working with?** If they have a tight deadline or need a quick turnaround, you may be able to negotiate more favorable terms by offering expedited delivery or flexibility.

Example:

A visual artist learns that a retail company wants to use their design for an exclusive holiday collection. Understanding the company's timeline and need for exclusivity, the artist negotiates a higher licensing fee in exchange for granting exclusive rights for that season.

5. Negotiate Fair Payment Terms

Compensation is one of the most important aspects of any licensing agreement, and negotiating fair payment terms ensures that you're properly compensated for your work. Whether you're asking for a flat fee, royalties, or both, make sure the payment structure reflects the value of your intellectual property.

Key payment structures to consider:

- **Flat Fee**: A one-time payment for the use of your work. This is common for short-term or single-use licenses. Make sure the flat fee compensates you adequately for the full scope of the license.

- **Royalties**: A percentage of the licensee's revenue generated by the use of your work. Royalties are ideal for ongoing use, such as in products, software, or media that generate continuous sales.

- **Advance + Royalties**: You receive an upfront payment (the advance) in addition to future royalty payments. The advance guarantees immediate compensation, while the royalties provide long-term revenue based on performance.

- **Tiered Royalties**: Royalties can be structured in tiers based on sales performance. For example, you might receive 5% for the first 10,000 units sold and 7% for every unit sold after that.

Example:
A software developer licenses a program to a tech company and negotiates an advance of $10,000 plus 3% royalties on the company's future sales of the software. This ensures the developer gets paid upfront while also benefiting from the product's long-term success.

6. Keep Communication Professional and Positive

Successful negotiations are built on strong communication and a positive working relationship. Even when advocating for your own interests, it's important to remain professional, respectful, and solution-oriented. Building rapport with the licensee can lead to smoother negotiations and even future collaborations.

Tips for effective communication:

- **Be Transparent**: Clearly explain your terms and why they matter to you. Transparency helps build trust and reduces misunderstandings.

- **Listen Actively**: Take the time to understand the licensee's concerns and objections. By listening actively, you can address their needs while still protecting your interests.

- **Offer Creative Solutions**: If negotiations hit a roadblock, be prepared to offer creative solutions. For example, if the licensee's budget is lower than expected, suggest alternative payment structures or reduced scope for the license.

Example:

A graphic designer maintains a positive and professional tone during negotiations with a small startup, understanding their budget limitations while still advocating for fair compensation. The designer proposes a lower upfront fee in exchange for higher royalties once the startup's product launches successfully.

7. Put Everything in Writing

Once the terms are agreed upon, it's essential to put everything in writing. A formal, written licensing agreement protects both parties and ensures that there are no misunderstandings about the terms of the deal. Include every key element, from payment terms to usage restrictions, in the final contract to avoid future disputes.

Elements to include in the written agreement:

- **Scope of the license** (usage, territory, duration)

- **Payment terms** (flat fee, royalties, advance payments)

- **Attribution and credit** requirements

- **Restrictions** (modifications, sublicensing, etc.)

- **Termination** clauses (for breach of contract or end of term)

Example:

An author licenses their short story to a magazine and ensures that all terms discussed during negotiations—payment, rights to reprint, and attribution—are clearly spelled out in a written agreement. This written contract provides legal protection if any issues arise later.

Conclusion: Mastering the Art of Licensing Negotiations

Negotiating a licensing agreement requires careful preparation, clear communication, and a willingness to compromise. By understanding the value of your work, identifying your priorities, and being flexible in your approach, you can negotiate licensing terms that protect your intellectual property while maximizing your financial returns. Remember to put everything in writing and maintain a positive working relationship with the licensee to ensure a smooth and successful licensing deal.

In the next section, we'll explore common pitfalls in licensing agreements and provide tips on how to avoid these mistakes to ensure that your agreements are legally sound and beneficial to both parties.

Avoiding Common Licensing Pitfalls

While licensing agreements can be a lucrative way to monetize your intellectual property, there are common pitfalls that can undermine your rights, limit your control over your work, or result in financial losses. By understanding these potential mistakes and how to avoid them, you can create strong licensing agreements that protect your interests and maximize the value of your creations. In this section, we'll highlight some of the most frequent licensing pitfalls and provide tips on how to steer clear of them.

1. Granting Overly Broad Rights

One of the most common mistakes is granting overly broad rights to the licensee without realizing the potential long-term consequences. When you give the licensee more rights than necessary, you may lose control over how your work is used, leaving you unable to license it to others or use it for your own purposes.

How to avoid this pitfall:

- **Limit the scope**: Be specific about how, where, and for what purpose the licensee can use your work. For example, if you're licensing an image for use on a product, specify which products it can be used on (e.g., mugs or t-shirts) and whether the licensee can use it in digital advertising or social media.

- **Retain unused rights**: Clearly state that any rights not explicitly granted to the licensee remain with you. This protects your ability to license the work for other uses in the future.

Example:

A writer licenses a short story to a magazine for publication in a single issue. The agreement specifies that the magazine cannot use the story in any future editions, digital versions, or marketing materials without further permission. This prevents the magazine from using the work beyond the original scope.

2. Failing to Specify Payment Terms

Another common mistake is vague or incomplete payment terms. Without clearly defined payment structures, you risk delayed payments, underpayment, or disputes over how much you're owed.

How to avoid this pitfall:

- **Be specific**: Clearly outline how and when you will be paid. If you're receiving royalties, specify the percentage, how it will be calculated (e.g., based on gross or net sales), and when you will receive royalty statements and payments.

- **Include late fees**: To avoid delays in payment, include a clause that specifies penalties for late payments, such as interest or late fees.

- **Request an advance**: If possible, negotiate for an advance payment to guarantee immediate compensation, particularly in long-term or royalty-based agreements.

Example:

A musician licenses a track to a film production company. The agreement states that the musician will receive a $5,000 upfront payment and 3% of the film's soundtrack sales, with royalties paid quarterly. The contract includes a late payment clause, which charges the company a 5% penalty if payments are delayed beyond 30 days.

3. Ignoring Territorial Restrictions

Licensing agreements should include territorial limitations that define where the licensee can use your work. Failing to specify territory can result in your work being used globally without appropriate compensation or control.

How to avoid this pitfall:

- **Set clear territorial boundaries**: Clearly define the geographic regions where the licensee can use your work. For example, limit usage to specific countries or regions, such as North America, Europe, or Asia.

- **Consider multiple licenses**: If you want to maximize revenue, you can issue different licenses for different regions, allowing multiple licensees to use the work in separate markets.

Example:

A software developer licenses a program to a company for distribution in North America only. The agreement specifies that the company does not have the right to distribute the software outside of this region, allowing the developer to license the software to other companies in Europe and Asia.

4. Allowing Unlimited Modifications

Many creators make the mistake of allowing unrestricted modifications to their work. This can result in the licensee altering your work in ways that misrepresent your vision, dilute its value, or damage your reputation.

How to avoid this pitfall:

- **Restrict modifications**: Include a clause that prohibits the licensee from modifying, altering, or adapting your work without your explicit permission. If you're comfortable with minor modifications (such as resizing or color adjustments), specify what changes are allowed.

- **Require approval**: If modifications are allowed, require the licensee to seek your approval before making any changes. This ensures that you retain creative control over how your work is presented.

Example:

An artist licenses an illustration to a marketing agency for use in a product campaign. The agreement states that the agency cannot modify the illustration in any way, including cropping, recoloring, or adding text, without the artist's written approval.

5. Overlooking Sublicensing and Third-Party Use

Sublicensing occurs when the licensee grants a third party the right to use your work. If your agreement doesn't address sublicensing, you could find your work being used by companies you didn't intend to work with, often without additional compensation.

How to avoid this pitfall:

- **Prohibit sublicensing**: Include a clause that explicitly prohibits the licensee from sublicensing your work to third parties without your permission.

- **Allow controlled sublicensing**: If you're open to sublicensing, include terms that require your approval for any sublicenses and specify how you will be compensated (e.g., a percentage of sublicensing revenue).

Example:

A software developer licenses an application to a tech company. The agreement prohibits the company from sublicensing the software to other firms or developers without the developer's written approval. This ensures the developer retains control over who uses their work.

6. Ignoring Termination and Renewal Clauses

Failing to include termination and renewal clauses can leave you stuck in an undesirable agreement or prevent you from reclaiming your rights after the license term ends. Without these clauses, you may lose control over your work indefinitely.

How to avoid this pitfall:

- **Set clear termination terms**: Include a clause that specifies how and when the agreement can be terminated. This might include termination for breach of contract (e.g., failure to pay royalties) or mutual agreement.

- **Include a renewal option**: If the licensee wants to continue using your work after the term ends, include a renewal clause that outlines the conditions for renewing the agreement, such as renegotiating payment terms.

- **Define what happens after termination**: Specify what happens to the licensed work after the agreement is terminated. For example, the licensee must stop using the work immediately or within a certain period.

Example:
A graphic designer licenses a logo to a startup for one year. The agreement includes a renewal option, allowing the startup to renew the license for an additional year with a renegotiated fee. If the license is not renewed, the startup must stop using the logo within 30 days.

7. Failing to Put the Agreement in Writing

Verbal agreements or informal understandings can lead to misunderstandings and disputes. Without a written agreement, it's difficult to enforce the terms or prove that the licensee is in breach of contract.

How to avoid this pitfall:

- **Always use a written contract**: Ensure that every licensing agreement is in writing, signed by both parties, and includes all key elements, such as the scope of the license, payment terms, and restrictions on usage.

- **Seek legal review**: If you're unsure about the legal language or the terms of the agreement, consult an attorney to review the contract before signing. This will help ensure that your rights are fully protected.

Example:

A photographer negotiates a licensing deal for one of their images with a travel company. To avoid any confusion, they draft a formal written agreement outlining the terms, including usage rights, payment, and attribution. Both parties sign the contract, ensuring that the terms are enforceable.

Conclusion: Protecting Yourself from Licensing Pitfalls

Avoiding common licensing pitfalls is essential for protecting your intellectual property, maintaining control over how your work is used, and ensuring that you're fairly compensated. By granting appropriate rights, specifying payment terms, limiting modifications, and using clear written agreements, you can create strong licensing deals that safeguard your interests while allowing the licensee to benefit from your creative work.

In the next chapter, we'll dive into how to protect your work in the digital age, exploring the unique challenges and opportunities of licensing and enforcing your rights in an increasingly online world.

Quick Tips and Recap

- **Limit the scope of the license**: Be specific about how, where, and for what purpose your work can be used to avoid losing control over your intellectual property.

- **Clearly define payment terms**: Outline how and when you will be paid, whether through flat fees, royalties, or advances, and include penalties for late payments.

- **Set territorial boundaries**: Specify the geographic regions where the licensee can use your work, and consider issuing separate licenses for different regions.

- **Restrict modifications**: Prohibit or limit the licensee's ability to modify your work without permission, ensuring you retain control over its presentation and use.

- **Address sublicensing**: Either prohibit sublicensing or establish clear terms for third-party use, including additional compensation for sublicensed work.

- **Include termination and renewal clauses**: Clearly define how and when the license can be terminated, and set terms for renewal to maintain control over your work after the license expires.

- **Always use a written contract**: Verbal agreements can lead to disputes. Make sure every licensing deal is documented in a formal, written agreement that both parties sign.

By following these tips, you can avoid common licensing pitfalls and ensure that your agreements protect your rights, offer fair compensation, and maintain your creative control.

Seal the Deal: Drafting Effective Licensing Contracts

"Drafting a contract is like drawing a map. It guides the journey of a business relationship, ensuring all parties know the route and the destination clearly."— INDRA NOOYI, FORMER CEO OF PEPSICO

Chapter Twelve, "Seal the Deal: Drafting Effective Licensing Contracts," is where we put on our finest legal attire and get down to business. It's the ultimate guide to crafting contracts that aren't just legally sound, but also as tight as a drum. After all, a good contract is the secret recipe behind every successful licensing deal.

In this chapter, we'll arm you with the skills to draft contracts that speak louder than words. We're talking crystal-clear clauses, bulletproof protections, and escape hatches for those "just in case" scenarios. You'll learn to articulate every expectation, obligation, and ounce of compensation with the precision of a poet and the acumen of a seasoned lawyer.

By the end of this foray into the fine print, you'll not only be able to spot the difference between a benign contract term and a potential backstabber, but you'll also wield the pen like a sword—ready to carve out deals that leave both parties smiling. So, sharpen your pencils (or boot up your word processors) and let's turn those handshake agreements into ironclad commitments that stand the test of time.

Essential Clauses: What Every Licensing Contract Needs

Drafting an effective licensing contract requires attention to detail and a comprehensive understanding of the essential elements that protect both your intellectual property and your financial interests. A well-written contract will clearly define the rights, obligations, and expectations of both parties. In this section, we'll walk through the essential clauses that should be included in every licensing agreement, ensuring your contract is legally sound and protects your work.

1. Scope of the License

The scope of the license defines the specific rights you are granting to the licensee, detailing how, where, and for what purpose your intellectual property can be used. This is one of the most critical clauses, as it determines the limits of the licensee's control over your work.

Key points to include:

- **Type of Use**: Specify exactly how the licensee is allowed to use your work (e.g., commercial, non-commercial, digital, print, broadcast). Define if they can reproduce, distribute, display, or create derivative works.

- **Medium**: Clarify the media in which the work can be used (e.g., social media, television, websites, physical products).

- **Exclusivity**: State whether the license is exclusive or non-exclusive. Exclusive licenses prevent you from granting the same rights to other parties, while non-exclusive licenses allow you to license the work to multiple entities.

Example:

A photographer licenses an image to a travel company for use in their digital marketing materials. The contract specifies that the image can only be used on the company's website and social media channels, and not in print materials or advertisements.

2. Duration of the License

The duration clause specifies how long the licensee is allowed to use your work. Whether the license is temporary or perpetual, it's essential to clearly state the start and end dates, as well as any options for renewal or extension.

Types of duration clauses:

- **Fixed-Term License**: Grants the licensee rights for a specific period (e.g., six months, one year, or three years). After the term ends, the licensee must stop using the work unless the license is renewed.

- **Perpetual License**: Grants the licensee rights to use the work indefinitely. While this type of license offers stability for long-term partnerships, it may limit your ability to reclaim or re-license the work in the future.

- **Renewal Options**: If you or the licensee want the option to continue using the work after the term ends, include a renewal clause that outlines the conditions for renewing the license, such as renegotiating payment terms.

Example:

A writer licenses an article to a magazine for a period of one year, after which the magazine can no longer publish or distribute the article. The contract includes a renewal option, allowing the magazine to extend the license for another year with renegotiated terms.

3. Payment Terms

The payment terms clause defines how you will be compensated for the use of your work. This is one of the most important clauses, as it ensures that you receive fair compensation for the rights you are granting.

Common payment structures:

- **Flat Fee**: A one-time payment for the license, typically used for single-use or short-term licenses.

- **Royalties**: Ongoing payments based on the licensee's sales or revenue generated from using your work. Royalty rates should be clearly defined, along with the frequency of payments (e.g., monthly, quarterly).

- **Advance + Royalties**: A combination of an upfront payment (the advance) and ongoing royalties based on the performance or sales of the work.

- **Milestone Payments**: Payments made at specific stages of the project or once certain goals are met (e.g., after the product is launched or when a sales target is reached).

Example:

A musician licenses a track to a game developer for a flat fee of $10,000. The contract also includes a 5% royalty on all sales of the game's soundtrack, with royalties paid quarterly based on the developer's sales reports.

4. Territory

The territory clause defines the geographic area where the licensee is allowed to use your work. This is especially important for intellectual property that can be distributed internationally, such as software, media content, or merchandise.

Options for territory clauses:

- **National License**: Limits the use of the work to a specific country or region (e.g., U.S. only, or European Union).

- **Global License**: Grants the licensee rights to use the work worldwide. While this may increase the licensee's reach, it may limit your ability to license the work in specific regions to other parties.

- **Regional Licenses**: If you want to maximize revenue, you can issue different licenses for different territories. For example, you might grant an exclusive license in one region and a non-exclusive license in another.

Example:

A software developer licenses an application to a company for distribution in North America. The contract clearly states that the company cannot distribute the software in Europe or Asia, allowing the developer to pursue separate licensing deals in those regions.

5. Attribution and Credit

Proper attribution ensures that you receive public recognition for your work. This clause specifies how your name or brand will be credited whenever the licensee uses your intellectual property.

What to include in the attribution clause:

- **Location of Credit**: Specify where the attribution will appear (e.g., in the credits of a film, on a product label, or in an online description).

- **Format of Credit**: Provide the exact wording or format you require for your credit (e.g., "Photography by [Your Name]" or "Written by [Your Name]").

- **Non-Attribution**: If you don't want to be credited, include a clause that waives attribution requirements.

Example:

A graphic designer licenses a logo to a retail company. The contract specifies that the designer's name must appear in all marketing materials that feature the logo, with the attribution "Design by [Designer's Name]."

6. Restrictions on Use

The restrictions on use clause protects your intellectual property from being used in ways that you do not approve of or that could damage its value. This clause can limit how the work is used, modified, or sublicensed to third parties.

Common restrictions:

- **No Modifications**: Prohibit the licensee from modifying or altering your work without your written consent. If modifications are allowed, clearly define what changes can be made.

- **No Sublicensing**: Prevent the licensee from sublicensing your work to third parties without your approval, ensuring that you maintain control over who uses your intellectual property.

- **Field of Use**: Restrict the use of the work to a specific industry or product category. For example, you might license a design for use on clothing but prohibit its use on other products, such as stationery or home goods.

Example:
A visual artist licenses an illustration to a publisher for use in a children's book. The contract specifies that the publisher cannot modify the illustration or use it in other products, such as coloring books or posters, without the artist's approval.

7. Intellectual Property Ownership

The intellectual property ownership clause is critical for ensuring that you retain ownership of your work. This clause should state clearly that you are granting a license, not transferring ownership, and that all rights not explicitly granted to the licensee remain with you.

Key elements to include:

- **Retention of Ownership**: State that you retain all ownership rights to the intellectual property and that the licensee is being granted limited use rights only.

- **No Transfer of Rights**: Clarify that the license does not transfer ownership, sell, or assign any rights in your intellectual property to the licensee.

- **Ownership of Derivative Works**: If the licensee creates derivative works based on your original work, specify who will own the rights to these new works. In most cases, you should retain ownership of any derivative works.

Example:

A software developer licenses a piece of code to a tech company for integration into their software product. The contract states that the developer retains ownership of the code and that the company has a limited, non-exclusive license to use it in their product.

Conclusion: Building a Strong Licensing Contract

By including these essential clauses in your licensing contract, you can ensure that both parties have a clear understanding of their rights and obligations. A well-drafted contract will protect your intellectual property, provide fair compensation, and set clear boundaries for how your work is used. With these elements in place, you can confidently move forward with licensing agreements that benefit both you and the licensee.

In the next section, we'll explore how to avoid ambiguity in contract terms and draft precise language that leaves no room for misinterpretation, ensuring your contract is enforceable and easy to understand.

Avoiding Ambiguity: Writing Clear and Precise Terms

One of the most critical aspects of drafting an effective licensing contract is ensuring that the language is clear and precise. Ambiguous or vague terms can lead to misunderstandings, disputes, and legal complications, which can undermine the agreement and damage the relationship between you and the licensee. In this section, we'll explore how to avoid ambiguity when drafting contract terms, helping you create contracts that are easy to understand, enforceable, and beneficial to both parties.

1. Use Specific Language

The first rule of drafting a clear contract is to use specific and straightforward language. Avoid legal jargon or overly complex terms that may confuse the licensee or obscure the meaning of the agreement. Each clause should be written in a way that leaves no room for interpretation, ensuring that both parties know exactly what is being agreed upon.

Tips for writing clear language:

- **Avoid vague terms**: Words like "reasonable," "appropriate," or "as needed" are open to interpretation. Instead, use precise terms that clearly define expectations. For example, rather than stating the licensee must make "reasonable efforts" to promote the work, specify the exact actions they must take, such as including the work in social media posts, newsletters, or print advertisements.

- **Define key terms**: If the contract uses industry-specific terms or unique phrases, include a definitions section at the beginning of the contract that explains what each term means in the context of the agreement. This prevents confusion about the meaning of critical terms.

- **Be explicit with numbers and dates**: Instead of saying "within a few months," specify "within 90 days." Rather than stating "a percentage of sales," clarify whether this refers to gross sales or net sales and state the exact percentage.

Example:

In a contract licensing an image for a company's social media campaign, avoid vague terms like "prominent placement." Instead, state that the image must appear as the main visual in at least 75% of the company's social media posts during the campaign period.

2. Define the Scope of Use Clearly

One of the most common sources of ambiguity in licensing agreements is the scope of use. To avoid disputes over how the licensee can use your work, you must clearly define the boundaries of the license. This includes the specific media, platforms, and types of use permitted under the agreement.

How to define scope clearly:

- **List specific uses**: Rather than granting the licensee the vague right to "use the work," specify the exact ways the work can be used. For example, "the licensee may use the image in digital marketing materials, including website banners, social media posts, and email newsletters."

- **State what is not permitted**: It's equally important to state what the licensee **cannot** do with the work. For example, if the licensee is not allowed to modify the work or use it in certain media, such as print advertising, include these restrictions in the contract.

- **Include limitations on duration and geography**: Clearly define the **duration** of the license (start and end dates) and the territory in which the licensee can use the work (e.g., North America only, or worldwide). If the licensee has the right to extend the agreement, specify the conditions for renewal.

Example:

A software developer licenses an application to a business for use in a specific project. The contract states, "The licensee is permitted to use the software only in the development and operation of the 'Project Alpha' mobile app, for distribution in the United States. The license does not extend to any other products or services offered by the licensee."

3. Clarify Payment Terms

Ambiguity in payment terms can lead to disputes about how and when you will be compensated. Clear payment clauses should specify the amount, structure, and timing of payments, as well as any penalties for late payments or missed deadlines.

How to write clear payment terms:

- **State exact amounts**: Avoid vague language such as "a fair percentage" or "a reasonable fee." Clearly define the exact amount the licensee will pay, whether it's a flat fee or a royalty percentage.

- **Outline the payment schedule**: If payments will be made over time, state the specific dates or intervals when payments are due (e.g., "payments will be made quarterly on the 15th of January, April, July, and October").

- **Specify royalty calculations**: If royalties are based on sales, define how the royalties will be calculated (e.g., "royalties will be calculated as 5% of net sales after deducting taxes, shipping, and handling").

- **Include penalties for late payments**: To prevent delays, include a penalty clause for late payments, such as "late payments will incur a fee of 5% per month after the due date."

Example:

A musician licenses a song to a streaming service. The contract specifies, "The licensee will pay an upfront fee of $5,000 within 30 days of signing the agreement, followed by a royalty of 3% of gross revenue generated by the song's use on the platform, payable quarterly. Royalties are due on the 1st of March, June, September, and December."

4. Specify Ownership and Intellectual Property Rights

Another area where ambiguity often arises is in ownership and intellectual property rights. It's essential to make it clear who owns the intellectual property and what rights are being transferred to the licensee. Ambiguity in this area can lead to legal disputes over ownership or unauthorized use of your work.

How to clarify ownership and rights:

- **State that ownership is retained**: If you are not transferring ownership of the work, explicitly state that you retain full ownership of the intellectual property and that the licensee is only being granted limited usage rights.

- **Define the rights being granted**: Specify whether the licensee has the right to reproduce, distribute, or modify the work. Be clear about whether they can create derivative works or sublicense the work to third parties.

- **Include a reversion clause**: If the license has a set duration, include a clause stating that all rights revert back to you once the agreement expires, ensuring that the licensee cannot continue using your work without permission.

Example:

A software developer licenses a codebase to a company. The contract states, "The licensor retains all ownership rights to the code. The licensee is granted a non-exclusive, non-transferable license to use the code for the development of the

'XYZ App.' The licensee is not permitted to modify, sublicense, or create derivative works based on the code without written permission from the licensor."

5. Avoid Overly General Termination Clauses

Termination clauses are another area where vague language can lead to disputes. If the contract doesn't clearly define the conditions under which either party can terminate the agreement, it may be difficult to end the contract without conflict.

How to avoid vague termination clauses:

- **Specify conditions for termination**: Clearly state the specific reasons for which either party can terminate the agreement. Common reasons include failure to pay, breach of contract, or mutual agreement between the parties.

- **Include a notice period**: Specify how much notice each party must give before terminating the contract (e.g., "either party may terminate the agreement with 30 days written notice").

- **Define consequences of termination**: Clearly state what happens once the contract is terminated. For example, the licensee must stop using the work immediately or within a specified time frame, and any outstanding payments must be made.

Example:

An author licenses the film rights to their book. The contract includes a termination clause that states, "Either party may terminate this agreement in the event of a material breach, such as failure to pay royalties or unauthorized use of the work. The breaching party must be given 30 days to rectify the breach before termination. Upon termination, the licensee must immediately cease all use of the work and pay any outstanding royalties."

Conclusion: Precision is Key to a Strong Contract

Avoiding ambiguity is essential for creating a strong, enforceable licensing contract that protects your intellectual property and clearly defines the rights and responsibilities of both parties. By using specific language, defining key terms, and addressing potential areas of confusion, you can draft a contract that is fair, transparent, and legally sound. This will help prevent disputes and ensure that both you and the licensee understand and fulfill your obligations.

In the next section, we'll explore legal protections you can build into your contract, such as indemnity clauses, non-compete clauses, and breach of contract terms, to further safeguard your rights and ensure your work is used appropriately.

Legal Protections: Building Safeguards Into Your Contract

When drafting a licensing agreement, it's not enough to simply define how your work will be used—you also need to protect yourself from potential risks and ensure that your intellectual property is safe. Legal protections act as safeguards, preventing misuse, ensuring that both parties fulfill their obligations, and providing recourse if something goes wrong. In this section, we'll explore key legal protections you should consider including in your licensing contract, such as indemnity clauses, non-compete agreements, and breach of contract terms.

1. Indemnity Clauses: Protecting Yourself from Liability

An indemnity clause shifts responsibility for legal claims or damages from one party to the other. In the context of licensing agreements, this clause protects you (the licensor) from liability if the licensee's use of your work results in legal claims or financial losses. For example, if the licensee uses your work in a way that infringes on someone else's rights, the indemnity clause can prevent you from being held accountable for their misuse.

What to include in an indemnity clause:

- **Licensee's responsibility**: The clause should specify that the licensee is responsible for any legal claims, damages, or costs that arise from their use of your work. This can include intellectual property infringement, breach of third-party contracts, or damages caused by improper use of the work.

- **Duty to defend**: Include language that requires the licensee to defend you against any legal claims or lawsuits related to their use of your work.

This protects you from having to cover legal costs or manage the dispute on your own.

- **Limits of indemnity**: Clearly state the limitations of the indemnity clause. For example, the licensee may not be responsible for claims resulting from your own actions, such as providing faulty work or violating a third-party contract.

Example:

A software developer licenses a program to a tech company. The indemnity clause in the contract states, "The licensee agrees to indemnify, defend, and hold harmless the licensor from any claims, damages, or losses arising out of the licensee's use of the software, including but not limited to intellectual property infringement or breach of third-party agreements."

2. Non-Compete Clauses: Protecting Your Market

If you're concerned about the licensee using your intellectual property in ways that might compete with your own business, a non-compete clause can help protect your market position. This clause restricts the licensee from using your work in ways that directly compete with your products or services, preventing them from undermining your brand or revenue.

How to use non-compete clauses effectively:

- **Define the scope**: Clearly define the scope of the non-compete clause. For example, the licensee may be restricted from using your work in certain industries, geographical regions, or product categories.

- **Specify duration**: State how long the non-compete clause will remain in effect. This is often tied to the duration of the licensing agreement but can also extend beyond the contract's expiration, depending on the circumstances.

- **Limit the competition**: The non-compete clause should be tailored to your specific needs. For example, if you're licensing a design to a fashion company, you might prevent them from using the design to create a competing line of products that could harm your existing business.

Example:

A graphic designer licenses a pattern to a fashion brand for use on clothing. The contract includes a non-compete clause stating, "The licensee may not use the licensed pattern or any variations thereof to create home decor products or accessories that directly compete with the licensor's existing product lines during the term of this agreement and for one year thereafter."

3. Confidentiality Clauses: Keeping Sensitive Information Secure

A confidentiality clause (also known as a non-disclosure agreement, or NDA) is important if you're sharing sensitive information with the licensee as part of the licensing deal. This clause prevents the licensee from disclosing proprietary information, trade secrets, or other confidential materials that you share with them during the course of the agreement.

What to include in a confidentiality clause:

- **Define confidential information**: Clearly state what constitutes confidential information, such as business plans, product designs, financial data, or customer lists.

- **Scope of confidentiality**: Specify how the confidential information can and cannot be used by the licensee. For example, the licensee may be allowed to use the information only for purposes directly related to the licensing agreement.

- **Duration of confidentiality**: State how long the confidentiality obligation will last. In some cases, it may continue even after the licensing agreement has ended to ensure long-term protection of sensitive information.

Example:

An author licenses the film rights to their novel to a production company. The confidentiality clause in the contract specifies, "The licensee agrees not to disclose any plot details, character designs, or other proprietary information provided by the licensor, except for purposes directly related to the development and production of the licensed film."

4. Breach of Contract Clauses: Defining Consequences for Non-Compliance

A breach of contract clause specifies what happens if either party fails to meet their obligations under the licensing agreement. This clause ensures that there are clear consequences if the licensee doesn't follow the terms of the contract, such as failing to pay royalties or using your work in unauthorized ways. By defining the consequences of a breach, you create a legal framework for resolving disputes or terminating the agreement.

Elements of a breach of contract clause:

- **Define the breach**: Clearly outline what constitutes a breach of the contract. This could include failure to make payments, unauthorized use of the work, or violation of any of the agreed-upon terms (such as sublicensing or modifying the work).

- **Notice and cure period**: Include a provision that requires the party in breach to be given written notice of the breach and a cure period (e.g., 30 days) to fix the issue before more serious consequences are triggered.

- **Consequences of breach**: Specify what will happen if the breach is not cured. This could include termination of the agreement, financial penalties, or legal action to recover damages.

Example:

A musician licenses a song to a film studio. The breach of contract clause states, "If the licensee fails to make royalty payments within 30 days of the due date or uses the song in unauthorized media, the licensor may terminate this agreement upon written notice. The licensee will have 15 days from receipt of notice to cure the breach. Failure to cure will result in immediate termination, and the licensee will be liable for any damages resulting from unauthorized use."

5. Termination Clauses: Managing the End of the Agreement

A termination clause allows both parties to end the licensing agreement under certain conditions. This clause should be carefully drafted to ensure that the termination process is clear, fair, and enforceable. Termination clauses are especially important if the licensee breaches the contract or if either party wants to exit the agreement early.

What to include in a termination clause:

- **Termination for cause**: Specify the circumstances under which either party can terminate the agreement "for cause," such as a material breach of the contract or failure to fulfill obligations.

- **Termination for convenience**: If you want the option to end the agreement without cause, include a "termination for convenience" clause. This allows either party to terminate the contract with a set notice period, such as 30 or 60 days.

- **Post-termination obligations**: Clearly state what happens after the contract is terminated. This might include the licensee ceasing all use of your work, returning any confidential information, and paying any outstanding royalties or fees.

Example:

A visual artist licenses a series of illustrations to a publishing company for use in a book. The termination clause states, "Either party may terminate this agreement for cause with 30 days written notice in the event of a material breach. Upon termination, the licensee must immediately cease all use of the illustrations and return any confidential materials provided by the licensor."

Conclusion: Safeguarding Your Licensing Agreement with Legal Protections

Incorporating legal protections into your licensing contract is essential for ensuring that your intellectual property is used appropriately and that you're shielded from potential risks. Indemnity clauses, non-compete agreements, confidentiality provisions, breach of contract terms, and termination clauses all serve as critical safeguards that protect your rights and set clear expectations for the licensee. By building these protections into your contract, you can confidently enter into licensing agreements that protect both your creative work and your business interests.

In the next section, we'll explore **escape clauses**, discussing how to handle breaches, disputes, and terminations effectively, ensuring that both parties can exit the agreement smoothly if needed.

Escape Clauses: Handling Breaches and Termination

In any licensing agreement, things may not always go as planned. Whether it's a breach of contract, changes in business needs, or unforeseen circumstances, having escape clauses in place ensures that both you and the licensee have a clear path to exit the agreement smoothly. These clauses provide mechanisms for handling disputes, breaches, and terminations, protecting your interests while maintaining a fair and professional relationship. In this section, we'll explore how to draft escape clauses that allow for flexibility while ensuring that your intellectual property remains protected.

1. Termination for Breach: Responding to Non-Compliance

A termination for breach clause allows you to end the agreement if the licensee fails to meet their contractual obligations. This clause is essential for protecting your rights and provides a clear process for addressing issues like non-payment, unauthorized use of your work, or other breaches of the agreement.

Key components of a termination for breach clause:

- **Define the breach**: Clearly outline what constitutes a breach of contract. Common breaches include failure to make payments, violating the terms of use, or unauthorized sublicensing.

- **Cure period**: Give the breaching party a specific time frame to remedy the breach after receiving written notice. For example, a 30-day cure period allows the licensee time to correct their actions before the contract is terminated.

- **Consequences of breach**: Specify what happens if the breach is not resolved within the cure period. This could include immediate termination of the agreement, payment of damages, or forfeiture of the licensed work.

Example:

A writer licenses an article to a website. The termination clause states, "In the event of a material breach, including failure to make payments or unauthorized modification of the work, the licensor may terminate the agreement upon 30 days written notice. If the breach is not cured within the notice period, the agreement will terminate, and the licensee will cease all use of the work."

2. Termination for Convenience: Ending the Agreement Early

Sometimes, either party may wish to end the licensing agreement for reasons that don't involve a breach of contract. A termination for convenience clause provides flexibility by allowing either party to terminate the agreement early, usually with a set notice period. This type of clause is particularly useful when business needs change or if the project is no longer viable.

How to draft a termination for convenience clause:

- **Notice period**: Specify the amount of notice required to terminate the contract for convenience. This is typically 30, 60, or 90 days, depending on the nature of the agreement.

- **Obligations upon termination**: Clearly state what both parties must do after the agreement is terminated. This may include stopping all use of the work, returning any confidential materials, or paying outstanding fees.

- **No penalties**: Ensure that there are no penalties or additional costs for terminating the contract early, as long as the notice period is followed.

Example:

An illustrator licenses a set of designs to a retail company for use on merchandise. The termination for convenience clause states, "Either party may terminate this agreement for any reason by providing 60 days written notice. Upon termination, the licensee will immediately cease production of merchandise featuring the designs and pay any outstanding royalties due to the licensor."

3. Force Majeure: Handling Unforeseen Circumstances

A force majeure clause protects both parties in the event of unforeseen circumstances that make it impossible to fulfill the terms of the contract. This clause typically covers events like natural disasters, government actions, or other significant disruptions that are beyond the control of either party. By including a force majeure clause, you ensure that neither party is held liable for failing to meet their obligations under extreme circumstances.

What to include in a force majeure clause:

- **Definition of force majeure events**: Clearly define what qualifies as a force majeure event. This could include natural disasters (e.g., earthquakes, floods), government actions (e.g., new regulations), labor strikes, or pandemics.

- **Effect on obligations**: Specify that the affected party is temporarily excused from fulfilling their obligations under the contract during the force majeure event.

- **Notice requirement**: Require the affected party to notify the other party in writing as soon as they become aware of the force majeure event. This allows both parties to plan accordingly and avoid misunderstandings.

Example:

A filmmaker licenses music for a documentary but encounters delays due to a government-mandated shutdown. The force majeure clause states, "Neither party shall be liable for failure to perform any obligations under this agreement due to events beyond their control, including but not limited to natural disasters, government actions, or pandemics. The affected party must notify the other party within 10 days of becoming aware of the event."

4. Dispute Resolution: Handling Conflicts Amicably

Disputes can arise even in well-drafted agreements, which is why a dispute resolution clause is essential. This clause outlines the process for resolving conflicts before they escalate to legal action. Common methods include mediation, arbitration, or negotiation. By including a dispute resolution clause, you can avoid lengthy and expensive court battles, while providing a clear path to settling disagreements.

Elements of a dispute resolution clause:

- **Method of resolution**: Specify how disputes will be resolved. Options include negotiation, where both parties work together to find a solution; mediation, where a neutral third party helps facilitate an agreement; or arbitration, where a neutral arbitrator makes a binding decision.

- **Location of dispute resolution**: Define where the dispute resolution process will take place (e.g., in a specific city or jurisdiction) to avoid confusion if both parties are in different locations.

- **Enforceability**: If arbitration is chosen, include a clause stating that the arbitrator's decision is final and enforceable in court.

Example:

A software developer licenses a program to a tech company. The dispute resolution clause states, "In the event of any dispute arising from this agreement, the parties agree to first attempt to resolve the matter through negotiation. If the dispute cannot be resolved within 30 days, the parties will submit to binding arbitration in the state of California. The arbitrator's decision shall be final and enforceable in a court of law."

5. Post-Termination Obligations: Ensuring a Clean Exit

Once a contract is terminated, either for breach or convenience, both parties still have certain post-termination obligations. These obligations ensure that the transition out of the agreement is smooth and that both parties fulfill any remaining duties, such as returning materials, stopping the use of licensed work, or settling any outstanding payments.

What to include in post-termination obligations:

- **Cessation of use**: State that the licensee must immediately stop using your intellectual property after the contract is terminated. If they continue using the work, this could result in legal action.

- **Return of materials**: Require the licensee to return any materials related to your intellectual property, such as digital files, prototypes, or confidential documents.

- **Outstanding payments**: Include a clause that requires the licensee to pay any outstanding fees or royalties within a specified time frame after termination.

Example:

An artist licenses a logo to a business for a specific product line. The post-termination obligations clause states, "Upon termination of this agreement, the licensee must immediately cease all use of the licensed logo and return all digital files related to the work. Any outstanding payments must be made within 30 days of termination."

Conclusion: Creating a Smooth Exit Strategy

Escape clauses are a critical part of any licensing agreement, providing clear paths for both parties to exit the contract if needed. Whether it's termination for breach, force majeure events, or dispute resolution, these clauses ensure that the agreement can be dissolved without unnecessary conflict or financial loss. By building in escape mechanisms, you protect your intellectual property and maintain control over how your work is used, even when the agreement ends.

In the next chapter, we'll explore real-world examples of successful licensing deals, showcasing how different types of contracts can lead to profitable and sustainable partnerships in various creative industries.

Quick Tips and Recap

- **Termination for Breach**: Clearly outline what constitutes a breach of contract and provide a cure period (e.g., 30 days) for the licensee to correct the issue before termination.

- **Termination for Convenience**: Allow either party to end the agreement early with a specific notice period (e.g., 30 or 60 days) to provide flexibility for changing business needs.

- **Force Majeure Clause**: Protect both parties from liability in cases of unforeseen events (e.g., natural disasters, government regulations) that prevent fulfillment of the contract.

- **Dispute Resolution**: Specify methods for resolving conflicts, such as negotiation, mediation, or arbitration, to avoid expensive legal disputes.

- **Post-Termination Obligations**: Ensure both parties know their responsibilities after termination, such as ceasing use of the licensed work, returning materials, and settling outstanding payments.

- **Cure Period for Breaches**: Establish a grace period (usually 30 days) for the breaching party to resolve any issues before the contract is terminated.

- **Notice Requirements**: Include clear notice requirements for termination, such as how and when each party should inform the other of the intention to end the agreement.

- **Return of Confidential Information**: Ensure that the licensee is required to return or destroy any confidential information shared during the contract upon termination.

- **Consequences for Continued Use**: Clarify what happens if the licensee continues to use the licensed work after termination, including legal consequences or financial penalties.

By including these essential escape clauses, your licensing agreements will be more flexible, enforceable, and prepared for any scenario, helping you protect your intellectual property and business interests.

Keeping Track: Managing Licensing Agreements

"Managing licensing agreements is like conducting an orchestra; each contract plays a different instrument, and it's your job to ensure they all harmonize to create a symphony of success." — ANNE WOJCICKI, CO-FOUNDER AND CEO OF 23ANDME

Chapter Thirteen, "Keeping Track: Managing Licensing Agreements," is akin to herding cats—if each cat were a critical legal document with a penchant for wandering off when least expected. Here, we delve into the glamorous world of ongoing management of licensing agreements, because the real fun begins after the ink dries.

In this chapter, we equip you with the strategies to monitor, enforce, and renew your licensing agreements. Think of it as setting up a surveillance system, but for paperwork. We'll show you how to keep your agreements working for you, not against you, with a keen eye on compliance, a steady hand on performance metrics, and a nifty trick or two for dealing with those pesky breaches.

Whether you're juggling two licenses or two hundred, this section will turn you from overwhelmed to overlord in the realm of contract management. By the end, you'll have the tools to not just keep track of every agreement but also ensure they're as profitable and hassle-free as they were intended to be. Get ready to whip your contracts into shape and keep them there—your business depends on it!

Organizing Your Agreements: Building a Contract Management System

Managing multiple licensing agreements can quickly become overwhelming if you don't have a structured system in place. Whether you're dealing with a few contracts or a large portfolio, having a reliable contract management system is crucial for keeping track of terms, deadlines, payments, and compliance. In this section, we'll explore the key steps to organizing your licensing agreements efficiently, using digital tools, contract management software, or even simple manual systems.

1. Centralize Your Contracts

The first step in building an effective contract management system is to centralize all of your licensing agreements. Having a single, easily accessible location for all contracts ensures that nothing gets lost, and it simplifies tracking multiple agreements at once. Whether you choose to use a digital solution or physical filing, the goal is to have everything in one place.

Options for centralizing contracts:

- **Digital storage**: Use cloud-based storage platforms like Google Drive, Dropbox, or OneDrive to store all your contracts in organized folders. Digital storage allows you to access contracts from anywhere, ensures backups, and makes it easier to share documents with legal or financial teams.

- **Contract management software**: For those managing a large number of agreements, contract management software (e.g., DocuSign,

PandaDoc, or ContractWorks) provides advanced features like automated reminders, digital signatures, and comprehensive tracking tools.

- **Physical filing systems**: If you prefer hard copies, set up a structured filing system with clearly labeled folders for each agreement. Organize contracts by client, project, or year to make retrieval quick and efficient.

Example:

A publishing company uses cloud-based storage to manage contracts with its authors. Each folder is labeled by author name and contains all related agreements, amendments, and correspondence. The system is accessible by the company's legal and finance teams, ensuring everyone is up to date on the terms of each contract.

2. Categorize Your Contracts

Once you've centralized your contracts, the next step is to categorize them in a way that makes it easy to manage specific types of agreements. Grouping contracts by key characteristics allows you to quickly locate and reference agreements based on their terms, deadlines, or parties involved.

Ways to categorize contracts:

- **Type of license**: Group contracts by the type of license (e.g., exclusive vs. non-exclusive, short-term vs. long-term). This helps you track which agreements grant more extensive rights and which ones are more limited.

- **Industry or sector**: If you work across multiple industries (e.g., publishing, media, fashion), create categories for each sector. This ensures that you can quickly access relevant agreements for a specific industry when needed.

- **Expiration dates**: Sort contracts based on expiration or renewal dates. This helps you stay on top of upcoming deadlines and ensure you're ready to renegotiate or renew agreements in a timely manner.

Example:

An artist categorizes their licensing contracts into three main groups: exclusive, non-exclusive, and temporary usage rights. They also use color-coded labels in their digital filing system to highlight contracts that are up for renewal within the next three months.

3. Use Templates and Standardized Forms

Creating contract templates and using standardized forms for common types of agreements can streamline the contract creation process and reduce errors. This is particularly useful if you're frequently negotiating similar types of deals, such as licensing agreements for artwork, music, or written content.

Benefits of using templates:

- **Consistency**: Using templates ensures that all contracts follow the same structure and include the necessary legal protections. This minimizes the risk of overlooking key clauses or terms.

- **Efficiency**: Templates save time by reducing the need to draft contracts from scratch each time. Instead, you can make minor adjustments to the template based on the specifics of the deal.

- **Customization**: Templates can be customized to fit the needs of individual agreements while maintaining a standardized framework. This allows you to easily adapt contracts for different clients or projects.

Example:
A musician who frequently licenses their tracks to filmmakers creates a standardized licensing agreement template. The template includes key clauses for royalty payments, usage rights, and duration, and can be quickly modified to suit each new deal.

4. Automate Key Deadlines and Reminders

Staying on top of contract deadlines is critical for ensuring compliance and maintaining control over your intellectual property. Missed deadlines, such as renewal dates or payment schedules, can result in lost revenue or the inadvertent extension of rights to a licensee. To avoid these issues, consider using automation tools to track important dates.

Tools for automating contract reminders:

- **Calendar tools**: Use digital calendars (e.g., Google Calendar, Outlook) to set reminders for key deadlines like contract renewals, payment due dates, or reporting requirements. Color-code these reminders based on priority.

- **Contract management software**: Many contract management platforms come with built-in features that automatically track deadlines and send reminders via email or SMS. These platforms often allow you to assign tasks to team members to ensure accountability.

- **Task management apps**: For a more lightweight solution, use task management apps like Trello, Asana, or Monday.com to create lists of contract deadlines and assign tasks related to compliance or follow-up actions.

Example:

A software developer uses contract management software to track their licensing agreements with multiple clients. The system automatically sends them email reminders 60 days before each contract is set to expire, allowing them ample time to renegotiate or terminate agreements as needed.

5. Maintain a Contract Summary or Dashboard

A contract summary or dashboard gives you a high-level overview of all your active agreements. This summary provides a snapshot of the key terms of each contract—such as parties involved, rights granted, payment terms, and renewal dates—allowing you to monitor your contracts at a glance. This is particularly useful if you're managing a large portfolio of agreements.

Key elements to include in a contract summary:

- **Parties involved**: List the names of the licensor and licensee, along with contact information.

- **Scope of the license**: Provide a brief summary of the rights granted in the contract (e.g., exclusive rights for digital media use).

- **Payment terms**: Include the payment structure, such as royalties or flat fees, and the schedule of payments.

- **Key dates**: Track the contract's start date, expiration date, and any renewal deadlines.

- **Special conditions**: Note any unique conditions or obligations in the agreement, such as marketing requirements or usage restrictions.

Example:

A publishing company maintains a contract dashboard in a spreadsheet format. Each row represents a contract, with columns summarizing the author's name, rights granted, royalty percentage, payment schedule, and expiration date. The dashboard helps the company stay organized and ensures they don't miss important deadlines.

Conclusion: Staying Organized and Efficient

A well-organized contract management system is essential for keeping track of your licensing agreements and ensuring that they continue to work for you long after they're signed. By centralizing your contracts, categorizing them, automating key reminders, and using contract summaries, you'll gain greater control over your portfolio, minimize the risk of missed deadlines, and streamline the ongoing management process.

In the next section, we'll explore how to monitor compliance with your licensing agreements to ensure that licensees adhere to the terms and conditions you've set, protecting your intellectual property and maximizing revenue.

Monitoring Compliance: Ensuring Licensees Adhere to Terms

After signing a licensing agreement, ensuring that the licensee adheres to the terms is critical to protect your intellectual property and ensure that the deal remains profitable. Monitoring compliance requires a proactive approach, from tracking how your work is being used to verifying that payments are made on time. This section will guide you through the steps needed to ensure that your licensees comply with the terms of the agreement, helping you to avoid potential breaches and maximize the value of your licensing contracts.

1. Regularly Review Licensee Activity

To ensure compliance, it's essential to regularly review how the licensee is using your intellectual property. This includes checking whether the work is being used according to the agreed-upon scope and conditions. Depending on the type of agreement, this might involve reviewing marketing materials, product designs, or even digital usage data to ensure that the licensee is following the rules.

How to review licensee activity:

- **Conduct audits**: Periodically review the licensee's use of your intellectual property. For example, if you've licensed a logo, check to see how it's being displayed in marketing campaigns or on products. If you've licensed software, request reports showing how many users have accessed it.

- **Set reporting requirements**: Include a clause in the licensing agreement that requires the licensee to provide regular reports on their use of the licensed work. For instance, they might need to submit quarterly updates on how your work is being used, including sales figures or distribution data.

- **Monitor online presence**: For digital media, regularly search for your licensed work on the internet, including social media, websites, or online stores. This can help you spot any unauthorized usage or violations of the agreement, such as improper attribution or exceeding the allowed usage limits.

Example:

An artist who licensed a series of illustrations to a home decor company conducts an annual audit of the company's product line to ensure the illustrations are only being used on products specified in the agreement. They also verify that proper credit is being given in product descriptions and marketing materials.

2. Track Payment and Royalties

One of the most important aspects of monitoring compliance is ensuring that the licensee is paying you on time and in the correct amounts. Royalty payments can be complex, especially when based on sales or revenue, so it's essential to have a system in place to track payments and verify that you're receiving the full amount owed.

Steps for tracking payments and royalties:

- **Request detailed royalty statements**: Include a clause in the contract requiring the licensee to provide detailed royalty reports, showing how payments are calculated. These reports should outline gross and net sales, deductions, and the final royalty amount.

- **Verify calculations**: Review the royalty statements to ensure that the calculations are accurate. This may involve cross-referencing the licensee's sales figures with your own records or conducting an independent audit if discrepancies arise.

- **Set payment reminders**: Use calendar tools or contract management software to set reminders for upcoming payment deadlines. This ensures that you're following up promptly if a payment is missed or delayed.

Example:

A musician who licenses their song to a streaming platform receives quarterly royalty reports from the platform. The musician cross-references the reported streaming numbers with publicly available data to ensure the payment calculations are accurate. If any discrepancies arise, they contact the platform's finance team for clarification.

3. Enforce Usage Restrictions

In many licensing agreements, you may impose restrictions on how the licensee can use your intellectual property. These restrictions may cover geographic regions, types of media, or even modifications to your work. To protect your rights, it's important to regularly check that the licensee is adhering to these usage restrictions.

How to enforce usage restrictions:

- **Check geographic boundaries**: If your agreement limits the licensee's use of your work to a specific territory (e.g., North America), monitor how your work is being distributed globally. This can involve tracking product sales, web traffic, or social media mentions to ensure that your work isn't being used outside the permitted region.

- **Limit media formats**: If you've restricted the licensee to using your work in specific formats (e.g., print, not digital), check that your work isn't being used outside the allowed mediums. This could involve checking online platforms, streaming services, or physical products.

- **Ensure no unauthorized modifications**: If the licensee is not permitted to modify or adapt your work, keep an eye on how your work is being presented. For example, you might want to ensure that a licensed logo isn't being altered in color or design without your approval.

Example:

A photographer who licensed an image to a travel company for use in print ads checks online advertisements and the company's website to verify that the image hasn't been used digitally, which would violate the licensing agreement. They also confirm that the image has not been altered in any way, such as through cropping or recoloring.

4. Conduct Compliance Audits

For more comprehensive monitoring, you can include a compliance audit clause in your licensing agreements. This clause gives you the right to audit the licensee's use of your work and their financial records to ensure full compliance with the agreement. Audits can be conducted periodically or in response to specific concerns, such as missing payments or unauthorized usage.

Elements of a compliance audit clause:

- **Audit frequency**: Specify how often you are entitled to conduct audits (e.g., annually or biannually). You may also allow for audits on-demand if you suspect a breach of the agreement.

- **Scope of the audit**: Define the areas of the licensee's business that are subject to the audit, such as sales records, distribution channels, or product designs.

- **Cost of the audit**: Typically, the licensor (you) bears the cost of the audit unless the audit reveals significant underpayments or breaches. In such cases, the licensee may be required to cover the cost of the audit.

Example:

A software developer includes a compliance audit clause in their licensing agreements, allowing them to audit the licensee's usage of the software and financial records annually. If the audit reveals that the licensee has underpaid royalties by more than 10%, the licensee is required to cover the audit costs.

5. Address Non-Compliance Quickly

When you identify non-compliance, it's important to address the issue promptly to avoid further breaches and protect your rights. Non-compliance can range from missed payments to unauthorized use of your work, and how you handle these issues can affect the relationship with the licensee and your legal position.

Steps for addressing non-compliance:

- **Send a written notice**: If you discover a breach, send a formal notice to the licensee outlining the specific issue and referencing the relevant clause in the licensing agreement. This notice should request that the breach be remedied within a set time frame (typically 30 days).

- **Offer an opportunity to cure**: Most licensing agreements include a cure period, giving the licensee time to correct the breach. If the issue is resolved within this time frame, the agreement continues as normal. However, if the breach is not cured, further action may be required.

- **Terminate the agreement if necessary**: If the licensee fails to remedy the breach, you may have the right to terminate the agreement. Be sure to follow the termination procedures outlined in the contract, and consult legal counsel if needed to protect your interests.

Example:

An author who licensed the film rights to their novel notices that the licensee has missed two royalty payments. The author sends a written notice to the licensee, referencing the payment terms in the contract and requesting that the overdue royalties be paid within 30 days. If the licensee fails to comply, the author may terminate the agreement and reclaim the film rights.

Conclusion: Staying on Top of Compliance

Monitoring compliance with your licensing agreements is an essential part of protecting your intellectual property and ensuring that licensees fulfill their obligations. By regularly reviewing the licensee's activities, tracking payments, enforcing usage restrictions, and conducting audits, you can safeguard your rights and maximize the value of your contracts. When non-compliance occurs, addressing it quickly and professionally helps maintain control over your work while protecting your legal interests.

In the next section, we'll explore tracking payments and royalties, covering how to set up efficient systems to ensure that you receive accurate and timely compensation for your licensed work.

Tracking Payments and Royalties: Keeping Finances in Check

One of the most critical aspects of managing licensing agreements is ensuring that payments, particularly royalties, are tracked and collected accurately. Whether you're receiving a one-time fee or ongoing royalty payments, having a solid system in place to manage finances is essential to maximizing the value of your agreements. In this section, we'll explore how to effectively track payments and royalties, ensuring that you receive your fair share on time, every time.

1. Set Clear Payment Terms in the Contract

The foundation of tracking payments and royalties starts with having clear, unambiguous payment terms in the licensing agreement. This ensures that both parties are on the same page regarding how and when payments should be made, leaving no room for misunderstandings.

Key elements of clear payment terms:

- **Payment schedule**: Specify whether payments are made upfront, on a recurring basis (e.g., quarterly, annually), or as royalties based on sales or usage. Include exact dates or time frames (e.g., "payment due on the 15th of each quarter").

- **Royalty rates**: Clearly define how royalties will be calculated—whether as a percentage of gross or net sales, or based on a fixed amount per unit sold or use. Be specific about any deductions, such as taxes, shipping, or returns, that will be factored into the calculation.

- **Payment method**: Specify how payments will be made (e.g., via bank transfer, check, or PayPal), ensuring that it's easy for both parties to comply with the terms.

Example:

A software developer licenses an application to a tech company, with the agreement stating, "Licensee agrees to pay a royalty of 5% of net sales on a quarterly basis, with payments due on the 15th of January, April, July, and October. Net sales are defined as gross sales minus taxes and shipping fees."

2. Implement a Royalty Tracking System

For agreements that involve ongoing royalties, it's essential to implement a royalty tracking system. This allows you to monitor sales data and payments, ensuring that royalties are calculated correctly and that you receive payments on time.

Options for tracking royalties:

- **Spreadsheets**: For smaller agreements or simple royalty structures, a spreadsheet can be a useful tool for tracking payments. Create a table that includes the royalty rate, total sales, deductions, and the final royalty amount. Be sure to update this regularly based on the reports provided by the licensee.

- **Royalty tracking software**: For more complex or large-scale agreements, consider using royalty management software (e.g., RoyaltyTracker, MetaComet) that automates the process. These platforms can track sales, calculate royalties, and generate reports, reducing the risk of manual errors.

- **Third-party royalty auditors**: If your licensing agreements involve significant sums or complex financial terms, you may want to hire a third-party auditor to ensure that the royalty calculations are accurate. Auditors can review sales data, payments, and contracts to verify that you're receiving the correct amount.

Example:

A musician uses royalty management software to track the performance of their songs on multiple streaming platforms. The software automatically pulls data from each platform, calculates royalties based on the agreed percentage, and generates quarterly reports for the musician to review.

3. Review Royalty Statements for Accuracy

Many licensing agreements require the licensee to provide detailed royalty statements, showing how payments are calculated. These statements should outline the total sales or usage, any deductions, and the resulting royalties owed. Reviewing these statements regularly is essential for catching any discrepancies or underpayments.

What to look for in royalty statements:

- **Sales or usage figures**: Verify that the reported sales or usage data matches your own expectations. If the numbers seem unusually low or high, investigate further to ensure accuracy.

- **Deductions**: Review any deductions (e.g., returns, taxes, marketing costs) to ensure they're in line with the terms of the agreement. Unjustified or excessive deductions can reduce your royalties.

- **Payment breakdown**: Ensure that the royalty rate is being applied correctly to the sales figures and that the final amount matches what is stated in the contract.

Example:

An author receives a royalty statement from their publisher showing 10,000 copies of their book sold during the last quarter. The statement includes deductions for returns and shipping costs, resulting in a final royalty payment. The author cross-references the sales figures with the publisher's sales reports to verify accuracy before accepting the payment.

4. Set Up Payment Tracking and Reminders

To avoid missed payments or late fees, it's important to have a payment tracking system in place that keeps you informed of when payments are due and when they've been received. This is especially important for ongoing royalty agreements where payments are made regularly.

How to track payments:

- **Use calendar reminders**: Set up calendar reminders or alerts in your email or task management system (e.g., Google Calendar, Outlook, Asana) to notify you of upcoming payment deadlines. This ensures that you're aware when payments are due and can follow up if they're missed.

- **Maintain a payment log**: Keep a log of all payments received, including the date, amount, and the corresponding royalty period. This helps you track which payments have been made and identify any outstanding amounts.

- **Follow up on late payments**: If a payment is missed, send a polite reminder to the licensee, referencing the terms of the agreement and requesting prompt payment. If payments continue to be delayed, consider enforcing penalties (as outlined in the contract) or seeking legal advice.

Example:

A visual artist sets up quarterly calendar reminders for when their licensing fees are due from a retail company. Each reminder prompts them to check their bank account for the payment and update their payment log with the details. If a payment is late, the artist follows up with a polite reminder email to the company's accounting department.

5. Conduct Regular Audits for High-Value Agreements

For high-value licensing agreements or those involving complex royalty structures, it's a good idea to conduct regular audits to ensure that payments are accurate and all financial terms are being followed. Audits can help you identify discrepancies, underpayments, or non-compliance with the contract's financial terms.

Steps for conducting audits:

- **Include an audit clause**: Your licensing agreement should include a clause that gives you the right to audit the licensee's financial records. Specify how often audits can occur (e.g., annually) and who bears the cost of the audit.

- **Review sales and royalty data**: During the audit, review all sales data, royalty calculations, and deductions. Verify that the licensee is following the payment terms outlined in the contract and that the reported figures match actual sales.

- **Address discrepancies**: If the audit reveals underpayments or discrepancies, notify the licensee and request that they correct the issue. Depending on the terms of the contract, the licensee may also be required to pay interest or penalties on late payments.

Example:
A fashion designer licenses their patterns to a large clothing retailer and includes an audit clause in the contract. Every year, the designer hires a financial auditor to review the retailer's sales data and royalty calculations, ensuring that the payments match the agreed terms. If the audit finds any discrepancies, the retailer is required to make up the difference.

6. Address Discrepancies Promptly

When discrepancies arise—whether it's a miscalculation in royalties or a late payment—it's important to address the issue promptly to maintain control over your licensing agreement. By acting quickly, you can prevent further issues and ensure that you're compensated fairly for your work.

How to address discrepancies:

- **Send a formal notice**: If you discover a payment discrepancy or underpayment, send a written notice to the licensee, outlining the specific issue and referencing the relevant clause in the agreement. Request that the discrepancy be resolved within a set time frame.

- **Offer a resolution**: In some cases, discrepancies may result from misunderstandings or clerical errors. If this is the case, offer a clear resolution, such as recalculating royalties or setting up a payment plan for overdue amounts.

- **Take legal action if necessary**: If the licensee refuses to resolve the issue or if underpayments continue, consult legal counsel to explore your options for enforcing the terms of the agreement or terminating the contract.

Example:

An author discovers that their publisher has underreported ebook sales for the past quarter, resulting in lower royalties. The author sends a formal notice to the publisher, requesting that the discrepancy be corrected within 30 days. The publisher acknowledges the error and agrees to make the necessary adjustments in the next royalty payment.

Conclusion: Staying on Top of Payments and Royalties

Effectively tracking payments and royalties is essential for ensuring that your licensing agreements remain profitable and that you're compensated fairly for your intellectual property. By setting clear payment terms, implementing tracking systems, reviewing royalty statements, and addressing discrepancies promptly, you can maintain control over your finances and avoid potential issues. Regular audits and proactive communication with licensees also ensure that payments are accurate and on time, giving you peace of mind as you manage your agreements.

In the next section, we'll cover renewals, amendments, and terminations, providing strategies for managing the contract lifecycle and ensuring that your agreements evolve with your business needs.

Renewals, Amendments, and Terminations: Managing the Contract Lifecycle

As part of effectively managing your licensing agreements, understanding how to navigate renewals, amendments, and terminations is crucial. Each of these stages in the contract lifecycle requires careful attention to ensure that your interests are protected and that the agreement continues to align with your evolving business goals. In this section, we'll explore strategies for managing these key aspects of your contracts, helping you stay in control of your licensing deals.

1. Managing Contract Renewals

Many licensing agreements include a **renewal option**, which allows the licensee to extend the contract beyond its initial term. Renewals can be automatic or require renegotiation, depending on the agreement's terms. Managing renewals effectively ensures that the contract continues to benefit both parties while giving you the opportunity to reassess the terms.

Key considerations for contract renewals:

- **Automatic vs. negotiated renewals**: Some contracts include automatic renewal clauses, meaning the contract renews for another term unless either party opts to terminate. In other cases, the agreement requires negotiation before renewal, allowing you to adjust terms such as payment rates, scope of use, or territory.

- **Review performance before renewal**: Before agreeing to renew a contract, review the licensee's performance during the initial term. Consider factors like payment history, compliance with the agreement, and overall value. If the licensee has met their obligations and the deal remains profitable, renewal may be a good option.

- **Renegotiate if necessary**: When renewing an agreement, it's a good opportunity to revisit the terms. If your work has increased in value or if market conditions have changed, consider renegotiating key terms such as royalty rates, usage restrictions, or geographic scope.

Example:

An author's contract with a publishing company is up for renewal. Before agreeing to an automatic renewal, the author reviews the publisher's payment history and marketing efforts. The author decides to renegotiate the royalty rate based on increased book sales and secures a higher percentage for the new term.

2. Handling Amendments

Over time, the terms of a licensing agreement may need to be modified to reflect changing circumstances or new business goals. Amendments allow you to adjust specific clauses without needing to terminate the entire agreement. However, it's essential to handle amendments carefully to avoid misunderstandings or unintended consequences.

Steps for managing contract amendments:

- **Identify the need for amendment**: Common reasons for amending a contract include expanding the license to cover new uses or territories, adjusting royalty rates, or changing the duration of the agreement. Discuss these changes with the licensee and ensure that both parties are in agreement before proceeding.

- **Document all changes**: Any amendments to the contract must be documented in writing and signed by both parties. Verbal agreements or informal modifications can lead to confusion and may not be enforceable. Use clear, precise language when drafting amendments to avoid ambiguity.

- **Ensure amendments are consistent with the original agreement**: When adding or modifying terms, review the entire contract to ensure the amendment aligns with the existing clauses. This helps prevent conflicting terms and ensures that the agreement remains legally sound.

Example:

A visual artist licenses an illustration to a magazine for print use but later agrees to allow the magazine to use the illustration in its online edition. The artist and the magazine draft a formal amendment that expands the usage rights to include digital media, with an updated payment structure to reflect the additional use.

3. Planning for Contract Terminations

At some point, you may decide to terminate a licensing agreement, either because the contract has run its course or due to a breach by the licensee. Understanding how to manage terminations is essential for protecting your intellectual property and ensuring a smooth transition.

Types of contract termination:

- **Termination for cause**: This occurs when one party breaches the terms of the contract, such as failing to make payments or using the licensed work outside the agreed-upon scope. In this case, you must provide written notice of the breach and give the licensee a specified period to remedy the issue (the cure period). If the breach is not resolved, you have the right to terminate the agreement.

- **Termination for convenience**: Some agreements allow for termination for convenience, meaning either party can end the contract without cause, typically by providing written notice within a specified time frame (e.g., 30 or 60 days). This offers flexibility if business goals change or if the agreement is no longer beneficial.

- **End-of-term termination**: When a licensing agreement reaches its expiration date, both parties may choose not to renew. In this case, the contract is terminated according to its natural timeline, and the licensee must stop using the licensed work.

Steps for managing terminations:

- **Follow the termination procedure**: Whether terminating for cause or convenience, follow the procedure outlined in the contract, including providing proper notice and adhering to any cure periods.

- **Reclaim your intellectual property**: Upon termination, the licensee must stop using your intellectual property and return or destroy any materials related to the work. Make sure to enforce this clause to protect your rights and prevent unauthorized use after the agreement ends.

- **Settle outstanding payments**: Before terminating the agreement, ensure that all payments, including royalties or fees, have been made. If the licensee has missed payments, request that they settle these amounts before the contract is formally terminated.

Example:

A photographer licenses a series of images to a travel company, but after repeated late payments, the photographer decides to terminate the agreement for cause. The photographer sends written notice to the company, giving them 30 days to resolve the payment issue. When the company fails to comply, the photographer terminates the contract and reclaims the rights to the images.

4. Preparing for Post-Termination Obligations

After a contract is terminated, both parties have certain post-termination obligations. These obligations help ensure a clean break and protect your intellectual property from further use. Failing to manage these obligations can lead to ongoing disputes or unauthorized use of your work.

Key post-termination obligations:

- **Cessation of use**: The licensee must immediately stop using your intellectual property upon termination, whether the contract ends naturally or due to a breach. This includes removing the work from any products, websites, or marketing materials.

- **Return or destruction of materials**: If the licensee holds any physical or digital materials related to your work, such as master files or promotional assets, the contract should require them to return or destroy these materials upon termination.

- **Final payments**: Ensure that any outstanding payments, such as royalties or licensing fees, are settled before the contract is fully terminated. This prevents financial disputes and ensures that you've been properly compensated for the duration of the agreement.

Example:

An author terminates a licensing agreement with an audiobook producer. The contract requires the producer to stop selling the audiobook and to destroy all digital copies within 30 days of termination. The author also ensures that all outstanding royalties are paid before the termination is finalized.

Conclusion: Navigating the Contract Lifecycle with Confidence

Effectively managing renewals, amendments, and terminations ensures that your licensing agreements continue to serve your best interests. By proactively handling renewals, negotiating amendments when necessary, and preparing for smooth terminations, you can protect your intellectual property and maintain control over how your work is used. A well-managed contract lifecycle helps you adapt to changing business needs while ensuring that you remain in the driver's seat throughout the life of the agreement.

In the next chapter, we'll explore best practices for enforcing your rights when a licensee breaches the agreement or violates your intellectual property, helping you safeguard your creative work and navigate legal challenges.

Quick Tips and Recap

- **Plan for Renewals**: Review the licensee's performance before renewing a contract. If necessary, renegotiate key terms like payment rates, scope of use, or duration to better reflect the current value of your work.

- **Handle Amendments Carefully**: Document all changes in writing, ensuring that both parties sign the amendment. Make sure amendments align with the original contract to prevent conflicts or confusion.

- **Prepare for Termination**: Whether terminating for cause or convenience, follow the termination procedures outlined in the contract, including providing proper notice and enforcing any cure periods.

- **Reclaim Your Intellectual Property**: Upon termination, ensure the licensee stops using your work immediately and returns or destroys any related materials to prevent unauthorized use.

- **Track Outstanding Payments**: Before terminating an agreement, confirm that all royalty payments and fees have been settled to avoid financial disputes after the contract ends.

- **Review Renewal Clauses Early**: Start reviewing contracts several months before they expire to give yourself time to renegotiate or terminate if necessary.

- **Monitor Licensee Compliance**: Ensure that the licensee adheres to any post-termination obligations, such as stopping the use of your intellectual property and removing it from products or marketing.

- **Enforce Post-Termination Obligations**: After termination, verify that the licensee has complied with the agreement by ceasing all use of your work and settling any final payments.

By managing renewals, amendments, and terminations effectively, you can stay in control of your licensing agreements, ensure they continue to serve your business interests, and protect your intellectual property throughout the contract lifecycle.

Cash In on Creativity: Royalties and Revenue Models

"Royalties are not just a revenue stream; they're a recognition of your creativity's worth. Mastering them ensures your art sustains both your soul and your livelihood." — BEYONCÉ, SINGER-SONGWRITER AND BUSINESSWOMAN

Chapter Fourteen, "Cash In on Creativity: Royalties and Revenue Models," is where your creativity meets its payday. In this exhilarating chapter, we break down the seemingly cryptic world of royalties into bite-sized, bankable delights. It's time to turn those artistic strokes, literary plots, and musical hooks into cold, hard cash.

Think of royalties as the golden geese of the creative world. Here, we'll teach you how to nurture them, from understanding different royalty structures to negotiating rates that make your wallet as happy as your heart. We'll explore a smorgasbord of revenue models, each tailored to squeeze the most juice out of every copyright, license, and deal you ink.

Whether you're a lone artist or a bustling creative enterprise, this chapter will arm you with the know-how to ensure that every ounce of your creativity is not just recognized, but also richly rewarded. Get ready to roll up your sleeves and dive into the nuts and bolts of turning your creative outputs into steady income streams. It's not just about making art—it's about making a living.

Types of Royalties: Breaking Down the Revenue Streams

Understanding the different types of royalties is key to maximizing your earnings as a creator. Royalties are payments you receive for allowing someone else to use your work, and they come in various forms depending on the type of creative output. In this section, we'll break down the major types of royalties, explaining how each works and how they can contribute to your overall revenue stream.

1. Mechanical Royalties: Earnings from Music Reproduction

Mechanical royalties are payments to songwriters and music publishers for the reproduction of their music. These royalties are earned whenever a song is reproduced in a physical format (like CDs or vinyl) or distributed digitally through streaming services and downloads.

How mechanical royalties are generated:

- **Physical media**: When a song is pressed onto physical formats such as CDs, vinyl records, or cassette tapes, the creator earns a royalty for each copy produced.

- **Digital downloads and streaming**: Mechanical royalties are also earned when music is downloaded from platforms like iTunes or streamed on services like Spotify, Apple Music, and Pandora.

Example:

A songwriter earns mechanical royalties every time their song is streamed on Spotify or purchased as a digital download. These payments are typically collected through a music rights organization like the Harry Fox Agency.

2. Performance Royalties: Payments for Public Use

Performance royalties are earned whenever your work is performed publicly. For music creators, this includes radio plays, live performances, and TV broadcasts. For writers and other creators, public performances can include staged readings, theater productions, or public screenings of films.

Where performance royalties come from:

- **Broadcast and live performances**: Songwriters and composers earn performance royalties when their songs are played on the radio, during live concerts, or in public venues like restaurants and clubs.

- **Television and film**: If your music or written work is used in a TV show, movie, or advertisement, performance royalties are paid every time it's broadcasted to the public.

- **Streaming services**: Similar to mechanical royalties, performance royalties are also generated through streaming platforms when your work is made available for public consumption.

Example:

A composer who writes the score for a television show earns performance royalties every time the show airs. These royalties are collected by performance rights organizations (PROs) such as ASCAP, BMI, or SESAC.

3. Licensing Royalties: Compensation for Intellectual Property Use

Licensing royalties are earned when you grant another party the right to use your intellectual property in a specific way. This could involve allowing your work to be featured in films, commercials, or merchandise. Licensing royalties are often negotiated as part of a broader agreement, where you license your work for a limited time or specific use.

Examples of licensing royalties:

- **Music licensing**: Artists can license their songs for use in commercials, video games, or movies. In exchange, they earn royalties based on how often the work is used and how widespread the distribution is.

- **Visual art and photography**: Artists can license their designs or photographs to companies for use in advertising campaigns, product packaging, or even as part of fashion lines. Licensing agreements usually specify the usage rights, territory, and duration, with royalties paid accordingly.

- **Literary and film licensing**: Writers and filmmakers can license their works to be adapted for stage plays, movies, or television series, earning royalties based on box office revenue, ticket sales, or distribution.

Example:

A photographer licenses an image to a travel company for use in a global ad campaign. The licensing agreement stipulates that the photographer will receive a percentage of the company's profits from the ad, or a flat fee based on usage and territory.

4. Print Royalties: Income from Publishing

Print royalties apply primarily to authors and illustrators, who earn these royalties from the sale of their published works, such as books, magazines, or graphic novels. These royalties are typically paid based on the number of copies sold or distributed, and are negotiated as part of a publishing contract.

How print royalties are calculated:

- **Percentage of sales**: Most print royalties are paid as a percentage of the sale price of each book or publication. The exact percentage depends on the publishing deal but can range from 5% to 15% for traditional book publishing.

- **Advance against royalties**: In some publishing agreements, authors receive an advance payment upfront. Once the book is published, royalties are earned once the advance has been recouped through sales.

Example:

An author who signs a book deal with a major publishing house might receive a 10% royalty on each book sold. If the book sells for $20, the author would earn $2 per copy sold, minus any advance that was initially paid.

5. Resale Royalties: Ongoing Income from Secondary Markets

Resale royalties (sometimes known as droit de suite) are earned when your work is sold again in the secondary market. This is most common for visual artists whose works are resold at auction or through galleries. Resale royalties ensure that creators continue to earn revenue from the appreciation of their work's value over time.

Where resale royalties apply:

- **Art auctions and galleries**: In many countries, visual artists are entitled to a percentage of the resale price when their work is sold at auction or by a gallery. This allows artists to benefit from the increased value of their work over time, especially if they become more well-known.

- **Other intellectual property**: Some industries, such as software and design, also have provisions for resale royalties, where creators earn revenue when their work is resold or repurposed in different formats or mediums.

Example:

A painter who sold a piece to a private collector for $5,000 may later earn resale royalties when the piece is resold at auction for $50,000, ensuring they benefit from the artwork's increased market value.

Conclusion: Maximizing Revenue Through Diverse Royalty Streams

Understanding the different types of royalties is crucial to maximizing your revenue as a creator. Each royalty stream offers unique opportunities to monetize your work across various platforms and industries. By tapping into mechanical, performance, licensing, print, and resale royalties, you can create a diverse and sustainable income model that ensures your creative output generates ongoing returns.

In the next section, we'll explore revenue models and help you choose the right strategy for your work, ensuring that you not only earn royalties but optimize your overall income potential.

Revenue Models: Choosing the Right Strategy for Your Work

Selecting the appropriate revenue model for your creative work can significantly impact how much you earn and how consistently you generate income. Whether you're a musician, author, visual artist, or filmmaker, choosing the right revenue strategy allows you to maximize your earnings and reach the right audience. In this section, we'll explore a variety of revenue models, breaking down the advantages of each and helping you decide which approach fits your creative business best.

1. Flat Fees: One-Time Payments for Immediate Cash

The flat fee model involves charging a single, upfront payment for the use of your work. This approach can be beneficial if you want to secure guaranteed income without relying on long-term performance or sales data. Flat fees are often used in situations where the usage of your work is limited in scope or duration, such as in advertisements, short-term licenses, or commissioned projects.

Advantages of flat fees:

- **Immediate payout**: You receive a lump sum payment, which can be helpful for covering immediate expenses or funding your next creative project.

- **No dependency on sales**: Your income isn't dependent on how well the work performs after the deal is signed, reducing uncertainty.

- **Simplicity**: Flat fee agreements tend to be simpler to negotiate and manage compared to royalty-based models.

When to use a flat fee model:

- For one-time uses of your work (e.g., a photo in a single advertising campaign).

- For short-term projects where the scope of use is limited.

- When you prefer upfront payment without depending on ongoing performance.

Example:

A filmmaker licenses a short clip to a TV network for a flat fee of $5,000, with no further obligations or payments. This ensures immediate cash flow, while the network has the right to use the clip for the duration of the campaign.

2. Percentage-Based Royalties: Earning a Share of Sales

Percentage-based royalties are one of the most common revenue models for creative work. In this model, you earn a percentage of sales or revenue generated from your work. This approach is especially popular in industries like music, publishing, and licensing, where your earnings scale with the success of the product or project.

Advantages of percentage-based royalties:

- **Scalability**: As the product or project becomes more successful, your earnings increase proportionally.

- **Long-term income**: You can continue earning royalties for years as long as the work remains in use, offering passive income opportunities.

- **Potential for higher earnings**: If the product or project performs well, your total income can far exceed a flat fee model.

When to use a percentage-based royalty model:

- For creative works that have the potential for high sales volume or long-term use (e.g., books, songs, or films).

- When you believe in the future success of the project and want to share in the upside.

- For collaborations where the success of the work depends on factors outside your control (e.g., publishing a book with a major publisher).

Example:

An author negotiates a 10% royalty on the sale of each copy of their book. If the book sells for $20, the author earns $2 per sale. As the book gains popularity, the author's earnings scale with the number of copies sold.

3. Subscription Models: Recurring Revenue for Ongoing Access

The subscription model is becoming increasingly popular for digital content creators, especially in music, publishing, and online platforms. With a subscription model, customers pay a recurring fee (monthly or yearly) for ongoing access to your work, whether it's streaming music, access to articles, or membership to an exclusive creative community.

Advantages of subscription models:

- **Predictable income**: Subscription models provide consistent, recurring revenue, making it easier to plan your finances.

- **Customer loyalty**: Subscribers often remain loyal over time, giving you a dedicated audience and a reliable revenue base.

- **Flexibility**: You can offer tiered subscriptions, providing access to different levels of content, from basic to premium offerings, which helps diversify your income streams.

When to use a subscription model:

- For digital creators who produce regular content (e.g., musicians, writers, bloggers).

- For creatives looking to build a loyal, ongoing customer base.

- For those offering exclusive or premium content to fans (e.g., behind-the-scenes footage, early access to music or chapters).

Example:

A musician launches a subscription service where fans pay $10 per month for early access to new songs, exclusive behind-the-scenes videos, and digital downloads. This model provides the musician with a steady monthly income while rewarding their most loyal fans.

4. Freemium and Ad-Supported Models: Maximizing Reach While Earning from Advertisers

The freemium and ad-supported models are commonly used by digital content creators and platforms. In a freemium model, the base product is offered for free, with optional premium content or features available for purchase. The ad-supported model involves offering your work for free or at a reduced cost, while earning revenue through advertising.

Advantages of freemium and ad-supported models:

- **Wider reach**: Offering free content allows you to attract a larger audience, which can later be monetized through ads or upselling to premium content.

- **Low entry barrier for users**: Users are more likely to engage with free content, increasing your overall exposure and potential customer base.

- **Advertising revenue**: For creators with a large audience, ad-supported models can generate significant income through ads on websites, videos, or podcasts.

When to use a freemium or ad-supported model:

- When your primary goal is to grow your audience quickly and monetize through upsells or ads.

- For content that can be easily segmented into free and premium tiers (e.g., apps, software, or online courses).

- For creators in industries where advertising partnerships are readily available (e.g., YouTube creators, bloggers).

Example:

A podcaster offers free episodes supported by advertising. Additionally, listeners can pay for a premium subscription to access ad-free episodes and bonus content. This dual revenue model allows the podcaster to monetize both free users and paying subscribers.

5. Licensing and Merchandising: Expanding Income Beyond the Original Work

Licensing and merchandising offer a way to extend the life of your creative work and generate revenue through additional products or formats. Licensing involves granting another party the right to use your work in exchange for royalties, while merchandising refers to selling products based on your creative output (e.g., branded merchandise, prints, or spin-off products).

Advantages of licensing and merchandising:

- **New revenue streams**: Licensing and merchandising allow you to monetize your work in new ways, often through minimal additional effort.

- **Broad reach**: Licensing your work to other platforms or markets helps you reach a wider audience without direct involvement in distribution.

- **Brand extension**: Merchandising turns your creative work into a brand, allowing you to sell related products (e.g., t-shirts, posters, or collectibles).

When to use licensing and merchandising:

- When your work has strong brand potential or fan appeal (e.g., popular films, books, or artwork).

- For creators looking to diversify their income by partnering with brands or creating physical products.

- When you want to reach new audiences or markets through collaborative deals.

Example:

A comic book artist licenses their characters to a toy manufacturer, receiving royalties from the sale of action figures. At the same time, the artist sells branded merchandise (e.g., t-shirts and posters) through their own online store.

Conclusion: Choosing the Right Revenue Model for Your Work

Selecting the right revenue model depends on the nature of your creative work, your goals, and the potential for ongoing income. Whether you prefer the simplicity of flat fees, the scalability of percentage-based royalties, or the consistency of subscription models, the key is to align your strategy with your long-term vision. By combining different revenue models, such as licensing, merchandising, and ad-supported content, you can diversify your income streams and create a sustainable financial foundation for your creative business.

In the next section, we'll dive into negotiating royalty rates and share tips on how to secure the best deals for your work, ensuring that your creativity is properly compensated.

Negotiating Royalty Rates: Securing the Best Deal

Negotiating the best royalty rates is crucial to ensuring that your creative work is fairly compensated. Whether you're licensing music, art, writing, or other intellectual property, the negotiation process directly impacts your long-term earnings. In this section, we'll explore strategies for successfully negotiating royalty rates, giving you the tools to secure a deal that reflects the true value of your work.

1. Understand the Industry Standards

Before entering any negotiation, it's essential to have a clear understanding of industry standard royalty rates. Different industries have widely varying expectations, and knowing these benchmarks will help you establish a fair starting point for negotiations. Research the standard rates for your specific field— whether it's publishing, music, visual arts, or software licensing—to better gauge the market.

Common industry royalty standards:

- **Book publishing**: Authors typically earn between 5% and 15% of the retail price for print books and 25% for ebooks. Self-publishing platforms may offer different terms, with higher royalties (up to 70%) on digital sales.

- **Music industry**: Songwriters and music publishers often receive mechanical royalties in the range of 9-12 cents per song reproduction, while streaming platforms offer lower per-play rates. Performance royalties are also paid via rights organizations like ASCAP and BMI, with varying rates depending on usage.

- **Visual arts**: Licensing artwork for use in advertising, merchandise, or products usually involves a flat fee or royalty based on sales, typically ranging from 5% to 15%.

Example:

An author negotiating a book deal with a traditional publisher may aim for a 10% royalty on print book sales, but may push for a higher rate on ebook sales, understanding that industry standards are often higher for digital formats.

2. Know Your Work's Value

Understanding your work's unique value is critical to negotiating effectively. This goes beyond industry benchmarks and takes into account factors like your reputation, the demand for your work, and the scope of the project. If your work has a proven track record of success or a dedicated fanbase, you may be able to justify higher royalty rates.

Factors that impact the value of your work:

- **Past success**: If you've had successful past projects, such as a best-selling book, popular artwork, or hit songs, you can leverage this success to negotiate higher royalty rates.

- **Market demand**: High-demand works, such as popular themes or genres, often command higher rates. For example, a song used in a blockbuster film might justify a larger royalty share than one used in a smaller, niche project.

- **Brand strength**: If you've built a strong personal brand or a loyal following, your work becomes more valuable to potential licensees. The more recognizable and marketable your work, the more leverage you have in negotiations.

Example:

A visual artist with a large online following may negotiate a higher royalty rate for a licensing deal with a fashion brand, knowing that their name and reputation will help drive sales of the products featuring their artwork.

3. Consider Flat Fees vs. Royalties

Depending on the project, you may be offered either a flat fee or a royalty-based deal. Flat fees offer immediate income without any dependency on the project's performance, while royalty deals provide ongoing payments based on sales or usage. In some cases, you may be able to negotiate a hybrid approach, combining both a flat fee and a royalty rate to secure the best of both worlds.

When to push for royalties:

- **Long-term projects**: If you believe the project has the potential for high sales over time, a royalty-based deal will likely provide better long-term earnings.

- **Limited upfront budget**: If the licensee has a limited budget but expects high performance, a royalty deal allows you to share in the success of the project as it grows.

When to choose a flat fee:

- **Short-term or one-time use**: For projects with limited scope or one-time use (e.g., a single commercial campaign), a flat fee can provide immediate, guaranteed income.

- **Uncertain performance**: If you're unsure about the project's commercial viability or sales potential, a flat fee may provide more security than a royalty-based deal.

Example:

A photographer licensing an image for a local advertising campaign might opt for a flat fee due to the limited scope of the project. However, if the same image is licensed for a global brand's digital campaign, the photographer might negotiate a combination of a flat fee plus royalties based on online impressions.

4. Negotiate for Escalating Royalties

An effective way to increase your earnings over time is to negotiate for escalating royalties. This structure allows your royalty rate to increase as sales or usage of your work reach certain thresholds. Escalating royalties incentivize the licensee to promote and distribute your work more widely, knowing that both parties will benefit from the success.

How escalating royalties work:

- **Tiered royalty rates**: You start with a base royalty rate, which increases once sales or revenue surpass a predetermined amount. For example, you might negotiate an 8% royalty for the first 10,000 units sold, which escalates to 10% for sales beyond that point.

- **Milestones and bonuses**: In addition to escalating royalties, you can negotiate performance-based bonuses. These bonuses are paid when the project reaches certain milestones, such as hitting a sales target or winning a major award.

Example:
An author negotiating a book deal could start with a 7% royalty on the first 5,000 copies sold, escalating to 10% for sales beyond that threshold. This incentivizes the publisher to invest more in marketing and distribution as sales increase.

5. Protect Your Interests with a Minimum Guarantee

When negotiating royalty rates, consider including a minimum guarantee clause in the agreement. A minimum guarantee ensures that, regardless of how the project performs, you will receive a set amount of payment. This is particularly useful when you're licensing your work for use in high-visibility projects or with companies that have uncertain sales projections.

Benefits of minimum guarantees:

- **Risk reduction**: A minimum guarantee protects you from poor project performance, ensuring that you earn a baseline income even if royalties fall short.

- **Leverage for higher rates**: Negotiating a minimum guarantee demonstrates confidence in the value of your work, which can help you secure a higher royalty rate or additional compensation.

Example:

A musician licensing their song for a film might negotiate a minimum guarantee of $10,000, regardless of how many copies of the soundtrack are sold. This ensures that the musician is compensated fairly even if the film's performance is less than expected.

6. Factor in Exclusivity and Territory

The exclusivity and territory of the licensing agreement can have a significant impact on your royalty rate. Exclusive deals, where the licensee is the only party allowed to use your work, often command higher rates than non-exclusive agreements. Similarly, if the license covers a large territory (e.g., global rights), the royalty rate should reflect the broader scope of use.

Negotiating exclusivity and territory:

- **Exclusive vs. non-exclusive**: Exclusive licenses typically come with higher royalty rates because you're limiting your ability to license the work to others. If the license is non-exclusive, you may be able to negotiate a lower rate but retain the right to license the work to other parties.

- **Territorial rights**: If the licensee is seeking rights to distribute your work globally, be sure the royalty rate reflects the increased exposure and potential revenue from multiple markets. You can also negotiate different rates for different territories.

Example:

A designer licenses a pattern to a clothing brand for exclusive use in North America. In return, the designer negotiates a higher royalty rate, knowing that they cannot license the same pattern to another company in that region.

Conclusion: Securing the Best Royalty Deal

Negotiating royalty rates requires a careful balance between understanding industry standards, recognizing the unique value of your work, and being strategic about the terms of the deal. By researching typical rates, considering factors like exclusivity and territory, and pushing for terms like escalating royalties or minimum guarantees, you can secure a deal that maximizes your earnings while protecting your creative rights.

In the next section, we'll discuss tracking and auditing royalties, giving you the tools to ensure that you receive accurate payments and stay on top of your earnings.

Tracking and Auditing Royalties: Ensuring You Get Paid

After successfully negotiating a royalty deal, the next critical step is making sure you actually receive the payments you've earned. Tracking and auditing royalties is essential for ensuring that your work is properly monetized and that you're compensated according to the terms of your contract. In this section, we'll explore how to effectively track royalties and conduct audits to verify that everything is accurate and transparent.

1. Set Up Clear Reporting Requirements

One of the most important things you can do to stay on top of your royalty income is to establish clear reporting requirements in your licensing agreements. These requirements should outline how and when the licensee will report royalties, sales figures, and any other data relevant to your earnings.

Key elements of royalty reporting:

- **Frequency of reports**: Specify how often the licensee must provide royalty reports (e.g., quarterly, biannually, or annually). Regular reports help you keep track of income and address any discrepancies before they become larger issues.

- **Detailed breakdown**: Require that the royalty report includes detailed information, such as units sold, price per unit, deductions (e.g., taxes or returns), and the total royalty amount. This transparency ensures you can cross-reference the data with any independent metrics you have.

- **Payment deadlines**: Make sure the agreement specifies when royalty payments are due, and ensure that payments are tied to the delivery of reports. Late payments can be addressed with penalty clauses, if necessary.

Example:

A musician includes a clause in their licensing agreement that requires the licensee to provide quarterly royalty reports, showing the number of streams and downloads for each song, the revenue generated, and the final royalty amount due. Payments must be made within 30 days of the report being issued.

2. Use Digital Tools to Track Royalties

Manually tracking royalties can become time-consuming, especially if you're dealing with multiple licensing agreements or platforms. Fortunately, there are various digital tools and software solutions that can help automate this process, making it easier to manage your earnings.

Recommended royalty tracking tools:

- **Spreadsheets**: For smaller-scale operations, a well-organized spreadsheet can be an effective way to track your royalties. Create columns for key data points such as sales, royalty percentages, and payment dates.

- **Royalty tracking software**: For larger or more complex deals, royalty management software (e.g., MetaComet, Royalty Exchange) can automate much of the tracking process. These platforms can generate reports, calculate royalties, and send alerts for missed payments.

- **Third-party platforms**: For musicians, authors, and other creators, platforms like TuneCore, CD Baby, and Amazon KDP provide built-in royalty tracking and reporting, making it easier to monitor income from various sources.

Example:

An author uses a royalty management platform to automatically track ebook sales across multiple online stores. The software generates detailed reports that show how many copies were sold on each platform and calculates the total royalties owed, helping the author stay on top of their earnings.

3. Compare Reports with Independent Data

To ensure the accuracy of the royalty reports you receive, it's important to cross-check them with independent data sources whenever possible. For example, if your work is available on a public platform (such as a streaming service, retail website, or app store), you can often access sales data or performance metrics directly. Comparing this data with the licensee's reports allows you to verify that the numbers match and that you're being paid correctly.

Ways to cross-check royalty data:

- **Streaming platforms**: If your music is streamed on platforms like Spotify or Apple Music, compare the royalty reports with the publicly available play counts or streaming data. Any significant discrepancies should be investigated.

- **Sales figures**: For physical products, check the licensee's sales figures against publicly available sales rankings or retailer data to ensure consistency.

- **Direct reports**: For digital products, such as apps or ebooks, platforms like Amazon or Apple may provide direct sales reports. Use these reports to verify that the licensee is reporting sales accurately.

Example:

A photographer licenses a series of images for use in an online gallery. The photographer cross-checks the licensee's quarterly royalty reports with the number of image downloads listed on the website's public analytics page. When discrepancies are found, the photographer contacts the licensee for clarification.

4. Conduct Royalty Audits

Even with detailed reports and tracking systems in place, mistakes or discrepancies can still occur. A royalty audit allows you to review the licensee's financial records to ensure that royalties are being calculated and paid correctly. Audits can be conducted periodically or in response to specific concerns about underpayment or misreporting.

Steps to conducting a royalty audit:

- **Include an audit clause**: Make sure your licensing agreement includes a clause that gives you the right to audit the licensee's financial records. This clause should specify how often audits can occur (e.g., once a year) and outline any notice requirements before conducting the audit.

- **Hire a professional auditor**: Royalty audits often require specialized knowledge, so it's best to hire a professional auditor who has experience with intellectual property and licensing agreements. The auditor will review the licensee's sales, royalty calculations, and payments to ensure everything is accurate.

- **Negotiate audit costs**: Some agreements stipulate that the licensee must cover the cost of the audit if significant underpayment is discovered (e.g., more than 5% discrepancy). If no significant issues are found, the licensor typically covers the audit costs.

Example:

An author suspects they are being underpaid by their publisher and decides to conduct an audit. After notifying the publisher in advance, the author hires a royalty auditor who reviews the publisher's sales and royalty payments over the past two years. The audit reveals an 8% underpayment, which the publisher agrees to rectify.

5. Address Discrepancies Promptly

If you discover discrepancies in royalty payments or reports, it's important to address the issue as soon as possible. Delayed responses can lead to further miscalculations or financial losses. Contact the licensee with clear evidence of the discrepancy and request an explanation or adjustment.

How to handle discrepancies:

- **Document the issue**: Keep detailed records of the discrepancy, including the original report, any independent data, and communications with the licensee. This documentation is essential if you need to escalate the issue to legal action.

- **Request adjustments**: Politely but firmly request that the licensee adjust the royalty payment to reflect the accurate figures. Most discrepancies can be resolved quickly if both parties communicate openly.

- **Take legal action if necessary**: If the licensee refuses to address the issue or if discrepancies continue to occur, consider seeking legal advice to enforce the terms of your contract. You may need to pursue litigation or terminate the agreement if the licensee is unwilling to cooperate.

Example:

A songwriter notices that their royalty payments from a licensing deal are lower than expected. After cross-checking the licensee's report with streaming data, the songwriter contacts the licensee and provides evidence of the discrepancy. The licensee acknowledges the mistake and adjusts the next royalty payment to reflect the accurate figures.

Conclusion: Staying on Top of Your Royalty Income

Tracking and auditing royalties is a vital part of managing your creative business. By setting up clear reporting requirements, using digital tools, and cross-checking reports with independent data, you can ensure that you're paid fairly for your work. When discrepancies arise, acting quickly and conducting audits will help you maintain control over your earnings and protect your financial interests.

With these tools and strategies in place, you'll be well-equipped to manage royalty income effectively, ensuring that every piece of your creative work earns its full potential.

In the next chapter, we'll explore managing multiple revenue streams, discussing how to diversify your income sources to build a stable and sustainable creative business.

Quick Tips and Recap

- **Set Clear Reporting Requirements**: Ensure your licensing agreement includes detailed, regular reporting on sales, royalties, and payment deadlines to keep track of your income.

- **Use Digital Tools**: Utilize royalty tracking software or spreadsheets to automate tracking and manage multiple royalty streams with ease.

- **Cross-Check Reports with Independent Data**: Verify royalty reports by comparing them with external sources like public streaming data or sales rankings to ensure accuracy.

- **Include an Audit Clause**: Make sure your agreement allows for royalty audits, and conduct periodic checks to ensure that royalties are being calculated and paid correctly.

- **Hire a Professional Auditor**: For larger or more complex deals, hire a royalty auditor to review financial records and verify the accuracy of payments.

- **Address Discrepancies Quickly**: If you find discrepancies in your payments, document the issue and contact the licensee for resolution. Act promptly to avoid further financial losses.

- **Request Adjustments or Legal Action**: If the licensee refuses to correct discrepancies, be prepared to request payment adjustments or seek legal advice to enforce your contract.

- **Track Payment Deadlines**: Set reminders for royalty payments to ensure they arrive on time, and follow up with the licensee if payments are late.

By implementing these strategies, you'll be able to track and audit your royalties effectively, ensuring that you get paid fairly and on time for your creative work.

Power in Partnership: Collaborations and Partnerships

"Collaboration is the secret ingredient that amplifies success. When we combine our strengths, we don't just add value—we multiply it."
— SATYA NADELLA, CEO OF MICROSOFT

Chapter Fifteen, "Power in Partnership: Collaborations and Partnerships," is all about the magic that happens when creative minds collide. Think of it as a mixer where the industry's brightest stars and hidden gems come together to create something that's greater than the sum of its parts.

In this chapter, we explore the art of choosing the right partners, the kind who complement your strengths, forgive your weaknesses, and double your chances at the snack table of success. We'll guide you through crafting partnerships that aren't just about sharing resources but multiplying them. From handshake deals to written contracts, we'll lay out the do's and don'ts, ensuring your collaborations sparkle without any unexpected sparks.

Whether you're joining forces for a single project or forging a long-term alliance, this section provides the blueprint for a partnership that not only works but thrives. Get ready to amplify your creative impact through the power of collaboration—because sometimes, it really does take a village to raise a masterpiece.

Choosing the Right Collaborators: Finding the Perfect Fit

In the world of creative partnerships, finding the right collaborator is key to turning a good project into a great one. The right partner can complement your strengths, fill in your gaps, and help bring your creative vision to life in ways you might not be able to achieve alone. But collaboration is more than just pairing up with someone talented—it's about finding someone who aligns with your goals, values, and working style. In this section, we'll explore how to choose the right collaborator, ensuring that your partnership is set up for success.

1. Look for Complementary Skills and Strengths

When choosing a collaborator, it's important to find someone whose skills complement, rather than mirror, your own. You want to partner with someone who brings something new to the table, filling in areas where you may be weaker or less experienced. By combining your respective strengths, you can create a partnership that's greater than the sum of its parts.

Key questions to ask:

- What are your own strengths and weaknesses?
- What skills or expertise does the project require that you don't have?
- Can this potential collaborator bring those missing elements to the table?

Example:
If you're a writer with a strong voice but struggle with marketing, you might seek a collaborator who excels at building audiences and promoting content. Together,

you'll have both the creative and business sides covered, increasing the chances of your project's success.

2. Align on Goals and Creative Vision

Creative collaborations thrive when both parties share a common goal or vision for the project. Misaligned goals can lead to conflicts and frustration down the road, so it's crucial to ensure that you and your potential partner are on the same page from the beginning. Take the time to discuss your expectations for the project and what success looks like for each of you.

Things to align on:

- The scope and scale of the project: Are you both aiming for the same level of ambition?

- Creative direction: Does your partner share your vision for how the project should look, sound, or feel?

- Long-term objectives: Do you both agree on the desired outcome, whether it's commercial success, artistic recognition, or simply personal growth?

Example:

Two musicians decide to collaborate on an album. One wants to experiment with avant-garde sounds, while the other envisions a more mainstream, radio-friendly project. Before committing, they discuss their creative vision and decide to blend their styles, finding a middle ground where they can both express themselves while staying true to the project's goals.

3. Consider Work Style and Communication

No matter how talented or aligned you are creatively, a partnership won't work if your working styles and communication habits clash. It's essential to consider how you and your potential collaborator approach deadlines, feedback, and problem-solving. A great partner should have a compatible work ethic and communication style, ensuring smooth collaboration throughout the project.

Factors to consider:

- **Work pace**: Do you both work at a similar speed, or will one person constantly be waiting on the other to catch up?

- **Feedback style**: Are you comfortable with direct, honest feedback, or do you prefer a gentler, more supportive approach?

- **Problem-solving**: How do you handle creative disagreements? Can you compromise and find solutions together?

Example:

A graphic designer and a writer team up to create a visual storytelling project. The designer prefers to work on tight deadlines and makes quick decisions, while the writer takes a slower, more methodical approach. To avoid frustration, they agree to establish clear milestones and regular check-ins, ensuring they're both comfortable with the project's pace and progress.

4. Evaluate Professionalism and Commitment

Beyond skills and vision, your collaborator's professionalism and commitment are critical to the success of the partnership. You want to work with someone who is reliable, meets deadlines, and is fully committed to the project. A partner who is constantly distracted or unable to deliver on their promises can derail the collaboration, no matter how aligned you are creatively.

Things to assess:

- **Past experience**: Have they successfully completed similar projects in the past? Do they have a track record of reliability?

- **Commitment level**: Are they as invested in the project as you are? Will they prioritize it, or is this a side project for them?

- **Reputation**: Do they have a good reputation in the industry? Have others had positive experiences working with them?

Example:

An author looking to collaborate with an illustrator checks the artist's portfolio and speaks to past collaborators. After learning that the illustrator consistently meets deadlines and maintains good communication, the author feels confident moving forward with the partnership.

Conclusion: Building the Right Foundation

Choosing the right collaborator is about more than just finding someone with talent—it's about finding someone who complements your skills, shares your vision, and matches your work ethic. By carefully considering the factors of complementary strengths, aligned goals, compatible work styles, and professional commitment, you can build a strong foundation for a successful creative partnership.

In the next section, we'll explore crafting win-win agreements, helping you structure clear and fair partnerships that set the stage for a thriving collaboration.

Crafting Win-Win Agreements: Structuring Fair and Clear Partnerships

Once you've chosen the right collaborator, the next step is to formalize your partnership with a clear, mutually beneficial agreement. Whether it's a casual project or a long-term collaboration, having a structured partnership agreement is essential for setting expectations, avoiding misunderstandings, and ensuring that both parties are protected. A win-win agreement ensures that both collaborators feel valued and that the terms are fair, allowing the partnership to flourish without unnecessary friction.

In this section, we'll explore how to craft an agreement that covers all the key elements of your collaboration, from creative control to financial splits, and set you up for a smooth and successful working relationship.

1. Clearly Define Roles and Responsibilities

A successful partnership starts with a clear understanding of who is responsible for what. Defining roles early on helps to avoid confusion, prevent tasks from being duplicated, and ensure that nothing falls through the cracks. Both parties should feel confident in their contributions and understand how they fit into the larger project.

How to define roles:

- **Outline specific tasks**: List out the individual responsibilities of each partner in the agreement. For example, one person might handle content creation while the other takes on marketing and distribution.

- **Clarify creative control**: Define who has the final say over creative decisions. Will one partner have more control over certain aspects, or will all decisions be made jointly?

- **Agree on timelines**: Include a schedule or timeline for each stage of the project, so both parties know what to expect and can manage their time accordingly.

Example:

In a partnership between a writer and an illustrator for a graphic novel, the writer is responsible for creating the storyline and dialogue, while the illustrator handles the artwork. Both agree to review each other's work regularly, with creative decisions being made jointly, ensuring the final product reflects both visions.

2. Establish Financial Terms and Revenue Sharing

Finances are often the trickiest part of any partnership, so it's crucial to be explicit about how money will be handled from the start. The financial terms should cover everything from how expenses will be divided to how profits will be shared. By clearly outlining financial responsibilities, both partners can avoid potential conflicts and feel secure in their contribution to the partnership.

Key financial considerations:

- **Revenue splits**: Determine how profits will be shared. Will it be a 50/50 split, or will one partner receive a higher percentage based on their level of involvement or expertise?

- **Expense sharing**: Discuss how project costs will be divided. Will both partners contribute equally to expenses like marketing, production, and materials, or will one party cover more costs in exchange for a higher revenue share?

- **Advance payments or royalties**: If the project involves upfront payments or future royalties (e.g., for book sales, licensing deals, or product sales), specify how those payments will be divided.

Example:

A songwriter and music producer collaborate on an album. They agree to a 60/40 split, with the songwriter receiving 60% of any revenue from streaming or album sales and the producer receiving 40%. Both partners will cover production costs equally, ensuring that the financial burden is shared fairly.

3. Address Intellectual Property Rights

One of the most important aspects of any creative partnership is determining who will own the intellectual property (IP) created during the collaboration. Intellectual property rights dictate how the work can be used, licensed, or sold in the future. A well-structured agreement should clarify who owns the IP, whether it's shared, and how it can be exploited beyond the initial project.

Ways to structure IP ownership:

- **Joint ownership**: Both parties share equal ownership of the work, with all decisions about its use requiring mutual consent.

- **Sole ownership with usage rights**: One partner owns the IP but grants the other partner usage rights, allowing them to use, display, or profit from the work under certain conditions.

- **Separate ownership**: Each partner owns their individual contributions (e.g., one owns the written content, and the other owns the visuals), and both retain control over how their work is used or licensed independently.

Example:

A photographer and a fashion designer collaborate on a photo shoot. They agree that the photographer will retain ownership of the images, but the designer will have the right to use the photos for marketing materials and social media promotion. Any future licensing of the photos must be agreed upon by both parties.

4. Include Dispute Resolution and Exit Clauses

Even the best partnerships can run into challenges, and it's important to plan for how conflicts will be handled if they arise. Including a dispute resolution clause in your agreement ensures that both parties have a process for resolving disagreements without damaging the relationship. Similarly, an exit clause provides a way for either partner to leave the project if things aren't working out, without leaving the other partner in a difficult position.

How to structure dispute resolution:

- **Mediation or arbitration**: If conflicts arise that can't be resolved between the partners, you can agree to seek mediation or arbitration. This involves a neutral third party who helps resolve the dispute in a fair manner.

- **Vote or decision-maker**: For joint projects where both parties need to make decisions, you might agree on a method for resolving deadlocked decisions. For example, you could designate a trusted third party or mentor to act as a tiebreaker.

How to structure an exit clause:

- **Notice period**: Include a requirement that either party must give a certain amount of notice (e.g., 30 days) before exiting the partnership, allowing the other partner time to adjust or find a replacement.

- **Exit terms**: Clearly define what happens to the work, profits, and intellectual property if one partner leaves. Will the remaining partner have full rights to continue the project, or will the project be shelved?

Example:

Two filmmakers partner on a documentary. They agree that if one person wants to exit the project, they must give 60 days' notice. Any disputes over creative control will be settled by a mediator they both trust. If the partnership ends, they agree that both will have access to the footage, but future use of the material will require mutual consent.

5. Put It in Writing: The Importance of a Written Agreement

No matter how well you and your partner get along, it's essential to formalize your partnership in writing. A written agreement provides clarity, outlines expectations, and offers legal protection for both parties. Even for smaller or more casual collaborations, having a written contract helps prevent misunderstandings and ensures that both parties are treated fairly.

Key benefits of a written agreement:

- **Clarity**: A written agreement leaves no room for confusion or ambiguity. Both parties know exactly what they're responsible for and how profits or ownership will be handled.

- **Legal protection**: If disputes arise or the partnership falls apart, a written agreement provides legal recourse and ensures that both parties are held to the agreed terms.

- **Professionalism**: A contract signals that both parties are serious about the partnership, helping to establish trust and a sense of responsibility from the start.

Example:

A visual artist collaborates with a marketing agency to design a series of campaign posters. They create a written contract that outlines the scope of the project, payment terms, and intellectual property rights, ensuring that both parties are aligned before starting the work.

Conclusion: Structuring Partnerships for Success

Crafting a win-win agreement is about more than just dividing up tasks and profits—it's about creating a strong foundation for a successful partnership. By clearly defining roles, establishing fair financial terms, addressing intellectual property, and planning for disputes or exits, you can ensure that your collaboration runs smoothly and benefits both parties.

In the next section, we'll explore how to maximize creative synergy, providing strategies for working together in a way that enhances each partner's strengths and brings your shared vision to life.

Maximizing Creative Synergy: Working Together for Greater Impact

When two (or more) creative minds join forces, the potential for something truly extraordinary emerges. However, to achieve the full power of creative synergy, collaborators need to foster an environment where ideas flow freely, strengths complement one another, and both parties work in harmony. In this section, we'll explore how to cultivate a productive, inspiring collaboration that allows both partners to shine and elevates the overall project.

1. Play to Each Other's Strengths

The foundation of a great partnership is recognizing and leveraging each person's unique talents. Successful collaborations happen when both partners are not only aware of each other's strengths but actively play to those strengths throughout the project. This involves dividing tasks based on each person's expertise and ensuring that everyone contributes in a way that maximizes the overall outcome.

How to identify and use strengths:

- **Evaluate complementary skills**: Have an open conversation at the start of the project to identify what each partner is good at. One person might be excellent at technical execution, while the other excels in ideation and strategy. Organize the project in a way that allows each of you to focus on what you do best.

- **Encourage specialization**: Let each person take the lead in areas where they are strongest. When you trust your collaborator to handle their responsibilities with expertise, you not only create better work but also build a sense of ownership and accountability.

Example:

A filmmaker partners with a composer to score a documentary. The filmmaker has a strong sense of visual storytelling but no musical background, while the composer is skilled in creating emotionally resonant music. Instead of trying to dictate the music, the filmmaker trusts the composer to create a score that enhances the film's narrative, resulting in a richer, more cohesive project.

2. Foster Open Communication and Idea Sharing

Creative synergy flourishes when both partners feel comfortable sharing their ideas and providing feedback. Open communication creates a collaborative environment where creativity is nurtured, and different perspectives can come together to form something greater than either partner could create alone.

Strategies for open communication:

- **Create regular check-ins**: Set up regular meetings or touchpoints where both partners can discuss the progress of the project, share new ideas, and provide feedback. These check-ins help keep the project on track and ensure both partners are aligned.

- **Encourage honest feedback**: Constructive criticism is key to growth, so both partners should feel safe giving and receiving feedback. Frame critiques in a positive, solution-focused way that helps the project move forward without discouraging creativity.

- **Value each other's contributions**: Make an effort to acknowledge and appreciate each other's ideas, even if they don't always make it into the final version. Feeling valued motivates both partners to continue contributing their best work.

Example:

Two designers collaborating on a product line hold weekly meetings to review each other's work and discuss new ideas. One designer offers constructive feedback on color choices, while the other suggests incorporating new materials. Through open dialogue, they blend their strengths and refine the product line to be more innovative and marketable.

3. Embrace Flexibility and Adaptation

Creative projects are rarely linear, and collaborations often require a level of flexibility that allows both partners to adapt to new ideas, unexpected challenges, or changing directions. Rather than rigidly sticking to a predefined plan, be open to evolving the project in response to new insights or inspiration that arises during the process.

How to foster flexibility:

- **Be open to change**: Both partners should approach the project with a mindset that welcomes new ideas and is willing to pivot if needed. If one person comes up with a better approach halfway through the project, don't be afraid to shift gears and explore it.

- **Adjust roles if necessary**: Sometimes, as the project evolves, one partner's role might change. Be willing to shift responsibilities or adapt the initial division of tasks to reflect the current needs of the project.

- **Learn from experimentation**: Encourage each other to experiment with different techniques, ideas, or approaches. Even if something doesn't work out, the lessons learned can inspire the next iteration.

Example:

An author and an illustrator are collaborating on a children's book. Initially, the plan was to have minimal illustrations, but midway through, they realize that more detailed, immersive illustrations would enhance the storytelling. They agree to shift focus, allowing the illustrator to take more creative control over the visuals, which results in a more compelling final product.

4. Balance Autonomy with Collaboration

One of the most challenging aspects of working together is striking the right balance between autonomy and collaboration. While both partners need to contribute equally, it's also important to give each other the freedom to work independently within their areas of expertise. Striking this balance ensures that each partner feels empowered while still maintaining a cohesive vision for the project.

How to balance autonomy and collaboration:

- **Delegate specific tasks**: Give each partner ownership over specific tasks or phases of the project. This allows each person to take the reins in their areas of expertise while ensuring that the project remains cohesive.

- **Check in regularly**: Even when working independently, regular check-ins help maintain alignment and ensure that both partners are still on track with the overall vision.

- **Trust each other's judgment**: Once you've delegated tasks, trust your partner to execute them without micromanaging. Let them bring their unique flair to the work, knowing that it will contribute to the larger creative vision.

Example:

A marketing strategist partners with a graphic designer to create a campaign. The strategist takes charge of developing the overall concept and messaging, while the designer is responsible for creating the visuals. They work independently on their respective tasks but hold regular check-ins to ensure the messaging and visuals align for a cohesive campaign.

5. Encourage Experimentation and Risk-Taking

Creativity thrives on innovation, and the most impactful collaborations are often those that take risks and push boundaries. By encouraging each other to step out of your comfort zones and experiment with new ideas or techniques, you can elevate the project beyond what either partner could achieve alone.

How to encourage experimentation:

- **Create a safe space for risks**: Both partners should feel comfortable taking creative risks without fear of judgment or failure. Establish a partnership where new ideas are welcomed and celebrated, even if they don't always work out as planned.

- **Test new approaches**: Allow time in the project to experiment with different approaches, tools, or styles. Even if you decide to return to the original plan, the experimentation phase can lead to unexpected insights.

- **Celebrate successes and failures**: Whether an experiment succeeds or fails, take the time to reflect on what worked and what didn't. Learning from both outcomes helps both partners grow and improves future projects.

Example:

Two photographers collaborating on an exhibition decide to experiment with mixed media by incorporating digital elements into their traditional photography.

While some ideas don't pan out, the ones that do add a fresh, innovative dimension to the final exhibition, setting their work apart from typical photography displays.

Conclusion: Creating Creative Synergy for Success

Maximizing creative synergy means fostering a collaborative environment where each partner's strengths are celebrated, ideas are shared openly, and risks are embraced. By focusing on playing to each other's strengths, maintaining open communication, and balancing autonomy with collaboration, you can create a partnership that produces far greater results than either person could achieve on their own.

In the next section, we'll cover navigating challenges in creative partnerships, exploring how to resolve conflicts, manage expectations, and maintain a healthy working relationship even when things get tough.

Navigating Challenges: Conflict Resolution and Managing Expectations

No matter how well-matched a partnership may be, every collaboration will face its share of challenges. Creative projects can bring out differing opinions, working styles, and expectations, which may lead to conflict. Navigating these challenges effectively is critical to maintaining a strong, productive partnership. This section will cover strategies for resolving conflicts, managing expectations, and maintaining a healthy working relationship even when tensions arise.

1. Set Clear Expectations from the Start

Many conflicts in creative partnerships stem from misaligned expectations. To avoid misunderstandings, it's important to set clear expectations at the outset of the collaboration. This includes defining roles, responsibilities, deadlines, and goals for the project, so both partners know what to expect from each other.

How to manage expectations:

- **Discuss goals upfront**: Before starting the project, have a detailed conversation about what each partner wants to achieve. Ensure that your goals are aligned and that you both agree on the direction of the project.

- **Establish boundaries**: Be clear about your availability, workload capacity, and preferred communication style. Setting these boundaries early prevents frustration later on if one partner feels overwhelmed or neglected.

- **Set realistic deadlines**: Discuss timelines and ensure that both partners agree on them. Avoid overpromising or setting unrealistic deadlines, which can lead to stress and friction.

Example:

A freelance graphic designer and a writer team up to create a series of infographics. They agree on specific deadlines and clarify that the designer will need a week's notice before any revisions. This upfront communication ensures that both parties know what to expect, preventing last-minute stress or rushed changes.

2. Address Issues Early and Directly

When conflicts arise, it's important to address them early—before they escalate. Ignoring small issues can lead to resentment, which can damage the partnership over time. Direct communication is key to resolving conflicts quickly and keeping the project on track.

How to address conflicts:

- **Have an open conversation**: If something is bothering you, bring it up calmly and constructively. Avoid blaming or attacking your partner; instead, focus on finding a solution that works for both of you.

- **Listen actively**: When discussing an issue, give your partner the chance to express their concerns as well. Listening to their perspective can help you understand where they're coming from and find common ground.

- **Stay solution-focused**: Rather than dwelling on the problem, work together to find a solution. Keep the focus on moving forward and how to prevent similar issues from arising in the future.

Example:

Two musicians collaborating on an album hit a creative block when they disagree on the direction of a track. Instead of avoiding the issue, they meet to discuss their differing ideas. By listening to each other's perspectives, they find a compromise and agree to incorporate elements of both styles, allowing the project to progress smoothly.

3. Use a Mediator or Third Party When Needed

In some cases, conflicts may be too complex or emotionally charged to resolve on your own. When you find yourselves at an impasse, bringing in a neutral third party can help mediate the situation and offer an unbiased perspective. This can be especially useful for resolving deadlocked decisions or ongoing disagreements.

When to bring in a mediator:

- **Stalemates**: If you and your partner can't agree on a critical decision and discussions are going in circles, a mediator can help break the deadlock by offering a fresh perspective.

- **Ongoing conflicts**: If the same issues keep arising and you're unable to resolve them on your own, a mediator can help identify the root cause and suggest solutions that benefit both parties.

- **Objectivity**: A third party can provide a neutral, objective view of the situation, helping to de-escalate tensions and foster a productive conversation.

Example:
A visual artist and a curator disagree on how to present an upcoming gallery show. After weeks of unresolved debates, they bring in a gallery director to mediate the discussion. The director helps them reach a compromise, ensuring that the final presentation satisfies both their artistic visions.

4. Be Willing to Compromise

Collaboration is inherently about compromise. While both partners may have strong ideas about how the project should progress, being too rigid can lead to conflict. Successful partnerships require a willingness to adjust your vision, listen to your partner's ideas, and find solutions that work for both of you.

How to embrace compromise:

- **Prioritize the project**: Remember that the goal is to create something great together, not to "win" every argument. Focus on what's best for the project rather than sticking rigidly to your personal preferences.

- **Be flexible**: Understand that your partner brings a unique perspective to the table. While you may not agree with every idea, being open to compromise can lead to a stronger, more cohesive final product.

- **Choose your battles**: Not every disagreement needs to be a dealbreaker. Sometimes, it's worth compromising on smaller issues to maintain harmony and save your energy for more important decisions.

Example:

Two filmmakers collaborating on a documentary disagree on the narrative structure. While one prefers a traditional timeline, the other suggests a non-linear approach. After discussing the pros and cons, they agree to compromise by incorporating a mix of both styles, creating a more dynamic and engaging final film.

5. Know When to Walk Away

While most conflicts can be resolved with communication and compromise, there are situations where a partnership simply isn't working. Knowing when to walk away is important for protecting your well-being and ensuring that the project isn't derailed by an unworkable collaboration. If efforts to resolve conflicts have failed, it may be best to part ways amicably and pursue other opportunities.

When to consider ending the partnership:

- **Irreconcilable differences**: If you and your partner have fundamentally different visions for the project and can't find a compromise, continuing the collaboration may do more harm than good.

- **Repeated conflict**: If the same issues keep arising despite efforts to resolve them, it may be a sign that the partnership isn't a good fit.

- **Unprofessional behavior**: If your partner consistently misses deadlines, fails to communicate, or behaves unprofessionally, it may be time to end the collaboration to protect your own reputation and work.

Example:

A writer and an editor collaborating on a novel continually clash over creative direction, with disagreements becoming more frequent and heated. After multiple attempts to resolve the conflict, they mutually decide to end the partnership. The writer finds a new editor who aligns more closely with their vision, and the project moves forward smoothly.

Conclusion: Navigating Challenges with Confidence

Creative collaborations are rewarding but often come with challenges. By setting clear expectations, addressing issues early, being willing to compromise, and knowing when to seek help, you can navigate these challenges and maintain a healthy, productive partnership. Remember, conflict is a natural part of the creative process—what matters is how you handle it.

With these strategies in place, you'll be better equipped to resolve conflicts, manage expectations, and ensure that your collaboration continues to thrive. In the next chapter, we'll explore how to leverage partnerships for growth, covering how strategic collaborations can help expand your creative reach and unlock new opportunities.

Quick Tips and Recap

- **Set Clear Expectations**: Discuss goals, roles, and responsibilities upfront to avoid misalignment and misunderstandings.

- **Address Issues Early**: Don't let small problems fester—bring them up promptly and discuss them openly to find solutions.

- **Encourage Open Communication**: Foster a collaborative environment by sharing ideas freely and giving constructive feedback.

- **Be Willing to Compromise**: Focus on the project's success and find middle ground where both partners' visions can shine.

- **Use a Mediator if Necessary**: If you reach an impasse, consider bringing in a neutral third party to help resolve the conflict.

- **Stay Solution-Oriented**: When addressing challenges, prioritize moving forward and resolving issues rather than dwelling on past problems.

- **Know When to Walk Away**: If the partnership isn't working despite your best efforts, it's okay to part ways and pursue new opportunities.

By keeping these tips in mind, you can navigate challenges, resolve conflicts, and maintain a successful creative partnership that enhances your project and personal growth.

PART FOUR

Leadership Persona Development

Welcome to Part Four: "Leadership Persona Development," where we take the raw clay of your professional demeanor and sculpt it into the commanding figure you're meant to be. This isn't just about putting on a suit and calling it leadership; it's about crafting a persona that resonates authority, fosters respect, and occasionally, makes coffee runs look like strategic moves. Here, you'll learn to balance the fine line between being approachably human and decisively superhuman. We'll tweak, tailor, and sometimes completely overhaul how you present yourself, ensuring that when you speak, others don't just listen—they lean in. Get ready to transform into not just any leader, but a leader with flair, inspiring loyalty and sparking innovation with just a raise of your eyebrow.

Digital Defense: Digital Rights Management (DRM)

"Digital rights management is not just about control; it's about ensuring
your content's integrity while maintaining trust with your audience."
— GINNI ROMETTY, FORMER CEO OF IBM

Chapter Sixteen, "Digital Defense: Digital Rights Management (DRM)," is where we armor up in the digital realm. Think of DRM as your electronic guard dog, trained to protect your creative works from the grabby hands of the Internet's less scrupulous surfers.

Here, we'll introduce you to the invisible shields and digital moats designed to keep your content safe within the castle walls of your choosing. Whether it's music, books, or software, DRM ensures your digital darlings stay put, or at least ask for your permission before they go gallivanting off into someone else's hard drive.

We'll dissect the hows and whys of these digital defenses, balancing the tightrope between protection and user-friendliness. Too much, and your users might revolt; too little, and you're the digital world's equivalent of a free buffet. By the end of this chapter, you'll be equipped to deploy DRM with the precision of a cybersecurity ninja, ensuring that your content does exactly what you want it to— no more, no less. Ready your digital armor; it's time to protect your creative kingdom.

What is DRM? Understanding the Basics of Digital Rights Management

Digital Rights Management (DRM) is a crucial tool for creators in the digital age, providing a protective layer for digital content such as music, books, videos, software, and more. Essentially, DRM is the digital equivalent of locking your doors to prevent unauthorized access, copying, and sharing of your creative works. It helps ensure that the people enjoying your content do so in a way that aligns with your terms, whether that's purchasing a song, renting a movie, or downloading software.

In this section, we'll break down the basics of what DRM is, why it's important, and how it works to safeguard your creative assets.

1. What is DRM?

At its core, DRM refers to a set of technologies and systems used to control how digital content is accessed, used, and distributed. It's a way for creators and businesses to protect their intellectual property in a world where copying and sharing digital files is as easy as a click.

DRM ensures that only authorized users—those who have purchased, rented, or obtained a legitimate license—can access and use the content. By embedding restrictions within the digital file, DRM can limit:

- Who can access the file (e.g., only those who have paid for it).

- How the file can be used (e.g., preventing copying, printing, or editing).

- How long the file can be accessed (e.g., subscription or rental periods).

Example:

If you purchase an ebook from an online retailer, DRM might prevent you from copying and distributing that ebook to others or converting it to a different format. The DRM ensures that the retailer—and by extension, the author—gets paid for each legitimate download or purchase.

2. Why is DRM Important?

With the explosion of the internet and digital distribution, protecting intellectual property has become more challenging than ever. While the digital world has made it easier to distribute and share content globally, it has also opened the door to piracy and unauthorized sharing. DRM helps creators and rights holders retain control over their digital assets, ensuring that they get properly compensated for their work.

Key benefits of DRM:

- **Prevents unauthorized distribution**: By restricting how files can be copied or shared, DRM reduces the risk of illegal downloads or file-sharing.

- **Ensures compliance with licensing terms**: DRM can enforce usage restrictions, such as allowing content to be used for a limited time or only on certain devices.

- **Protects revenue streams**: For digital content creators, DRM helps protect sales and subscriptions by limiting free, unauthorized access to their work.

Example:

In the music industry, DRM is often used to prevent a purchased song from being copied and shared across multiple devices or platforms. This helps artists and record labels protect their revenue by ensuring that each listener pays for access to the music.

3. How Does DRM Work?

DRM works by embedding access controls directly into the digital content file. These controls dictate who can access the content and how it can be used. While DRM technologies can vary depending on the type of content (e.g., ebooks, music, software), the general process involves:

- **Encryption**: The content is encrypted, meaning it's scrambled and unreadable until the proper authorization is provided (usually after purchase or subscription).

- **Licensing**: A user must obtain a license (usually by paying for the content) to access the encrypted file. The license serves as the "key" to unlock the content.

- **Usage restrictions**: Once unlocked, DRM can apply additional restrictions, such as limiting how many times a file can be copied, printed, or shared, or limiting access to specific devices (e.g., only allowing playback on a single computer or smartphone).

Example:

In the world of video streaming services like Netflix or Amazon Prime, DRM ensures that users can only access content through their subscription, limiting the ability to download or record shows for offline sharing. DRM may also restrict how many devices can access the same account simultaneously.

4. The Evolution of DRM: From CDs to Streaming Services

DRM has evolved alongside digital content itself, growing more sophisticated as technology advances. Early examples of DRM can be seen in the copy protection systems used in CDs and DVDs, where companies embedded codes that prevented users from copying or ripping the content to their computers.

As digital distribution expanded with the rise of MP3s, ebooks, and streaming services, DRM technology adapted to protect a wider array of content. Now, DRM systems are integrated into platforms like Apple's iTunes, Amazon Kindle, and Spotify to control the usage and distribution of digital media.

Example:

In the early 2000s, iTunes used DRM to prevent songs purchased from the store from being copied to more than five devices. While Apple later removed DRM from its music files, other forms of DRM still exist across its movies, books, and apps.

Conclusion: The Role of DRM in Digital Content Protection

DRM plays an essential role in protecting digital content by controlling access and limiting unauthorized use. Whether you're a musician, author, software developer, or video creator, DRM provides a safeguard for your digital assets, ensuring that you retain control over how your content is shared and consumed.

In the next section, we'll dive deeper into the types of DRM and how specific protections are applied across different industries, from music and books to software and streaming media.

Types of DRM: Tailoring Protection for Different Media

Digital Rights Management (DRM) systems are not one-size-fits-all. Each type of media—whether it's music, ebooks, software, or video—requires a different approach to protection based on how it's consumed, shared, and distributed. In this section, we'll explore the various types of DRM and how they are tailored to meet the specific needs of different forms of digital content. By understanding the unique challenges each type of media faces, you can better choose the right DRM strategy to safeguard your work.

1. DRM for Music and Audio: Protecting Soundtracks and Songs

The music industry has long been a battleground for DRM, especially with the rise of digital downloads and streaming services. DRM in music aims to prevent unauthorized copying and sharing while allowing consumers to legally purchase or stream songs on different devices.

How DRM works in music:

- **Encryption and licensing**: Digital audio files are encrypted and require a license (or permission) for playback. This can limit how many times the file is shared or on how many devices it can be played.

- **Streaming services**: Platforms like Spotify, Apple Music, and Tidal use DRM to control access. While users can stream music freely with a subscription, they typically can't download and share files for offline use outside the app.

- **Device limitations**: Some services restrict the number of devices a user can link to their account or the number of downloads allowed for offline listening. This prevents large-scale sharing or unauthorized duplication.

Example:

A user subscribes to a streaming service like Apple Music. While they can download songs for offline listening, the DRM ensures that those downloads are tied to the Apple Music app and can't be transferred to other devices or shared with others.

2. DRM for Ebooks: Protecting Digital Texts

With the rise of ebooks, DRM has become a crucial tool for protecting authors, publishers, and retailers from unauthorized sharing and piracy. DRM in ebooks typically focuses on preventing copying, sharing, and printing of the text, ensuring that readers who access the content have legally purchased or licensed it.

How DRM works in ebooks:

- **Device and platform restrictions**: Ebooks purchased from platforms like Amazon Kindle, Apple Books, or Google Play Books are often restricted to specific devices or apps. For example, a Kindle ebook can typically only be read on Kindle devices or in the Kindle app, and can't be easily transferred to other e-readers.

- **Usage controls**: DRM can prevent users from printing large sections of an ebook, copying text, or sharing the file with others. This protects the intellectual property of the author and publisher.

- **Subscription models**: Platforms like Scribd or Kindle Unlimited offer subscription-based access to ebooks, where users can "borrow" titles temporarily. DRM ensures that when the subscription or borrowing period ends, the user no longer has access to the book.

Example:

An author publishes an ebook on Amazon Kindle. DRM ensures that readers who purchase the ebook can only access it on their Kindle devices or apps and prevents them from sharing or distributing unauthorized copies.

3. DRM for Video: Protecting Films, TV Shows, and Streaming Media

The video industry—especially with the explosion of streaming services—relies heavily on DRM to protect content from piracy and unauthorized sharing. Whether it's a Hollywood blockbuster or a TV series, video DRM controls how content is streamed, downloaded, and accessed across devices.

How DRM works in video:

- **Streaming services**: Platforms like Netflix, Hulu, and Disney+ use DRM to encrypt video content, ensuring that it can only be streamed or downloaded by authorized users. Even when users download content for offline viewing, the DRM prevents them from copying or sharing the file outside of the app.

- **Geographic restrictions**: DRM also helps enforce geographic restrictions, preventing content from being accessed in regions where it hasn't been licensed for distribution.

- **Playback controls**: DRM can limit how many devices or accounts can access the video at the same time, reducing the risk of password-sharing or unauthorized streaming.

Example:

A user subscribes to Netflix and downloads a movie for offline viewing. The DRM ensures that the downloaded movie can only be viewed through the Netflix app, and access expires after a set period or when the subscription ends. Additionally, the video cannot be shared with others or copied to external storage.

4. DRM for Software and Games: Protecting Digital Applications

For software developers and game creators, DRM is critical in preventing piracy, unauthorized installations, and copying of applications or games. DRM in this space often focuses on ensuring that only legitimate users can access the software, and preventing widespread sharing or installation of the product across multiple devices without proper licensing.

How DRM works in software and games:

- **License keys**: Software products often use unique license keys or activation codes that are required for installation. This ensures that only those who have purchased the software can use it.

- **Online verification**: Many modern software applications and games use online DRM, where the product must periodically verify its license with the server. This prevents unauthorized copies from being used offline or without proper licensing.

- **Limited activations**: Some software limits the number of devices on which a product can be installed, ensuring that a single purchase isn't used across multiple devices without additional licenses.

Example:

A user purchases a copy of a popular game on Steam, a digital game distribution platform. The game is protected by DRM, which requires the user to be online and logged into their Steam account to play. This prevents the game from being copied and shared with others who haven't purchased it.

5. DRM for Images and Art: Protecting Visual Creations

Visual artists, photographers, and designers also rely on DRM to protect their digital works from unauthorized use, duplication, and distribution. DRM for visual media typically focuses on watermarking, usage restrictions, and access controls.

How DRM works for images and art:

- **Watermarking**: Many artists use digital watermarks to protect their work from being copied or used without permission. Watermarks serve as a visible deterrent to unauthorized use.

- **Licensing restrictions**: DRM can be used to control how digital artwork is accessed and shared. Licensing agreements may include restrictions on how many times an image can be downloaded or printed.

- **Metadata**: DRM systems often embed metadata into digital files, which helps track the origin and ownership of the content, ensuring that proper attribution is maintained.

Example:

A photographer uploads high-resolution images to a stock photo website. DRM tools, such as watermarks and download restrictions, ensure that only those who purchase the license can download and use the images without the watermark.

Conclusion: Tailoring DRM for Your Creative Work

The type of DRM you choose depends on the nature of your digital content and how you want to protect it. By understanding the specific needs of different media—whether it's music, ebooks, video, software, or visual art—you can select the right DRM strategy to safeguard your work while maintaining a seamless user experience.

In the next section, we'll cover the balance between protection and user experience, ensuring that you protect your content without alienating your audience with overly restrictive DRM measures.

Balancing Protection and User Experience: Avoiding the DRM Backlash

While Digital Rights Management (DRM) is essential for protecting your content from piracy and unauthorized use, it can also lead to frustration if implemented too restrictively. If users find the DRM too limiting or intrusive, it can create a negative experience, driving them away from your content—or worse, pushing them toward pirated versions without such limitations. In this section, we'll explore how to balance DRM protection with a positive user experience, ensuring that your content stays secure without alienating your audience.

1. Understand the User's Perspective

One of the most important aspects of balancing DRM and user experience is understanding the user's point of view. While creators and businesses want to protect their work, users are primarily concerned with accessing and enjoying content seamlessly. They want convenience and flexibility, and overly restrictive DRM can interfere with that.

Key user concerns:

- **Ease of access**: Users expect to access the content they've paid for quickly and easily. Lengthy authentication processes, frequent license checks, or the need for constant internet access can create unnecessary barriers.

- **Device compatibility**: Users want flexibility in accessing content across different devices. DRM systems that restrict content to a single device or platform can frustrate users who expect to switch between their phone, tablet, and computer without hassle.

- **Fair usage**: Users often expect to be able to make personal copies of purchased content for backup purposes or offline access. DRM systems that prevent copying, even for personal use, can be seen as too restrictive.

Example:
A user purchases an ebook from a major retailer but finds that it can only be read on one specific app, making it impossible to access the book on their preferred e-reader. This creates a frustrating experience and may cause the user to avoid purchasing from that retailer in the future.

2. Keep DRM Transparent and Unobtrusive

To avoid alienating users, DRM should be as transparent and unobtrusive as possible. When DRM becomes too visible or interferes with the user experience, it can lead to negative feedback and backlash. The goal is to protect your content without users feeling like they're being restricted at every turn.

Tips for unobtrusive DRM:

- **Limit interruptions**: Avoid DRM that constantly interrupts the user, such as frequent license checks or requiring reauthentication every time they access the content. Once a user has purchased or licensed the content, allow them to enjoy it without unnecessary disruptions.

- **Allow offline access**: While DRM often requires online verification, it's important to give users the flexibility to access their content offline, especially for items like ebooks, music, or videos. If users can't access their content while traveling or in areas without internet, they may become frustrated.

- **Streamline the process**: Make sure the DRM system works smoothly, without causing delays or glitches. Users should be able to download, install, and access the content quickly and efficiently, without complicated steps.

Example:

A music streaming service allows users to download songs for offline listening, but the DRM only requires online verification once a month. This gives users flexibility without constantly interrupting their experience, ensuring they can enjoy their music on the go.

3. Allow Flexibility with Devices and Platforms

One of the main complaints users have about DRM is its tendency to lock content to specific devices or platforms. In today's world, users expect to switch between multiple devices—phones, tablets, laptops, and TVs—seamlessly. To maintain a positive user experience, it's important to allow some flexibility in how users access your content across different platforms.

Tips for device flexibility:

- **Allow multi-device access**: If possible, allow users to access the content they've purchased on multiple devices. This is especially important for content like ebooks, movies, and music, where users may want to switch between devices throughout the day.

- **Avoid strict platform locks**: If you're distributing content through multiple channels (e.g., an app store and a website), ensure that users can access their content across both platforms. Restricting access to just one platform can frustrate users who want more options.

- **Consider device limits carefully**: While it's reasonable to limit the number of devices that can access the content, make sure the limit is generous enough to accommodate most users. A restrictive limit (e.g., one or two devices) can feel suffocating, especially for families or users with multiple devices.

Example:

An ebook retailer allows users to read their purchased books on up to five different devices, including smartphones, tablets, and computers. This flexibility ensures that users can enjoy their books wherever they are without feeling restricted by the DRM.

4. Educate Users About DRM and Their Rights

One way to avoid DRM backlash is by being transparent with users about how DRM works and what rights they have. Often, users become frustrated with DRM because they don't understand why certain restrictions are in place or how they can use the content they've purchased. By educating your audience, you can reduce confusion and ensure a smoother user experience.

How to educate users about DRM:

- **Provide clear information**: When users purchase or license content, make sure they are aware of any restrictions, such as device limits or time-based access. Being upfront about these details helps set clear expectations and prevents users from feeling blindsided.

- **Offer help and support**: Provide resources or customer support that explain how DRM works and how users can get the most out of their content. If users have issues accessing or transferring their content, offer solutions to ensure they remain satisfied with their purchase.

- **Reassure users about fair use**: Make sure users know that the DRM isn't intended to prevent legitimate use, such as accessing their content across devices. Let them know what they can do with the content they've purchased and how they can enjoy it without issues.

Example:

An app developer includes a clear FAQ section on their website that explains the DRM restrictions on their software, how many devices it can be installed on, and how users can transfer their license to a new device. By providing this information upfront, they reduce confusion and prevent negative feedback from users who might otherwise feel frustrated by the limitations.

5. Find the Right Balance Between Protection and Convenience

Ultimately, balancing DRM protection with user experience is about finding the sweet spot where your content remains secure without creating unnecessary barriers for legitimate users. Too much DRM can push users away, while too little protection can leave your content vulnerable to piracy. By focusing on convenience, flexibility, and transparency, you can ensure that your DRM strategy serves both your interests and your users' needs.

Key points to consider:

- **Assess the level of protection needed**: Depending on the type of content you're distributing; you may not need the strictest DRM measures. Consider the risks of piracy versus the potential impact on user experience, and tailor your DRM approach accordingly.

- **Listen to user feedback**: Pay attention to how users respond to your DRM policies. If you're receiving consistent feedback about restrictions or usability issues, consider adjusting your DRM settings to improve the user experience.

- **Prioritize loyal users**: Protecting your content is important, but it's equally important to cultivate a positive relationship with your audience. When users feel trusted and valued, they're less likely to seek unauthorized access or pirated versions of your work.

Example:

A software developer uses a simple DRM system that requires a one-time activation upon installation. Users can install the software on multiple devices, but the license must be verified once per device. This approach protects the software from widespread piracy while ensuring that legitimate users have a seamless experience.

Conclusion: Finding the Right Balance for Your DRM Strategy

Balancing protection and user experience is crucial for any DRM strategy. While it's important to safeguard your content, overly restrictive DRM can frustrate your audience and lead to a negative user experience. By keeping DRM unobtrusive, allowing device flexibility, educating users, and prioritizing convenience, you can protect your digital assets without alienating the people who support your work.

In the next section, we'll explore DRM tools and technologies, providing practical guidance on how to implement effective DRM solutions that meet your specific needs.

DRM Tools and Technologies: How to Protect Your Digital Assets

Now that we've covered the importance of balancing protection and user experience, let's dive into the practical side of implementing Digital Rights Management (DRM). The right DRM tools and technologies can help you secure your digital content while ensuring that users can access it without frustration. In this section, we'll explore a range of DRM tools and platforms designed to protect various forms of digital content, from ebooks to music, video, and software.

1. DRM for Ebooks: Protecting Digital Texts

Ebook creators and publishers need DRM solutions that prevent unauthorized copying and sharing while allowing readers to access content across devices. Many DRM platforms for ebooks also integrate with popular online retailers, making it easy for creators to distribute and protect their work.

Recommended DRM tools for ebooks:

- **Adobe Digital Editions**: Adobe's DRM solution is widely used by ebook retailers and libraries to protect digital content. It allows you to control how many devices can access the ebook and limit sharing, printing, or copying.

- **Amazon Kindle DRM**: Kindle's proprietary DRM system automatically protects ebooks sold through the Kindle store. This DRM ties purchased ebooks to a user's Amazon account, ensuring that books can only be accessed via Kindle devices or apps.

- **Google Play Books DRM**: Google's DRM technology protects ebooks sold on the Google Play platform, allowing readers to access their purchases across devices while preventing unauthorized sharing.

Example:

An author publishes a novel on Amazon Kindle and uses Amazon's built-in DRM to ensure that the ebook can only be accessed through the Kindle platform. This prevents readers from sharing the ebook file with others or converting it to another format without permission.

2. DRM for Music and Audio: Securing Sound Files

With the popularity of streaming services, the music industry relies heavily on DRM to prevent illegal downloads and unauthorized sharing. DRM for music typically focuses on controlling access to streaming content and ensuring that downloaded files cannot be distributed outside the authorized platform.

Recommended DRM tools for music:

- **Apple FairPlay**: Apple's FairPlay DRM system is used for music, movies, and other media distributed through iTunes and Apple Music. It encrypts audio files and ties them to a user's Apple ID, ensuring that the music can only be played on authorized Apple devices.

- **Microsoft PlayReady**: This DRM solution is commonly used in streaming services to protect audio and video content. It supports multiple media types and devices, allowing creators to control how content is distributed and used.

- **Widevine**: Acquired by Google, Widevine is a DRM technology used by many streaming services, including Spotify, to protect audio content.

It ensures that songs can be streamed but not downloaded or shared without permission.

Example:

A record label releases a new album on Apple Music, using Apple's FairPlay DRM to ensure that the songs can be streamed but not downloaded as standalone files. This prevents users from copying and distributing the music illegally.

3. DRM for Video: Safeguarding Streaming and Downloadable Content

With the rise of video streaming platforms like Netflix, Hulu, and YouTube, protecting video content has become critical for filmmakers, content creators, and broadcasters. Video DRM systems focus on controlling access, preventing copying, and ensuring that only authorized users can view the content.

Recommended DRM tools for video:

- **Google Widevine**: Widely used by major streaming platforms like Netflix, Hulu, and Amazon Prime Video, Widevine DRM ensures secure streaming of video content. It supports multiple levels of protection, from standard streaming to high-definition and 4K.

- **Microsoft PlayReady**: PlayReady is another popular DRM solution for video, used by services like HBO Go and Vimeo. It encrypts video files, controls access, and limits sharing or copying of content.

- **Verimatrix**: This DRM tool is designed for protecting video content across a range of platforms, from on-demand streaming services to live TV broadcasts. It helps broadcasters and filmmakers prevent piracy and unauthorized distribution.

Example:

A filmmaker releases their movie on a popular streaming platform like Netflix, which uses Widevine DRM to ensure that the video can only be streamed through the platform's app and not downloaded or shared without authorization.

4. DRM for Software and Games: Securing Applications and Digital Tools

For software developers and game creators, DRM is essential for preventing piracy, unauthorized installations, and the distribution of cracked versions. DRM for software often involves license keys, activation processes, and online verification to ensure that only legitimate users can access the product.

Recommended DRM tools for software and games:

- **Denuvo**: Widely used in the gaming industry, Denuvo DRM protects games from being pirated. It employs encryption and authentication processes that make it difficult for unauthorized users to copy or crack the game.

- **Flexera**: This DRM solution helps software developers manage licenses and prevent unauthorized usage of their products. It offers features like online verification, limited activations, and subscription management to ensure that users follow the licensing terms.

- **Wibu-Systems**: Known for its CodeMeter DRM solution, Wibu-Systems protects software by encrypting code and controlling how applications are installed and used. It also offers cloud-based licensing options, making it easy to manage software across devices.

Example:
A game developer releases a new video game using Denuvo DRM, which requires users to authenticate their purchase through an online server. This prevents the game from being copied or pirated and ensures that only legitimate customers can play.

5. DRM for Images and Visual Content: Protecting Photography and Artwork

Visual artists, photographers, and graphic designers face the challenge of protecting their digital artwork from unauthorized use and distribution. DRM tools for images typically focus on watermarking, embedding metadata, and controlling access to high-resolution files.

Recommended DRM tools for images:

- **Digimarc**: Digimarc offers a DRM solution specifically designed for protecting digital images. It embeds a unique watermark or digital fingerprint in the image file, making it easy to track and identify unauthorized usage.

- **Pixsy**: Pixsy not only helps photographers protect their images but also provides tools for tracking unauthorized use across the web. It enables users to take action against image theft and secure compensation for illegal use.

- **Adobe Photoshop DRM**: Adobe Photoshop offers tools to protect visual content by adding watermarks, restricting editing permissions, and embedding metadata that identifies the creator and usage rights of the file.

Example:

A photographer uploads their portfolio to a stock photo website, using Digimarc to embed a digital watermark in each image. This watermark prevents unauthorized copying and ensures that the photographer retains control over how their work is used.

Conclusion: Choosing the Right DRM Tools for Your Content

Selecting the right DRM tools and technologies depends on the type of content you're protecting and how you want to distribute it. From ebooks to music, video, software, and images, there are a wide variety of DRM solutions available to help you safeguard your creative work while providing a seamless experience for legitimate users. By leveraging the appropriate DRM tools, you can maintain control over your digital assets and ensure that your content is protected from piracy and unauthorized use.

With the right DRM strategy in place, you'll be well-equipped to protect your creative work and maximize its value across digital platforms. In the next chapter, we'll explore how to monitor and enforce DRM, ensuring that your content remains secure and your rights are upheld in the digital space.

Quick Tips and Recap

- **Choose the Right DRM for Your Media**: Tailor your DRM strategy based on the type of content—ebooks, music, video, software, or images—to ensure optimal protection.

- **Keep DRM User-Friendly**: Balance protection with a seamless user experience by ensuring that DRM doesn't overly restrict legitimate access or usage.

- **Use Trusted DRM Tools**: Platforms like Adobe Digital Editions, Apple FairPlay, Google Widevine, and Denuvo offer reliable solutions for protecting different types of digital content.

- **Protect Multiple Devices**: Allow flexibility for users to access content across multiple devices while maintaining security through DRM controls.

- **Embed Metadata and Watermarks**: For visual content, using watermarks and metadata can help track and control unauthorized use.

- **Monitor Online Access**: For software and games, require license keys and online verification to prevent unauthorized usage and ensure compliance.

- **Stay Updated on DRM Technologies**: The digital landscape changes rapidly, so regularly review and update your DRM tools to keep your content secure.

By implementing the right tools and balancing protection with convenience, you can safeguard your digital assets while maintaining a positive experience for your users.

Tech Meets Copyright: Impact of New Technologies on Copyright

"As technology continues to evolve, so too must our approach to copyright. It's about staying ahead of the curve to ensure our creations are protected in a digital age." — ELON MUSK, CEO OF SPACEX AND TESLA

Chapter Seventeen, "Tech Meets Copyright: Impact of New Technologies on Copyright," is where the old school meets the new wave, and trust me, it's not just a polite handshake—it's a full-blown dance-off. As technology evolves at a breakneck pace, so too must our understanding of copyright law, lest our creative works get left doing the Macarena while everyone else is flossing.

In this chapter, we'll explore the wild frontier of emerging tech—from blockchain proving copyrights to AI creating artworks that could fool even the keenest eye.

How do we apply century-old laws to creations made by machines? And what happens when 3D printing can replicate anything, including your most cherished inventions?

Prepare to have your mind expanded and possibly a little boggled as we navigate the tricky waters where technology disrupts tradition. By the end, you'll not only understand these innovations but be ready to harness them, ensuring that your copyright strategy is as cutting-edge as the tech that challenges it. Grab your gear; it's time to future-proof your creative rights.

AI and Machine-Generated Content: Who Owns the Copyright?

As artificial intelligence (AI) becomes more sophisticated, its ability to create music, art, literature, and even software that rivals human-made content raises a fundamental question: Who owns the copyright to works created by AI? This question is at the heart of a growing debate as machine-generated content becomes increasingly common in the creative industries. In this section, we will explore the complexities of copyright ownership when the creator is not a human but a machine, and how this emerging challenge is reshaping the legal landscape of intellectual property.

1. The Rise of AI-Created Works

AI systems like OpenAI's GPT (the technology behind this text), DALL·E, and DeepMind's AlphaGo have demonstrated remarkable creativity in generating text, art, music, and even writing code. These AI tools are capable of learning from vast amounts of data and applying that knowledge to produce original works. However, because AI is not human, it does not fall within traditional frameworks of copyright law, which have always been based on human authorship.

Examples of AI-generated content include:

- **Music**: AI systems like AIVA and Amper Music can compose entire symphonies or background music, raising questions about who owns the resulting tracks.

- **Art**: Programs like DALL·E and Deep Dream create original artworks based on inputs, generating images that mimic human creativity.

- **Writing**: AI systems like GPT can produce original articles, stories, and scripts, challenging the definition of "author."

Example:

In 2018, a portrait created by an AI program named Edmond de Belamy was sold at auction for $432,500. The work was generated by a machine learning algorithm, sparking debate over whether the creators of the algorithm, the AI itself, or the people behind the sale owned the copyright.

2. Copyright Law's Definition of Authorship

Traditionally, copyright law requires that a work be created by a human to qualify for protection. Under most legal systems, including U.S. copyright law, works produced by non-humans are generally not eligible for copyright protection. The U.S. Copyright Office has explicitly stated that copyright cannot be granted to works "produced by a machine or mere mechanical process that operates randomly or automatically without any creative input or intervention from a human author."

However, the challenge arises when humans and AI collaborate to create content. For instance, if a human provides the inputs or initial parameters that guide the AI's creative process, can that human be considered the author of the resulting work? In some cases, copyright may be awarded to the person who guided the AI, but the rules around this are not yet fully developed.

Key considerations:

- **Human involvement**: Copyright laws may grant ownership to the person who actively guided or programmed the AI, as long as there is significant human creative input.

- **Ownership of the AI itself**: Some argue that the owner or developer of the AI tool should hold the copyright, as they created the technology that made the work possible.

Example:

An AI-assisted art generator creates a painting based on parameters set by a human user. While the AI generated the final image, the human input in defining the style, subject, and colors might qualify them as the author, giving them the copyright under current laws.

3. The Debate Around Machine Authorship

As AI becomes more autonomous, the question of machine authorship becomes even more pressing. Some legal scholars and futurists have suggested that AI systems could, in theory, be granted copyright themselves, much like how corporations (legal entities) can own copyright. However, this raises philosophical and ethical questions about whether a non-human entity should be treated as a "creator" with legal rights.

Challenges of machine authorship:

- **Responsibility and liability**: If AI holds copyright, who is responsible for enforcing it? Can a machine sue for infringement? These legal responsibilities traditionally fall on the human creator or owner.

- **Originality**: Copyright law requires that a work be "original" to its creator. If an AI system is merely processing and remixing existing content, can it truly create something "original"? AI often uses massive datasets of existing works to generate new content, blurring the line between creation and reproduction.

Example:

In 2019, a group of musicians and AI developers used AI to compose music in the style of Beethoven. While the music is technically new, it heavily relies on analyzing and mimicking Beethoven's style. Does this count as an original work, and if so, who owns it—the developers, the AI, or no one?

4. Current Legal Approaches and Future Considerations

As of now, most copyright systems do not grant AI authorship. Instead, the human creators, programmers, or users involved in guiding the AI's output typically retain copyright ownership, though this area of law is still in flux. In some cases,

AI-generated works fall into the public domain because they lack human authorship, which means anyone can use them without restriction.

Legal responses so far:

- **The United States**: U.S. law does not recognize AI as an author. Human input is necessary for a work to be protected by copyright. The U.S. Copyright Office has rejected attempts to register works created entirely by machines without human involvement.

- **The European Union**: EU copyright law similarly requires human authorship. However, the EU is actively exploring the implications of AI-generated content, and future reforms may address this issue.

- **Japan**: Japan has been more open to AI-generated works, suggesting that the legal owner of the AI or its creator could hold the copyright in cases where a human's involvement is minimal.

What's next?

- **Legal reforms**: As AI continues to evolve, we may see future reforms that provide clearer guidelines on who owns the rights to AI-generated works. This could involve assigning copyright to the programmers, users, or even the AI itself in certain circumstances.

- **Global harmonization**: With AI-generated works becoming more common globally, there may be a need for international standards to address these questions consistently across borders.

Example:

In 2020, the UK government proposed reforms that could grant copyright protection to certain AI-generated works, but the idea remains controversial. Some fear it could limit access to creative content or stifle innovation if AI-generated works are granted the same protections as human-made content.

Conclusion: Navigating AI and Copyright Ownership

The intersection of AI and copyright law is one of the most complex and rapidly evolving areas of intellectual property. While current laws generally favor human authorship, the increasing role of AI in creative processes is challenging traditional notions of ownership and creativity. As AI technology continues to advance, copyright laws will need to evolve to address these new realities, ensuring that creators—whether human or machine—are properly recognized and rewarded.

In the next section, we'll explore how blockchain technology is being used to secure copyright ownership and protect digital works in the evolving digital landscape.

Blockchain and Copyright: Securing Ownership in the Digital Age

The rise of blockchain technology has revolutionized several industries, from finance to supply chain management, and is now poised to impact the way we handle copyright protection. In an increasingly digital world where content is easily duplicated and distributed, ensuring ownership and tracking usage has become a major challenge for creators. Enter blockchain—a decentralized, immutable ledger technology that can help creators secure ownership and track the usage of their intellectual property. In this section, we'll explore how blockchain is transforming copyright management and what it means for the future of protecting creative works.

1. What is Blockchain?

At its core, blockchain is a type of distributed ledger technology (DLT) that records transactions across a network of computers in a way that ensures transparency, security, and immutability. Each piece of data, or "block," is linked to the previous one, creating a "chain" of data that cannot be altered without consensus from the entire network.

Blockchain's unique features make it particularly well-suited for copyright protection, as it allows for:

- **Secure ownership records**: Once ownership of a creative work is recorded on a blockchain, it cannot be altered or tampered with. This provides an immutable record of who created or owns a piece of content.

- **Transparency and traceability**: Blockchain allows for the transparent tracking of content usage, licenses, and royalties, enabling creators to see how and where their work is being used.

Example:

A musician uploads their song to a blockchain-based platform, where the blockchain records the time of creation, the identity of the artist, and the terms of the license. This record is permanent and can be referenced at any time to prove ownership or track how the song is used across the internet.

2. How Blockchain Can Secure Copyright Ownership

Blockchain offers a groundbreaking solution for proving ownership and establishing the origin of creative works in the digital world. By recording an artwork, song, book, or other creative product on a blockchain, creators can generate an immutable proof of ownership. This record can then serve as evidence in legal disputes over copyright infringement or unauthorized use.

Key ways blockchain secures ownership:

- **Timestamping and verification**: When a creator uploads their work to a blockchain, the date and time of the upload are securely recorded. This creates a tamper-proof timestamp that can be used to prove when the work was created, providing an indisputable record of authorship or ownership.

- **Smart contracts**: Blockchain also enables the use of smart contracts, which are self-executing contracts with the terms of the agreement written directly into code. For creators, this means that licensing agreements and royalty payments can be automated. Once certain conditions are met (e.g., someone downloads a song), the smart contract can automatically transfer payment to the creator.

- **Global recognition**: Because blockchain operates on a decentralized global network, ownership records on the blockchain are accessible from anywhere in the world. This makes it easier for creators to prove ownership and enforce their rights across international borders.

Example:

A photographer uploads their images to a blockchain-based copyright platform that issues a unique digital certificate of ownership. If the photographer later finds their images being used without permission, they can refer to the blockchain record as evidence of their ownership and take legal action.

3. Blockchain and Licensing: Automating Rights Management

One of the most powerful applications of blockchain in copyright management is the automation of licensing and royalty payments through smart contracts. Traditionally, managing licenses and ensuring that creators receive proper compensation has been a complex and time-consuming process. Blockchain simplifies this by automating the entire lifecycle of licensing agreements.

How smart contracts work:

- **Pre-programmed terms**: Creators can encode their licensing terms into a smart contract, specifying the conditions under which their work can be used (e.g., the cost of a license, duration of use, etc.).

- **Automatic execution**: When someone purchases a license to use the work, the smart contract automatically executes the transaction, transferring funds to the creator's account and granting the user access to the content.

- **Royalty tracking**: For works like music, smart contracts can automatically distribute royalties to all involved parties based on pre-determined splits (e.g., a composer, producer, and artist). This eliminates the need for intermediaries and ensures creators are paid fairly and on time.

Example:

A musician encodes the terms of their song's licensing into a smart contract on a blockchain platform. When a film producer buys the rights to use the song, the smart contract automatically transfers the agreed-upon payment to the musician and issues a license for the song's use. The process is transparent, instant, and secure.

4. Blockchain and Copyright Infringement: Tracking and Enforcing Rights

Beyond securing ownership and automating licensing, blockchain can also be used to track usage and detect potential copyright infringement. By embedding unique identifiers or "fingerprints" into digital files (e.g., music, videos, images), blockchain allows creators to track how their content is distributed and used across the internet.

Ways blockchain helps enforce copyright:

- **Content tracking**: Digital files can be embedded with blockchain-verified identifiers that make it easy to track their distribution. If unauthorized copies of the content appear online, the blockchain record can be used to trace the origin of the infringement and take action.

- **Automatic takedown notices**: In cases of copyright infringement, smart contracts can be programmed to automatically issue takedown notices or cease-and-desist letters when the blockchain detects unauthorized use of the content.

- **Proof of infringement**: In legal disputes, blockchain provides creators with immutable proof of ownership and can help prove when and where the infringement occurred.

Example:

An artist uploads their digital artwork to a blockchain-based platform that assigns a unique identifier to each image. When the artist discovers that their work is being sold without permission on another website, they use the blockchain record to prove that they own the original artwork and issue a takedown notice to the infringing site.

5. Challenges and Limitations of Blockchain in Copyright

While blockchain offers exciting possibilities for copyright protection, it's important to recognize that the technology is still relatively new, and there are several challenges and limitations that need to be addressed.

Challenges of blockchain in copyright:

- **Adoption and accessibility**: For blockchain to become a standard tool for copyright management, it needs to be widely adopted by creators, businesses, and legal systems. Currently, the technology is still niche, and many creators may not be familiar with how to use it.

- **Energy consumption**: Some blockchain networks, particularly those that use proof-of-work consensus mechanisms (like Bitcoin), consume large amounts of energy. This has raised concerns about the environmental impact of blockchain technologies.

- **Legal recognition**: While blockchain provides a secure record of ownership, the legal systems in many countries are still catching up to the technology. In some cases, blockchain-based evidence may not yet be recognized in court as definitive proof of ownership.

Example:

A writer uses blockchain to timestamp their manuscripts, ensuring that they can prove ownership if their work is ever copied or stolen. However, when a dispute arises, the court is unsure how to treat the blockchain record, leading to delays in resolving the case.

Conclusion: The Future of Blockchain in Copyright Protection

Blockchain technology offers a promising new frontier for copyright protection, enabling creators to secure ownership, automate licensing, and track usage with unprecedented transparency and security. While the technology is still evolving, its potential to revolutionize copyright management is clear. As blockchain continues to gain traction, creators who embrace it early will be well-positioned to protect their intellectual property in the digital age.

In the next section, we'll explore how 3D printing is raising new copyright challenges, particularly in the realm of physical and digital design.

3D Printing and Copyright: Protecting Physical and Digital Designs

The rise of 3D printing has revolutionized manufacturing, design, and even art, allowing anyone with the right equipment and files to create physical objects from digital blueprints. While this technology offers incredible possibilities, it also introduces new challenges for copyright protection, as digital files for 3D-printed objects can be easily shared, modified, and replicated. In this section, we will explore how 3D printing affects copyright law, the difficulties of protecting physical and digital designs, and what creators can do to safeguard their intellectual property in this rapidly evolving space.

1. The Basics of 3D Printing and Copyright Challenges

3D printing, also known as additive manufacturing, involves creating three-dimensional objects by layering material based on a digital blueprint or CAD (Computer-Aided Design) file. These digital design files can be easily shared online, raising concerns about the unauthorized use and replication of copyrighted designs.

While traditional copyright law covers the protection of creative works, it was not designed with 3D printing in mind, leaving many creators and companies struggling to protect their physical and digital designs. The ability to 3D-print physical objects from digital files makes it easier than ever for individuals to infringe on copyright by duplicating or modifying designs without permission.

Challenges of protecting designs with 3D printing:

- **File sharing**: Once a CAD file is uploaded or shared online, it can be downloaded and used by anyone with access to a 3D printer, making it difficult to control or monitor the distribution of digital designs.

- **Design modification**: Digital files can be easily altered, allowing users to tweak or modify a copyrighted design and claim it as their own, blurring the lines between original and derivative works.

- **Physical replication**: While copyright law traditionally applies to creative works like literature, music, and visual art, it is less clear how it applies to physical objects. This raises the question of whether a 3D-printed object based on a copyrighted design infringes on that design's copyright.

Example:

A toy designer creates a unique action figure and uploads the 3D design file online. Without permission, others download the file, print the toy, and sell it on their own, violating the designer's copyright. The designer is left with little control over how the digital and physical versions of the toy are being distributed.

2. Copyrighting 3D Design Files: Protecting the Digital Blueprint

One of the primary ways to protect intellectual property in the 3D printing world is through the copyrighting of digital design files (CAD files). Since the design file itself is a creative work, it is eligible for copyright protection just like other forms of intellectual property such as music or art.

How copyright applies to digital design files:

- **Originality**: The digital blueprint must be an original creation, meaning it cannot be a direct copy of another person's work. Copyright protection applies to the expression of the idea (the design itself), not the idea of the object being created (e.g., a chair or a toy).

- **File distribution**: Once a design file is copyrighted, the creator has exclusive rights to control its distribution, reproduction, and modification. Unauthorized sharing or selling of the file constitutes copyright infringement.

- **Digital watermarks**: To track the use of digital files, creators can embed watermarks or other identifiers into the design files, making it easier to trace unauthorized copies or modifications. Watermarks can serve as evidence in legal disputes over copyright ownership.

Example:

A jewelry designer creates a 3D design file for a custom ring and copyrights the file. They sell the digital file on a platform where customers can download it and print the ring. If the file is shared without permission or modified and re-uploaded as a different design, the designer can take legal action to protect their copyright.

3. Protecting Physical Designs: 3D Printing and Design Patents

While copyright protects the digital design files used for 3D printing, design patents are often more effective for protecting the physical objects themselves. Design patents provide legal protection for the unique, ornamental features of a physical object, preventing others from producing or selling a similar design without permission.

How design patents protect physical designs:

- **Ornamental designs**: A design patent applies to the unique visual appearance of an object rather than its functional features. This makes it particularly useful for protecting the aesthetic aspects of products, such as furniture, jewelry, or fashion items.

- **Exclusive rights**: Once a design patent is granted, the patent holder has exclusive rights to produce, sell, and license the design for a set period (usually 15 years in the U.S.). Unauthorized replication or sale of the design is considered patent infringement.

- **Broader protection**: While copyright may not always cover physical objects, a design patent extends protection to the 3D-printed replicas of a design, providing creators with a legal tool to combat infringement in the physical world.

Example:
An industrial designer creates a unique lamp design and secures a design patent for its ornamental features. If someone prints a 3D replica of the lamp using a modified version of the original design file, the designer can take legal action to stop the production and sale of the knockoff lamps, citing patent infringement.

4. Digital Rights Management (DRM) for 3D Printing: Limiting Unauthorized Use

Just as Digital Rights Management (DRM) is used to protect music, video, and software from unauthorized distribution, DRM tools are also being developed to safeguard 3D design files and prevent them from being used without permission.

DRM technology can restrict how design files are shared, printed, or modified, giving creators more control over their intellectual property.

How DRM works for 3D printing:

- **License management**: Creators can set specific terms for how their design files can be used, such as allowing a file to be printed a limited number of times or only on specific 3D printers. DRM systems ensure that these conditions are enforced.

- **Anti-copying measures**: DRM can prevent unauthorized copying of design files or block modifications that alter the original work without the creator's consent.

- **Tracking and reporting**: DRM tools can track the distribution and usage of digital design files, alerting creators to potential infringement or unauthorized replication of their designs.

Example:

A fashion designer uses DRM technology to protect a 3D-printed shoe design. The DRM restricts the file to being printed only three times by licensed 3D printers. If the file is shared or used beyond these limits, the DRM blocks further printing and notifies the designer of the violation.

5. Legal Frameworks and Future Considerations

While copyright and design patents offer some protection for digital and physical designs in the world of 3D printing, the legal frameworks governing this area are still evolving. As 3D printing becomes more widespread, legislators and courts will need to address the unique challenges it poses to intellectual property rights.

Key legal considerations for the future:

- **Defining infringement**: Courts will need to clarify when the replication of a 3D-printed object constitutes copyright or patent infringement, especially in cases where designs are modified.

- **International enforcement**: 3D printing operates in a global marketplace, making it difficult to enforce copyright or patent protections across borders. International treaties and legal cooperation will be necessary to protect creators' rights worldwide.

- **Balancing innovation and protection**: As 3D printing continues to drive innovation, legal systems must strike a balance between encouraging creativity and protecting the rights of original creators. Overly strict regulations could stifle experimentation, while too little protection could lead to rampant infringement.

Example:

A startup develops a new line of 3D-printed medical devices and secures design patents to protect their unique features. However, they discover that manufacturers in another country are producing knockoff versions of the devices without permission. Enforcing their patent rights internationally becomes a complex and expensive process, highlighting the need for stronger global IP enforcement mechanisms.

Conclusion: Navigating Copyright in the 3D Printing Era

3D printing presents exciting opportunities for creators but also significant challenges in terms of copyright and intellectual property protection. By understanding how to secure copyright for digital design files, pursuing design patents for physical objects, and leveraging DRM technologies, creators can better safeguard their designs in this new landscape. However, the legal frameworks governing 3D printing are still developing, and future reforms will likely be needed to ensure robust protection for both digital and physical designs.

In the next section, we'll look at how copyright law is adapting to these and other technological disruptions, exploring what changes may be on the horizon as tech continues to evolve.

The Future of Copyright Law: Adapting to Technological Disruption

As technology continues to evolve at a rapid pace, the world of copyright law finds itself constantly playing catch-up. Emerging technologies like AI-generated content, blockchain, and 3D printing challenge traditional notions of intellectual property, and existing laws are often ill-equipped to handle these new complexities. This final section will explore how copyright law is adapting to these technological disruptions, what changes we can expect in the future, and how creators can stay ahead of the curve.

1. The Push for Legal Reforms

Many legal systems around the world are beginning to recognize the challenges posed by new technologies and are pushing for reforms to ensure that copyright law remains relevant. Legislators are considering ways to update copyright frameworks to address issues such as machine-generated content, digital asset tracking, and cross-border enforcement.

Key areas for reform:

- **AI-generated content**: As AI continues to create art, music, and literature, lawmakers are grappling with the question of authorship and ownership. Should AI-generated works be eligible for copyright protection, and if so, who owns the copyright—the developer, the user, or the machine itself?

- **Blockchain and smart contracts**: Blockchain technology is pushing the boundaries of copyright enforcement, allowing for automated royalty payments and immutable ownership records. Legal reforms may need to formally recognize blockchain-based copyrights and smart contracts as valid tools for managing intellectual property.

- **Digital content and fair use**: As digital media continues to dominate; issues of fair use and user rights are increasingly coming under scrutiny. Lawmakers may need to clarify how fair use applies in a world where content is easily copied, remixed, and shared across platforms.

Example:
The European Union recently updated its Copyright Directive, which aims to address the challenges posed by online platforms and digital content. The directive includes provisions to hold tech platforms accountable for copyright violations and ensure that creators are compensated for their work, reflecting a growing recognition of the need for legal reforms in the digital age.

2. Global Harmonization of Copyright Laws

As technologies like AI, blockchain, and 3D printing operate in a global marketplace, the need for international cooperation in copyright enforcement is becoming increasingly important. Many creators face challenges in protecting their works across borders, as different countries have varying levels of copyright protection and enforcement mechanisms.

Why global harmonization matters:

- **Cross-border enforcement**: In today's digital age, copyrighted works are often shared and distributed internationally, making it difficult to enforce intellectual property rights across multiple jurisdictions. Harmonizing copyright laws and enforcement mechanisms would make it easier for creators to protect their work globally.

- **Consistency for digital platforms**: Major digital platforms like YouTube, Spotify, and Amazon operate across many countries, each with its own copyright rules. A more unified global copyright system would simplify compliance for these platforms and ensure that creators receive consistent protection no matter where their content is accessed.

Current global efforts:

- **The Berne Convention**: One of the most important international treaties governing copyright, the Berne Convention establishes basic protections for creators worldwide. However, as new technologies emerge, updates to this and other treaties may be necessary to address modern challenges.

- **WIPO (World Intellectual Property Organization)**: WIPO is actively engaged in exploring how new technologies are impacting copyright, including AI and blockchain. Through international discussions, WIPO seeks to create frameworks that help harmonize copyright laws across different countries.

Example:
A filmmaker based in the U.S. discovers that their movie is being illegally streamed on a website hosted in another country with weak copyright

enforcement. Without strong international cooperation, it becomes difficult to stop the infringement and protect their intellectual property rights across borders.

3. Protecting Creativity in the Age of Automation

One of the most significant challenges for copyright law in the future will be how to protect human creativity in an age where machines can generate content. As automation and AI take on larger roles in content creation, it's important to ensure that human creators are still incentivized and rewarded for their contributions.

Challenges of automation:

- **Displacement of human creators**: As AI systems become more adept at generating high-quality art, music, and writing, human creators may find themselves competing with machines for recognition and compensation. Copyright law may need to adapt to ensure that human creativity remains valuable and protected.

- **New definitions of originality**: Copyright law has traditionally required that a work be original to its creator. However, as AI becomes more involved in the creative process, the definition of originality may need to evolve. If AI-generated content is derived from existing works, where does the line between derivative work and original creation lie?

Example:

A company uses an AI program to generate custom logos for businesses, replacing the need for human designers. While this technology offers efficiency and cost savings, it raises questions about how copyright law should address AI-generated logos and whether human designers will still be able to compete in this space.

4. The Role of Creators in Shaping the Future

As copyright law evolves to meet the demands of the digital age, creators have an important role to play in shaping the future of intellectual property protection. By staying informed about legal developments, advocating for their rights, and embracing new technologies, creators can ensure that they remain at the forefront of the copyright landscape.

How creators can take charge:

- **Stay informed**: Creators should actively follow changes in copyright law and emerging technologies that may impact their work. By understanding the legal landscape, they can better protect their intellectual property and make informed decisions about how to manage their rights.

- **Advocate for reform**: Many creators are actively pushing for copyright reforms that address the challenges posed by new technologies. By engaging with lawmakers, participating in industry groups, and voicing their concerns, creators can help shape laws that protect their rights while fostering innovation.

- **Embrace new tools**: Technologies like blockchain, smart contracts, and AI can be powerful tools for creators. By adopting these technologies early, creators can gain a competitive edge and ensure that their work is protected and monetized in new ways.

Example:

A group of musicians advocates for legislation that would establish clear guidelines on the use of AI in music production, ensuring that human artists are properly credited and compensated when AI is used to generate derivative works based on their original compositions.

Conclusion: The Future of Copyright in a Tech-Driven World

As technology continues to disrupt traditional notions of creativity and ownership, copyright law must evolve to protect both human creators and the innovative works generated by machines. From AI-generated content and blockchain-based copyright protection to the challenges posed by 3D printing, the future of copyright law will be defined by how it adapts to these technological shifts. By staying informed and embracing new tools, creators can ensure that their work remains protected, even in the face of rapid change.

In the next chapter, we'll explore practical strategies for monitoring and enforcing copyright in the digital age, ensuring that your intellectual property rights are upheld in an increasingly complex and interconnected world.

Quick Tips and Recap

- **AI-Generated Content**: Current copyright laws favor human authorship, but AI's role in content creation is growing. Stay informed about future legal developments regarding ownership of AI-generated works.

- **Blockchain for Copyright**: Use blockchain technology to create immutable records of ownership and automate royalty payments via smart contracts, ensuring transparency and security in your digital rights management.

- **3D Printing and Copyright**: Protect your digital designs with copyright and design patents. Consider using DRM technologies to prevent unauthorized sharing and replication of 3D design files.

- **Global Harmonization**: As technology operates globally, pushing for consistent international copyright laws is essential for cross-border enforcement of intellectual property rights.

- **Stay Informed About Legal Reforms**: Keep up with changes in copyright law to ensure your intellectual property is protected, especially as new technologies challenge traditional frameworks.

- **Advocate for Change**: Creators should engage with lawmakers and industry groups to help shape future copyright reforms that balance innovation with the protection of intellectual property.

- **Embrace New Tools**: Explore technologies like blockchain, DRM, and AI to enhance the protection and management of your creative works in the digital age.

By staying ahead of technological trends and understanding their impact on copyright, you can ensure that your intellectual property remains protected and monetized in the future.

Pirates Ahoy: Dealing with Digital Piracy

"Digital piracy isn't just a nuisance; it's a direct challenge to intellectual property rights and a threat to creators everywhere. We must adapt and enforce with vigilance to protect our works in the digital age." — SUNDAR PICHAI, CEO OF GOOGLE

Chapter Eighteen, "Pirates Ahoy: Dealing with Digital Piracy," is your guide to navigating the choppy waters of the Internet, where digital pirates lurk behind every click, ready to plunder your precious content. This isn't about walking the plank; it's about being the captain who outsmarts the scallywags and safeguards their treasure.

In this chapter, we'll deploy tactics that are more cunning than a barrel of monkeys and as effective as a cannonball barrage. You'll learn how to spot a pirate ship from a mile away and the best strategies for repelling boarders— figuratively speaking, of course. From encryption to watermarking, and the legal avenues open to you when your work is hijacked, we'll cover all the bases.

Prepare to fortify your digital assets like a fortress and use every tool in your arsenal to keep the pirates at bay. After all, in the vast ocean of the Internet, it's better to be the feared admiral than the easy target. So hoist the sails, ready the cannons, and let's make sure those pirates get nothing but a good view of your stern as you sail into the sunset.

Identifying Digital Pirates: How to Spot and Monitor Online Piracy

The first step in combating digital piracy is knowing how to identify when and where it's happening. In the vast ocean of the internet, digital pirates can hide behind the anonymity of websites, social media platforms, and peer-to-peer networks. In this section, we'll explore how to recognize the signs of piracy, the tools available to monitor unauthorized use of your content, and how to take proactive measures to stop pirates in their tracks.

1. Common Types of Digital Piracy

Digital piracy can take many forms, from unauthorized downloads to illegal streaming services, making it essential to recognize the various ways your content could be compromised. Below are the most common types of digital piracy:

- **File-sharing websites**: Piracy often occurs on file-sharing platforms where users upload and download copyrighted material without authorization. These sites may offer everything from books and music to movies and software.

- **Torrents and peer-to-peer (P2P) networks**: Torrent sites and P2P networks like BitTorrent enable users to share large files quickly, making them popular among pirates. These networks decentralize the distribution process, making it harder to track the original uploader.

- **Streaming websites**: Unauthorized streaming websites provide access to pirated movies, TV shows, and music. These platforms often operate under different domain names and can be difficult to shut down.

- **Social media and forums**: Pirates sometimes use social media groups, forums, and messaging apps to share links to pirated content or distribute copyrighted material directly.

Example:

An author notices their book being offered for free on a file-sharing website, despite it being available for purchase only on legitimate platforms. This is a common form of piracy, where digital copies of ebooks are illegally uploaded and shared.

2. Tools and Methods for Monitoring Piracy

Once you know where digital pirates may be hiding, the next step is to monitor these platforms and detect unauthorized use of your content. Fortunately, there are tools and services designed to help creators keep an eye on their work across the internet.

Tools for identifying digital piracy:

- **Google Alerts**: Set up Google Alerts for your name, brand, or specific content titles. This free tool will notify you whenever your content is mentioned online, making it easier to spot potential piracy.

- **Reverse image search**: For visual content like artwork or photographs, tools like Google's Reverse Image Search or TinEye can help you track where your images have been posted online. This is particularly useful for photographers, designers, and illustrators whose work might be illegally shared without permission.

- **Copyright monitoring services**: Services like Digimarc, PiracyTrace, and MUSO offer comprehensive piracy monitoring, scanning the web, torrent sites, and social media for unauthorized use of your content. These services often provide detailed reports on where your work is being pirated and assist in issuing takedown notices.

Example:

A musician uses MUSO, a piracy monitoring service, to track where their songs are being shared on illegal torrent sites. MUSO provides daily reports, allowing the musician to quickly issue takedown requests and stop the spread of pirated content.

3. Spotting Signs of Piracy

While monitoring tools are essential, you can also identify piracy manually by keeping an eye out for certain red flags:

- **Unusual spikes in traffic**: If you notice an unexplained spike in downloads or streams on your legitimate platforms, it could be a sign that your content has been pirated elsewhere. Pirates often attract traffic to illegitimate copies, which can impact your legitimate sales.

- **Fake copies or listings**: Scammers sometimes create fake listings of your digital products on websites like Amazon or eBay. If you find listings for your work at prices much lower than usual—or offered for free—there's a good chance your content has been pirated.

- **User reports**: Loyal fans or customers may alert you to instances of piracy. Creators often receive emails or messages from fans who have seen unauthorized copies of their work circulating online. Always follow up on these reports and investigate further.

Example:

An independent filmmaker notices a sudden drop in views on their official streaming platform, despite previously consistent traffic. After some investigation, they find their film being illegally streamed on a free movie website. This is a common sign that piracy is siphoning off legitimate traffic.

4. Proactive Monitoring on Social Media and Forums

Digital piracy isn't limited to file-sharing websites. Pirates often promote their content via social media platforms, discussion forums, or messaging apps. These platforms can act as hubs for pirates to share links to unauthorized copies of your work, and they can sometimes reach thousands of users in a short time.

Tips for monitoring social media and forums:

- **Social media searches**: Regularly search for mentions of your work on social media platforms like Twitter, Instagram, and Facebook. Look for suspicious links or posts offering your content for free.

- **Join relevant groups**: If you suspect piracy is occurring in niche forums or social media groups, join these communities to monitor activity. You can also enlist the help of fans to report instances of piracy.

- **Use anti-piracy bots**: Platforms like Discord and Reddit sometimes allow the use of bots to detect and report piracy. These bots can be programmed to monitor channels for specific keywords or suspicious links and notify you when they detect piracy-related content.

Example:

A software developer finds that pirated versions of their app are being distributed in a Discord community. They use an anti-piracy bot to monitor the server for any mention of their software, allowing them to quickly take action and report the illegal activity.

5. Partnering with Anti-Piracy Organizations

If piracy becomes a recurring issue, you may want to consider partnering with anti-piracy organizations. These organizations work on behalf of creators to monitor piracy, issue takedown notices, and take legal action against infringers.

Anti-piracy organizations include:

- **The Copyright Alliance**: This organization advocates for creators' rights and provides resources to help protect intellectual property from piracy.

- **The Recording Industry Association of America (RIAA)**: For musicians and the music industry, the RIAA is heavily involved in fighting digital piracy by monitoring peer-to-peer networks, issuing takedown requests, and taking legal action against large-scale infringers.

- **The Motion Picture Association (MPA)**: Filmmakers can seek assistance from the MPA, which actively monitors illegal streaming sites and helps protect film content from piracy.

Example:

A game developer struggling with piracy enlists the help of an anti-piracy organization to monitor torrent sites for illegal copies of their game. The organization issues multiple takedown notices and helps the developer regain control over the distribution of their software.

Conclusion: Stay Vigilant and Proactive

Identifying digital pirates is the first step in protecting your work from unauthorized use. By understanding where piracy occurs, using monitoring tools, and keeping an eye out for red flags, you can stay ahead of potential threats and take action before piracy impacts your revenue. Regular monitoring and proactive measures, such as partnering with anti-piracy organizations, will help you maintain control over your digital assets.

In the next section, we'll explore preventive measures like encryption, watermarking, and DRM that can help you secure your work before pirates even have the chance to strike.

Preventive Measures: Encryption, Watermarking, and DRM

In the fight against digital piracy, the best offense is a strong defense. By employing preventive measures such as encryption, watermarking, and Digital Rights Management (DRM), you can deter potential pirates from stealing or misusing your content. These tools not only help protect your work from unauthorized access and distribution but also make it easier to track and enforce your intellectual property rights. In this section, we'll explore how these three critical technologies can be used to safeguard your digital assets and prevent piracy before it even begins.

1. Encryption: Locking Down Your Content

Encryption is the process of converting data into a secure code that only authorized users can unlock. By encrypting your digital content—whether it's an ebook, music file, software, or video—you can prevent unauthorized users from accessing or sharing it without your permission. Encryption serves as the first line of defense against piracy by ensuring that only those who have purchased or licensed your content can use it.

How encryption works:

- **Data encryption**: When your content is encrypted, it's converted into a code that is unreadable without the appropriate decryption key. This key is typically provided when a legitimate user purchases or subscribes to your content.

- **Public and private keys**: Some encryption systems use a combination of public and private keys to protect content. The public key is used to encrypt the data, while the private key (held by the user) is needed to decrypt it. This ensures that only authorized users can unlock the content.

- **End-to-end encryption**: This method ensures that content remains encrypted during transmission, such as when streaming video or transferring files between devices. It prevents unauthorized parties from intercepting the content.

Example:

A software developer uses encryption to protect their app's source code. When a user purchases the app, they receive a unique key that allows them to unlock and install the software. If the file is shared with others, the encryption remains in place, preventing unauthorized use.

2. Watermarking: Tagging Your Digital Content

Watermarking involves embedding visible or invisible markers into digital content that identify the owner or creator. Watermarks serve as a digital signature that makes it harder for pirates to steal your work without leaving a trace. Watermarks can be applied to a wide variety of content, including images, videos, documents, and audio files.

Types of watermarks:

- **Visible watermarks**: These are obvious markers, such as a logo or text overlay, that are placed directly on the content. Visible watermarks deter unauthorized use by clearly identifying the work as your own. They are commonly used in photography, design, and stock imagery.

- **Invisible watermarks**: These are embedded into the digital file's metadata and cannot be seen by users. Invisible watermarks are often used to track and verify ownership in case of a dispute, and they can be detected with specialized tools.

- **Forensic watermarking**: This technique embeds unique identifiers into each copy of the digital content, allowing creators to trace the source of unauthorized distribution. Forensic watermarks are especially useful for high-value content like films, software, and confidential documents.

Example:

A photographer uploads their images to a stock photo website with a visible watermark overlay on each image. If someone attempts to use or distribute the images without purchasing a license, the watermark serves as a clear indicator of unauthorized use. Meanwhile, the photographer also uses invisible watermarks to track where the images are shared.

3. Digital Rights Management (DRM): Controlling Access and Usage

Digital Rights Management (DRM) is a technology that helps creators and companies control how their digital content is accessed, distributed, and used. DRM tools can restrict actions such as copying, sharing, printing, or modifying the content, ensuring that it remains within the boundaries set by the creator. DRM is widely used for ebooks, music, software, and video, and it plays a crucial role in preventing digital piracy.

Key DRM features:

- **Access control**: DRM systems ensure that only authorized users can access the content by requiring authentication (such as a password, license key, or subscription) before the content is unlocked.

- **Usage restrictions**: DRM can prevent users from copying or sharing the content with others. For example, it may limit the number of times a file can be downloaded or restrict playback to certain devices.

- **License management**: DRM tools allow creators to manage different types of licenses, such as pay-per-view, rental, or lifetime access. They can automate payments and ensure that users comply with the licensing terms.

- **Geographic restrictions**: DRM can enforce regional licensing by restricting content access based on a user's geographic location, ensuring that content is only accessible where it is licensed for distribution.

Example:

An ebook author uses DRM to protect their book on Amazon Kindle. The DRM system ensures that readers who purchase the ebook can only access it on Kindle devices or apps. It also prevents readers from sharing the ebook file with others or converting it to another format.

4. Combining Preventive Measures for Maximum Protection

While encryption, watermarking, and DRM are powerful tools on their own, they become even more effective when used together. By layering these preventive measures, creators can build a comprehensive defense against piracy that addresses multiple aspects of content protection.

How to combine preventive measures:

- **Encrypt and watermark**: By encrypting your content and embedding watermarks (either visible or invisible), you can ensure that pirates can't easily steal or share your content without leaving behind traces of their activity.

- **Apply DRM with encryption**: Combining encryption with DRM ensures that your content is protected both from unauthorized access and unauthorized usage. For example, encrypted video files can be restricted to only authorized users, while DRM prevents them from copying or sharing the content.

- **Use forensic watermarking with DRM**: For high-value content like movies or software, forensic watermarking can be used alongside DRM to trace the source of any unauthorized copies that might be circulating online.

Example:

A filmmaker releases their latest movie on a streaming platform using DRM to control access and encryption to protect the file from unauthorized downloads. They also apply forensic watermarking, allowing them to trace any illegal copies of the film that might appear on torrent sites.

5. Staying Ahead of Pirates with Regular Updates

Preventive measures need to be regularly updated to stay ahead of evolving piracy tactics. Pirates are constantly finding new ways to bypass DRM, encryption, and watermarking, so it's important to stay vigilant and update your tools as new technologies become available. Keeping your preventive measures current will ensure that your digital assets remain secure in the face of new threats.

Example:

A video game developer regularly updates their DRM system to protect against newly developed piracy tools that target game cracks. By staying ahead of the pirates, the developer ensures that their game remains secure and that legitimate users continue to support the product.

Conclusion: Proactively Defend Your Digital Content

Encryption, watermarking, and DRM are essential tools in the fight against digital piracy. By proactively implementing these measures, you can significantly reduce the risk of unauthorized access, copying, and distribution of your content. Combining these technologies and regularly updating them will provide a strong defense that protects your work from digital pirates.

In the next section, we'll dive into the legal side of dealing with digital piracy, exploring how to issue takedown notices, cease and desist letters, and pursue lawsuits against pirates who steal your work.

Taking Legal Action: Takedown Notices, Cease and Desist, and Lawsuits

When preventive measures aren't enough to stop digital pirates, it's time to take legal action. From sending takedown notices to filing lawsuits, there are several legal avenues available to protect your intellectual property and assert your rights. In this section, we'll explore how to use these legal tools effectively, what each one entails, and how to escalate your response when necessary to protect your work.

1. Takedown Notices: Using the DMCA to Remove Infringing Content

The Digital Millennium Copyright Act (DMCA) is a powerful tool for removing infringing content from the internet. It provides a legal process for sending takedown notices to websites and platforms that host or distribute unauthorized copies of your work. If the infringing content is on a platform that complies with the DMCA, such as YouTube, social media sites, or file-sharing platforms, the website must remove the content upon receiving a valid DMCA notice.

How to issue a DMCA takedown notice:

- **Identify the infringing content**: Before issuing a takedown notice, locate the specific URLs or files where your copyrighted work is being infringed. It's important to be precise to ensure that the platform can easily identify and remove the content.

- **Submit a DMCA notice**: Most platforms have an online form or contact method for submitting DMCA takedown requests. Your notice should include:

  - A description of the copyrighted work being infringed.

  - The URLs or locations of the infringing content.

  - A statement confirming that you are the copyright owner or authorized to act on behalf of the owner.

  - A request for the removal of the infringing content.

- **Monitor compliance**: After submitting the notice, the platform must respond promptly, typically by removing the content. Some platforms will notify the infringing user, who has the right to issue a counter-notice if they believe the takedown was wrongful.

Example:

An author finds a website offering free downloads of their ebook without permission. They submit a DMCA takedown notice to the website's hosting provider, requesting that the unauthorized ebook be removed. The hosting provider complies, and the infringing content is taken down within a few days.

2. Cease and Desist Letters: A Formal Warning to Pirates

A cease and desist letter is a formal legal document that demands a person or organization stop engaging in unlawful activity—in this case, distributing or using your copyrighted content without permission. It serves as a warning to the infringer that if they do not comply, you may take further legal action, such as filing a lawsuit.

How to write a cease and desist letter:

- **Identify the infringer**: Ensure you have the correct contact details for the person or entity responsible for the infringement. This could be an individual, a company, or even the administrator of a website where your content is being distributed.

- **Explain the infringement**: Clearly state how your copyrighted material is being used without permission. Include details about the content in question, the specific instances of infringement, and the platform or location where it is occurring.

- **Demand immediate action**: Specify the actions you want the infringer to take, such as removing the infringing content or stopping further distribution. Provide a deadline for compliance, typically 10–14 days.

- **Include legal consequences**: Warn the infringer that failure to comply with the cease and desist letter may result in legal action, including lawsuits and the potential for financial damages.

- **Optional: Consult a lawyer**: While cease and desist letters can be written by the copyright holder, having a lawyer draft or review the letter can give it added weight and ensure that it complies with legal standards.

Example:

A graphic designer finds their artwork being sold as prints on an unauthorized website. They send a cease and desist letter to the website's owner, demanding the removal of the prints and a halt to further sales. The letter warns that legal action will follow if the infringing activity continues.

3. Filing a Lawsuit: Taking Pirates to Court

If takedown notices and cease and desist letters fail to stop the infringement, you may need to escalate the situation by filing a copyright infringement lawsuit. This step should be considered when the piracy is causing significant financial harm or if the infringer refuses to comply with previous warnings. Filing a lawsuit can result in monetary damages, court orders to stop the infringement, and even criminal penalties in extreme cases.

Steps for filing a copyright infringement lawsuit:

- **Consult an attorney**: Copyright law is complex, and you'll need a qualified intellectual property attorney to help you navigate the legal process. Your attorney will assess the strength of your case and advise on the best course of action.

- **Gather evidence**: Before filing a lawsuit, you'll need to gather comprehensive evidence of the infringement. This includes screenshots, links, purchase records, and any communication with the infringer. The more detailed your evidence, the stronger your case will be in court.

- **File the lawsuit**: Once the evidence is gathered, your attorney will file the lawsuit in the appropriate jurisdiction. The infringer will be served with legal documents and will have an opportunity to respond. The case may go to trial, or the infringer may settle out of court to avoid further legal costs.

- **Seek damages**: If your lawsuit is successful, the court may award you damages for the infringement. This can include compensation for lost revenue, statutory damages (in cases of willful infringement), and legal fees. In some cases, the court may issue an injunction, requiring the infringer to stop using or distributing your work.

Example:

A software company discovers that their program has been pirated and distributed through multiple torrent websites. After sending several cease and desist letters that are ignored, the company files a copyright infringement lawsuit against the website's operators, seeking damages for lost sales and the immediate shutdown of the infringing sites.

4. Weighing the Costs and Benefits of Legal Action

While legal action can be an effective way to stop piracy and recover financial damages, it's important to weigh the costs and benefits before proceeding. Lawsuits can be time-consuming, expensive, and emotionally draining, especially if the infringer is difficult to locate or operating in another country.

Factors to consider:

- **Severity of the infringement**: If the piracy is causing significant financial harm or damaging your reputation, legal action may be worth pursuing. However, if the infringement is minor or the content is being distributed on a small scale, the costs of a lawsuit may outweigh the potential benefits.

- **Likelihood of success**: Consult with an attorney to assess your chances of winning the case. If the infringer is operating anonymously or from a country with weak copyright enforcement, it may be difficult to achieve a favorable outcome.

- **Alternative solutions**: In some cases, reaching a settlement or negotiating a licensing agreement with the infringer may be more practical than going to court. This approach can save time and money while still protecting your rights.

Example:

A musician finds that their song is being illegally used in an advertisement by a small company. Rather than filing a lawsuit, the musician's attorney negotiates a licensing agreement with the company, allowing them to use the song legally in exchange for fair compensation.

Conclusion: Know When to Fight

Taking legal action is often the last resort when dealing with digital pirates, but it can be an effective way to stop infringement and protect your rights. Whether you choose to issue a DMCA takedown notice, send a cease and desist letter, or file a lawsuit, it's essential to understand your legal options and consult with an attorney when necessary. Knowing when and how to escalate your response will help you defend your intellectual property and ensure that pirates are held accountable for their actions.

In the next section, we'll explore how to build a strong defense by educating your audience about piracy and using technology to bolster your defenses against future threats.

Building a Strong Defense: Educating Your Audience and Leveraging Technology

While legal actions and preventive measures like DRM and encryption can protect your digital content, one of the most effective ways to fight digital piracy is by educating your audience and using cutting-edge technology to bolster your defenses. In this final section, we'll explore how fostering a culture of respect for intellectual property among your fans and leveraging the latest tech innovations can create a proactive, long-term strategy against piracy.

1. Educating Your Audience: The Power of Awareness

A significant portion of digital piracy stems from a lack of awareness rather than malicious intent. Many users don't realize the impact piracy has on creators or mistakenly believe that if content is available for free online, it's legal to download. By educating your audience, you can help reduce piracy by fostering a culture of respect and understanding around intellectual property rights.

Tips for educating your audience:

- **Explain the impact of piracy**: Use your platform—whether it's a website, blog, or social media channel—to share how piracy directly affects you as a creator. Show your audience that illegal downloads or unauthorized sharing reduce your ability to continue producing content, which can resonate with those who want to support your work.

- **Encourage legal alternatives**: Promote legal ways for your audience to access your work. Whether it's through a subscription service, purchasing from your online store, or streaming on a legitimate platform, provide clear paths for your audience to enjoy your content legally.

- **Offer free samples or previews**: One of the reasons people turn to pirated content is the desire to "try before they buy." By offering free samples, chapters, or demo versions of your content, you can give your audience a taste of your work without resorting to illegal downloads.

- **Engage with your audience**: Engage with your fans and customers through social media and blogs, responding to questions and addressing concerns about pricing or availability. Building strong relationships with your audience fosters loyalty, and loyal fans are less likely to seek out pirated copies of your work.

Example:

A filmmaker regularly posts on social media, explaining the financial challenges of independent filmmaking and how piracy undermines their ability to fund future projects. By creating an emotional connection with their audience, they encourage fans to purchase or stream the movie legally to support the project.

2. Leveraging Technology: Staying Ahead of Pirates

While education is essential, leveraging the latest technology to protect your content is equally important. Pirates are constantly evolving their tactics, so it's critical to stay one step ahead by using advanced tools to secure your intellectual property and monitor potential infringements.

Technological tools to protect your content:

- **Blockchain for copyright tracking**: As mentioned earlier, blockchain technology can be used to create immutable records of ownership, ensuring that your work is protected and easily traceable. By embedding your content in a blockchain ledger, you can verify ownership and monitor distribution across the internet.

- **Artificial Intelligence (AI) for monitoring**: AI-powered tools can scan the web for unauthorized copies of your content, identifying potential infringers faster than manual searches. These tools can monitor social media, file-sharing sites, and streaming platforms in real-time, alerting you when your content is pirated and helping you take immediate action.

- **Content recognition systems**: Platforms like YouTube Content ID and Facebook Rights Manager allow creators to automatically track where their content is used on those platforms. These tools can detect unauthorized uploads of your work and either block the content or monetize it on your behalf.

- **Watermarking and digital fingerprints**: As mentioned earlier, embedding invisible watermarks or unique digital fingerprints into your content allows you to trace its origins if it's shared without permission. These technologies help identify the source of unauthorized distribution and provide evidence in legal disputes.

Example:

An author uses Digimarc to embed invisible watermarks in their ebook. When pirated copies of the book appear on file-sharing sites, the watermarks allow the author to trace the origin of the illegal files and take action to remove them.

3. Incentivizing Legal Access: Rewarding Your Supporters

Another effective strategy for reducing piracy is incentivizing legal access to your content. Offering perks, rewards, or exclusive content to paying customers can encourage your audience to support you through legitimate means rather than seeking out pirated versions.

Ways to incentivize legal access:

- **Exclusive content or early access**: Offer paying customers early access to new releases, exclusive behind-the-scenes content, or bonus material that isn't available through illegal downloads. This creates a sense of value and reward for those who support you legally.

- **Membership or subscription models**: Create membership tiers that offer perks like premium content, live Q&A sessions, or signed merchandise. Fans are more likely to avoid piracy when they feel like part of a community that directly supports the creator.

- **Discounts and special offers**: Periodically offering discounts, bundle deals, or limited-time offers can attract customers who might otherwise turn to pirated content because of pricing concerns.

Example:

A musician offers exclusive behind-the-scenes videos, early access to new singles, and discounted concert tickets to fans who purchase their music through the official website. This approach fosters loyalty and discourages fans from seeking out pirated copies.

4. Building Partnerships with Platforms and Anti-Piracy Organizations

Finally, you don't have to fight piracy alone. Partnering with online platforms and anti-piracy organizations can significantly strengthen your defenses by providing you with the tools and support you need to combat piracy on a larger scale.

How to build partnerships:

- **Work with online platforms**: Major platforms like YouTube, Amazon, and Spotify have dedicated anti-piracy systems in place. By registering your content with these platforms, you can ensure that they help monitor and take down unauthorized copies of your work.

- **Join anti-piracy organizations**: Organizations like the Copyright Alliance, RIAA, and MPA provide resources and legal assistance for creators dealing with piracy. These organizations can monitor piracy on your behalf, issue takedown notices, and even initiate legal action against large-scale infringers.

- **Use anti-piracy software**: Services like MUSO, PiracyTrace, and Digimarc offer tools to monitor and protect your content across the web. These services can automate much of the piracy detection process, saving you time and ensuring that infringements are addressed quickly.

Example:

A software developer partners with PiracyTrace, an anti-piracy service that monitors torrent sites for unauthorized versions of the developer's app. The service automatically issues takedown notices to websites hosting the pirated software, helping the developer maintain control over their product's distribution.

Conclusion: A Comprehensive Approach to Piracy Defense

Fighting digital piracy requires a multi-faceted approach that includes educating your audience, leveraging advanced technologies, and building partnerships with platforms and anti-piracy organizations. By fostering a culture of respect for intellectual property and using the latest tools to protect your content, you can significantly reduce the risk of piracy and ensure that your work remains secure.

In the next chapter, we'll explore how to maintain ongoing copyright protection by keeping up with changes in copyright law, technology, and enforcement strategies.

Quick Tips and Recap

- **Educate Your Audience**: Build awareness about the negative impacts of piracy by explaining how it affects your ability to create content and offering legal alternatives for access.

- **Promote Legal Access**: Provide exclusive content, early access, or discounted offers to incentivize your audience to support you through legitimate means.

- **Use Blockchain and AI**: Leverage blockchain for secure ownership tracking and AI-powered tools to monitor the web for unauthorized copies of your work.

- **Apply Watermarks and DRM**: Protect your content with invisible watermarks and Digital Rights Management (DRM) to deter and track piracy.

- **Partner with Platforms**: Work with platforms like YouTube, Facebook, and Amazon that offer built-in anti-piracy tools to help monitor and remove infringing content.

- **Engage Anti-Piracy Services**: Use services like MUSO, PiracyTrace, or Digimarc to automate piracy detection and enforcement, freeing up your time to focus on content creation.

- **Create a Loyal Fanbase**: Strengthen your relationship with your audience by offering exclusive perks and fostering a community that values and supports your work.

By combining education, technology, and strategic partnerships, you can effectively combat digital piracy and maintain control over your intellectual property.

Social Media Scrutiny: Copyright Challenges on Social Platforms

"Social media is the new frontier for copyright law; navigating it requires a clear understanding of both its power and its pitfalls. Creators must be vigilant to protect their work while engaging with this dynamic platform."— MARK ZUCKERBERG, CEO OF FACEBOOK

Chapter Nineteen, "Social Media Scrutiny: Copyright Challenges on Social Platforms," is where we dissect the frenetic dance of sharing, posting, and reposting that defines our digital lives. It's like navigating a high school reunion; you want to look your best, share your highlights, but avoid any embarrassing faux pas—especially those that could lead to legal drama.

In this jungle of hashtags and handles, understanding the copyright rules isn't just smart—it's survival. We'll explore the minefield of memes, the quagmire of quotables, and the vortex of viral videos, pinpointing exactly where admiration crosses into infringement. You'll learn the ins and outs of what can (and just as importantly, cannot) be shared, ensuring that your next post isn't just lit but also legally sound.

From the subtleties of user-generated content to the harsh realities of takedown notices, this chapter ensures you're not only trending but also treading carefully. So, tighten up your privacy settings and sharpen your content strategies; it's time to conquer the social media arena with confidence and compliance!

Memes, GIFs, and Viral Content: Understanding Fair Use and Copyright

Social media thrives on memes, GIFs, and viral content, with users sharing and resharing these pieces of pop culture across platforms. However, what feels like innocent fun can quickly land creators and brands in murky legal waters. In this section, we'll explore the copyright implications of using and sharing memes, GIFs, and viral content, and how **fair use** can—or cannot—protect you.

1. The Nature of Memes and GIFs: A Copyright Minefield

Memes and GIFs often consist of images, video clips, or audio that originated elsewhere—typically from movies, TV shows, or music—making them subject to copyright protection. When these materials are reposted or repurposed into new formats (e.g., adding text to a meme or looping a short video into a GIF), the original creator or copyright holder retains their rights over the content. Even though memes and GIFs are seen as part of internet culture, the original material is still someone's intellectual property.

Why memes and GIFs may infringe copyright:

- **Derivative works**: Memes and GIFs typically modify or transform existing works (images, videos, or audio), which can qualify them as **derivative works** under copyright law. Creating or sharing a derivative work without permission may constitute copyright infringement.

- **Unauthorized sharing**: If the meme or GIF is based on copyrighted content (such as a movie clip or song), sharing it without the owner's permission—even for humorous purposes—could be an infringement.

Example:

The popular "Distracted Boyfriend" meme, based on a stock photo by Antonio Guillem, became viral on social media. While it seemed like harmless fun, Guillem retained the copyright to the image and could technically pursue legal action against those using his work without permission.

2. Fair Use: When Memes and GIFs Might Be Protected

Many creators assume that their use of memes, GIFs, and viral content falls under fair use, a legal doctrine that allows limited use of copyrighted material without permission in certain circumstances. While fair use can apply, it's a narrow and complex defense, especially on social media where content is shared widely and quickly.

Factors determining fair use:

- **Purpose and character of use**: Fair use tends to favor transformative works that add new meaning or purpose to the original content, such as parody, criticism, or commentary. Memes and GIFs that significantly alter or recontextualize the original material might qualify, but simple reposting without transformation likely will not.

- **Nature of the copyrighted work**: Fair use is more likely to apply if the original work is factual rather than highly creative. However, memes and GIFs often originate from creative works (e.g., films, music, or art), making this factor less favorable.

- **Amount and substantiality used**: Using small, non-essential portions of a copyrighted work may favor fair use. Memes and GIFs that utilize brief clips or images may qualify under this criterion, but if they feature significant portions of a copyrighted work, it could be harder to defend as fair use.

- **Effect on the market**: If the meme, GIF, or viral content negatively affects the market for the original work or its potential licensing opportunities, it's less likely to be considered fair use. For example, if a GIF is shared widely and diminishes the commercial value of the original video, it could lead to legal trouble.

Example:

A short clip from a movie turned into a viral GIF might be considered fair use if it's used in a highly transformative way, such as to critique or parody the film. However, if the GIF is simply a loop of a popular scene with no added commentary, it's unlikely to qualify as fair use.

3. The Role of Platforms: Content Sharing and Copyright Compliance

Social media platforms like Facebook, Instagram, and Twitter provide users with tools to share content, but they also have strict policies regarding copyright compliance. Platforms often implement content filtering systems and rely on DMCA takedown notices to address copyright violations. While platforms offer a safe harbor from liability as long as they remove infringing content when notified, creators are still responsible for the content they upload and share.

Platform responsibilities:

- **Automated content detection**: Many platforms use content identification tools (like YouTube's Content ID) to detect copyrighted material in posts. If a meme or GIF contains copyrighted elements, it might be flagged and removed automatically.

- **DMCA takedowns**: Copyright holders can file DMCA takedown notices if they find their material being used without permission. If a meme or GIF you've posted is flagged, the platform is required to remove it or face legal consequences.

- **Reposting with caution**: Just because something has gone viral or has been reposted thousands of times doesn't make it safe to use. Always be mindful of the potential copyright implications when sharing viral content, and where possible, seek permission or use content licensed for reuse.

Example:

A Twitter user posts a meme using a GIF from a popular TV show, and it goes viral. Shortly after, the user receives a DMCA takedown notice from the network that owns the show, asking the platform to remove the infringing content.

4. Best Practices: Staying Safe While Sharing Memes and GIFs

To avoid copyright issues while still engaging in social media fun, there are several best practices you can follow when sharing memes, GIFs, and viral content.

Best practices to follow:

- **Create your own memes**: Use original images or free-to-use content to create your own memes. Many platforms offer stock images or public domain content that can be safely used for creative purposes.

- **Use licensed content**: If you want to share copyrighted material, look for content that is licensed for public use. Websites like Giphy offer GIFs that have been cleared for sharing under specific terms, making it easier to avoid infringement.

- **Transform content**: If you're repurposing existing content, ensure that your work is transformative enough to qualify for fair use. This might involve adding commentary, changing the meaning of the original, or using it for parody or critique.

- **Credit the original creator**: While giving credit doesn't automatically shield you from copyright infringement, it's a good practice to acknowledge the original creator. In some cases, creators may allow you to share their work if properly credited.

Example:

A small business owner creates their own meme using a royalty-free image from an online stock photo site. By adding their unique branding and humorous text, they avoid any copyright issues and create engaging, original content for social media.

Conclusion: Sharing Safely in the Meme Culture

Memes, GIFs, and viral content are integral to social media culture, but they often straddle the line between creativity and copyright infringement. By understanding the nuances of fair use, being mindful of platform policies, and using content responsibly, you can navigate this space without risking legal issues. Whether you're creating or sharing, it's essential to respect copyright law while participating in the fast-paced world of social media.

In the next section, we'll dive into user-generated content (UGC) and discuss how to navigate the copyright challenges around reposting and owning content created by others on social platforms.

User-Generated Content: Rights, Permissions, and Ownership

User-Generated Content (UGC) has become the lifeblood of social media, with brands, influencers, and creators increasingly relying on posts, images, videos, and reviews shared by users to promote products and engage audiences. However, the legal landscape surrounding the rights, permissions, and ownership of UGC is often complex and can lead to copyright issues if not handled properly. In this section, we'll explore the copyright implications of UGC, who owns the content, and how to navigate the legalities of sharing or repurposing user-created content.

1. What is User-Generated Content?

UGC refers to any content—such as posts, photos, videos, comments, and reviews—created and shared by users on social media platforms rather than by the brands or organizations themselves. For businesses, UGC is a powerful tool for building community, increasing engagement, and providing authentic content that resonates with audiences.

However, while UGC is often publicly shared, that does not necessarily mean it is free for commercial use. Just because users post content on social platforms doesn't mean they relinquish their copyright over it, making it important to understand how to navigate permissions and ownership issues.

Examples of UGC:

- A customer posts a picture of themselves wearing a brand's clothing and tags the brand on Instagram.

- A fan creates a fan art illustration based on a movie and shares it on Twitter.

- A user writes a detailed review of a product and uploads it as a video on YouTube.

2. Who Owns User-Generated Content?

The general rule of copyright law is that the original creator of a work automatically owns the copyright to that work, regardless of whether it's posted on social media or another public platform. This means that users who create content—whether a photo, video, or piece of writing—own the rights to that content, even after posting it online. As the copyright owner, they have exclusive rights to control how the content is used, distributed, and monetized.

Key points about UGC ownership:

- **Copyright remains with the user**: Users retain copyright ownership of the content they create, even if it is posted publicly on platforms like Instagram, Twitter, or Facebook. Sharing content publicly does not transfer copyright ownership.

- **Social media platforms don't own UGC**: While platforms may have licensing agreements in their terms of service (allowing them to host and display the content), they do not gain copyright ownership. Platforms merely have the right to showcase the content within the confines of their service.

- **Brands don't own UGC**: If a brand wants to use user-generated content for commercial purposes—such as reposting, sharing on a website, or using in an ad campaign—it must obtain permission from the content's creator, even if the user has tagged the brand or mentioned them in a post.

Example:

A beauty influencer posts a photo of themselves using a makeup product and tags the makeup brand on Instagram. While the brand may wish to repost the photo on its own Instagram account, it doesn't automatically have the legal right to do so without seeking permission from the influencer, who owns the photo.

3. Requesting Permission to Use UGC

To legally use UGC for commercial purposes, brands and individuals must obtain explicit permission from the content's creator. This is often done through direct messages, emails, or official permissions processes, depending on the platform and context. Simply giving credit or tagging the original creator is not enough to avoid copyright infringement.

How to obtain permission:

- **Ask directly**: Reach out to the user who created the content and request permission to use their photo, video, or post. This can be done via direct message or email. Be clear about how you intend to use the content (e.g., reposting on social media, using it in a marketing campaign, etc.).

- **Provide a clear licensing agreement**: If the UGC is to be used in a broader commercial context, such as an advertising campaign, provide a simple licensing agreement that outlines how the content will be used and what rights the creator is granting. The agreement should cover issues such as the duration of use, geographic restrictions, and whether the creator will be compensated.

- **Screenshot consent**: If you're obtaining permission through social media DMs or comments, keep a screenshot of the user's consent as proof that permission was granted. This can serve as legal protection in case there is any dispute later.

Example:

A restaurant sees a customer's Instagram post showing a photo of a beautifully plated dish and wants to share it on their official social media account. The restaurant messages the customer, asking for permission to repost the photo. Once permission is granted, the restaurant saves the conversation and credits the customer when they share the photo.

4. Platforms and Terms of Service: Implied Permissions

Some social media platforms have terms of service agreements that give platforms and other users limited permissions to repost or share content within the ecosystem of the platform. For example, if someone posts content on Twitter, other users can retweet it without needing explicit permission, as this falls under the platform's functionality. However, this does not extend to taking content outside of the platform or using it for commercial purposes without permission.

Key points about platform terms of service:

- **Limited use on-platform**: Platforms may allow for limited sharing and reposting of content within the platform itself (e.g., retweets, story shares). This is typically built into the terms of service, but it does not mean users can download and use content outside the platform without permission.

- **No commercial use**: Just because content can be reshared within a platform doesn't mean it can be repurposed for commercial use. If you want to use UGC in marketing materials or ads, you'll still need explicit permission from the content creator.

Example:
A Twitter user posts a meme that goes viral, and many other users retweet it. This kind of sharing is allowed within Twitter's platform, but if a company wants to use the meme in a marketing campaign, they need to ask for the creator's permission before doing so.

5. UGC Contests and Hashtags: Establishing Terms

Many brands encourage users to post content related to their products or services by creating UGC contests or campaigns with specific hashtags. In these cases, it's important to establish clear terms and conditions that specify how the UGC will be used and what rights the user is granting to the brand by participating in the campaign.

How to establish terms for UGC contests:

- **Create clear guidelines**: Specify in the contest rules that by submitting content (via hashtag or submission form), users are granting the brand a license to use their content for specific purposes. Make sure the terms are clear about where and how the content will be used (e.g., social media, website, advertising).

- **Ensure participants agree to terms**: Before a user participates in the UGC contest, ensure they have acknowledged and agreed to the terms and conditions. This might involve directing them to a webpage that explains the rights they are granting.

Example:

A clothing brand runs an Instagram contest asking users to post photos of themselves wearing the brand's clothing with a specific hashtag. The contest rules state that by participating, users are granting the brand permission to use their photos on social media and the brand's website. Users are required to agree to these terms before entering.

Conclusion: Navigating UGC with Care

User-generated content is a powerful tool for brands and creators, but it's essential to respect copyright law and the ownership rights of the content creators. By obtaining permission, clearly outlining terms in UGC campaigns, and understanding the limits of platform-based sharing, you can safely and legally leverage UGC to build your brand or engage with your audience.

In the next section, we'll explore takedown notices and platform policies, diving into how copyright infringement is handled on social media and what you can do if your content is used without permission.

Takedown Notices and Platform Policies: Navigating DMCA in the Social Media World

In the fast-paced, content-driven world of social media, it's easy for copyrighted material to be shared, reposted, or used without permission. Whether it's a photo, video, or piece of music, unauthorized use of your work can lead to significant consequences, including loss of revenue or damage to your brand. Fortunately, platforms and copyright laws, such as the Digital Millennium Copyright Act (DMCA), provide ways to take action. In this section, we'll explore how to navigate DMCA takedown notices, the policies of social media platforms, and how to deal with infringement on social platforms.

1. What is a DMCA Takedown Notice?

The DMCA is a U.S. copyright law enacted to protect creators from unauthorized use of their content on the internet. A key component of the DMCA is the takedown notice, which allows copyright holders to request the removal of infringing content from websites or social media platforms. If your copyrighted work has been used without permission on a social platform, a DMCA takedown notice is often the most effective first step in having the content removed.

How a DMCA takedown notice works:

- **Identify the infringing content**: Before filing a takedown notice, locate the specific post, video, image, or other content that is infringing your copyright. Make sure to note the URLs, usernames, and platforms where the infringement occurs.

- **Submit the notice**: Platforms like YouTube, Facebook, Instagram, and Twitter allow users to file DMCA takedown requests via their support centers or help pages. The notice must include:

    o   A description of your copyrighted work.

    o   The location (URL) of the infringing content.

    o   A statement affirming that the use of the content is unauthorized and infringes your copyright.

    o   Your contact information and a statement made under penalty of perjury that the information in the notice is accurate.

- **Removal of content**: Once the platform receives the takedown notice, it will typically remove the infringing content within a short period. The infringer may also receive a notification from the platform, giving them the opportunity to file a counter-notice if they believe the takedown is unjustified.

Example:

A photographer discovers that their image has been reposted on Instagram without permission by a popular account. The photographer files a DMCA takedown notice with Instagram, requesting that the platform remove the image. Instagram complies, and the post is taken down within a few days.

2. Platform Policies: DMCA Compliance and Copyright Enforcement

Each social media platform has its own set of policies and processes for handling copyright infringement claims, but all major platforms adhere to the DMCA's basic framework. Understanding the specific policies of the platform where the infringement occurs can help you file a more effective takedown request.

Platform-specific DMCA policies:

- **YouTube**: YouTube uses an automated system called Content ID to detect and manage copyrighted material. Content ID matches uploaded videos to a database of copyrighted content, flagging any potential infringement. Copyright holders can also file DMCA takedown requests manually if their work is used without permission.

- **Instagram**: Instagram has a copyright infringement form available on its help page, allowing users to file DMCA notices. If the notice is valid, Instagram will remove the infringing post and notify the user who posted it.

- **Twitter**: Twitter also allows users to submit a DMCA takedown request through its help center. Once received, Twitter reviews the claim and removes the content if it is found to infringe upon the copyright holder's rights.

- **Facebook**: Facebook's Rights Manager provides creators with tools to protect their content, automatically identifying and removing unauthorized uses. Facebook also accepts traditional DMCA takedown notices if your content is used without permission.

Example:

A musician finds their song used in a YouTube video without permission. The musician files a manual DMCA takedown request, and YouTube removes the video. In the future, the musician opts to enroll in YouTube's Content ID program to automatically detect unauthorized use of their music.

3. What Happens After a Takedown Notice?

After a DMCA takedown notice is filed, the platform will remove or disable access to the infringing content. However, the process doesn't always end there. The user who posted the content has the option to file a counter-notice if they believe the takedown was made in error.

What to expect after filing a takedown notice:

- **Notification of removal**: Once the platform takes down the content, you will receive confirmation that your request has been fulfilled. The platform will also notify the infringing user that their content was removed.

- **Counter-notice process**: The user who posted the content may file a counter-notice claiming that the content does not infringe on your copyright (e.g., if they believe it falls under fair use). If a counter-notice is filed, the platform will restore the content unless you take further legal action.

- **Legal options**: If you believe the counter-notice is unjustified, you may need to take legal action to resolve the dispute. In some cases, this can involve filing a lawsuit to assert your copyright and prevent the infringer from continuing to use your work.

Example:

A YouTube content creator posts a video using clips from a copyrighted film without permission. The film studio files a DMCA takedown notice, and YouTube removes the video. The creator files a counter-notice, claiming the use of the clips qualifies as fair use for a review. The studio chooses not to pursue further legal action, and YouTube reinstates the video.

4. Protecting Yourself from False Claims and Abuse of the DMCA

While the DMCA provides an essential tool for copyright protection, it's not uncommon for the system to be misused. Some users file false DMCA claims or abuse the process to remove legitimate content, such as criticism or parody. If you find yourself the target of a wrongful takedown request, it's important to know how to respond.

How to protect yourself from false DMCA claims:

- **File a counter-notice**: If you receive a DMCA takedown notice for content you believe is not infringing (such as fair use or content you own), you can file a counter-notice with the platform. The counter-notice should explain why you believe the takedown was incorrect and request that the content be restored.

- **Gather evidence**: Collect evidence to support your case, such as proof of ownership, documentation of licensing agreements, or an explanation of how the content qualifies under fair use. This can help bolster your counter-notice and protect your rights.

- **Avoid repeated violations**: Some platforms penalize users for repeated DMCA takedown notices. If your content is consistently flagged, it's important to review your practices to ensure you're complying with copyright laws and not inadvertently infringing on others' work.

Example:

A YouTuber creates a parody video using short clips from a popular movie. The movie studio files a DMCA takedown notice, but the YouTuber believes their video is protected under fair use as a parody. They file a counter-notice with YouTube, explaining their argument for fair use, and YouTube reinstates the video.

5. Best Practices for Using Copyrighted Material on Social Media

To avoid potential copyright issues on social media, it's crucial to follow best practices when sharing or using content created by others. While DMCA takedown notices are an effective remedy for infringement, it's always better to prevent issues before they arise.

Best practices for avoiding copyright infringement:

- **Create original content**: Whenever possible, create your own original content rather than using material owned by others. This eliminates the risk of infringing on someone else's copyright and ensures you retain full ownership of your work.

- **Seek permission**: If you want to use copyrighted content, always seek permission from the creator or copyright holder. This might involve reaching out to the creator or purchasing a license to use the material legally.

- **Understand fair use**: Familiarize yourself with the principles of fair use, particularly if you create content that involves commentary, parody, or criticism. Make sure your use of copyrighted material falls within the bounds of fair use before posting it on social media.

Example:

A social media manager for a brand wants to use a popular song in a promotional video. Instead of using the song without permission, they reach out to the artist and secure the proper licensing rights, ensuring the video is both creative and legally compliant.

Conclusion: Navigating the DMCA with Confidence

DMCA takedown notices provide a vital mechanism for protecting your content on social media, but it's important to understand how to file them correctly and respond to counter-notices when necessary. By familiarizing yourself with each platform's policies, using best practices for copyright compliance, and being proactive in protecting your rights, you can confidently navigate the challenges of social media copyright issues.

In the next section, we'll explore monetizing social media content and the legal considerations you need to keep in mind when collaborating with brands, creating sponsored posts, or turning your social media presence into a revenue stream.

Monetizing Social Media Content: Legal Considerations for Creators

In today's digital landscape, social media is not just a platform for connection—it's also a powerful tool for monetization. Whether you're an influencer, a brand ambassador, or a content creator, making money from your posts, videos, and collaborations is a common goal. However, monetizing social media content comes with its own set of legal challenges and responsibilities. In this section, we'll explore the key legal considerations for creators who want to monetize their social media presence, ensuring that your revenue streams are not only profitable but also legally sound.

1. Sponsored Content and Brand Collaborations

One of the most popular ways to monetize social media is through sponsored content and brand collaborations. Creators partner with brands to promote products or services in exchange for compensation, which can range from free products to significant financial payouts. While these partnerships are lucrative, they also come with legal obligations, including adhering to disclosure requirements and ensuring the content meets copyright standards.

Key legal considerations for sponsored content:

- **Disclosure rules**: Most countries have strict regulations requiring transparency in advertising. In the U.S., the Federal Trade Commission (FTC) mandates that creators clearly disclose their relationship with a brand whenever they are paid or receive free products in exchange for promotion. Use hashtags like #ad or #sponsored, or simply state "This post is sponsored by [brand]" to make sure your followers know when a post is an advertisement.

- **Contracts with brands**: Ensure you have a written contract in place for all brand collaborations, outlining the terms of the agreement, including compensation, content deadlines, and usage rights. This protects both you and the brand from misunderstandings or disputes later.

- **Copyright and intellectual property**: If you're using a brand's logo, products, or proprietary material in your sponsored content, make sure you have permission to do so. Conversely, if you create original content for the brand, clarify whether the brand owns the rights to that content or if you retain ownership.

Example:

An Instagram influencer partners with a fitness brand to promote their new workout gear. The influencer posts a photo wearing the gear and includes the hashtag #ad to comply with FTC guidelines. The influencer also ensures that the agreement with the brand specifies how long the post will remain active and whether the brand can repurpose the photo in its own marketing materials.

2. Licensing and Using Third-Party Content

If your social media content involves the use of third-party materials, such as music, photos, videos, or graphics created by others, it's crucial to understand the licensing and copyright issues at play. Unauthorized use of copyrighted material can lead to takedown notices, loss of monetization, or even legal action. To monetize your content safely, make sure you have the appropriate rights or licenses to use any third-party content in your posts.

Legal considerations for using third-party content:

- **Licensing music for videos**: If you use music in a video or post, you must obtain the proper license unless the music is in the public domain or is licensed under a royalty-free agreement. Some platforms, like YouTube, offer a library of music that creators can use without infringing copyright, but using popular songs without permission can lead to demonetization or copyright claims.

- **Stock images and videos**: When using stock images or videos, make sure you're purchasing them from reputable platforms that provide the correct licensing terms for commercial use. Free stock libraries often offer content under Creative Commons licenses, but you need to verify whether commercial use is allowed and if attribution is required.

- **User-generated content**: If you want to use UGC in your social media monetization strategy, obtain explicit permission from the creator to avoid copyright issues. Even when the content is posted publicly, you still need the creator's consent to use it for commercial purposes.

Example:

A YouTube creator includes a popular song in the background of their travel vlog without securing the proper license. As a result, YouTube's Content ID system flags the video, and the creator loses the ability to monetize it. To avoid this in the future, the creator switches to using royalty-free music from YouTube's audio library.

3. Protecting Your Own Content: Copyright and Trademarks

As a content creator, it's essential to protect your own intellectual property, especially if you're monetizing your social media presence. Your original content—photos, videos, graphics, and even slogans—can be vulnerable to theft, misuse, or unauthorized sharing. Taking steps to register copyrights and trademarks for your brand and content can provide legal recourse if someone infringes on your rights.

How to protect your content:

- **Copyright registration**: While your original work is automatically protected by copyright law as soon as it's created, registering your content with the U.S. Copyright Office or a similar agency in your country can strengthen your legal position in case of infringement. This allows you to file a lawsuit and seek damages if someone uses your content without permission.

- **Trademark your brand**: If you've developed a recognizable brand name, logo, or slogan, consider trademarking it. A trademark gives you exclusive rights to use your brand identity in commerce and prevents others from using it without your permission.

- **Monitor for infringement**: Regularly monitor social media platforms and the web for unauthorized use of your content. Services like Google Alerts and anti-piracy tools can help you identify when someone is using your content without permission, allowing you to take action with a takedown notice or legal claim.

Example:

A YouTuber creates a series of tutorial videos and uses a unique tagline that becomes associated with their brand. To protect the tagline, the YouTuber files for a trademark. Later, when another creator starts using the same tagline, the YouTuber sends a cease-and-desist letter, backed by the registered trademark, to stop the infringement.

4. Revenue-Sharing Models on Social Platforms

Many social media platforms offer built-in monetization features that allow creators to earn revenue directly from their content. These include ad revenue sharing, paid subscriptions, and tipping features. Each platform has its own policies regarding how revenue is shared and what type of content qualifies for monetization. It's important to understand these rules to avoid inadvertently violating platform guidelines and risking demonetization.

Platform monetization models:

- **YouTube AdSense and Partner Program**: YouTube allows creators to earn money through ad revenue as part of the YouTube Partner Program. However, content must comply with YouTube's copyright and community guidelines to remain eligible for monetization. Using copyrighted music or footage without permission can lead to demonetization or copyright strikes.

- **Instagram and Facebook**: Instagram and Facebook offer monetization options such as branded content partnerships, in-stream ads, and fan subscriptions. To use these features, creators must meet specific eligibility criteria, such as having a certain number of followers and adhering to platform policies on branded content disclosures.

- **Twitch and TikTok**: Twitch offers revenue-sharing options through ads, subscriptions, and donations from fans. TikTok also allows creators to monetize their videos through virtual gifts and sponsorships, but creators must ensure that all content meets platform guidelines for copyright and appropriate use.

Example:

A Twitch streamer gains a large following and begins earning money through donations and ad revenue. To protect their income stream, the streamer carefully ensures that all music and visuals used in their streams are properly licensed, preventing any potential copyright claims that could lead to demonetization or takedown notices.

Conclusion: Monetize with Confidence and Compliance

Monetizing your social media content offers exciting opportunities for financial success, but it's essential to navigate the legal landscape carefully. Whether you're collaborating with brands, using third-party content, or protecting your own intellectual property, understanding the legal considerations is key to maintaining a profitable and compliant social media presence. By adhering to copyright laws, disclosure rules, and platform guidelines, you can ensure that your content creation remains both creative and compliant.

In the next chapter, we'll discuss how to build a long-term strategy for protecting your intellectual property across different platforms and ensure that your digital rights are safeguarded in a rapidly evolving online world.

Quick Tips and Recap

- **Disclose Sponsored Content**: Always disclose sponsored posts using hashtags like #ad or #sponsored to comply with FTC guidelines and avoid legal issues.

- **Get Written Agreements**: Ensure all brand collaborations are backed by clear written contracts outlining compensation, usage rights, and content deadlines.

- **Obtain Licenses for Third-Party Content**: Before using music, images, or videos you don't own, obtain the necessary licenses or use royalty-free content to avoid copyright infringement.

- **Register Your Copyrights and Trademarks**: Protect your original content and brand assets by registering copyrights and trademarks to safeguard against unauthorized use.

- **Use Platform Monetization Tools**: Take advantage of monetization options on platforms like YouTube, Instagram, and Twitch, but ensure your content complies with copyright and platform guidelines.

- **Monitor for Unauthorized Use**: Regularly check for misuse or theft of your content and use DMCA takedown notices to address copyright infringements.

- **Understand Revenue-Sharing Models**: Familiarize yourself with the revenue-sharing models offered by social media platforms to maximize your earnings without violating any rules.

By following these tips, you can confidently monetize your social media content while staying within legal and platform guidelines.

CHAPTER TWENTY

Future Forward: Emerging Trends in Copyright Law

"Staying future forward in copyright law means continuously adapting to emerging trends and technological advancements to protect intellectual creativity in the digital age." — LAWRENCE LESSIG, PROFESSOR OF LAW AND LEADERSHIP AT HARVARD LAW SCHOOL AND A LEADING ADVOCATE OF COPYRIGHT REFORM

Chapter Twenty, "Future Forward: Emerging Trends in Copyright Law," is your crystal ball into the ever-evolving landscape of intellectual property rights. Strap in and buckle up—this isn't your grandma's copyright law; it's a rocket ship to the new frontiers where technology and legislation collide with a spectacular bang.

In this chapter, we'll zoom into the future, where AI creates art, drones deliver books, and virtual reality experiences are the new storytelling canvas. We'll dissect how copyright law is keeping pace (or panting behind) the rapid technological advancements, preparing you for a world where copyright battles might be fought in digital arenas or even over neural networks.

From blockchain securing digital assets to 3D printing challenging traditional manufacturing, we navigate the thrilling possibilities and potential pitfalls. With an eye on tomorrow, this chapter equips you to not just anticipate the future but to actively shape it, ensuring your creative endeavors stay protected and prosperous in the brave new world of copyright law. Ready your intellectual property phasers—future copyright challenges await!

AI-Generated Creations: Navigating Copyright for Machine-Made Content

As artificial intelligence (AI) continues to advance, the line between human and machine creativity is becoming increasingly blurred. AI-generated works—whether they are images, music, text, or even entire books—are raising critical questions about copyright ownership and intellectual property rights. In this section, we'll explore the challenges and uncertainties surrounding copyright law when it comes to AI-generated content and how creators and lawmakers are navigating this new frontier.

1. The Rise of AI-Generated Content

AI is no longer just a tool for automating tasks—it is now capable of generating original, creative works. From AI programs that compose symphonies to algorithms that design unique art pieces, machines are entering the creative domain. Platforms like OpenAI's GPT and DALL·E can produce written content and images that rival human-made creations, leaving us with a pivotal question: who owns the rights to works generated by AI?

Examples of AI-generated content:

- **Music**: AI systems like AIVA can compose classical music, creating symphonies and scores based on data from famous composers.

- **Art**: AI tools such as DeepArt and DALL·E create stunning visual artwork, often blending styles from famous artists or generating entirely new artistic expressions.

- **Writing**: AI models like GPT-4 can generate articles, poetry, stories, and even entire novels, raising questions about authorship and copyright ownership.

2. The Copyright Dilemma: Who Owns AI-Generated Works?

Traditional copyright law is designed to protect works created by humans, granting the creator the exclusive rights to use, distribute, and monetize their work. But when it comes to works generated by AI, the situation becomes murkier. Current copyright laws do not clearly define who owns the rights to machine-made creations, leaving a legal gray area that could lead to future disputes.

Potential copyright ownership scenarios:

- **The AI itself cannot own copyright**: Since copyright law generally only applies to human creators, an AI system cannot own the copyright to its creations. This leads to the question of whether the developer, user, or another entity holds the rights.

- **The AI developer**: One argument is that the developer of the AI should own the copyright, as they created the tool that made the work possible. However, this position can be complicated by the fact that the AI's outputs are often unpredictable and autonomous.

- **The user**: Another perspective is that the user of the AI—the person who inputs the prompts or guides the AI—should be considered the creator. The user plays a role in shaping the output, though the extent of their contribution is often minimal compared to traditional human authorship.

- **No copyright protection**: Some argue that AI-generated works should not be eligible for copyright protection at all, since they lack human authorship. In this case, such works would fall into the public domain, where anyone could use or distribute them freely.

Example:

A designer uses an AI tool to generate a series of abstract paintings, which they then sell as digital artwork. The designer inputs certain parameters to guide the

AI's creation but does not directly design the pieces themselves. In this case, who holds the copyright—the designer or no one?

3. The Current Legal Landscape

As of now, copyright laws around the world are grappling with how to address AI-generated content. In the U.S., the U.S. Copyright Office has stated that for a work to receive copyright protection, it must be created by a human. However, this stance may evolve as AI technology becomes more sophisticated, and the pressure to adapt copyright law increases.

Current legal approaches to AI-generated content:

- **United States**: U.S. copyright law currently requires human authorship for a work to be protected. The U.S. Copyright Office has denied copyright claims for AI-generated works, such as cases where AI created artwork without significant human intervention.

- **United Kingdom**: In the U.K., copyright law allows for some limited protection of computer-generated works, though it is often awarded to the individual who made the necessary arrangements for the creation of the work, such as the person operating the AI.

- **European Union**: The EU is exploring new frameworks for AI and copyright, with proposals to establish clearer guidelines on who owns AI-generated works. However, like other jurisdictions, it is still in the early stages of adapting existing laws to address AI advancements.

Example:

In 2019, the U.S. Copyright Office denied a copyright application for a work created by an AI system called Creativity Machine, stating that only works created by humans can be granted copyright protection. This decision highlights the current stance of U.S. law but also signals a need for future reform as AI-generated content becomes more prevalent.

4. Potential Solutions and Future Directions

As AI continues to push the boundaries of creativity, the copyright landscape will need to adapt. Some potential solutions include redefining authorship to accommodate AI-generated works or creating new categories of intellectual property protection specifically for machine-made content. In any case, lawmakers, creators, and the tech industry will need to collaborate to ensure that AI and copyright laws evolve in a balanced way.

Possible solutions for AI-generated copyright:

- **Joint authorship models**: One potential solution is a joint authorship model, where both the AI developer and the user share copyright ownership. This approach acknowledges both the human input and the machine's contribution to the creation.

- **New legal frameworks for AI**: Another possibility is the creation of an entirely new legal framework for AI-generated works, recognizing that these creations are fundamentally different from traditional human-made works. This could involve new types of intellectual property rights that apply specifically to machine-generated content.

- **Increased licensing and regulation**: As AI-generated content grows, there may be more emphasis on licensing and regulation of AI tools, ensuring that creators and users have clear guidelines on how to properly attribute and use machine-made content.

Example:

In the future, platforms that generate AI art or music might implement a licensing system where users pay for the right to use the AI's creations commercially. These licenses could outline who holds the rights to the content, potentially offering a solution to the current ambiguity around AI-generated works.

Conclusion: Navigating the AI-Copyright Frontier

As artificial intelligence continues to reshape the creative landscape, navigating the copyright implications of AI-generated content will be one of the major challenges facing creators and lawmakers. While the current legal framework is still catching up, understanding the key issues surrounding AI and copyright is crucial for anyone looking to harness the power of AI in their creative endeavors.

In the next section, we'll explore how blockchain technology and smart contracts are transforming the way digital assets are protected and managed, offering new solutions for creators in the digital age.

Blockchain and Smart Contracts: Securing Copyright in the Digital Age

As the world of digital content creation expands, creators are increasingly looking for ways to protect and manage their intellectual property in a secure and transparent manner. Blockchain technology and smart contracts are emerging as powerful tools in this arena, offering innovative solutions to some of the most persistent challenges in copyright law. In this section, we'll explore how blockchain is transforming copyright protection, from securing digital ownership to automating licensing agreements through smart contracts.

1. What is Blockchain, and How Does it Work for Copyright?

Blockchain is a decentralized, digital ledger technology that records transactions across multiple computers in a way that makes the information secure, transparent, and immutable. Each record (or block) is linked to the previous one, forming a chain, and is encrypted, ensuring that the data cannot be altered without consensus from the entire network.

For copyright protection, blockchain offers several key benefits:

- **Immutable proof of ownership**: Creators can register their digital works on a blockchain, creating an unchangeable record of ownership. This acts as a timestamped certification of who created the work and when, making it easy to prove ownership if disputes arise.

- **Transparent tracking of usage**: Blockchain allows for the tracking of how digital content is used. Each time the work is sold, licensed, or transferred, the transaction is recorded on the blockchain, providing a transparent, tamper-proof history of its usage.

- **Decentralized control**: Since blockchain operates without a central authority, creators can maintain direct control over their works without relying on intermediaries, such as publishing houses or distribution platforms.

Example:

An artist registers their digital paintings on a blockchain platform, creating a permanent, time-stamped record of ownership. When the artist sells a painting as a digital asset, the sale is recorded on the blockchain, ensuring a transparent transfer of ownership. If someone tries to claim the painting as their own, the artist can easily prove their rights using the blockchain record.

2. Smart Contracts: Automating Licensing and Royalties

One of the most revolutionary aspects of blockchain technology for copyright protection is the use of smart contracts. A smart contract is a self-executing contract with the terms of the agreement directly written into code. Once certain conditions are met, the contract automatically enforces itself without the need for intermediaries. In the context of copyright, smart contracts can streamline and automate processes such as licensing, royalty payments, and distribution.

How smart contracts can help copyright holders:

- **Automating licensing agreements**: Smart contracts can be programmed to automatically grant licenses to users who meet specific criteria, such as making a payment or agreeing to certain terms. This eliminates the need for manual paperwork and ensures that licensing is handled quickly and securely.

- **Instant royalty distribution**: With smart contracts, royalties can be automatically distributed to creators whenever their content is used or sold. For example, when a song is streamed on a platform, the smart contract can automatically allocate royalties to the artist, producer, and other rights holders, ensuring timely and transparent payments.

- **Built-in enforcement**: Smart contracts can also enforce licensing terms by restricting access to content if the terms of the agreement are violated. For example, if a user tries to share or use a work without proper authorization, the smart contract can automatically revoke their access or prevent further use.

Example:

A musician releases an album on a blockchain-based platform with a smart contract that automatically licenses the songs to listeners for a fee. Each time a listener purchases the album, the smart contract distributes the royalties to the musician, producer, and any collaborators. The contract also limits how the music can be shared, ensuring the artist's control over their work.

3. Blockchain for Copyright Registration and Protection

Blockchain is particularly well-suited for copyright registration and protection in the digital age. By using blockchain, creators can establish a clear and indisputable record of their rights to a work, making it easier to protect against infringement and unauthorized use. Several platforms have already emerged that offer blockchain-based copyright registration services, allowing creators to register their works in a secure and transparent way.

Benefits of blockchain-based copyright registration:

- **Immutable record of ownership**: Unlike traditional copyright registration, where disputes over ownership may arise, blockchain's immutable nature ensures that the ownership record cannot be altered or tampered with. This provides creators with a secure and verifiable way to prove their rights to a work.

- **Global accessibility**: Blockchain operates on a decentralized network, meaning that creators from anywhere in the world can register their works without relying on national copyright offices or legal systems. This makes copyright protection more accessible and efficient for creators operating in the digital economy.

- **Easy dispute resolution**: With a clear and time-stamped record of ownership stored on the blockchain, resolving disputes over copyright infringement becomes easier. Creators can use the blockchain record as **evidence** in legal cases, streamlining the dispute resolution process.

Example:

An independent game developer registers their game on a blockchain platform that offers copyright protection services. Each time the game is updated or sold; the transactions are recorded on the blockchain. If another developer tries to release a similar game and claim it as their own, the original developer can use the blockchain record to prove ownership.

4. Challenges and Considerations with Blockchain and Smart Contracts

While blockchain and smart contracts offer exciting new possibilities for copyright protection, there are still challenges to consider. The technology is still in its early stages, and many creators are unfamiliar with how to implement it effectively. Additionally, blockchain is not a substitute for traditional copyright law but rather a complementary tool.

Key challenges to consider:

- **Legal recognition**: Although blockchain provides strong evidence of ownership, not all legal systems recognize blockchain records as valid proof of copyright. Some jurisdictions may still require traditional copyright registration, so creators may need to use blockchain alongside existing legal frameworks.

- **Complexity of smart contracts**: Writing and deploying smart contracts requires technical expertise, and mistakes in the code can lead to unintended consequences. Creators should work with experts or platforms that specialize in smart contract deployment to ensure their contracts function as intended.

- **Environmental concerns**: Blockchain networks, especially those based on proof-of-work algorithms (such as Bitcoin), can consume large amounts of energy. However, newer blockchain systems like proof-of-stake aim to reduce the environmental impact of the technology.

Example:

A filmmaker uses a blockchain platform to register their short film and implement a smart contract for distribution. However, the platform is relatively new, and the filmmaker must also file for copyright with the national copyright office to ensure their work is fully protected in case of a legal dispute. Despite this extra step, the blockchain still provides an added layer of security and transparency for managing the film's distribution.

Conclusion: Blockchain as a Game-Changer for Copyright

Blockchain and smart contracts offer a promising new way for creators to protect, manage, and monetize their digital content. By providing immutable records of ownership and automating key processes like licensing and royalty payments, blockchain is transforming the way intellectual property is handled in the digital age. While there are challenges to overcome, the potential benefits of blockchain for copyright protection are undeniable, making it a game-changer for creators looking to secure their digital assets.

In the next section, we'll dive into the world of 3D printing and explore the legal challenges of protecting designs and physical objects in a world where replication is as simple as hitting "print."

3D Printing and Copyright: Protecting Designs in a Replicable World

The rise of 3D printing technology has revolutionized industries from manufacturing to healthcare, allowing individuals to create and replicate physical objects with remarkable precision. However, this innovation has also sparked new challenges in copyright law, as the ease of replication raises concerns about protecting designs, inventions, and artworks from unauthorized reproduction. In this section, we will explore how 3D printing intersects with copyright law and the strategies creators can use to protect their work in a world where replication is only a click away.

1. The Impact of 3D Printing on Copyright

At its core, 3D printing is a process that turns digital designs into physical objects. The printer reads a digital file, usually a Computer-Aided Design (CAD) file, and creates a physical version layer by layer. While this is a powerful tool for innovation, it also presents a legal dilemma: if a design can be easily downloaded and printed by anyone, how can copyright protect the original creator?

Challenges posed by 3D printing:

- **Easy replication**: Just like music, movies, or software, digital design files can be shared, downloaded, and copied without permission. Once a

CAD file is uploaded to the internet, it can be accessed by anyone with a 3D printer, leading to widespread unauthorized reproduction of physical objects.

- **Difficult enforcement**: Enforcing copyright in the world of 3D printing is particularly challenging because there are so many decentralized platforms where design files can be shared. Even if a file is taken down from one site, it can quickly appear on others.

- **Infringing on product designs**: 3D printing makes it easy to create copies of patented or copyrighted objects, such as toys, household items, and even medical devices. This raises significant concerns for businesses and creators who rely on the exclusivity of their designs.

Example:

A designer creates a custom phone case and sells it online. However, someone purchases the case, scans it, and uploads the CAD file to a free 3D printing website, where others can download it and print their own versions. The designer's original work is now being copied and distributed without permission, undermining their business.

2. Copyright Protection for 3D Designs and Objects

In many cases, the designs and blueprints used for 3D printing are considered intellectual property and can be protected under copyright law. However, there are nuances to how copyright applies to digital designs and physical objects.

How copyright applies to 3D printing:

- **Digital design files**: The CAD files or other digital blueprints used in 3D printing are treated like any other creative work. As long as they meet the threshold of originality, they are eligible for copyright protection. This means that only the creator of the file has the right to reproduce, distribute, or license the design.

- **Physical objects**: If the object being printed is aesthetic in nature (e.g., a sculpture, jewelry, or decorative item), it may be protected by copyright as a work of art. However, functional items (such as tools or devices) are not typically protected by copyright but may be covered under patent law or design patents.

- **Derivative works**: Modifying an existing CAD file or 3D design can result in a derivative work, which can be protected under copyright. However, permission from the original creator is often required to modify or create new versions of their work.

Example:

An artist creates a series of sculptures using 3D printing technology. The CAD files for the sculptures are protected by copyright, and the artist controls how the files are distributed and used. If someone downloads one of the files, prints the sculpture, and sells it without permission, they would be infringing the artist's copyright.

3. Licensing and Monetizing 3D Designs

To combat the challenges of unauthorized reproduction, creators are increasingly turning to licensing agreements as a way to maintain control over their designs while still allowing others to use them. Licensing allows the creator to specify the terms under which their designs can be printed, shared, or sold, offering a flexible way to monetize their work.

Types of licensing for 3D designs:

- **Personal use licenses**: A creator may license a CAD file for personal use, meaning that individuals can download and print the design for themselves but are not allowed to sell or distribute the printed objects.

- **Commercial licenses**: For businesses or individuals looking to sell printed objects based on a design, the creator can offer a commercial license. This allows the licensee to produce and sell the objects under specific terms, usually in exchange for a fee or royalties.

- **Open-source licensing**: Some creators choose to release their designs under an open-source license, which allows others to use, modify, and distribute the design freely, as long as they credit the original creator.

Example:

A 3D modeler creates a collection of intricate jewelry designs and licenses them for personal use only. Customers can purchase the CAD files, print the jewelry for themselves, and enjoy wearing it, but they are not allowed to sell or distribute the printed pieces. If a retailer wants to sell the jewelry commercially, they must negotiate a separate commercial license with the designer.

4. Enforcing Copyright in the World of 3D Printing

While licensing provides a way to control how designs are used, enforcing copyright in the 3D printing space can still be challenging. Creators need to be proactive about monitoring the use of their designs and taking action when infringement occurs.

Strategies for enforcing copyright:

- **Monitoring platforms**: Creators can monitor 3D printing marketplaces and file-sharing sites for unauthorized copies of their designs. Some platforms, like Thingiverse and MyMiniFactory, have systems in place for creators to file takedown notices if their designs are being shared without permission.

- **Using watermarks or encryption**: Some designers choose to embed digital watermarks or encryption in their CAD files, making it harder for others to distribute unauthorized copies. This also allows creators to track where their designs are being shared.

- **Legal action**: If infringement is widespread, creators may need to take legal action to enforce their copyright. This can include sending **cease and desist** letters, filing DMCA takedown notices, or pursuing lawsuits for damages.

Example:

A toy designer discovers that their copyrighted CAD file for a toy figurine has been uploaded to multiple 3D printing marketplaces without permission. They file takedown notices on each platform, requesting the removal of the infringing files. The designer also contacts the individuals selling the printed toys and sends cease and desist letters to stop further unauthorized sales.

5. The Future of Copyright in 3D Printing

As 3D printing technology continues to evolve, so too will the legal landscape surrounding copyright and intellectual property. Lawmakers and creators will need to adapt to ensure that designs and objects are adequately protected while still encouraging innovation and creativity.

Future considerations for copyright in 3D printing:

- **Global copyright enforcement**: Since 3D printing is a global phenomenon, there is a growing need for international copyright enforcement mechanisms. Standardized laws and procedures across borders could help creators protect their designs more effectively.

- **New forms of copyright protection**: Some experts predict that new forms of digital rights management (DRM) for CAD files will emerge, allowing creators to control how their designs are used and ensuring that licensing agreements are followed.

- **Evolving legal frameworks**: As 3D printing becomes more widespread, lawmakers may need to update existing copyright laws or create new frameworks to address the unique challenges of this technology.

Example:
A furniture designer uses 3D printing to create custom chairs and tables, selling both the printed products and the CAD files for others to print. As 3D printing grows, the designer advocates for stronger international copyright laws to protect their designs across multiple countries and marketplaces.

Conclusion: Protecting Designs in a 3D-Printed World

3D printing opens up incredible possibilities for creativity, but it also poses significant challenges for copyright law. Protecting digital designs and physical objects from unauthorized reproduction requires a combination of legal strategies, including copyright registration, licensing, and vigilant enforcement. As 3D printing technology continues to advance, creators must stay informed and proactive to ensure their designs remain secure and profitable.

In the next section, we'll explore how virtual and augmented reality (VR and AR) are pushing the boundaries of storytelling and creativity, and how copyright law is adapting to protect immersive digital content.

Virtual and Augmented Reality: New Frontiers for Copyright Protection

The rise of virtual reality (VR) and augmented reality (AR) is transforming the way we experience content, creating immersive environments where users can interact with digital elements in new and exciting ways. From virtual worlds to interactive AR filters, these technologies offer unprecedented opportunities for creators. However, with these innovations come new challenges in copyright protection, as digital assets become more integrated into both real and virtual spaces. In this section, we'll explore how VR and AR are reshaping copyright law and what creators can do to protect their work in these emerging fields.

1. The Evolution of Copyright in Virtual Worlds

In virtual reality environments, users can explore fully immersive digital worlds that are filled with artwork, music, architecture, and interactive elements. These virtual worlds are often built by multiple creators, each contributing their own copyrighted materials, such as 3D models, textures, soundscapes, and scripts. As a result, questions of copyright ownership and usage rights are more complex in VR than in traditional digital media.

Copyright challenges in virtual worlds:

- **Multiple layers of ownership**: A single VR environment may contain various types of copyrighted content, each owned by different creators. For example, a virtual art gallery might display digital paintings, sculptures, and music, all with separate copyrights. This requires careful coordination of licensing agreements and permissions to ensure that every element is used legally.

- **User-generated content (UGC)**: Many virtual worlds allow users to create and upload their own content, such as avatars, objects, or experiences. While this fosters creativity, it also raises questions about who owns the rights to this user-generated content and how it can be protected.

- **Infringement within virtual spaces**: Just as in the physical world, copyrighted material in VR can be infringed upon, whether through unauthorized duplication of digital assets or misuse of creative works. Enforcing copyright in a decentralized, virtual space presents new legal and technological challenges.

Example:

A game developer creates a popular virtual world where users can build their own virtual homes, filled with 3D objects like furniture, art, and décor. Some users begin copying designs from real-world furniture brands without permission, leading to potential copyright infringement issues within the virtual world. The developer must enforce rules to prevent unauthorized replication of copyrighted content.

2. Augmented Reality and the Blending of Real and Digital Worlds

Augmented reality (AR) overlays digital elements onto the real world, allowing users to interact with virtual objects through devices like smartphones or AR glasses. From AR filters on social media to interactive retail experiences, AR is becoming an essential part of the digital ecosystem. But as AR brings digital content into real-world settings, it raises questions about how copyright applies to these overlapping spaces.

Copyright challenges in augmented reality:

- **Use of copyrighted material in AR**: Many AR experiences rely on pre-existing copyrighted material, such as music, artwork, or logos. For example, an AR app might allow users to place virtual versions of famous sculptures in their physical space. Without proper licensing, this could lead to copyright infringement, even though the objects only exist digitally.

- **Protection of AR designs**: Just like VR, creators of AR content—such as filters, 3D models, and interactive experiences—need to ensure that their digital designs are protected from unauthorized use. Because AR content can be easily shared and accessed by anyone with a smartphone, it is vulnerable to misuse.

- **Blurring the line between real and virtual**: In AR, copyrighted digital elements are layered on top of the real world, creating new challenges for enforcement. For example, an AR filter that uses a copyrighted image or song might be experienced in a public space, raising questions about how and where copyright law applies.

Example:

A fashion brand creates an AR app that allows users to virtually "try on" clothes using their smartphone camera. The app overlays the brand's clothing designs onto the user's image in real-time. Another developer copies these virtual clothing designs and creates a competing AR app without permission, leading to potential copyright infringement.

3. Protecting Content in Virtual and Augmented Reality

To protect their intellectual property in VR and AR, creators need to adapt traditional copyright strategies to these new platforms. This includes securing proper licensing agreements, monitoring for infringement, and taking advantage of new technological protections to safeguard digital assets.

Strategies for copyright protection in VR and AR:

- **Registering digital assets**: Creators should register their digital assets— such as 3D models, textures, music, and interactive scripts—just as they would any other creative work. This provides a legal basis for enforcing copyright in case of infringement within virtual or augmented environments.

- **Licensing for immersive experiences**: In VR and AR, licensing agreements must cover both the use of content within the virtual environment and the real-world rights associated with it. This ensures that creators are compensated for their work, whether it's displayed in a virtual gallery or experienced through an AR filter.

- **Using digital rights management (DRM)**: DRM technologies can be used to control access to digital assets in VR and AR, preventing unauthorized copying or distribution. For example, DRM can restrict how many times a virtual object can be duplicated or whether it can be transferred between users.

Example:

A digital artist creates a series of interactive 3D sculptures for use in a VR art gallery. To protect their work, the artist uses DRM tools to limit how many times each sculpture can be purchased and shared. The artist also registers their designs with the copyright office to ensure they have legal protection in case of infringement.

4. Future Copyright Challenges in VR and AR

As VR and AR technologies continue to evolve, so too will the legal challenges surrounding copyright. Virtual and augmented environments are becoming more complex and immersive, creating new opportunities for creators but also raising questions about how copyright law will adapt to these digital frontiers.

Future considerations for copyright in VR and AR:

- **Cross-platform issues**: As VR and AR experiences become more connected across platforms, creators will need to navigate licensing and copyright laws across different devices, regions, and jurisdictions. This will require standardized rules for protecting content in global, interconnected virtual spaces.

- **Monetization of virtual assets**: The ability to sell and trade virtual goods in VR and AR is growing, but creators need clear guidelines for monetizing these assets while retaining control over their use. New laws may emerge to address the ownership and resale of digital assets in virtual worlds.

- **Legal recognition of virtual property**: As virtual worlds grow in complexity; the concept of virtual property rights will become more important. Legal systems may need to recognize virtual property as a legitimate form of ownership, with copyright laws protecting both the digital and physical aspects of virtual goods.

Example:

A company develops an AR experience that allows users to view virtual real estate models in real-world locations through their smartphones. As AR real estate becomes more common, questions arise about whether the virtual property rights should be treated the same as physical property rights, including how copyright laws apply to the virtual models.

Conclusion: Navigating Copyright in Virtual and Augmented Reality

Virtual and augmented reality are pushing the boundaries of how we create, share, and experience content, but they are also testing the limits of copyright law. As VR and AR become more integrated into our daily lives, creators must be proactive in protecting their intellectual property, using a combination of traditional copyright protection and new technologies like DRM and licensing agreements. By understanding the unique challenges posed by immersive digital environments, creators can ensure their work remains secure and legally protected in these exciting new frontiers.

In the next chapter, we'll discuss how to future-proof your intellectual property strategy and ensure your copyrights and digital assets are protected as technology and copyright law continue to evolve.

Quick Tips and Recap

- **Register Digital Assets**: Ensure that all VR and AR creations, such as 3D models, music, and interactive scripts, are registered to secure copyright protection.

- **Licensing for Virtual and Real Worlds**: Draft licensing agreements that cover both virtual environments and the physical world to avoid legal ambiguities and ensure proper use of your work.

- **Use DRM for Protection**: Implement Digital Rights Management (DRM) tools to restrict unauthorized copying, sharing, or resale of your virtual and augmented reality content.

- **Monitor for Infringement**: Actively monitor platforms and virtual marketplaces for unauthorized use of your work, and take swift legal action where necessary.

- **Understand User-Generated Content (UGC)**: If users can create or upload content within your virtual world, establish clear terms and conditions to manage ownership and prevent disputes.

- **Secure Cross-Platform Rights**: If your content is used across multiple VR or AR platforms, ensure you have rights secured for each one, as different platforms may have varying legal requirements.

- **Consider Future Proofing**: Stay informed about emerging copyright laws related to immersive technologies to protect your virtual and augmented content for the long term.

- **Guard Against Virtual Infringement**: Develop mechanisms to track and stop unauthorized replication or distribution of virtual objects and environments within VR and AR spaces.

These additional tips help creators manage the legal complexities of virtual and augmented reality, ensuring comprehensive protection of their intellectual property in these cutting-edge spaces.

Conclusion

*Navigating the Future of Copyright
in a Creative World*

As we reach the final chapter of "Beyond the Pen: Copyright Strategies for Modern Creators," it's clear that the landscape of intellectual property has transformed dramatically. What once applied solely to written words, music, and visual arts now stretches across new frontiers—encompassing digital designs, AI-generated content, virtual and augmented realities, and much more. In today's world, where technology blurs the lines between physical and digital, creators face both incredible opportunities and significant challenges. Understanding and applying copyright law is no longer a luxury; it's a necessity for protecting your creative work, ensuring fair compensation, and maintaining control over your artistic output.

Throughout this book, we've taken a comprehensive journey through the evolving world of copyright, from the foundational principles of ownership to the cutting-edge tools of blockchain and smart contracts. Along the way, we've explored practical applications of fair use, handled disputes with cease-and-desist letters, and tackled the ever-present threat of digital piracy. With each chapter, the goal has been to equip you—the creator—with the knowledge and strategies needed to thrive in this dynamic environment, where your work is not only your passion but also your livelihood.

The Power of Ownership

At the heart of copyright lies the concept of ownership. It is through this legal framework that creators can control how their work is used, who benefits from it, and how it is distributed. We began by establishing the importance of registering your copyright and staking your claim to your work. As creators, understanding the nuances of ownership ensures that you can navigate challenges like joint authorship, derivative works, and licensing agreements with confidence. It is essential to remember that copyright is not just about defense—it is about empowerment. When you control your creative output, you gain the freedom to build your brand, monetize your efforts, and protect your artistic legacy.

Innovation, Technology, and the Changing Face of Copyright

We live in an era where technological advancements constantly reshape the ways in which we create and consume content. Technologies like AI, blockchain, 3D printing, and virtual/augmented reality present exciting new opportunities for creators, while simultaneously introducing complex legal questions. Who owns the rights to AI-generated content? How can blockchain secure your digital assets across platforms? What happens when physical objects can be replicated at the click of a button?

As copyright law races to catch up with these rapid innovations, it's crucial that creators stay ahead of the curve. This book has provided insights into how you can leverage these technologies to protect your work, whether through smart contracts for automated licensing or DRM tools for controlling access to digital creations. The future of copyright will be shaped by those who embrace these technologies, using them not only for creation but also for security and monetization.

Fair Use, Licensing, and Monetization: Mastering the Balance

One of the most important topics we've explored is the delicate balance between fair use and infringement. In a world where content is shared, reposted, and remixed at lightning speed, understanding when and how your work can be used by others is key. Navigating fair use isn't just about avoiding legal pitfalls; it's about ensuring that your rights as a creator are respected. Knowing when to license your content, and under what terms, allows you to maximize its value while retaining control.

Whether you're offering commercial licenses for 3D designs, setting up smart contracts for royalty payments, or using social media to promote your brand, the ability to monetize your work effectively is a cornerstone of success. Today's digital platforms offer countless ways to earn revenue from your creations, but each comes with its own legal considerations. With this book, you now have the tools to make informed decisions about how to license your work, structure agreements, and protect your royalties.

Protecting Your Work in a Global, Digital Ecosystem

In the final chapters, we examined the dark side of creativity in the digital age: infringement, piracy, and disputes. As much as technology facilitates creativity, it also opens the door to new forms of copyright violations. From identifying digital pirates to issuing DMCA takedown notices, understanding the mechanics of copyright enforcement is essential for any creator operating in the digital space.

Global platforms and decentralized networks have made it more challenging to control the distribution of your work, but they've also brought tools like blockchain and DRM to the forefront of copyright protection. With the right strategies, you can actively defend your creations against theft and misuse, maintaining the integrity and value of your intellectual property.

Looking to the Future

Copyright is an ever-evolving field, shaped by new technologies, global trends, and creative innovation. As a modern creator, you are part of this transformation, and your work will help define the future of intellectual property. The skills you've gained from this book—understanding ownership, mastering licensing, and using cutting-edge technology—are not just tools for today; they are your roadmap for tomorrow.

The future of creativity lies at the intersection of law and innovation, and by staying informed, you can continue to protect your work in a landscape that is constantly shifting. Whether you're creating music, writing novels, designing digital art, or building virtual worlds, your ability to navigate the complexities of copyright will determine the impact of your creations.

Final Thoughts: Owning Your Future as a Creator

"Beyond the Pen" is not just a guide to copyright; it's a manifesto for modern creators who want to protect, profit from, and promote their work in a world that's more connected—and competitive—than ever before. The lessons learned here will serve you across industries and platforms, giving you the confidence to make decisions that support your creative vision while safeguarding your rights.

Remember, as a creator, you wield the power to shape culture, influence thought, and inspire change. But with that power comes the responsibility to understand the legal framework that protects your work. The future of your creative career depends not just on your talent, but on your ability to own and defend your intellectual property. As you move forward, let this book be your compass, guiding you through the ever-changing terrain of copyright law and creative innovation.

The future is yours to create—and protect.

Where Do We Go from Here?

As you close the chapter on "Beyond the Pen: Copyright Strategies for Modern Creators," you're now equipped with the knowledge and tools to protect and maximize the value of your creative work. But in the world of business and law, the journey doesn't stop with copyright. If you're a creator looking to build a career or business around your work, understanding the legal aspects of the publishing industry is just as important as knowing your intellectual property rights.

That's why the next installment in the Empire Builders Series: Masterclasses in Business and Law is "Legal Ink: Navigating the Legalese of Publishing." While "Beyond the Pen" focused on protecting and managing your creative assets, "Legal Ink" will dive deep into the complex legal world of publishing—whether you're self-publishing, signing a deal with a major publisher, or exploring hybrid publishing models.

In "Legal Ink," we'll explore:

- **Publishing Contracts**: What to look for, what to avoid, and how to negotiate the best terms for your work. You'll learn how to decipher complex legal jargon and ensure that your rights, royalties, and future opportunities are fully protected.

- **Traditional vs. Self-Publishing**: The legal implications of choosing between these two paths. We'll break down the benefits and challenges of each model, helping you make informed decisions about how to distribute and monetize your work.

- **Distribution and Rights Management**: Beyond just getting your book or content to market, you'll need to navigate the intricacies of foreign rights, film and television adaptations, and digital distribution. "Legal Ink" will help you secure your place in the broader publishing ecosystem while maximizing the reach of your work.

- **Handling Disputes**: From contractual breaches to plagiarism, we'll cover common legal disputes in the publishing industry and teach you how to handle them with confidence and clarity.

The Empire Builders Series was designed with the modern creator and entrepreneur in mind, providing not only the legal expertise but also the strategic insight to build and protect your creative empire. While *Beyond the Pen* armed you with the tools to protect your creations, "Legal Ink" will show you how to navigate the publishing world's legal terrain and transform your content into a thriving business.

This upcoming book will be the final installment in the Empire Builders Series, offering a full circle of knowledge that combines copyright strategy with the practicalities of the publishing industry. From contracts and royalties to distribution and branding, "Legal Ink" will be your guide to ensuring that your publishing journey is as smooth and profitable as possible.

With both books in hand, you will have a comprehensive legal toolkit to help you thrive as a modern creator and business owner. You've already mastered the art of protecting your intellectual property—now it's time to take the next step and dive into the world of publishing law, where your creative vision becomes a tangible reality.

Stay tuned for "Legal Ink: Navigating the Legalese of Publishing," and continue building your creative empire with confidence and clarity.

Together, these two volumes—"Beyond the Pen" and "Legal Ink"—will form the cornerstone of your mastery over the legal and business strategies essential for long-term success. As you embark on the next phase of your journey, remember that knowledge is your greatest asset, and with it, you can build, protect, and grow your empire.

READ ON for a bonus chapter!

The Future of Copyright: Predictions and Emerging Trends for the Next Decade

"As we look ahead, the evolution of copyright will increasingly intersect with technology, requiring adaptive legal frameworks to manage the balance between protecting creators and enabling innovation." — TIM WU, PROFESSOR AT COLUMBIA LAW SCHOOL AND A PROMINENT ADVOCATE FOR ANTITRUST AND INTERNET POLICIES

Welcome to the Bonus Chapter: "The Future of Copyright: Predictions and Emerging Trends for the Next Decade." Buckle up and don your prophetic spectacles—this is where we play Nostradamus with the law books, forecasting the twists and turns in copyright legislation as we plunge into the roaring 2030s.

Imagine a world where every tweet and TikTok could be a minable asset, and where holographic performances are the subject of fierce copyright debates. We'll explore how the blending of physical and digital realities might stretch current laws to their breaking points and beyond. Expect to hear about laws adapting to the challenges posed by AI-generated content, the global harmonization of copyright protections, or the potential backlash that might swing the pendulum towards more open, shared creative commons.

This chapter isn't just a peek into the crystal ball; it's a speculative map to navigating the uncharted waters of copyright's future. With wit and a bit of wisdom, we'll sketch out the possible, the probable, and the wildly optimistic scenarios of the coming decade. By the end, you won't just be a spectator of these changes—you'll be an informed, ready, and witty participant in the dialogue shaping the future of creative rights. Let's dive into the next chapter of copyright, where the only constant is change—and plenty of it!

AI and Machine Learning: Shaping the Future of Authorship and Ownership

As artificial intelligence (AI) and machine learning (ML) advance at an unprecedented pace, the boundaries of creativity are being stretched in ways we could scarcely imagine just a decade ago. These technologies are no longer simply tools to assist human creators—they have become creators in their own right, capable of generating everything from music and visual art to written content and even entire virtual environments. However, as AI begins to take on the role of author, new questions arise about ownership, authorship, and copyright protection in this brave new world of machine-generated content.

1. Who Owns AI-Generated Content?

Perhaps the most pressing question in the era of AI-driven creativity is: Who owns the copyright to works generated by AI? Traditional copyright law is built on the assumption that creative works are the product of human intellect and effort, granting copyright protection to human authors. But AI-generated works— whether they are visual art created by algorithms, music composed by neural networks, or stories written by language models—challenge these assumptions.

There are several potential paths that the law might take in answering this question:

- **The User as Owner**: One approach is to assign ownership to the human user who directs the AI. In this scenario, the person who inputs commands, defines parameters, or otherwise "guides" the AI is considered the author, since they played a role in shaping the outcome, even if the AI did the heavy lifting.

- **The AI Developer as Owner**: Another possible approach is to assign copyright ownership to the developers or companies that created the AI systems themselves. After all, without their technology, the creative work wouldn't exist. This approach treats AI as an advanced tool, and the rights would go to those who created the tool, not those who use it.

- **No Copyright Protection**: A more radical position is that AI-generated works shouldn't be eligible for copyright protection at all. Since there is no human creator involved in the process, these works could fall into the public domain immediately upon creation, allowing anyone to use, share, or modify them without restriction. This approach would have major implications for industries where AI-generated content is becoming increasingly common.

Example:

An artist uses AI software like DALL·E to generate digital artworks. While the artist selects certain themes, styles, and prompts for the AI to work with, the final creative output is produced entirely by the AI. Should the artist own the copyright to the resulting images? Or should the developers behind DALL·E hold the rights since their technology created the work?

2. Legal Precedents and Current Copyright Laws

Current copyright laws around the world are not fully equipped to handle the complexities of AI-generated content. Most legal systems still require human authorship for copyright protection. In the United States, for instance, the U.S. Copyright Office has made it clear that copyright is reserved for works "created by a human being." Similarly, in Europe, the Berne Convention defines an "author" as a human creator, and most national copyright laws reflect this.

Recent court cases and legal challenges are beginning to shape how the law approaches AI-generated works:

- In 2019, the U.S. Copyright Office rejected a copyright application for an artwork created by an AI system called Creativity Machine, stating that works generated by AI without human involvement could not receive copyright protection.

- In contrast, the U.K. has a slightly more flexible approach, allowing for some level of copyright protection for computer-generated works, but attributing authorship to the person who made the "necessary arrangements" for the work to be produced.

These legal precedents suggest that the debate over AI-generated content is far from settled. As AI technology continues to evolve, legal systems will need to adapt to determine how machine-made creations are treated under copyright law.

3. The Role of AI in Collaborative Creativity

AI is not always an autonomous creator. In many cases, AI works collaboratively with humans to produce creative content. This raises new questions about joint authorship and ownership. When AI assists in the creation of a work—such as generating music based on a composer's input or providing text suggestions for a writer—who should be credited as the author? Should the AI receive a co-authorship role, or does its contribution merely support the human creator, who retains full ownership?

The increasing prevalence of AI-assisted creativity could lead to a redefinition of what it means to be an author in the 21st century. As AI tools become more integral to the creative process, creators may need to negotiate new forms of joint authorship agreements, outlining the extent to which the AI is credited for the work.

Example:
A filmmaker uses an AI tool to automatically generate background music for their film. The AI analyzes the mood and pacing of the scenes to create an original score. In this case, is the filmmaker the sole author of the music, or does the AI (or its developer) deserve some form of co-authorship?

4. Future Directions: Legislative Reforms and Global Impact

Looking forward, it's clear that legislative reform will be necessary to address the complexities of AI-generated content. Some potential paths include:

- **New Legal Categories for AI-Generated Content**: Governments may create entirely new legal frameworks for AI-generated works, separate from traditional copyright law. This could include recognizing AI-generated content as a unique class of work, with its own set of rules for ownership, licensing, and distribution.

- **Increased Use of Smart Contracts**: As AI-generated content becomes more common, we may see a rise in the use of smart contracts to manage the ownership, licensing, and monetization of these works. These contracts could automate royalty payments, ensuring that both human creators and AI developers are compensated fairly.

- **Global Harmonization of AI and Copyright Law**: Given the global nature of digital content creation and distribution, international cooperation may be necessary to establish consistent standards for how AI-generated works are treated under copyright law. The rise of AI could spur new agreements on the global stage, akin to the Berne Convention, that clarify ownership and authorship rights for AI-generated content.

Example:

Imagine a future where AI-generated content—whether it's artwork, music, or even a screenplay—can be automatically licensed via smart contracts, with royalties being split between the AI developers, the users, and any other stakeholders involved in the creation. Such a system could revolutionize the way we manage copyright in the digital age.

Conclusion: The Shifting Boundaries of Creativity

As AI and machine learning continue to push the boundaries of creativity, the concept of authorship is being redefined. The future of copyright law will need to address these challenges, ensuring that both human creators and AI technologies are recognized fairly. Whether through legislative reform, new legal categories, or emerging technologies like blockchain, the next decade will likely see significant changes in how we define and protect creative works.

The era of AI-generated content is here, and the law must evolve to keep pace with this rapidly changing landscape. As a creator, understanding the implications of AI on authorship and ownership will be crucial to navigating the future of intellectual property and ensuring that your rights are protected in the age of intelligent machines.

In the next section, we'll explore how blockchain and smart contracts are playing a pivotal role in revolutionizing copyright protection, offering new ways to secure ownership and automate the licensing of digital content across the globe.

Blockchain and the Decentralized Copyright Revolution

As the world becomes increasingly digital, creators face the challenge of protecting their intellectual property in a fast-paced, borderless online environment. Enter blockchain technology, a decentralized and transparent system that is revolutionizing the way creators secure and manage copyright. Initially known for its use in cryptocurrencies like Bitcoin, blockchain has evolved into a powerful tool for managing and verifying digital assets, including music, art, videos, and written content. In this section, we'll explore how blockchain is leading a decentralized copyright revolution and reshaping the future of intellectual property rights.

1. What is Blockchain, and How Does it Apply to Copyright?

At its core, blockchain is a distributed ledger technology that allows data to be recorded across a network of computers in a secure, immutable, and transparent manner. Each piece of data, or "block," is linked to the previous one, forming a chain. Once a block is added to the blockchain, it cannot be altered or deleted without consensus from the entire network. This system creates a tamper-proof record of transactions or ownership that can be publicly verified, making it an ideal solution for managing copyright and intellectual property.

How blockchain applies to copyright:

- **Immutable Proof of Ownership**: By registering a creative work (such as music, artwork, or a novel) on a blockchain, creators can establish an immutable record of ownership. This record serves as a digital timestamp, proving when the work was created and who owns the rights to it. In the event of a copyright dispute, this blockchain record can provide indisputable evidence of authorship.

- **Decentralized and Transparent**: Unlike traditional copyright systems, which often rely on centralized authorities like government agencies or collecting societies, blockchain operates on a decentralized network. This means that creators can manage their own copyright without the need for intermediaries, and anyone can verify ownership and usage rights through the public ledger.

- **Global Accessibility**: Because blockchain is decentralized, it is not restricted by national borders. Creators from anywhere in the world can register their works on the blockchain and have their rights protected globally, making it easier to enforce copyright across jurisdictions.

Example:

A digital artist uploads their artwork to a blockchain-based platform that provides copyright registration services. The moment the artwork is uploaded, the blockchain generates a timestamp and a unique cryptographic hash, creating an immutable proof of ownership. If someone else tries to claim the artwork as their own or sell unauthorized copies, the artist can point to the blockchain record to prove their authorship.

2. Smart Contracts: Automating Licensing and Royalty Payments

One of the most exciting applications of blockchain for copyright management is the use of smart contracts. A smart contract is a self-executing contract with the terms of the agreement directly written into code. These contracts automatically enforce themselves when predefined conditions are met, removing the need for intermediaries such as lawyers or licensing agencies.

In the context of copyright, smart contracts can automate the process of licensing creative works and distributing royalties, ensuring that creators are paid fairly and efficiently.

How smart contracts work for copyright:

- **Automating Licensing Agreements**: A smart contract can be set up to automatically grant licenses to users who meet specific conditions, such as paying a fee or agreeing to certain usage terms. For example, a musician can use a smart contract to license their song for use in a video game. Once the game developer pays the licensing fee, the smart contract executes, granting the developer the right to use the song under the agreed-upon terms.

- **Instant Royalty Payments**: Smart contracts can also automate the distribution of royalties. When a licensed work is sold, streamed, or used, the smart contract automatically divides the revenue and distributes royalties to the relevant parties—whether that's the creator, collaborators, or rights holders. This system eliminates delays in royalty payments and ensures that creators are compensated in real time.

- **Built-In Enforcement**: Smart contracts can also include enforcement mechanisms. If a user violates the terms of a licensing agreement—such as sharing a work without permission or exceeding the licensed usage—the smart contract can automatically revoke access or impose penalties.

Example:
A filmmaker licenses a song for use in a documentary through a smart contract. The contract specifies that the filmmaker can use the song in a single production for a one-time fee. Once the filmmaker pays the fee, the smart contract grants the license and ensures that the royalties are automatically split between the songwriter, the performer, and the producer. If the filmmaker tries to use the song in another project without paying, the smart contract prevents them from accessing the file.

3. Blockchain Platforms for Copyright and Creative Rights

Several blockchain-based platforms have emerged that offer copyright protection and management services for creators. These platforms provide a decentralized alternative to traditional copyright registration systems, allowing creators to protect and monetize their work more effectively.

Some popular blockchain platforms for copyright management include:

- **Ascribe**: Ascribe is a blockchain platform that allows creators to register their digital art, designs, and written content, providing proof of authorship and ownership. It also enables creators to sell and license their work through smart contracts.

- **SingularDTV**: SingularDTV is a blockchain-based platform for filmmakers, musicians, and other content creators. It allows creators to fund, produce, and distribute their work using blockchain technology, with smart contracts handling licensing and royalty payments.

- **OpenSea**: OpenSea is a decentralized marketplace for digital assets, including artwork, music, and virtual goods. It uses blockchain to track ownership of these assets and allows creators to set up smart contracts for sales and licensing.

These platforms are part of the growing decentralized economy, where creators can retain greater control over their work and bypass traditional gatekeepers like record labels, studios, and publishing houses.

Example:

A musician registers their latest album on SingularDTV and uses smart contracts to handle the licensing of individual tracks. Each time a track is purchased or streamed, the smart contract ensures that royalties are automatically split between the musician, the producer, and any collaborators. The blockchain provides a transparent record of all transactions, making it easy for the musician to track how their work is being used and monetized.

4. The Challenges and Future of Blockchain in Copyright

While blockchain offers promising solutions for copyright management, it also faces certain challenges and limitations that need to be addressed for widespread adoption.

Challenges of blockchain for copyright:

- **Legal Recognition**: Although blockchain provides an immutable record of ownership, not all jurisdictions recognize blockchain records as legally binding. In some countries, traditional copyright registration may still be required for legal enforcement, meaning that blockchain should be seen as a complement to, rather than a replacement for, existing legal systems.

- **Scalability**: Blockchain networks can struggle with scalability, particularly when handling large volumes of transactions. This can be a limitation for creators who need to manage high-frequency sales or licensing agreements.

- **Complexity**: While blockchain technology holds great potential, it can be technically complex for creators to use. Platforms and tools that make blockchain more user-friendly will be essential for its widespread adoption in the creative industries.

Despite these challenges, blockchain's potential to transform copyright is undeniable. As the technology matures, it is likely to become a cornerstone of the decentralized creative economy, offering creators greater control, transparency, and security.

Future Trends in Blockchain for Copyright:

- **Increased Adoption by Creators**: As more user-friendly platforms emerge; creators will increasingly turn to blockchain to protect and monetize their work. This shift could lead to a more decentralized creative industry, where artists, writers, musicians, and filmmakers maintain greater control over their intellectual property.

- **Integration with Traditional Copyright Systems**: In the future, we may see blockchain technology integrated with traditional copyright systems, creating a hybrid model where blockchain provides proof of ownership and real-time transactions, while traditional systems handle legal enforcement.

- **Smart Contract Ecosystems**: The rise of smart contracts could lead to the development of ecosystems where creators can easily license, sell, and monetize their work across multiple platforms, all while ensuring that royalties are paid fairly and automatically.

Example:

In the future, a global network of smart contracts might allow creators to license their work to users across the world, with each transaction recorded on a blockchain. These smart contracts could automatically handle everything from royalty distribution to usage rights enforcement, creating a seamless, decentralized ecosystem for copyright management.

Conclusion: A Decentralized Future for Copyright

Blockchain is at the forefront of a decentralized copyright revolution, offering creators unprecedented control over their work. By providing immutable proof of ownership, automating licensing and royalties, and bypassing traditional gatekeepers, blockchain has the potential to reshape the way we manage intellectual property in the digital age.

While challenges remain, the future of blockchain in copyright is bright. As the technology matures and gains legal recognition, it will become an invaluable tool for creators looking to protect and profit from their work in a transparent and efficient way.

In the next section, we'll examine the legal challenges and opportunities presented by 3D printing, another disruptive technology that is redefining copyright in both digital and physical realms.

Global Harmonization of Copyright Laws: Toward a Unified Framework?

In an increasingly interconnected digital world, creative works often cross international borders in the blink of an eye. Whether it's a viral meme shared across continents, a song streamed on multiple platforms globally, or a bestselling novel translated into numerous languages, creators today face the challenge of protecting their intellectual property in a global marketplace. Unfortunately, copyright laws vary significantly from country to country, leading to confusion, legal loopholes, and inconsistent protections. In this section, we will explore the potential for global harmonization of copyright laws and what a unified framework could mean for creators, businesses, and consumers alike.

1. The Current State of Global Copyright Laws

While there are international agreements that provide a baseline level of copyright protection, national copyright laws can differ in significant ways. For instance, what qualifies as "fair use" in one country might be considered infringement in another, and the length of copyright protection can vary dramatically depending on where the creator is located.

Some key international agreements that currently influence global copyright protection include:

- **The Berne Convention (1886)**: One of the oldest and most important international copyright treaties, the Berne Convention established the principle that works created in one member country must be protected in all other member countries without the need for registration. It also introduced the idea of automatic copyright protection, which means a work is protected upon creation, without the need for formal registration.

- **The World Trade Organization (WTO) Agreement on Trade-Related Aspects of Intellectual Property Rights (TRIPS)**: TRIPS established minimum standards for copyright, trademark, and patent protection that all WTO members must comply with. It built upon the Berne Convention and introduced enforcement mechanisms to ensure that member countries uphold these standards.

- **The WIPO Copyright Treaty (WCT) (1996)**: The World Intellectual Property Organization (WIPO) Copyright Treaty specifically addressed the challenges of protecting digital content in the internet age, including provisions for protecting works in digital formats and preventing the circumvention of digital rights management (DRM) systems.

Despite these agreements, the actual implementation of copyright law still varies widely by jurisdiction. Some countries are more aggressive in enforcing copyright laws, while others may have more relaxed approaches or less infrastructure for enforcement. Additionally, different cultural and economic contexts influence how copyright laws are written and applied.

Example:

A U.S. songwriter releases a song that becomes popular on global streaming platforms. While the U.S. and many other countries provide strong protections for the song under copyright law, the artist may struggle to enforce their rights in countries with weaker copyright enforcement or inconsistent protections, leading to piracy or unauthorized use of the song in those regions.

2. The Need for a Unified Global Copyright Framework

With the rise of global digital platforms such as YouTube, Spotify, TikTok, and Netflix, content created in one country is now instantly accessible to audiences around the world. This global reach creates both opportunities and challenges for creators. On the one hand, creators have the ability to reach larger audiences than ever before, but on the other, they face the difficulty of navigating different copyright laws and enforcement mechanisms across multiple countries.

A unified global copyright framework could address many of these challenges by providing consistent rules and standards across jurisdictions, simplifying the process of protecting and enforcing copyright for creators operating in the global digital economy.

Benefits of a unified copyright framework:

- **Simplified Enforcement**: Creators would no longer need to navigate the complex web of differing national copyright laws, as a unified framework would ensure consistent protection and enforcement across borders.

- **Clearer Rules for Digital Platforms**: With harmonized laws, digital platforms could apply the same copyright policies and enforcement measures globally, leading to more consistent treatment of content creators and users.

- **Increased Protection for Creators**: In many parts of the world, copyright laws are either underdeveloped or poorly enforced. A global framework could ensure that creators receive the same level of protection and compensation, regardless of where their work is accessed.

Example:

An independent filmmaker from India creates a documentary that is distributed globally through an online streaming platform. Under a unified global copyright framework, the filmmaker would have confidence that their work is protected in every country where the platform operates, and they would be able to enforce their rights and receive royalties from international audiences without having to navigate multiple legal systems.

3. Challenges to Global Harmonization

Despite the many potential benefits of harmonizing copyright laws globally, there are significant challenges that stand in the way of achieving this vision.

Key challenges to global copyright harmonization:

- **Cultural Differences**: Different countries and regions have diverse cultural attitudes toward creativity, ownership, and sharing. For instance, some countries may prioritize the open sharing of knowledge and culture over strict enforcement of intellectual property rights, while others may take a more protective approach. These cultural differences can make it difficult to create a one-size-fits-all copyright framework.

- **Economic Considerations**: Countries at different stages of economic development may have varying priorities when it comes to intellectual property laws. Developing countries may be more focused on promoting access to information and knowledge sharing, while wealthier nations with strong creative industries might prioritize economic incentives for creators and businesses.

- **Sovereignty Issues**: Many nations are reluctant to cede control over their intellectual property laws to a global authority. Copyright laws often reflect national policies and priorities, and any move toward global harmonization could be seen as a threat to national sovereignty.

- **Enforcement Capabilities**: Even if global copyright laws were harmonized, enforcement would remain a challenge in countries with limited legal or technological infrastructure. Without the ability to effectively enforce copyright, the benefits of harmonization would be diminished.

Example:

A visual artist from Brazil has their work stolen and reproduced without permission by a company in China. Under current global copyright conditions, enforcing their rights could be complicated by differences in the two countries' copyright enforcement practices and legal frameworks. A harmonized global copyright system might streamline the process, but challenges related to economic and cultural differences could still arise.

4. Potential Paths Toward Global Harmonization

Despite these challenges, there are several potential paths that could lead to greater global harmonization of copyright laws in the coming decade. Some of these paths include:

- **Strengthening International Treaties**: Existing international agreements, such as the Berne Convention and the WIPO Copyright Treaty, could be expanded and modernized to address the needs of the digital economy. This could involve creating clearer guidelines for digital content, cross-border enforcement mechanisms, and new rules for AI-generated works and other emerging technologies.

- **Regional Harmonization**: While full global harmonization may be difficult to achieve, regional efforts could pave the way. For example, the European Union (EU) has made significant progress in harmonizing copyright laws across its member states. Similar efforts could take place in other regions, such as Southeast Asia, Africa, or the Americas, creating a patchwork of harmonized regions that could eventually coalesce into a global system.

- **Industry-Led Initiatives**: In the absence of global government action, the tech and media industries could take the lead in creating standardized copyright policies that apply across their platforms. Large digital platforms like YouTube, Apple, and Spotify already operate globally, and they could help push for more consistent copyright laws by establishing common practices for content management, licensing, and enforcement.

- **Technology-Driven Solutions**: Blockchain and smart contracts could play a role in simplifying the enforcement of copyright across borders. By creating transparent, tamper-proof records of ownership and usage rights, these technologies could help create a de facto system of global copyright protection, even if legal frameworks remain fragmented.

Example:

A group of countries in Southeast Asia works together to harmonize their copyright laws and create a regional intellectual property enforcement body. This regional framework simplifies the process for creators within these countries to protect and monetize their works across borders. Over time, similar regional efforts in other parts of the world could contribute to a larger movement toward global harmonization.

Conclusion: A Global Vision for Copyright

As the world becomes more interconnected and content crosses borders with unprecedented speed, the need for global harmonization of copyright laws is more urgent than ever. A unified framework could simplify copyright protection for creators, ensure fair compensation across jurisdictions, and reduce the legal uncertainty that comes with operating in a global marketplace.

However, achieving global harmonization will not be easy. Cultural, economic, and political differences between nations will continue to shape how copyright laws are written and enforced. Nonetheless, efforts to harmonize copyright laws— whether through strengthened international treaties, regional cooperation, or industry-led initiatives—will be essential in creating a more equitable and efficient system for protecting creative works in the digital age.

In the next section, we'll explore the future of user-generated content (UGC) and how the explosive growth of platforms like YouTube, TikTok, and Instagram will drive changes in copyright law, particularly when it comes to fair use and licensing.

The Rise of User-Generated Content (UGC) and the Future of Fair Use

As the digital landscape has evolved, user-generated content (UGC) has become one of the defining features of the internet. Platforms like YouTube, TikTok, Instagram, and Twitch have empowered millions of creators to share their work with a global audience, leading to an explosion of content creation. From viral memes and reaction videos to remixes and fan art, UGC is a driving force behind the internet's most dynamic and engaging content. However, this rise in user-driven creativity also brings about new challenges and questions around copyright and fair use—questions that will shape the future of content creation and ownership.

In this section, we'll explore how the increasing volume of UGC is disrupting traditional notions of copyright, the potential changes in fair use doctrine, and how creators can navigate this evolving legal landscape.

1. The Growth of User-Generated Content and Its Impact on Copyright

The rise of social media platforms and content-sharing sites has democratized creativity in unprecedented ways. Today, anyone with a smartphone and an internet connection can create and distribute content, from short-form videos to livestreams and memes. This explosion of UGC has blurred the lines between content creators, audiences, and rights holders, raising new questions about how copyright laws apply in a world where millions of users remix, share, and reimagine existing works daily.

Key challenges related to UGC and copyright include:

- **Use of Copyrighted Material**: A significant portion of UGC is built on the foundation of pre-existing, copyrighted works. Whether it's a YouTuber using clips from a movie in a review, a Twitch streamer playing music in the background of a gaming session, or a TikTok creator dancing to a popular song, the use of copyrighted material without permission raises concerns about infringement.

433

- **The Role of Platforms**: Platforms like YouTube, Instagram, and TikTok act as intermediaries between content creators and rights holders. These platforms must navigate the complex task of balancing the rights of copyright owners with the desire of users to create and share content freely. This has led to the rise of tools like YouTube's Content ID, which allows copyright holders to claim ad revenue or block infringing content automatically, but it remains an imperfect solution.

- **Legal Uncertainty for Creators**: Many creators who produce UGC operate in a legal gray area, uncertain whether their use of copyrighted material qualifies as fair use or constitutes infringement. This uncertainty can lead to legal disputes, demonetization, or takedown notices, making it difficult for creators to know where they stand.

Example:

A YouTuber creates a video essay analyzing the themes in a popular TV show, using clips from the show to illustrate their points. While the video is educational and transformative in nature, it still uses copyrighted material, raising questions about whether it qualifies as fair use or infringes on the TV show's copyright.

2. The Evolution of Fair Use in the Age of UGC

One of the central issues in the UGC landscape is fair use, a doctrine that allows the limited use of copyrighted material without permission under certain circumstances, such as for criticism, commentary, news reporting, education, or parody. Fair use is intended to strike a balance between protecting the rights of creators and promoting freedom of expression and innovation. However, with the rise of UGC, the boundaries of fair use are constantly being tested.

Factors of Fair Use: To determine whether a work qualifies as fair use, courts typically consider the following four factors:

- **Purpose and Character of the Use**: Is the new work transformative? Does it add something new or alter the original work in a significant way? Uses for criticism, commentary, and parody are more likely to be considered fair use.

- **Nature of the Copyrighted Work**: Some works, such as factual or educational materials, are more likely to be subject to fair use than highly creative works like films, music, and novels.

- **Amount and Substantiality**: How much of the original work is used? Using only a small portion of the work, or a portion that is not central to its "heart," may be more likely to qualify as fair use.

- **Effect on the Market**: Does the use of the copyrighted material harm the market for the original work? If the new use is seen as a substitute for the original, it is less likely to be considered fair use.

How UGC is Expanding the Boundaries of Fair Use:

- **Transformative Works**: Many UGC creators produce transformative content, such as commentary, parody, or remixes. This is where fair use is most likely to apply, as transformative works add new meaning, insights, or value to the original material. For instance, reaction videos, video essays, and meme culture often rely on repurposing existing content in creative ways that could be considered transformative.

- **Short-Form Content**: Platforms like TikTok and Instagram Reels popularized short-form videos that often incorporate copyrighted music or video clips. While these short clips may be less substantial in nature, they still raise questions about the balance between fair use and infringement, particularly when they go viral or reach massive audiences.

- **Educational and Informational Content**: Many creators produce educational content, whether it's tutorials, how-to videos, or historical analyses. These types of videos often incorporate copyrighted material under the assumption of fair use for educational purposes, but the commercial nature of many UGC platforms complicates the matter.

Example:

A TikTok creator uses a popular song as background music for a 15-second dance video. While the video is short and may seem insignificant, if the creator is monetizing their content, the use of copyrighted music without permission could lead to a copyright claim by the song's rights holder.

3. Platform Policies and the Role of DMCA Takedowns

To manage the overwhelming volume of UGC, platforms have had to develop automated systems for handling copyright claims and takedown notices. The Digital Millennium Copyright Act (DMCA) allows copyright holders to request the removal of infringing content from online platforms, but this system has become controversial in the UGC world.

Issues with the DMCA Takedown Process:

- **Automated Takedowns**: Platforms like YouTube use automated systems such as Content ID to detect copyrighted material in user-generated videos and issue takedown notices or monetize the content on behalf of the rights holder. While this system allows copyright owners to protect their work, it can lead to false positives or overly aggressive takedowns that harm creators using content legitimately under fair use.

- **Disproportionate Impact on Creators**: Smaller creators are often disproportionately affected by DMCA takedowns. A single takedown notice can lead to a loss of income, penalties, or even account suspension, even if the content qualifies as fair use. For UGC creators, the risk of false or unfair takedowns creates uncertainty and frustration.

- **Content Moderation vs. Free Expression**: The rise of DMCA takedowns has led to debates over content moderation and the impact of copyright enforcement on free expression. Creators argue that overly broad copyright enforcement stifles creativity and innovation, while copyright holders emphasize the need to protect their intellectual property from unauthorized use.

Example:

A YouTuber creates a video reviewing a new video game, using short clips of gameplay footage. The game's developer issues a DMCA takedown notice, even though the video could arguably fall under fair use for the purposes of commentary and criticism. The YouTuber's video is demonetized, and they lose ad revenue while disputing the claim.

4. The Future of Fair Use and UGC: What's Next?

As user-generated content continues to grow in volume and influence, copyright laws will need to adapt to protect both creators and rights holders. In the coming years, we may see significant changes to the way fair use is interpreted and enforced, as well as the development of new tools to manage UGC on digital platforms.

Potential Trends and Changes:

- **Clarification of Fair Use for UGC**: In the face of mounting legal disputes, lawmakers and courts may move to provide clearer guidance on how fair use applies to UGC. This could involve setting specific rules for short-form content, educational works, or commentary that would give creators more confidence in navigating copyright laws.

- **Expansion of Licensing Systems**: Some platforms are exploring ways to license copyrighted music and videos directly to UGC creators. For example, TikTok has struck deals with major music labels to allow users to incorporate licensed music into their videos legally. Expanding these types of agreements could help protect creators from copyright claims while ensuring that rights holders are compensated.

- **Technology-Driven Solutions**: New technologies like blockchain and smart contracts could provide innovative solutions for managing copyright in the UGC space. Blockchain could be used to track and verify ownership of digital content, while smart contracts could automate licensing agreements and royalty payments, making it easier for UGC creators to use copyrighted material legally.

- **Changes to DMCA**: As criticism of the current DMCA system grows, there may be calls for reforms that make it easier for UGC creators to dispute wrongful takedowns and assert their fair use rights without facing penalties.

Example:

In the future, a TikTok creator could use a platform feature that automatically licenses copyrighted music for their videos, with a portion of ad revenue or royalties going to the rights holder. This would allow creators to continue making content without fear of copyright claims while ensuring that the original artists are fairly compensated.

Conclusion: Navigating the Future of UGC and Fair Use

The rise of user-generated content has transformed the way we create and consume media, blurring the lines between professional creators, rights holders, and audiences. As UGC continues to shape internet culture, the need for clear and adaptable copyright laws becomes increasingly important. Creators must navigate the complexities of fair use, while platforms and rights holders work to balance copyright enforcement with creative freedom.

The future of fair use and UGC will likely involve a combination of legal reforms, new licensing models, and technological solutions that allow creators to thrive while protecting the intellectual property of rights holders. As a UGC creator, understanding your rights and responsibilities will be key to navigating this evolving landscape and continuing to create content that resonates with global audiences.

With these trends in mind, we move closer to a future where content creators, rights holders, and platforms can coexist in a digital ecosystem that values both creativity and ownership.

Quick Tips and Recap

- **Understand Fair Use**: Learn the four factors of fair use—purpose, nature, amount, and market impact—to determine when you can legally use copyrighted material in your content.

- **Transformative Content is Key**: Focus on creating transformative works (e.g., commentary, parody, reviews) that add new meaning to the original material, increasing the likelihood of qualifying for fair use.

- **Be Cautious with UGC**: When using copyrighted material in your user-generated content (UGC), always consider the potential for copyright claims and takedown notices, especially on platforms like YouTube and TikTok.

- **Licensing Options**: Where possible, explore licensing options for using music, videos, or other copyrighted content in your UGC to avoid infringement.

- **DMCA Takedowns**: Familiarize yourself with the DMCA process and know your rights to dispute wrongful takedowns. If your content qualifies for fair use, you can challenge a claim through the proper channels.

- **Use Platform Tools**: Platforms like YouTube offer tools like Content ID to help creators monitor copyright issues. Utilize these tools to stay compliant with copyright laws.

- **Seek Legal Guidance**: If you're unsure whether your content falls under fair use, consult with a legal expert to prevent potential legal disputes or infringements.

- **Stay Informed**: Keep up with changes to copyright laws, especially regarding UGC, as new legislation and court cases will likely shape the future of fair use and copyright enforcement.

By following these tips, you can better navigate the complexities of fair use and copyright law in the ever-growing world of user-generated content.

Resources

The Empire Builders and Blueprint Series

Welcome to the Resource section of the Empire Builders Series: Masterclasses in Business and Law. Here, we provide a carefully curated collection of practical tools and materials designed to complement the strategies and insights discussed throughout the series. This section is your gateway to deeper understanding and application, offering everything from sample agreements and checklists to detailed case studies and guidelines. Whether you're forging a new business, protecting intellectual property, or planning for expansion, these resources are intended to empower you with the necessary tools to effectively implement and navigate the complex landscape of business and law. Embrace these resources as your companion in building and sustaining a robust empire.

Empire Builders Series:
Masterclasses in Business and Law

In the dynamic world of business, where innovation intersects with opportunity, success often hinges not only on creativity but also on a deep understanding of the legal and operational landscapes. The Empire Builders Series is meticulously designed to arm aspiring entrepreneurs, seasoned business owners, creative professionals, and legal experts with the comprehensive knowledge and strategies needed to navigate these complexities and build lasting empires.

Each book in the series serves as a foundational pillar, offering expert guidance and actionable insights in specific areas of business and law; tailored to foster growth, innovation, and success in today's competitive marketplace:

1. **Brick by Brick**: This guide acts as your blueprint for building a business from the ground up. It offers essential strategies, legal insights, and operational tactics crucial for establishing a solid foundation for any business venture.

2. **Mark Your Territory**: Dive deep into the world of trademarks with this essential guide, designed to help you protect and effectively leverage your brand in today's competitive market.

3. **From Idea to Empire**: Transform your entrepreneurial dreams into reality with this exhaustive guide to business planning. Learn how to craft a compelling business plan that not only attracts investors but also sets the stage for a successful enterprise.

4. **Beyond the Pen**: Safeguard your creative works and master the intricacies of copyright law with this expert guide, tailored specifically for writers, artists, musicians, and digital content creators.

5. **Legal Ink**: Demystify the complex legal landscape of publishing with practical advice on negotiating contracts and protecting intellectual property, essential for authors and publishers.

The Empire Builders Series stands as a testament to the power of knowledge and the importance of mastering the strategic and legal aspects of business management. Each book is designed not merely to inform but to inspire action and lead to success. Embark on this journey to build your empire, one masterclass at a time.

Brick by Brick:
The Entrepreneur's Guide to Constructing a Company

The first book in the Empire Builders Series: Masterclass in Business and Law is "Brick by Brick: The Entrepreneur's Guide to Constructing a Company."

Summary: "Brick by Brick" is an indispensable resource for entrepreneurs who are poised to transform their innovative business ideas into successful enterprises. This comprehensive guide meticulously outlines the complexities of business formation, providing detailed, step-by-step instructions and vital insights into the legal, operational, and strategic aspects of starting and running a thriving company.

Part 1: Laying the Foundation – Focuses on selecting the appropriate business entity, delving into the legal implications of each option and the economic considerations vital for establishing a solid foundation for your business.

Part 2: Operational Mechanics – Discusses the operational aspects of setting up partnerships and LLCs, navigating corporate governance, maintaining corporate records, and managing capital and shareholder relationships effectively.

Part 3: Advanced Strategic Planning – Offers insights into managing structural changes, handling stock and ownership issues, expanding operations across state lines, and deploying tax strategies to ensure compliance and optimize financial performance.

Part 4: Implementation Tools and Resources – Provides practical tools such as sample agreements, startup task checklists, and comprehensive guidelines for drafting business plans and the incorporation process, enabling entrepreneurs to effectively implement their business strategies.

"Brick by Brick" not only serves as a guide but acts as a complete blueprint for building a robust business capable of thriving in today's competitive market. It arms aspiring entrepreneurs with the necessary knowledge and tools to navigate the complexities of business formation. From drafting your first business plan to preparing for incorporation, this book delivers invaluable insights and practical advice to establish a strong foundation and sustain growth.

Mark Your Territory:
Navigating Trademarks in the Modern Marketplace

The second book in the Empire Builders Series: Masterclass in Business and Law is "Mark Your Territory: Navigating Trademarks in the Modern Marketplace."

Summary: "Mark Your Territory" provides an indispensable resource for anyone involved in the branding and legal aspects of their business, offering a comprehensive guide to understanding, acquiring, and effectively managing trademarks. This book is crucial for ensuring that trademarks, which are vital assets to any business, are properly protected and leveraged.

Part 1: Fundamentals of Trademarks – Introduces the basics of trademarks, including their legal framework, the process of trademark selection and registration, and their importance in identifying business sources and ensuring product quality.

Part 2: Strategic Trademark Management – Focuses on the ongoing management of trademarks, detailing strategies for maintaining rights, monitoring for infringements, addressing challenges in digital marketing, and managing global trademark portfolios.

Part 3: Advanced Topics in Trademarks – Delves into more complex issues such as preventing trademark dilution, managing renewals, understanding the specific needs of service marks in advertising, and navigating the intricacies of trademark licensing and emerging legal trends.

Part 4: Practical Tools and Resources – Provides practical aids like sample trademark filings, management checklists, and insightful case studies, equipping readers with tangible tools and real-world examples to apply the concepts discussed effectively.

Designed for entrepreneurs, business owners, and legal professionals, "Mark Your Territory" equips readers with actionable strategies and essential tools for effective trademark management. It ensures that readers can maintain their brand's uniqueness and legal protections, thus securing a competitive edge in the marketplace.

From Idea to Empire:
Mastering the Art of Business Planning

The third book in the Empire Builders Series: Masterclass in Business and Law is "From Idea to Empire: Mastering the Art of Business Planning."

Summary: "From Idea to Empire" offers an indispensable roadmap for entrepreneurs eager to transform their innovative ideas into successful businesses. This comprehensive guide equips readers with a strategic blueprint for drafting robust business plans that attract investors and serve as a roadmap for navigating the transition from startup to thriving enterprise.

Part 1: Conceptualizing Your Business – This section lays the groundwork by assisting readers in defining their business vision, understanding market needs, analyzing competitors, and setting clear business objectives. It also guides readers in selecting an effective business model that aligns with their long-term goals.

Part 2: Strategic Planning – Delve into creating detailed marketing strategies, operational plans, and financial projections. This part covers risk management and technological integration, ensuring the business plan is both innovative and executable.

Part 3: Articulating Your Plan – Focuses on the actual drafting of the business plan, including how to write an engaging executive summary, develop compelling proposals, and master communication and negotiation tactics with potential investors and partners.

Part 4: Execution and Review – Outlines the necessary steps to launch the business successfully, monitor its performance, and make adjustments based on real-world feedback and market dynamics. This section also explores strategies for sustainable growth and long-term viability.

"From Idea to Empire" is more than a mere planning manual; it's a strategic guide that provides budding entrepreneurs with the necessary knowledge, tools, and confidence to build a business capable of facing today's market complexities. With practical advice, real-world examples, and essential resources, this book is a vital tool for anyone ready to evolve their business concept from idea to a profitable empire.

From Idea to Empire: Abridged Edition

The third book in the Empire Builders Series: Masterclass in Business and Law is "From Idea to Empire: Abridged Edition."

Summary: "From Idea to Empire: Abridged Edition" delivers the essential roadmap for turning business ideas into successful enterprises—streamlined for readers seeking concise and actionable insights. While the original edition provides an expansive resource with success stories and detailed case studies, this abridged version focuses solely on the strategic elements of business planning, offering the tools needed to conceptualize, design, and execute a winning business strategy.

By eliminating supplementary stories and focusing on the practical frameworks, this edition is perfect for readers eager to dive straight into the mechanics of business planning without distraction. It provides the knowledge required to develop robust business models, articulate compelling proposals, and successfully launch and grow a business in today's dynamic marketplace.

Part 1: Conceptualizing Your Business – Laying the Foundation – In this section, readers learn how to define their business idea, identify market needs, analyze competitors, and set clear objectives. It introduces essential business models and helps entrepreneurs align their vision with long-term goals.

Part 2: Strategic Planning – Mapping the Path to Success – Here, readers will discover how to design effective marketing strategies, operational plans, and financial projections. Topics like risk management and technological integration are covered to ensure every business plan is both realistic and innovative.

Part 3: Articulating Your Plan – Communicating with Precision and Impact – This section emphasizes the importance of clarity in communication. Readers will learn how to craft compelling executive summaries, develop strong proposals, and master negotiation strategies for working with investors and partners.

Part 4: Execution and Review – Launching and Scaling with Purpose – The final section covers essential steps for launching a business successfully, monitoring performance, and making real-time adjustments. It also addresses strategies for sustainable growth, long-term resilience, and market adaptation.

About This Edition:

The Abridged Edition is crafted for readers who prefer a focused, no-frills approach to business planning. By presenting the core methodologies from the original book in a concise format, this version allows entrepreneurs to absorb key concepts quickly and efficiently. Whether you're a first-time entrepreneur or a seasoned business owner, this streamlined guide provides the essential tools needed to transform an idea into a thriving business.

Why This Edition Matters:

"From Idea to Empire: Abridged Edition" underscores that great business planning doesn't require lengthy explanations—it requires clear strategies and actionable frameworks. This edition emphasizes the importance of focus, discipline, and adaptability in building a successful business.

Designed to complement busy entrepreneurs, it delivers the same powerful strategies as the original book but in a more accessible format. Readers can quickly refer to specific sections, apply the knowledge, and move forward with confidence in their business endeavors.

"From Idea to Empire: Abridged Edition" is the perfect companion for entrepreneurs who need to move swiftly from concept to execution. With straightforward advice and practical insights, this edition equips readers to create robust business plans and take decisive action toward building their own empire.

Beyond the Pen:

Copyright Strategies for Modern Creators

The fourth book in the Empire Builders Series: Masterclass in Business and Law is "Beyond the Pen: Copyright Strategies for Modern Creators."

Summary: "Beyond the Pen" serves as a crucial guide for artists, writers, musicians, and digital creators who seek to effectively navigate the complexities of copyright law and protect their creative assets. This comprehensive resource provides a deep dive into the mechanisms, legal frameworks, and strategic practices necessary to safeguard intellectual property in today's rapidly evolving digital landscape.

Part 1: Understanding Copyright Law – This section lays the groundwork by covering the essentials of copyright, including how to register works, the extent of legal protection available, and the nuances of international copyright laws. It equips creators with the crucial knowledge needed to assert and defend their rights.

Part 2: Navigating Use and Fair Use – Focuses on the vital concept of fair use, offering real-world scenarios and detailed guidance on how to handle copyright infringements and resolve disputes effectively without compromising creative freedom.

Part 3: Licensing and Monetization – Explores strategic approaches to structuring and managing licensing agreements, understanding diverse revenue models, and handling collaborations, ensuring creators can monetize their works effectively while maintaining control over their usage.

Part 4: Copyright in the Digital Age – Addresses the challenges and opportunities presented by new technologies, digital rights management, and online content sharing platforms. This part also examines the impact of social media on copyright and anticipates future trends that could influence creators' rights.

"Beyond the Pen" is more than just a legal manual; it is a strategic resource that empowers creators to protect, manage, and prosper with their intellectual property in today's interconnected market. Packed with practical examples, expert advice, and actionable strategies, this book is an indispensable tool for anyone looking to navigate the legal challenges and seize the opportunities in the modern creative landscape.

Legal Ink:
Navigating the Legalese of Publishing

The fifth book in the Empire Builders Series: Masterclass in Business and Law is "Legal Ink: Navigating the Legalese of Publishing."

Summary: "Legal Ink" offers an indispensable guide for authors seeking to navigate the complex world of publishing contracts. This comprehensive book demystifies legal jargon and provides a clear roadmap to understanding and managing the intricacies of publishing agreements effectively.

Part 1: The Grant of Rights – This section explains the various types of publishing rights, offering guidance on how to negotiate and manage these rights effectively to safeguard the author's interests.

Part 2: Your Obligations – Details the commitments authors must uphold under publishing contracts. It emphasizes the implications of these obligations for an author's literary career and advises on managing multiple contractual commitments.

Part 3: Getting Your Book to Market – Covers the practical aspects of the publishing process from the final manuscript preparation to marketing and distribution. This part ensures authors understand the steps involved and their roles in bringing their book to market.

Part 4: Follow the Money – Breaks down the financial components of publishing contracts, including advances, royalties, and accounting clauses. It offers crucial advice on how to negotiate for fair compensation.

Part 5: Parting Ways – Discusses strategies for effectively managing the conclusion of a publishing agreement, including rights reversion and contract termination, providing tactics for authors to regain control of their work.

"Legal Ink" acts as more than just a guide—it's a strategic tool for any author looking to deeply understand and master the legal framework of publishing contracts. With this book, writers are equipped to make informed decisions, negotiate better terms, and ensure their rights are protected throughout their publishing journey. It is an essential resource for anyone looking to confidently handle the legalities of publishing and secure the success of their work in the competitive marketplace.

The Empire Blueprint Series:
Case Studies for Business Success

Welcome to the Case Studies section of The Empire Blueprint Series: Case Studies for Business Success. This collection serves as an essential companion to the theoretical knowledge presented in the earlier volumes. Here, we delve into real-world applications and successful business practices through detailed case studies, showcasing how various entrepreneurs and businesses have navigated challenges, seized opportunities, and achieved success in their respective fields.

In this series, you will encounter a variety of scenarios that illustrate the practical implementation of business strategies and legal frameworks. Each case study not only highlights successes but also discusses the obstacles faced and lessons learned along the way. Whether you're a budding entrepreneur, a seasoned executive, or a legal professional, these insights will provide you with invaluable perspectives and tools to enhance your own business endeavors.

Each book in the series includes:

1. **70 Case Studies in Vision, Strategy, and Personal Branding**: This volume explores the journeys of entrepreneurs who have effectively crafted their visions and built strong personal brands. It highlights strategies for aligning personal values with business goals and creating a lasting impact in the marketplace.

2. **70 Case Studies in Leadership, Innovation, and Resilience**: This volume examines leaders who have driven innovation and fostered resilience within their organizations. The case studies showcase their approaches to overcoming challenges and inspire others to cultivate a culture of adaptability and forward-thinking.

3. **74 Case Studies in Growth, Digital Presence, and Legacy Building**: This volume delves into the strategies employed by businesses that have successfully navigated digital transformation and growth. It emphasizes the importance of establishing a strong online presence and building a legacy that resonates with future generations.

Each case study in The Empire Blueprint Series: Case Studies for Business Success is crafted to offer actionable insights and inspiration for readers. By examining these real-world examples, you will gain a deeper understanding of the strategies that drive business success and how to apply these lessons to your own ventures.

70 Case Studies in Vision, Strategy, and Personal Branding: The Foundations of Success, Volume 1

The first book in The Empire Blueprint Series: Case Studies for Business Success is "70 Case Studies in Vision, Strategy, and Personal Branding: The Foundations of Success," Volume 1

Dive deeper into the essential elements of business success with Volume 1: 70 Case Studies in Vision, Strategy, and Personal Branding. This volume not only presents a wealth of real-world examples but also serves as a practical toolkit for aspiring entrepreneurs and seasoned professionals alike. Here, you will find a curated collection of resources designed to complement the case studies and enhance your understanding of effective business practices.

From strategic planning templates and personal branding frameworks to time management guides and storytelling techniques, these resources empower you to implement the insights gleaned from the case studies. Explore practical tools for optimizing your online presence, launching impactful marketing campaigns, and engaging audiences across various platforms.

With a focus on innovation and adaptability, this resource section is your go-to companion for navigating the complexities of today's business landscape. Whether you're looking to craft an inspiring vision, develop effective strategies, or build a standout personal brand, the materials provided will equip you with the actionable insights needed to achieve meaningful success. Embrace the tools and inspiration within these pages, and take your entrepreneurial journey to new heights.

70 Case Studies in Leadership, Innovation, and Resilience: building a Thriving Enterprise, Volume 2

The second book in The Empire Blueprint Series: Case Studies for Business Success is "70 Case Studies in Leadership, Innovation, and Resilience: Building a Thriving Enterprise," Volume 2

Enhance your understanding of effective leadership with Volume 2: 70 Case Studies in Leadership, Innovation, and Resilience: Building a Thriving Enterprise. This resource section is designed to complement the rich insights presented throughout the volume, providing you with practical tools and frameworks to elevate your leadership journey.

Within this section, you'll find a variety of resources that address the core themes of this book—leadership, innovation, and resilience. From templates for developing effective communication strategies to guides on fostering a collaborative corporate culture, these materials are crafted to support your growth as a leader. Explore negotiation techniques, emotional intelligence assessments, and frameworks for ethical leadership that will help you build trust and loyalty within your teams.

The resources also include practical tips for embracing digital transformation and integrating innovative technologies into your business practices. Learn how to leverage these tools to drive growth, enhance customer engagement, and maintain a competitive edge in today's dynamic market.

With a focus on creating lasting value and building a legacy, this section equips you with actionable insights and strategies to navigate challenges with confidence. Whether you are an entrepreneur launching a new venture or an executive steering an established enterprise, these resources will empower you to lead with purpose and resilience.

Dive into these valuable tools and insights, and discover how to turn challenges into opportunities, fostering an environment where innovation and sustainable growth thrive.

74 Case Studies in Growth, Digital Presence, and Legacy Building: Strategies for Long-Term Success, Volume 3

The third book in The Empire Blueprint Series: Case Studies for Business Success is "74 Case Studies in Growth, Digital Presence, and Legacy Building: Strategies for Long-Term Success," Volume 3

Unlock the secrets to sustainable success with Volume 3: 74 Case Studies in Growth, Digital Presence, and Legacy Building: Strategies for Long-Term Success. This resource section is designed to enhance your understanding and application of the powerful insights shared throughout the volume, providing you with practical tools and strategies for thriving in today's competitive landscape.

Resources

In this section, you'll find a wealth of resources that align with the key themes of this book—growth, digital engagement, and legacy building. From templates for strategic goal-setting and growth frameworks to guides on optimizing digital marketing efforts, these materials will help you implement the actionable insights gained from the case studies.

Explore best practices for storytelling and community engagement in the digital realm, along with practical tips for leveraging social media to amplify your brand's presence. Discover frameworks for navigating the complexities of innovation and operational efficiency, ensuring your business not only grows but flourishes sustainably.

The resource section also emphasizes the importance of legacy building, offering tools for effective succession planning and community involvement. Learn how to align your everyday decisions with your long-term vision, ensuring that your enterprise leaves a lasting impact for future generations.

Whether you are an entrepreneur embarking on a new venture, an executive scaling operations, or a professional seeking to elevate your digital presence, these resources will empower you to lead with purpose and confidence. Dive into the practical tools and insights provided here, and equip yourself to navigate challenges, innovate boldly, and create a meaningful legacy.

In conclusion, the Resource section of the Empire Builders Series and Empire Blueprint Series serves as valuable extensions of the learning journey you've embarked upon. By utilizing these carefully chosen tools and materials, you are better equipped to apply the principles and strategies discussed in the series to real-world scenarios. Each resource has been tailored to enhance your understanding and effectiveness in the realms of business and law, ensuring you have the practical support necessary to navigate challenges and seize opportunities. We hope these resources prove instrumental in helping you build and sustain your business empire, transforming knowledge into actionable success.

L. A. Moeszinger also known as simply "L" is the face behind the AuthorsDoor Leadership Program: AuthorsDoor Series: *Publisher & Her World*, AuthorsDoor Advanced Series: *Publisher & Her World*, and AuthorsDoor Masterclass Series: *Publisher & Her World*. The program comprises, books, courses, and workbooks. The courses expand upon the books. The workbooks go into further detail, outlining step-by-step instructions. Courses are *free*; books and workbooks are available for purchase on Amazon and other retailer sites. She has been launching the careers of self-publishers since 2009, and she also writes the AuthorsRedDoor.com blog on writing, publishing, and marketing. L is also the co-founder of The Ridge Publishing Group and its imprints.

She is an American author, publisher, and creator who resides in Coeur d'Alene, Idaho, with her husband and two dogs. She writes under the pseudonyms: Ann Patterson and Ann Carrington for her business law pieces; L. A. Moeszinger for her writing, publishing, and marketing pieces; Lori Ann Moeszinger for her biblical books and personal pieces; and a handful of others for her Manhattan Diaries series. She believes strongly in faith, blessings, and working her butt off . . . and she thinks one of the best things about being an author-publisher—unlike the lawyer she used to be—is that she can let her passion out.

Original Package Design
© 2024 AuthorsDoor Leadership Program
Cover Design: Eric Moeszinger
Author Photo © 2023 Edwin Wolfe

Parent Website: https://www.RidgePublishingGroup.com and

    blog site https://www.PublisherAndHerWorld.com

Publisher Website: https://www.GuardiansofBiblicalTruth.com and

    blog site https://www.Jesus-Says.com

Author website: https://www.LAMoeszinger.com and New Youniversity sites:

    https://www.NewYouniversity.com, https://www.ManhattanChronicles.com

Bridge Website: https://www.AuthorsDoor.com and

    blog site https://www.AuthorsRedDoor.com

Entertainment website: https://www.EthanFoxBooks.com and

    blog site https://www.KidsStagram.com

Want More?

The ideas in this book are expanded upon throughout the AuthorsDoor Leadership Program of books, courses, and workbooks. Follow our Facebook page. Join our Facebook private group. Watch our YouTube channels (AuthorsDoor Group, Authors Red Door #Shorts, and Publisher and Her World at Ridge Publishing Group). Listen to our Podcast channel (Publisher's Circle); or email me: *Hello@AuthorsDoor.com*

AuthorsDoor Hubs

Get insights from the articles we write on our *website* (AuthorsDoor.com). You'll find more publications to help authors sell better, pitch better, recruit better, build better, create better, and connect better. You are also invited to visit our *blog* and find out what we're talking about now. Sign up for our *AuthorsDoor Leadership Program Newsletter* and join the conversations going on there with our private community (Publisher's Circle); visit: *www.AuthorsRedDoor.com*

Publisher & Her World Blogs

Enter a world where the sometimes shocking and often hilarious climb to the top as an author-publisher is exposed by a true insider. Faced with on-going trials and tribulations of the world of self-publishing, L. A. Moeszinger is witty and sometimes brutally candid in her postings. If you enjoy getting the inside scoop on the makings and thoughts behind self-publishing, this is the blog for you! *www.PublisherAndHerWorld.com*

This

book was art

directed by John Jared.

The art for both the cover and the

interior was created using pastels on toned

print making paper. The text was set in 10 point Times

New Roman, a typeface based on the sixteenth-century type designs

of Claude Garamond, redrawn by Robert Slimback in 1989.

The book was printed at Amazon and IngramSpark.

The Managing Editor was Jack Clark. The

Production was supervised by

Jason Reed and Ed

Warren.